THE CITY IN THE VALLEY

SBL
Society of Biblical Literature

Studies in Biblical Literature

General Acquisitions Editors

Benjamin D. Sommer,
Old Testament/Hebrew Bible

Sharon H. Ringe,
New Testament

Number 7

THE CITY IN THE VALLEY
Biblical Interpretation and Urban Theology

THE CITY IN THE VALLEY

Biblical Interpretation and Urban Theology

by
Dieter Georgi

Society of Biblical Literature
Atlanta

THE CITY IN THE VALLEY
Biblical Interpretation and Urban Theology

Copyright © 2005 by the Society of Biblical Literature

All rights reserved. No part of this work may be reproduced or transmitted in any form or by any means, electronic or mechanical, including photocopying and recording, or by means of any information storage or retrieval system, except as may be expressly permitted by the 1976 Copyright Act or in writing from the publisher. Requests for permission should be addressed in writing to the Rights and Permissions Office, Society of Biblical Literature, 825 Houston Mill Road, Atlanta, GA 30329 USA.

Library of Congress Cataloging-in-Publication Data

Georgi, Dieter.
    The city in the valley : biblical interpretation and urban theology / by Dieter Georgi.
        p. cm. — (Studies in biblical literature ; no. 7)
    ISBN 1-58983-099-7 (paper binding : alk. paper)
    1. Cities and towns—Religious aspects—Christianity. 2. Cities and towns—Biblical teaching. 3. Bible. N.T.—Criticism, interpretation, etc. 4. Theology, Doctrinal. I. Title. II. Studies in biblical literature (Society of Biblical Literature) ; 7.
    BR115.C45G46 2004
    270'.09173'2—dc22   2004004753

13 12 11 10 09 08 07 06 05   5 4 3 2 1

Printed in the United States of America on acid-free, recycled paper conforming to ANSI/NISO Z39.48-1992 (R1997) and ISO 9706:1994 standards for paper permanence.

Contents

Foreword vii
    Helmut Koester

Preface xi

1. Personal Reflections on an American
   Theological Perspective 1

2. Socioeconomic Reasons for the "Divine Man" as
   Propagandistic Pattern 11

3. Who Is the True Prophet? 25

4. The Urban Adventure of the Early Church 53

5. The Hour of the Gospel: Jesus and Caesar 69

6. On Paul's Image of the Human 93

7. Legal Dimensions of Money and Theological
   Consequences 103

8. Living with Chaos: Meditations on Paul's Ethics 135

9. Why Was Paul Killed? The Epistle to the Romans
   as a Document of Resistance......................................147

10. John's "Heavenly" Jerusalem 161

11. The Wrath of the Dragon: Patriarchy's Last Stand ...187

12. Should Augustine Have the Last Word on
    Urban Theology?..195

13. The Interest in Life-of-Jesus Theology as a Paradigm
    for the Social History of Biblical Criticism 221

14. The Religious Dimensions of the World Market:
    A Farewell to the Middle Ages..255

15. Is There Justification in Money? A Historical and
    Theological Meditation on the Financial Aspects of
    Justification by Christ..283

16. Bultmann Was Not First: Josiah Royce as
    Interpreter of Paul 309

17. Reason, Religion, Responsibility: Reflections on the
    Frankfurt Tillich 323

18. Praxis and Theory in Theological Education:
    Is Scholarship "Hot" or "Cold"? 337

19. En Route to an Urban Theology: Can Theology
    Help Us Understand Urban Society? 343

20. On Sojourning 367

FOREWORD

In the fall of the year 1954, shortly after the completion of my doctoral dissertation at the University of Marburg, I came to the University of Heidelberg in Germany to serve as research and teaching assistant to Günther Bornkamm, the professor of New Testament studies at that university. On one of my visits to my new boss, I ran into a heated debate that Professor Bornkamm had with one of his doctoral students about the project of a dissertation on the opponents of Paul in the Second Letter to the Corinthians. This doctoral student was Dieter Georgi, at that time serving as a minister of a church in Frankfurt. He argued strongly against the consensus of scholarship, especially among the students of Rudolf Bultmann, that Paul wrote 2 Corinthians against gnostic opponents. One of Bultmann's last students and my fellow student at the University of Marburg, Walter Schmithals, was at that time just about to publish his dissertation on Paul's gnostic opponents in the Corinthian correspondence, arguing strongly that Paul was writing against gnostic opponents in both letters to the Corinthians. But here was this young minister who argued with the director of his dissertation saying that the interpretation of our venerated master Rudolph Bultmann was entirely wrong and ill-conceived. I was flabbergasted.

Dieter and I soon became friends, and so did our families. His lovely and wonderful wife Barbara, my wife and I had known from the time of our studies together at the University of Marburg—she would become one of the first female ministers to be ordained in her church. Professor Bornkamm kindly invited me to help in the supervision and counseling of his numerous doctoral students, including Dieter Georgi. During those years I learned much from him. Established hypotheses needed to be tested, and renewed scrutiny of the texts in question was called for: What had been overlooked? What did the texts really reveal? Was the gnosticizing flavor of the language of 2 Corinthians caused by gnostic opponents, or was Paul himself using such language in his arguments against the super-apostles who had come to Corinth? What other phenomena of the Hellenistic and Jewish religious propaganda of the time could explain the behavior of these super-apostles? What did we know of the marketplace of religious competition in the Greek cities of Paul's missionary activities? Of course, as a student of Rudolf Bultmann I had learned much during my studies about such questions. But my younger friend Dieter Georgi forced me to enter into new fields and new levels of critical inquiry. And it must be said that our Heidelberg mentor of beloved memory, Gunther Bornkamm, himself a student of Bultmann, although critical of Dieter Georgi's endeavors, encouraged his somewhat revolutionary thoughts.

There was another important aspect of Dieter Georgi's work. He was and always remained the Christian minister devoted to the well-being and critical renewal of the church. But his commitment to the church was not inspired by conventional piety but rather by his understanding of religion as political engagement. For him, the task of the Christian church in this world should not be informed by a desire of establishing a safe haven of religious activity and piety but by engaging the Christian people in challenging the political and social complacency of the new structures that were wrought in Germany (and elsewhere!) after the disasters of the Second World War. For him, there was no exegetical or theological question that was not at the same time a question of political and social justice and equity in the world today. The just cause of the allied forces against the horrors of Nazi Germany and against Japanese imperialism seemed darkened for him by the American bombing of Dresden, which he witnessed personally, and by the atomic bombing of Japanese cities by American airplanes. The imperialist policy and economy of the decades after World War II troubled him deeply and inspired his scholarly efforts better to understand the politics and religion of the Roman imperial period and of early Christian documents.

Hermeneutics are often informed by political agendas. Dieter Georgi was deeply suspicious of such agendas. For him, hermeneutics should be based upon the results of historical-critical inquiry. That required that all available ancient sources should be investigated with the utmost care and empathy. I remember well a discussion in a seminar about an ancient writing for which a doctoral student had presented a report with a devastatingly negative criticism of the author's bias. Dieter Georgi, himself not very much liking what the author's purpose was, nevertheless protested and told the student and the participants of the seminar that it was our duty to listen carefully to the ancient author's words. We should put ourselves into the author's position and with empathy face the problems that this author tried to deal with. Dieter thoroughly rejected the modern interpreter's hubris that claims to possess already the knowledge of a more superior response to the problems that the ancient author face.

There are three areas in which Dieter Georgi's insistence upon empathy bore much fruit. First, there was the question of the opponents of Paul in 2 Corinthians. Dieter certainly had little sympathy with the christological position of the opponents. Their claim to possess the miracle-working powers of Christ was something he deeply rejected because for him, as for Paul, the humanity of Jesus and not the demonstration of supernatural powers was the key to understanding God's revelation. Nevertheless, he was able to present forcefully and with empathy the purpose and intentions of Paul's opponents and could therefore highlight Paul's arguments against them in a novel way, although he also saw the problems of the sometimes gnosticizing language that Paul used in his arguments against them. Second, Dieter Georgi had little room in his own thinking for the individualistic mysticism of Jewish wisdom theology that is especially present in the Wisdom of Solomon. But he was able to show the profound attraction of that world-denying wisdom movement and to highlight its merits and its power in the development of gnostic theology. This effort of his scholarship will be evident in the publication of his commentary on the Wisdom of Solomon, which should see the light of day soon as it is prepared, on the basis of the notes that he left, by one of his German students, Professor Angela Standhartinger, who is now holding the chair at the University Marburg that once was occupied by Rudolph Bultmann. Third, there is imperialist Rome, with which Dieter Georgi, a died-in-the-wool democrat, had no sympathy whatsoever. But more than anyone before him he was able to demonstrate empathetically the power of the eschatological visions of Vergil and Horace that inspired Augustus's political and legal reform programs.

In his career Dieter Georgi mirrored what the Epistle to the Hebrews says: we have no lasting city in this world. He was a wanderer, a gypsy, as he once confessed himself. After some years spent in Germany as a pastor in Frankfurt and teacher at the University of Heidelberg, he left for the United States—the country in which his mother was born. He came first for a brief sojourn as a visiting professor at Harvard University, then taught for several years at San Francisco Presbyterian Seminary in San Anselmo. From there he moved to Harvard University once more for a very fruitful and exciting fifteen-year period of teaching, which all doctoral students whose dissertations he supervised remember gratefully. The opportunity to become the founding dean to supervise the creation of new Protestant and Catholic theological faculties at the University of Frankfurt proved irresistible and enticed him to return to his home city's university. Briefly returning to the United States after his retirement to teach at Union Theological Seminary in New York, he then followed an invitation to teach in the Philippines for several years. Some of us, including myself, hoped that he would instead have stayed home in order to finish his commentary on Paul's Second Letter to the Corinthians. On the other hand, his constant awareness of political and social problems, especially as they related to the education of students of theology, not only left him restless and with the urgent feeling to help wherever he could, but it also inspired most of his thinking and writing. Much of this is documented in the essays of this volume.

Eventually he returned to the task of writing his commentaries on the Wisdom of Solomon and the Second Letter of Paul to the Corinthians. But he also continued his devotion to the education of preachers of the gospel with regular seminars for ministers and lay leaders, in which he inspired many to use critical exegesis for a better understanding of the message of the Bible for our troubled times. Alas, increasing health problems slowed down his efforts to complete these commentaries, and his untimely death ended this endeavor. Yet not only his monumental published works on *The Opponents of Paul in 2 Corinthians* and on *Paul and the Poor* but especially the essays in this volume will be a lasting legacy for future generations. These essays demonstrate eminently that Dieter Georgi was not only a nomad wandering between the continents of this earth, Europe, America, and Asia; his creative mind also constantly wandered from the ancient world of Jesus and Paul, Vergil and Augustus to our own time, from his field of New Testament studies to the fields of religion, politics, and economics past and present, from the established society and its elites to the poor and disadvantaged then and now, constantly seeking the genuine God-given true humanity that Jesus had proclaimed and lived.

Complacency and ignorance he despised as much as he rejected the kind of scholarship that glories in the mastery of a protected and isolated discipline. If it sometimes proved adventurous to delve into a related field of studies, he was always willing to take the risk. These essays are therefore a wake-up call as he during the years of his earthly sojourn always called and encouraged his friends, students, and colleagues to venture out into the perilous journey in the search of justice, equity, and peace in our world.

Helmut Koester
Harvard University
Cambridge, Massachusetts
August 2005

PREFACE

It was the best of times, it was the worst of times. It was the age of wisdom, it was the age of foolishness, it was the epoch of belief, it was the epoch of incredulity, it was the season of Light, it was the season of Darkness, it was the spring of hope, it was the winter of despair, we had everything before us, we had nothing before us, we were all going direct to Heaven, we were all going direct the other way. (Charles Dickens, *A Tale of Two Cities*[1])

Is there promise in metropolis? Do our cities still have lasting values? These questions imply a negative answer for many people. They seriously

---

1. This famous quote is the beginning of one of the most gripping descriptions of the period of the French Revolution. At the threshold of a new millennium this statement of Dickens has all the traces of an ominous prediction. Dickens's portrait of the French Revolution is a blend of sympathy with the fate of the exploited French masses and of utter horror about the irrational destruction that was the inevitable result of massive impoverishment caused by the arrogance and neglect of the exploiting circles. Dickens's narrative shows the potential of the city for catastrophe and dehumanization but also of the presence and power of humane imagination and courageous action. Dickens's fascinating portrait is also a prophecy of the results of globalization that makes the rich richer and the poor poorer and has the number of the latter increase in staggering fashion.

The essays of this book are written with the clear awareness that the fingers of the world clock inevitably and very soon move to High Noon. Will the billions of the world's poor move between twelve and one o'clock in one body to the ever-smaller islands of those who have amassed all the resources and all the power in their coffers and forts? No NATO would be able to stop those masses because the poor of today, in contrast to the poor before the French Revolution, possess excellent knowledge about the workings of the machines of the rich, and they can stop those engines and turn them around against those relatively few who claim to own them.

I wrote these lines in January 2000. At that time it showed already that, contrary to the 1980s, transformations tended to happen no longer peacefully but with increasing violence. However, I did not anticipate at all that my prediction of early 2000 would come true in a more gruesome way than I could have dreamed. The countryside attacked the city at its core doubt that there is either promise or values in the cities of today or any to be rediscovered, doubt that there is any chance that a sizable number of people could reidentify with the urban situation or that there is anyone ready to reassess, let alone reinvent, the livability of the city.

Any contrary assumption these people would consider unrealistic. The state of contemporary cities gives ample support to this pessimism. The plight of the megalopolis can be summarized as follows. The widening chasm between rich and poor is felt most in cities, and moreso the bigger the city. All too many urban settlements are quickly growing garbage dumps, suffocating in their sewage, not to mention increasing traffic jams and air pollution. Urban centers all around the globe exercise deficit management. Each rush hour already seems to contradict the hopes expressed above. All of this is accompanied by suicidal tendencies of the market, the major lifeline of any city since times immemorial. Competition on the market has already attained junglelike characteristics. The stronger gobble the weaker, and, in the end, the few remaining big ones will gulp down one another, thus destroying competitors, competition, and finally the market itself—all in the name of freedom of trade. States and the public hand are becoming poorer as well as weaker, and the private sector, richer and more powerful. The rather secretive deliberations and preparations for the Multilateral Agreement on Investment (MAI) are symptomatic for the topsy-turvy character of the present relationship between politics and economics. Discussion and drafting by twenty-nine member nations of the Organization for Economic Cooperation and Development (OECD) were stopped in the last minute but not yet for good. MAI would forbid any national restraints on foreign investments outside of the defense sector, and it would prohibit giving any preference to domestic companies over foreign investors. It would outlaw any national and even regional social protection that could infringe upon the interests of foreign investors. This would be the final end of what in Germany and Western Europe became known as the social-market economy.

---

in a most devilish fashion, proving that the countryside was manipulated and corrupted too. Would or could war be the proper response? a nation or nations against what? against a no-nation? and with what means? terror against terror? In the light of the issues discussed in this book, the observation becomes most relevant that the victims of the criminal destruction of the World Trade Center came not from the United States alone but from many member-nations of the United Nations. Therefore, the proper response and remedy need to come from the United Nations tower and not from the White House, a joined effort of all nations and societies toward social and economic change beyond national sovereignty and pride, a change that would not benefit the cities alone but bring peace and strength to the countryside as well and leading to the reconciliation between city and countryside, a reconciliation not yet achieved in the history of humanity.

Self-interest and profiteering, already sufficiently unrestrained, would finally triumph and add further moral corruption to the physical pollution of the cities with their unlimited suburban sprawl and bring about their suicidal doom.

Yet a contrary ground swell appears to be evolving. People in the Bronx and other deprived areas of New York have developed pride in their neighborhoods. Ecological conscience is growing and bringing back lively green into the urban stone deserts in Germany and elsewhere. Community organizers in Manila have taken up the fight for street vendors and other poor people against the big tycoons, although the latter seem to have the power and give the appearance that they have not only money on their side but with it also the officials and the law. The community welfare fighters do not fear that. They engage themselves for the poor, their houses, and for their right to keep their dwellings, dilapidated though they are. They battle for the right of the disenfranchised to maintain their minimal trades, to keep their pride, not only in themselves but also in their city as their home. Well-to-do people are starting to return from the suburbs to the urban centers as well, and not everywhere at the expense of the poor and not always into inner-city fortresses, "protected" by heavily armed security guards.

The hope of possibly developing the city into an antidote to the wolfish nature of the human race gains momentum as the growing communitarian movement, not only in the United States, proves. There are chances that urban conglomerates will cease to exist as the fulfillment of the bestial potential of humans. It is no longer unthinkable that the metropolis might turn into a neighborhood of neighborhoods. There are opportunities for the evolution of a really communicative and constructive marketplace, where global, regional, and personal concerns meet. This would bring to an end the fairly recent tendency to restrict the market to its commercial aspects. Thereby the threat of the worldwide suicide of the market might be abated only minutes before twelve. The various forms of peaceful protest outside and inside the conference rooms of the WTO in November 1999 in Seattle, Washington, against a hasty finalization of a global world-trade arrangement, were hopeful signs. They challenged and delayed the cementing of neoliberal globalization. The violent accompaniments were not central and could not mar the main objectives of the protest.[2]

---

2. The passionate plea by the chief editor of Le Monde Diplomatique, Ignacio Rammonet, in the editorial of the December 1997, issue to "unarm the markets" drew attention to the destructive as well as suicidal advances of the globalization efforts of neoliberalism and laid the base for the rallying of the movement Association pour une Taxation des Transactions

Such changes do not come about as a matter of course. They are cumbersome and full of risks. Considerable imagination, courage, energy, prudence, and sheer cleverness stand behind them and must increase much more if there is to be any hope for the cities of the day after tomorrow. A change of consciousness is needed that will allow a completely new view of things. An extensive strategy of consensus is required, reforming, indeed eliminating the present consensus, whose suicidal character has become sufficiently evident. This needs a lot of doing, and it takes time. It took hundreds of years to build the present consensus. It actually started almost two thousand years ago, with a major additional push in the tenth century. The building of the new consensus cannot wait that long, but it will take its time, and that will transcend our own life expectancy. Without patient as well as persistent working, thinking, and rethinking, nothing will change. The concrete signals of change, mentioned above, demonstrate a change in the realm and function of praxis, not predominant, yet subversive. A kind of praxis that is no longer subservient to theory takes roots in many places that superficially seem corrupt and desolate. Such new praxis takes its life in its own hands,

---

Financières pour l'aide aux citoyens, in short Attac, carried worldwide by people whom Peter Glotz, a well-known German politician and political philosopher, called "the early socialists of a new International" and clearly distinguishable from the old International.

This is proven by the fact that the warnings against the disastrous effects of the new economy on the health and vitality of the world at large have also reached the United Nations tower in New York. Two quotes from a commentary United Nations General Secretary Kofi Annan prove that. What he wrote for the *Asian Wall Street Journal* on 1 December 1999, is relevant support of the goals of the peaceful Seattle protesters: "It seems as though emerging economies are assumed to be incapable of competing honestly, so that whenever they produce something at a competitive price, they are automatically accused of dumping. In reality, it is the industrialized countries which are dumping their surplus food created by subsidies of $ 250 billion a year on the world market." "If industrial countries do more to open their markets, developing countries can increase their exports by far more than they receive now in aid." These quotes I found in an article by Sylvia L. Mayuga in the *Philippine Daily Inquirer*, 5 December 1999, an article basically in support of the Seattle protests, in which Filipino and Filipino activists had taken the role of essential initiators.

The terminological confusion about globalization is bewildering indeed. The opponents of the neoliberal manipulations and propaganda that go under the slogan of globalization call themselves antiglobalization people. However, they are the true globalists because the NGOs that they represent advocate the notion that industry as well as economy have to be related to and governed by the universality and complexity of global life, not the other way round. The neoliberal ideologues and their fellow travelers in industry, economy, politics, universities, and even churches are no globalists at all but particularists, indeed parochialists. They limit their perspective to industry, economy, and market as if this covered all of global life, its needs, and its gifts. There are so many things of global reality that they do not even touch. Thus, one can call the globalization ideologues and their fellow-travelers authentic antiglobalizers.

creatively and with cunning. This subversion needs to be assessed, strengthened, and advanced. It will dispute the theories that have resulted in the corrupt practice at hand, and it will inspire constructive theories that have their motivations laid open. This could bring about a theory that would truly grow out of praxis and, therefore, respect the common experience and enhance the conditions of the marginalized and the disenfranchised. It could at the same time stimulate the imagination and responsibilities of the powerful, making them realize that the real economic benefit for everyone, the powerful and the rich included, is in the greatest degree of welfare for the greatest number of people. The celebration of self-centeredness will cease because it is suicidal, unreasonable, irrational, and definitely unrealistic.

Thus, heavy work is ahead of us. It cannot succeed without reorientation and refocusing. No single person or group can do this alone, not even one country all by itself. One sweep would not suffice. Promising a blueprint for such a future would, therefore, be preposterous. Many experimental drafts are needed, and they must be debated and repeatedly redone. Right from the start, these drafts will not do without redrafting our knowledge about what was, what came to pass, what is, and why it is the way it is. No major change has happened in history without basic reconsideration of the past. This, by nature of the assignment, should be the job of historians and interpreters, including theologians. It requires a great number of people with an imaginative mind and with critical and hermeneutic skills.

They can fulfill that task only if they avoid being mere archivists. They need to keep a firm footing in their own situation and an eye on the future. Without critical assessment of their own predisposition and involvement, they cannot provide a sufficiently critical reassessment of the past nor reliable drafts for the future. Mixing the levels of time and freely traveling between them becomes an urgent necessity. Painstaking historical-critical attention to details as well as contemporary and prophetic political engagement need to be joined.

The following chapters constitute such drafts. They were drawn up in conscious awareness of urban and metropolitan situations around the Boston and San Francisco Bays and on the islands and peninsulas of New York. Los Angeles and Ann Arbor provided the author with further shades of urban experience. Considerations on this topic were, however, first made in postwar Germany in Frankfurt on Main, the hometown of the author, a city that has slowly grown into the hub of a major metropolitan area of the European continent. It is about to become officially what, in reality, it more or less already is, namely, the banking center of Europe, or more precisely, of the European Union. Frankfurt is nicknamed Bankfurt and Mainhattan with good reason.

These reflections are the expressions of a very conscious blending of detailed historical, philological, philosophical, and theological reflections with constant active engagement in academic, church, and general politics. After twenty years of active life in the United States, I have returned to my roots. In Frankfurt on Main, the final condensation of the insights evolved that I had gained in constant dialogue with past and present before and abroad. Prolonged visits to the United States and Canada during the last fifteen years have kept me in touch with the reality of the other continent. This introduction found its final form in the Philippines. I had been called to teach by Union Theological Seminary in Dasmariñas, Cavite, the oldest Protestant Seminary in the Philippines, 35 kilometers south of the urban sprawl of the Manila area. Day by day that sprawl is devouring more of some of the best rice-producing soil of the world, converting it into fortified housing areas for the well-to-do and into resort facilities for tourists from Europe and the United States. Huge golf courses are among the developments that steal water essential for the local tenant farmers. The stolen water of the rich ends up untreated in the streams and adds to their stench, completing the deterioration of the natural water flow into sewage channels started by the white man, Spanish as well as American, centuries ago. This experience added new aspects to my consciousness of urban and metropolitan reality with its tragedy as well as its hope. Together we started to develop programs that would add ecological consciousness to the training of ministers and expand awareness of the doctoral students of their previous and continuing praxis as basis for their evolving scholarly theories.

My profession as New Testament scholar should help me to participate in the reconsideration of the past so necessary for us today. My work entails historical-critical and theological-critical analysis of the Judeo-Christian textual sources in their historical, everyday contexts and of their subsequent history of reception and influence. Letting myself be nursed by contemporary insights and oriented toward the future, I see a new story of old evolving. Voices and faces of old, seemingly familiar, all too familiar in fact and thus no longer recognized and respected, are heard and seen anew. These old figures, their stories and their ancient lines, appear with new and challenging profiles and points, contrary to customary expectations. This often calls into question what seemed to have been settled long ago. These challenges are naturally detrimental to sacred cows. Indeed, the book covers rise and the pages tremble as the dead come to life and leave their golden cages, where they had been silenced by our pious embalming. They retell us their stories, which we had buried through the rites of sanctification and canonization.

This entombment of the past was achieved in the process of turning church officials into soothsayers of society, priests of the mighty, which eventually caused the present dismal state of affairs. Much of what we complain about now has been the result of certain misdispositions of theologians, clerics, and others who used church and theology as means of gaining advantage by means of deception. Such misdispositions overlooked and misinterpreted major concerns and tendencies of our heritage, ancient as well as recent.

In his trilogy on urban culture, *The Fall of Public Man* (1977), *Palais Royal* (1986), and *The Conscience of the Eye: The Design and Social Life of Cities* (1990), New York sociologist Richard Sennett critically addresses the dualisms of the Western mind and life as they express themselves in the cities of the Western world. They are characteristic for Christianity and for Western culture, shaped and influenced by the former. He sees these dualisms as causing continuous damage to the urban centers of the West. In his opinion, the relations of public and private, inside and outside, foreign and kindred, spiritual and secular, order and chaos are not realistically grasped and settled in the structure and lives of our cities. According to Sennett, these unresolved dualisms corrupt our cities. In them, Christianity has left as fatal heritage for modern society. In Sennett's judgment, these dualisms are not the least due to the influence of Augustine.

In my opinion, Sennett's view of such dualisms, their origin, nature, and effect, has an essential point but is overdrawn. Undoubtedly, what he calls dualisms are rather dualities that tended toward dualisms again and again, and still do. Dualism, however, is to be understood as an ideologically blown-up polarity of contrary factors. Whenever the dualities described by Sennett bordered on dualism, this evolution was not consciously intended and actually always denied. That did not make things better, as Sennett rightly observes. However, in general, instead of using the term *dualism, duality* would suffice.

These dualities, namely, unreconciled polarities, originated because Gentile Christianity in its breakaway from Judaism between 90 and 200 C.E. and in its increasing attempt to reconcile itself with the governing Roman society, lost hold of the ability of the early church to keep contrasts and paradoxes in creative tension. Keeping antitheses in creative tension is called dialectic. The dialectical dimensions of the message of the early church and its encompassing theology are represented especially by the letters of Paul, yet these are by no means the only expression of the early church's dialectic. The Pauline letters constitute dialogical communication with his congregations. Unfortunately, only some of these epistles have survived to prove the communicative dimension of a dialectic that was dialogical indeed, not the exercise of some abstract logic.

This dialectical approach was able to hold antitheses and even paradoxes in creative suspense, for instance that of the true representations of the bodily dimension of both human and divine existence, namely, that of the human person and that of the church community, understood as the body of Christ or, more precisely, Christ incorporated, the Christ as corporation.

As the Gentile church tried to make peace with the society around it and with its governing authorities, it transformed these dialectical phenomena into the dualities mentioned above, and there are many more, although these are less important for the line of inquiry that Sennett pursues and that the studies below will follow.

By emphasizing that Christianity caused and used such dualities, Sennett puts his finger on major problems and contradictions of the evolution of Christian praxis and theory, originally the main force behind the origin and development of the so-called Western world. The West is made up of and obsessed by such dualities. The relation of praxis and theory is illustrated, for instance, by the order in which they are found.

We are accustomed to put theory first and practice second and to understand the latter as the application of the former. This duality and its sequence had their origin in Plato and Aristotle;[3] the latter on occasion contradicted it significantly. The biblical tradition tends to put praxis first, understanding it in a more complex and comprehensive way than we are accustomed to, as creative as well as self-creative activity, initiating and changing the world around as much as oneself. The first chapter of the Bible, Gen 1, speaks of such creative activity. It does not limit itself to God alone but extends to humans as well. The creation narrative in Genesis also presupposes that God is changed by that universal creative action. He is no longer alone but is multiplied by creating humans in his image. The last chapter of the Bible, Rev 22, again insists on such creative action as essential for having future. "Doing righteousness" it is called in Rev 22:11. In the next verse, John of Patmos uses a phrase that Protestantism, not only in its Lutheran version, has disparaged: "to reward everyone as to his or her work" (22:12). John does not have a kind of working in mind that is mere hustle and bustle, but he thinks of the kind of creative activity that the first chapter of Genesis describes. "Work" in John's vision means "praxis," although the Greek

---

3. Plato is the first to speak extensively of this pair, but he tries to keep them in a dialectical relationship. Aristotle separates both concepts but is not all too consistent about that. A good and succinct discussion about the relationship between Plato and Aristotle concerning that pair is found in Edward Caird, *The Evolution of Theology in the Greek Philosophers: The Gifford Lectures, Delivered in the University of Glasgow in Sessions 1900–1 and 1901–2* (Glasgow: MacLehose, 1904; repr., New York: Kraus, 1968), 293–314. The scholastic resumption of Aristotle again took up this distinction of theory and practice and developed it further.

term does not occur here. But the term used, ἔργον, as a singular means "praxis," creative and socially relevant activity as a whole, comprising all of a person's life. Here as well in the visionary traditions of the First Testament, vision (*theoria*) is born in praxis and related to it as much as it creates praxis anew.

In a false literalism, Christian exegesis and theology, already prior to the Reformation, even more since then, have read Paul's criticism of the "works of the law" as censure of all action. It was completely overlooked and still is that Paul uses the singular "work" or, better, "praxis" always in a positive way to describe the whole engagement of Jesus Christ and of his followers as well. The phrase in 1 Thess 1:3 τὸ ἔργον τῆς πίστεως, "the praxis of trust" or, better, "trust as praxis," unfortunately has no place in most Christian theologies, although Paul has meant it as a comprehensive statement, together with the two other pairs "toil of love" and "endurance of hope," also very active concepts. The first and the last chapters of the Bible were written by banished people, Gen 1 by persons exiled in Babylon, Rev 22 by one arrested on the island of Patmos. Both texts are written by visionaries, Rev 22 in the literal sense of the word, Gen 1 in a derived sense. Neither chapter nor their contexts present "utopia" as a dream world, a substitute for their present deficiencies of life. Both texts and also the letters of Paul take their present situations seriously and develop out of them visionary challenges, "theories." Plato understands θεωρία not as mere contemplation or speculation or as systematically organized knowledge. Rather, he took "theory" to be vision, which he interrelated closely with "praxis."[4]

Medieval theology and philosophy misread Plato as much as the Bible, and they overinterpreted Aristotle. This led to a fatal reversal of the sequence praxis–theory to that of theory–practice, now understood as another irreconcilable polarity. *Theoria,* that is, vision, lost its imaginative, visionary qualities, and *praxis,* originally something very creative, turned into practice, a mere application of more or less abstract theory, most often stifled and sterile indeed. This polarity conditions the Western world to this present day.

Later the church pretended to possess active concern for the public as much as for personhood and persons. However, the public and the personal became, in reality, irreconcilable opposites. The church stressed spirituality. At the same time, it stressed its corporate character and claimed an interest in bodily concreteness. The relationship between both concerns, however, was not achieved by maintaining a dialogical interactive, indeed dialectical relation, between both but by the exercise of power. The result was hierarchical and centralized organization on one side as the basis of power and individualization on the other as the object of power.

Contrary to its claim, Christian theology had not been something completely new. It was rather a concrete rebirth of Jewish and pagan theologies, anything but unique. The historically unjustifiable claim of Christian uniqueness later functioned as a basic argument and evidence for the Christian imperialist hold on mind and society. This theology, strengthened by authoritarian minds such as Athanasius and Augustine, dominated the Christianized Roman world in East and West, and, after a period of decline, it again gained dominance in the Christian medieval society of Orient and Occident.

In that period the building of cities became a major preoccupation of Christian culture in the Mediterranean, in Western, and more and more also in Central Europe. In the first chapter of *The Conscience of the Eye*, Sennett describes the founding of towns in the West during the early Middle Ages. They were set up as protective fortresses, but the population protected was housed badly, crammed, and disorganized, and the houses and streets were narrow and crooked. The town centers were set apart from the garbage in the common streets. The centers were reserved for the holy place on which the church was built, a visible demonstration of divine order over and against the chaos of the secular world as represented by the utterly dirty remainder of the town around the church. As towns grew into cities, that contrast became merely more obvious. Elaborate and aesthetically more and more refined cathedrals in the city centers were clearly separated and distinguished from the chaos and filth around them where people lived and worked. Sennett refers to the fact that merchants and traders would set up their tables in town. Thus, the medieval market originated, initially rather decentralized. Sennett does not discuss the fact that the evolving market slowly turned into a major element of order on the horizontal level, whereas the church was the organizing element on the vertical level—another duality, rather eventful and fateful for the future.

The plight of the poor was real in those towns and cities, partly because of the outlays for churches and cathedrals. In order to receive attention, the poor had to come to the churches or other holy places established by monks and nuns. The latter would exercise a concern for the poor in the form of charity, in which the more fortunate could participate, too. This, however, took place mostly in and around the holy premises because clerics and monks would present much of the charity. The rest of town or city remained rather untouched by social concerns.

Such contradictions abounded, were indeed continuous. If they developed into dualisms, church and society usually first denied their existence. Then, if really and unavoidably confronted with this development, they tried to resolve the problem by emphasizing either one of the two contrary factors of the duality over the other, thus causing a reaction in the opposite direction in the not too distant future, thus in the end producing no balance at all. The occasional bordering of such dualities on dualisms revealed itself as a tragic dilemma basic for church and allegedly Christian society. It proved that they had thoroughly compromised themselves in their vying for political, social, and economic power—truly tragic in the ancient sense of conflict in the classical Greek tragedy, the problem of ὕβρις, "hubris," included. The repeated attempts of trying to get out of such dilemmas—through overemphasis of one side of the respective duality over the other—often turned tragedy into tragicomedy during the ensuing reversal, when the other, suppressed side again gained dominance.

Much of the proclamation that founded the Christ communities in the first century had used prevailing dualisms of the time—most of all of apocalyptic or gnostic nature—in order to exploit their critical potential and to meet societal and religious problems of the times head-on as those adopted ideologies had done before. Often enough, the sometimes-divisive and even energy-sapping nature of these dualisms was turned into imaginative and constructive dialectic. I am mainly thinking of the seven authentic letters of Paul and of the book of Revelation. Both authors were quite conscious of the urban situation and concentrated intentionally on that, thus turning their reflection into documents of urban theology. The Gospel of John is another, even more complex example of an urban theology as it skirts around Jerusalem and the conflict between (urban) Judea and (rural) Galilee in a paradigmatic fashion. The history of the origin and redaction of the works of Luke presents a further belaboring of problems of urbanity, more optimistic in the Acts of the Apostles, more pessimistic in the Gospel of Luke. All these writings demonstrate that within the early church tremendous efforts existed to confront societal issues and problems of the period and to come up with creative solutions, in praxis as much as in vision. As a creature of the Easter events, much of the early church had moved to the cities of the Mediterranean and developed concerns for them as centers of a strongly urbanized culture.

This urban concentration of the church declined contemporaneously with an increasing demise of the Mediterranean cities and towns starting in the second century C.E. Only the gnostic and gnosticizing branches of the church resisted that tendency. The other factions of the early church moved more and more out of the political arena and increasingly concentrated on heaven, souls, and the intricacies of theological grammar and vocabulary. This was the result of the growing loss of the dialogical and dialectical power and potential of the early church. It survived in Gnosticism but with heavy losses due to increasing individualism. There were also rare occasions of resurgence of the ability to confirm paradoxes as much as keeping them in dialectical suspense. The christological doctrine of the Council of Chalcedon represents such recurrence, a miracle of sorts.

In general, the dualities grew and remained unreconciled. The cause and reason for that development lie in the diffidence and distrust that the victorious branch of the church developed with regard to the actual socioeconomic state of human life in the Mediterranean, particularly with respect to people at the base of society. The dualities evolved in the church as it separated from Judaism around the turn of the first to the second century. Much of the church left the Mediterranean cities to themselves as they deteriorated. In terms of politics and social relevance, many of the leaders of the church set their eyes to the tops of society, intending coalition and alliance on that level.

A good number of these issues are picked up in the chapters below, which are reworked essays of mine. They all have in common a concern for urban theology. I start out with more exegetical studies, add reflections on themes from church history and theology relevant to the overarching themes of this collection, and end with discussions of more contemporary concerns, although the questions overlap often enough, as is natural. As far as the biblical side of the collection is concerned, I concentrate on the letters of Paul and the book of Revelation. In the latter part of the collection, streamlining is achieved by emphasis on the more economic and educational aspects of social history and history of theology, aspects present to this very day.

Urban theology is consciously contextual and situation-oriented. In my case, the association with variations and contrasts of various contemporary urban contexts has been highly formative. An essential element of these experiences has been my professional stay in the United States. They have found their concentrated expression in my farewell address to the Harvard Divinity School community originally under the heading "On Being an American Theologian," presently with the title "Personal Reflections on an American Theological Perspective." Here the reader will get an impression of the U.S.-American dimensions of my journeying as a theologian and how these experiences provided impetus to my heavy involvement and considerable engagement on both sides of the Atlantic, with a slight tilt to its Western shores. I could not conceive of my urban thinking and theologizing without this praxis of wandering.

I then turn to the topic of the book in particular. Any redrafting of the formative past of church and Western culture has to make up for the neglect theology and church have shown for the socioeconomic situation of the Hellenistic world, the cradle of Western civilization, an urban culture interested in achievement that is represented and traded on the market. This was the context that shaped the early church. A major factor in that social and cultural situation was hero-worship. It was the focus as well as the originator of much of the urban society evolving around the Mediterranean. In "Socioeconomic Reasons for the 'Divine Man' as a Propagandistic Pattern," the Mediterranean world during the Hellenistic-Roman period is described as an increasingly urban culture that centered on the market. This culture was given to the extraordinary and thoroughly miracle-oriented but saw in this no contradiction to rationalism. The expenditures for this worldwide experiment were tremendous; so was the fascination and, therefore, its missionary success. It drew both Rome and Carthage in its ban, with both cities competing in trying to best represent Hellenism.

The Romans finally inherited this achievement-oriented market society and improved it in many different ways. The Caesar religion became motor and protector of the growing world market and the cities and towns representing it. As this came about, a major shift occurred, which entailed a great social surprise. The leading figures of the Roman Empire defected from their cities, even the capital Rome, during the high point of Roman power and flirted with the countryside, first ideally and then more and more in fact. In "Who Is the True Prophet?" I discuss this surprising change, rather contrary to the development that the majority of urban people experienced all across the Mediterranean. I contrast the attitude of Horace, an official poet and prophet of the Caesar religion, thus a representative of the Roman elite, with the approach to concept, reality, and future of the city as expressed in the book of Revelation. Horace and John are set against each other with respect to the relevance and reality of their prophetic claims about the future of the city, proving that the prophet of Christ indeed showed more concern for the city than the prophet of Augustus.

Whereas Jesus and his disciples were people from the countryside and small towns, the so-called Easter events, especially the visions that were experienced during and after Easter, greatly changed the social situation for most of the adherents of Jesus. The majority of them went to larger cities, starting with Jerusalem, a city of world renown. They initiated "The Urban Adventure of the Early Church." In describing this adventure, I present major elements of the consciousness that was at the heart of these rather explosive moves covering the Mediterranean in less than half a century.

The major units of that adventure of the early church were the urban congregations confessing Jesus as the Christ. They understood themselves as incorporations of Jesus, the risen Christ and the living spirit. As such incorporations, they saw themselves as models for a truly urban life, where the ideals of the contemporary urban society, especially that of freedom, were realized. The new urban Christ communities knew of themselves as incorporated freedom, a challenge to their environment. Since they knew the Christ to be incorporated in their communities, they displayed great confidence vis-à-vis their major competitor, the Caesar religion, and laid claim to the epoch and its future.

Following the line of historical sequence, I then move to Paul. Besides John of Patmos, he most prominently represents the encounter with the Caesar religion and the critical as well as constructive dialogue with the larger society. In "The Hour of the Gospel: Jesus and Caesar" it is shown that in the early church, especially in Paul, the attempt to preach and organize the new society was done in a spirit of critical challenge to the Caesar religion. It is curious that Paul conceived much of the core of his urban theology in his address to the Galatian congregations, not inhabitants of cities but of small towns and hamlets striving to become, by way of accumulation, a city of their own. The essay "On Paul's Image of the Human" sheds further light on the anthropological challenge Paul develops vis-à-vis the urban situation that the communities he founded saw themselves in. "Legal Dimensions of Money and Theological Consequences" shows that the range of Paul's theological reflections on the urban situation of the Christ communities encompassed legal and economic dimensions.

The nature of Paul's theology and ethics evolving in these urban and political encounters was visionary, not doctrinaire; it was surely experimental as it behooved the needs of urban people Paul was dealing with. It was conscious "Living with Chaos." Under this title I present "Meditations on Paul's Ethics." They appear at first sight to be less historical, and they revive the spirit of the U.S. campuses of the late 1960s and early 1970s. This is done, however, for the purpose of gaining a deeper insight into the urban spirit of Paul and his communities. The clarifying potential of such a view from the distance is utilized both for a new view of an allegedly well-known topic and for bringing out its inspiring dimensions for the viewers' own time.

The visionary mood and gist of Paul's prophetic form of ethics is uncovered in these meditations. This kind of creative and constructive ethics has been brushed aside quite often in past and contemporary exegesis. Contrary to a common interpretation of Paul and the early church, they were anything but quietist or apolitical, let alone subservient to the governing authorities. Everyone talks about the reasons for Jesus' death, hardly anyone about the reasons for the execution of the author of Rom 13:1-7. "Why Was Paul Killed? The Epistle to the Romans as a Document of Resistance" makes up for that deficiency. The fact that Paul was tried, convicted, and executed by the highest court in the Roman Empire, that of the Caesar, is put into the perspective of the conscious encounter of Paul and Caesar. Apparently the urban theology Paul had developed brought about his demise. His advocacy of a healthy urban society was negatively answered by the governing urban powers. Their understanding of the course of society was defined by the religion and theology I described in "Who Is the True Prophet?"

Paul and John of Patmos were closer to each other in spirit than is usually assumed. John's irony matches that of Paul and has the same challenging character, directed negatively at the Caesar religion but encouraging the congregations to give reality to the urban ideas and dreams of Hellenistic-Roman society. John, the author of the book of Revelation, reflects the major trend of mission and activity of the early church, which started and maintained an urban concern. "John's 'Heavenly' Jerusalem" reflects on that in detail. It proves that John did not treat worldly issues in an escapist fashion but in a programmatic, constructive way. He conceived of the new Jerusalem, the city in the valley, not as the Jerusalem known but rather as ancient Babylon brought to life again. This Babylon revived looks much more radical than its ancient model, which in the meantime had turned into a demonic image. In John's portrayal, it has become a city that comprises the urban ideals of the Hellenistic world, the world viewed as a city.

As in the case of Paul, I also add a lighter note to the discussion of Revelation through the reprint of a public address, "The Wrath of the Dragon: Patriarchy's Last Stand." In his vision in Rev 12 of the earthly fate of the heavenly woman, John puts the faithful of the Christ communities of Western Asia Minor into a dramatic context of challenge and counter-challenge exceeding the everyday world. In his vision of the wrath of the dragon, John prepares the grounds for Rev 13, where he portrays the Caesar and the Caesar religion as the reincarnation of Satan, the dragon of Rev 12. This encounter is made relevant for today in this essay by being translated into a modern world governed by the ideology of nationalism. The continuous interplay of nationalism and urban bourgeoisie is addressed. This introduces issues that will be followed in later essays.

Entirely contrary to its Jewish beginnings, toward the end of the first century C.E. much of the church moved away from Judaism and more toward pagan society and state. These branches of the church gave up the sociocritical dimension of the early church praxis and the accompanying Christ-oriented theologies of the first century with their urban concern.[4]

---

4. The separation of the later dominant branch of the church from Judaism and the accompanying growth of anti-Judaism are parallel to the increase of deurbanization of that part of the church. This parallel development calls for further study with the possibility in mind that there was a causal connection behind this parallelism. The anti-Jewish nature of Augustine's theology would support such an assumption.

This detachment from urban interests climaxed in Augustine, who quite consciously took a distance to the city and despised any "urban theology." His view became influential for the next one and a half millennia; his reading of Paul became nearly canonical and affects us still. This needs to be challenged, which I do under the heading, "Should Augustine Have the Last Word on Urban Theology?"

What made the church follow Augustine and move away from Paul's urban approach and its socioeconomic theology? Why was the cult of the extraordinary, significant for Hellenistic-Roman society and its market economy, again put into the center of the church's concern and message? In "The Interest in Life-of-Jesus Theology as a Paradigm for the Social History of Biblical Criticism," this renewed fascination with the great personality as the center of theology is described and is drawn out into the present time. Thus, it intimates that we have not yet left the Middle Ages. It is important to note that the Middle Ages are not mere history now but are still with us. To this day life-of-Jesus theology is a strong part of theological interest, education, and church formation and therewith also of socioeconomic ideology. The latter has accompanied and steered life-of-Jesus theology from its beginnings. Contemporary biblical studies and theology at large are still informed by questions that shaped the bourgeois mind in medieval times. This life-of-Jesus theology definitely has cities and towns as its basis, the bourgeoisie as its adherents and advocates. It is tragic that for this kind of theology the cities are nevertheless of no concern, even less a focus; instead, a romanticized countryside plays a leading role. A kind of "Birkenstock" theology is still going strong worldwide.

However, in this theological and socioeconomic context, modern capitalist economy and its theory evolved, which is, in fact, nothing modern but, instead, quite medieval. "The Religious Dimensions of the World Market: A Farewell to the Middle Ages" describes this evolution and puts it into a contemporary theological perspective. In support of these inquiries and in contrast to much of contemporary economic thought and silent church complicity, I attempt to rethink the challenge that Paul's numerous reflections on the collection for Jerusalem present to us today. Paul's critical response to the urban society focused in particular on the market society of his days and on matters of economy and finance present in it. The strongest recognition of the socioeconomic dimensions of faith and church is found in the agreement between the Jerusalem and Antioch churches concerning a collection for Jerusalem and its execution by Paul. Later Paul identified himself and his congregations especially with this enterprise.

All this calls on us to develop a new urban theology. The economic aspects of this urban theology are treated in "Is there Justification in

Money? A Historical and Theological Meditation on the Financial Aspects of Justification by Christ." The relevance of these considerations of Paul is considerable for a theology that locates itself consciously in the centers of market and finance. Such theology takes a critical view with respect to obvious seduction and consequential tragedies of the buzzword "globalization," the fanfare of neoliberal ideology and practice. The claim of novelty and innovation accompanying neoliberal propaganda betrays thorough ignorance. Church and theology rightly understood have been *global*, that is, ecumene-oriented, from their very start and have collected positive and negative experiences *en masse* in the last two thousand years, unrecognized and unused by the alleged realists of neoliberalism. The church's experiences of old are called upon to be used in critical as well as constructive response to the present pseudogospel of globalization.

Two thinkers, Josiah Royce and Paul Tillich, prove that such concentration on the religious basis and dimension of urban communities and their global interaction has been a matter of contemplation on the American continent. Both thinkers are also connected with the continent I come from. I deal with Royce under the heading "Bultmann Was Not First: Josiah Royce as an Interpreter of Paul." Tillich is discussed under the title "Reason, Religion, Responsibility: Reflections on the Frankfurt Tillich."

Urban theology will be a major intellectual exercise in the universities and churches of tomorrow. It will, therefore, be a central element of an academic education in the future, in Asia even more than in Europe and the United States. Intellectual formation can no longer be surrendered to the dualities and dualisms of the past. In "Praxis and Theory in Theological Education: Is Scholarship 'Hot' or 'Cold'?" I intimate dimensions and goals of personal and intellectual development that grow out of praxis and into theory. I then present an example of such concrete theological enterprise in the context of a major metropolitan area that is the banking center of Europe, under the title "En Route to an Urban Theology: Can Theology Help Us Understand Urban Society?" An application of such program to the metropolitan areas of New York or Manila would not require too many changes.

My baccalaureate address "On Sojourning," presented to the seniors of Harvard Divinity School at the close of the 1976–77 academic year, is placed at the end of this collection of essays to provide a final upbeat. It demonstrates trust in the spoken word as a force that can move people and through them the world around them as we approach another millennium, an epoch in which the city will definitely dominate—for the better or the worse.

At the end of his *A Tale of Two Cities* Charles Dickens has Sidney Carter say as he faces the guillotine in place of another person he saves: "I see a beautiful city and a brilliant people rising from this abyss, and, in their struggles to be truly free, in their triumphs and defeats, through long years to come, I see the evil of this time and of the previous time of which this is the natural birth, gradually making expiation for itself and wearing out."

Union Theological Seminary
Dasmariñas, Cavite, Philippines
Dieter Georgi

1

PERSONAL REFLECTIONS ON AN AMERICAN THEOLOGICAL PERSPECTIVE

Urban Theology demands concreteness. Abstract generalization without personal, local, and regional specifics merely enhances the worldwide deterioration of the present urban mess. More than twenty years teaching in the United States and my present engagement as a visiting professor in the Philippines within an environment still heavily Americanized have formed much of my present perspectives and actions. The American hemisphere has increased the urban perspective, long before a matter of my theological consciousness already. In a way, between an American-born mother and an American-born son, I should be entitled to speak as an American myself.

Since 1964, with few interruptions, my family has been exposed to the experience of the huge crossroads called America, mostly of major urban knotpoints. Our prolonged stay in this busy intersection has led to the consequence that over there, in the old country, we Georgis are considered Americans.

Whether we are citizens in the technical sense here or there does not make that much of a difference in our days. In reality that counts, this is merely a bureaucratic quibble. Experience matters the most as determinator and qualifier. This particularly shows in the frustrating experiences when we express an original idea, something that just dawned on us and that we can claim true authorship for, and hear the German reaction: "typically American." However, we are accustomed to this pigeonholing experience. Often enough in the States, too, when we communicate an idea of our own, the reaction is: "typically German." This is all the more so, on either side of the ocean, if the idea expressed has a critical or challenging character. It is rarely perceived that empathy might be at the base of that challenge, even sympathy, cosuffering.

The upshot of all this is that whether you or I like it or not, over there, in the old country, I am an American theologian and shall remain that as long as I live. I believe my many years of experience of the crossroads America entitle me to consider myself an American theologian, and I am still taken as such by many. Thus, I shall use the "we" and the "us" as an American denominator.

Let me make a further point of definition. As I speak of "American," I try consciously to speak of the Americas at large, not only of the east-west connection Cambridge–San Francisco, which would circumscribe my academic engagement in the United States, but also of the north-south connection Canada–Argentina.[1] This would be very hard to understand for my German interlocutors, and—let us be honest—it is hard for us U.S. Americans as well. We may be intellectually aware of the fact that Canada is a larger country than the United States and that Brazil is larger than the United States, at least without Alaska. Existentially and experientially, we tend to give in to the very consequential sloppiness that identifies America with the United States. Thus, we give semantic credence to the ever-increasing perception and condemnation of the United States for chauvinism and imperialism.

You may be upset about this straightforward statement. However, before you part and denounce me as typically un-American, I want to tell you that I do not speak in abstract terms but in concrete ones. Staying here and debating whether the United States is imperialistic or collaborative, ugly or benign, is rather different from being abroad and outside of U.S. government compounds and then being discovered and identified as a U.S.-American taxpayer and professor—whether former or present does not make any difference. We Americans abroad are much more your ambassadors, your envoys, and your mediators than the official U.S. diplomats. Whereas they enjoy diplomatic immunity, we face the heat. We have to pay the price for what is done or not done, said or not said by the United States, particularly by the administration.

I am not overstating or betraying paranoia. We had not been long in the United States and already were identified in Germany with U.S. policies in Vietnam. Our opposition to the Johnson and Nixon policies did not help much. And it is even more so now in the age of the Pershing IIs and the international economic crisis. There is the guilt-by-association argument. There is our paying tax to the Internal Revenue Service for

---

1. Since I spoke this, the truth of that statement has come out even more perceptibly in our family. Our daughter has married a Mexican, our youngest son an Italian-Canadian. Our family has definitely become international. Six languages are spoken among our children and grandchildren.

over twenty years. This certainly constitutes heavy association. There is also the naive but pervasive belief that academicians have an effective role in society and that we professors, therefore, could have done more and earlier to change U.S. policies.

This being held accountable, not only for what I have or have not done, but also for what others that I am held to be associated with have done or not done, this has been the continuous story of my life. What I am sharing with you tonight grows out of that experience of not only identifying ourselves with the U.S.-American people and institutions but also of constantly being identified with them by others, often against our will and discounting our opposition. Stubbornly denying or defying those identifications does not help at all. Personal, institutional, or national pride are not good counselors either. This being identified by others is part of our historical existence and experience. We have to face it and work with it as much as with our own beliefs, actions, and nonactions.

The history of German chauvinism, anti-Semitism, Nazi atrocities, the Holocaust, the Vietnam war, white racism, American imperialism, anticommunism, the sins of Christian imperialism, and so forth will always be part of my history, no matter how much I am opposed to them and try to correct them. Since my boyhood, for instance, I have been interested in Native Americans, identifying with them against their white oppressors. But when I came to California, I realized that my residence there enjoyed the fruits of the oppression of American Indians and of the eradication of the "redskins." I was on the side of the "white man," whom I had always loathed when deep into the night I had read the stories by James Fenimore Cooper and others about the Mohicans, the Iroquois, the Commanches, the Sioux, the Apaches, and so on.

Thus, I have learned to face history realistically. I have grasped that I cannot associate merely with what I like around me and before me. We are always associated, too, with the sin and shame of ourselves as well as of others and also with the consequences of that.

Some of you may presume now that I am suffering from a gigantic guilt complex, but this historical realism I am talking about does not mean wallowing in guilt and negativity. It means facing up to our human complexity, not just that of ourselves alone but also the complexity of belonging, which is always more than our choosing. This complexity always also means complicity and compassion. Having gone through the experiences not only of the "ugly German" but also of the "ugly American," I feel entitled to speak to you tonight in terms of constructive encouragement. Our theological tradition helps us to find a middle way between the routes of stifling guilt complexes and of the covering up of past and present sins. We American theologians are learning slowly that forgiveness of sins and justification of faith are more than privatistic concepts and experiences. They are social phenomena too; they express the experience of the realities of loyalty and solidarity, not limited to privileged persons or groups, Christians, for instance. It does not mean whitewashing events. It means the experience of facing up and learning in full, being educated not from the top down but from the bottom up, our victims doing the teaching, the forgiving. We have to accept the loyalty and the solidarity from them—and we do. Thus, this lecture confesses to the fact that there is a place for hope.

As I reflect with you on what we American theologians can bring to the human family, I do not intend to distill a history of American theology. But out of a blending of the historical, the literary, the personal, and the current I present a critical fancy, heeding the words of Milton in *Paradise Lost*:

> But know that in the soul
> Are many lesser faculties than
> Reason as chief. Among these Fancy next
> Her office holds; of all external things,
> Which the five watchful senses represent,
> She forms imagination, airy shapes,
> Which Reason, joining or disjoining, frames....

A critical fancy I want to give, born out of the faculty, which has her office next to reason.

Is it too late for such a fancy? Chances are that the world clock points to two minutes to twelve due to our complicity. However, if we are ready to face this squarely—not covering this grim reality with any hurrah nationalism or scholarly neutralism—there are chances that the hands of the clock might still be halted. There are still two minutes left for corporate critical fancy of which this lecture is a part.

We American theologians participate in the lively fashion in which Americans relate to their past. In Europe, even intellectuals think that Americans have little past history or, as Native Americans, no sense of history at all, of which Europeans, of course, brag to have plenty. Europeans, therefore, claim that the American relationship to history is simple at best. The complexity of a William Faulkner or a Miguel Asturias are taken to be matters of personal idiosyncrasy alone, no reflections of complex historical consciousness, collective as well as personal. Yet there are many Ahabs pursuing their Moby Dicks in these American longitudes. The presence of an often-confusing if not demonic past is part of the American experience. There is also the interpretative reality of the tradition of the Hopis or of the lore of the African American spirituals, constructive offers of reconciliation of human and nature, human and history. Attempts at glorifying simplification in bourgeois mythification are, instead, rightly met constantly and quickly with critical scrutiny, which brings out the dark and even tragic dimensions in the American experience.

Within that lively relationship to the past, a solid element also of the literary tradition of the Americas, is the peculiar way of taking the Bible seriously. North American culture, the Canadians included, is the most Bible-dependent of all Western cultures. African American–inspired Bible reading is an essential part of the American experience. The Bible-related life of the Catholic base communities in Latin America proves that now the Bible is alive there even more. Therefore, the Bible is the nucleus of much of liberation theology too.

European Reformation led to an isolation of the Bible from public life and to a privatization of the biblical experience in Europe, even though there were some attempts at broadening it—in the pietistic experiments. All the spiritualists and other nonconformists who tried to relate the Bible to public life were persecuted, pushed into the ghetto, the underground, or abroad. English refugees who had fled to Frankfurt on Main in Germany, in the middle of the sixteenth century, already tried to give institutional expression to their understanding of obedience to Jesus Christ as Lord as they had learned it from a rediscovered Bible. Lutheran clergy drove these heretics out of Germany because they feared interference with clerical authority and even more a possible breakup of the dividing lines between the spiritual and the common, the secular. You know of these English refugees to and from Frankfurt on Main through more famous people, indirectly influenced by them, the Pilgrims of Plymouth fame. Their concrete and contemporizing interpretation of the biblical covenant is at the heart of American democracy.

It should not be forgotten either that Pauline and Johannine thoughts found expression in nonconformist spiritual practice and organization with the awareness that the spirit is given to the members of a community and that the spirit manifests itself in the meetings of the community and the dialogue and sharing that take place there. As we speak today of the spirit of a meeting we give credit to the spiritualist concept of the reality of direct guidance of the community—respectively the committee of whatever kind—by the Holy Spirit. The impact of the Gospel of John and of the letters of Paul reveals itself in this very concrete understanding of the spirit.

Thus, for us the limits between the religious and the secular are still transparent. Whereas medieval theology was under the motto of "fides quaerens intellectum," American theologians go further and say, "fides quarens societatem." Our social and political concern, criticism, and construction are heavily fed by biblical sources.

However, just as much as the biblical tradition moves us toward societal consent in ever-new forms of the covenant, this very tradition inspires also our critical dissent as we see the Bible turned into the tool of conformism or escapism. Here I see a major role of American biblical criticism, at the moment the pinnacle of biblical scholarship in the world. Here the historical dimensions of the Bible are explored as never before, including those of social, cultural, and political history. The economic aspects are scrutinized as well as those of religious history. We American exegetes see the Bible more and more in the widest possible context of the ancient world at large.

Sometimes we may bury the message with facts, but the urge to understand more than facts or ideas, to understand people, and to relate to people is strong. The seeming difference of the Bible to ourselves and our time slowly but forcefully turns into the questions of people wherever, questions long suppressed through processes of neutralization and domestication of unheard and unwanted challenges.

There is still a certain neutralism and historicism to be found in biblical scholarship, but also much resurrecting has taken place of dead and buried people, some in golden, some in unknown graves, among them many women and obviously many people of color. As they rise, they start to challenge us. They suggest new vistas, thus giving voice to what was before only half heard, misheard, silenced, forgotten, or suppressed. American biblical hermeneutics will slowly turn on us into a ministry of the dead. Rediscovering the Bible, hearing the witnesses speak anew, and discovering unknown martyrs have become spiritual experiences beginning to change churches and society, most prominently the Roman Catholic Church in the Americas. This is replacing the old biblical anti-intellectualism, which turned its back on biblical scholarship with the argument that it would interfere with spiritual life. Now biblical scholarship has even the stones crying out.

However, the orientation toward the past, particularly toward the biblical past, has always turned us American theologians to the future as well. The biblical concepts of the new world, the new humanity, the garden of Eden, the new Jerusalem, and many more have spurred individuals, groups, and whole countries in the north as well as in the south of the Americas. These and other images became code words for the Underground Railroad as well as images of sustenance and identity for those held back in slavery. Images from the First and Second Testaments of the exodus and of solidarity have fed liberation movements of this century, whether of Latin Americans or of black or red Americans or of American women.

These liberation movements are but the avant-garde of the Third World on the move from under the yoke of patriarchy, particularly that of the white man. Prophetic visions are shaping human togetherness and cooperation that defy the alleged necessity of old that says, "A working theory of the State must, in fact, be conceived in administrative terms. Its will is the decision arrived at by a small number of men to whom is confided the legal power of making decisions" (so in that ever-reprinted book by Harold J. Laski, *A Grammar of Politics*).

The liberation movements of today are the harbingers of tomorrow's frontiers, frontiers that will not turn into trenches like those of yesteryear. We are asked to be witnesses of the freedom of those still oppressed, even more of the freedom of those yet unborn. It is for them most of all that we want the clock to be reset, to take it out of the hand of those who are determined to make ourselves the last generation rather than to give free space and sufficient resources to the unheard-of generations. Our strife is for the common nationhood of all humans. Present-day nationhood and nationalism were not the first creatures of the modern age but are the last and most blatant remnants of those dark ages, their final devil's egg.

As we develop our utopias in exercising our prophetic heritage and mission, we realize that we do this with many voices, as though in concert. The crossroad called America has always been creative in communal experiments, almost none of them without a very heavy dose of utopianism.

The vision of authentic community has always been the best protection against the corruption thereof. Our loyalties crisscross, no doubt. There is no one with only one loyalty. The faith communities we belong to, for instance, have their loyalties beyond national boundaries, too.

Each of us individually and all of us together represent not just one voice but an orchestra involved in a concert of loyalties. Some of the parts, some of the orchestras are yet untried. So we are all listening as well as trying. Our conductor does not make it easy for us. She is not directing from a podium like the man in the White House. No, our American conductor is not just American, and he or she is playing a part while conducting, is one of us.

The Americas, and especially we American theologians as professional dreamers, are called successfully to demonstrate the experiment of pluralism, not with eyes fixed on the old pressure cookers of parochialism or its extended form of nationalism, both outdated remnants of the Dark Ages. Only if we allow our loyalties to the human family at large to be as powerful as those to our immediate neighbors and friends will the experiment succeed, the human family survive. We cannot ask anyone else to make the experiment for us. Neither selectivity nor controls nor power games, neither subordination nor exploitation will help to bring a humane twenty-first century around. They will stop it from coming.

The churches as experimental communities will have a major function in this exercise. However, respect for their integrity will demand respect for the integrity of others, openness for sharing, sharing also with communities of other integral centers, religious or godless. Our readiness for the day of the Lord requires first of all the readiness for one another, particularly the readiness for the enemy, not in order to kill but in order to embrace.

The wonderful life of the American crossroad has been made so colorful because the communities mentioned allowed personhood to develop. Commonhood created personhood. As in Paul's image of the body of Christ, the communal bodies excited and integrated individual gifts. Without them, the communities would have died. The creative play between communality and personality is something we American theologians need to give more attention to, not just in the context of spiritual communities but also in secular contexts. The arts and sports come into view here as much as education and, of course, society at large. We have learned a lot from sociologists in these respects, but the sociologists also want to learn something from us in exchange. Troeltsch needs more successors, a theologian from whom sociologists still learn. He needs company. The same is true with psychologists. We are indebted to them, but we American theologians also have a mission for them. Before I go further into future assignments for us theologians, let me stop and turn our attention to a local message, as it were.

Harvard College was founded for the purpose of training ministry candidates in rational theological discourse. These people, who were trained and who then trained others as well, were, however, accustomed to listening to the experience of their souls as well. Within the creative tensions described before as characteristic for us American theologians, the tensions between tradition and utopia, between community and person, within these creative tensions lies this other one—as its heart, so to speak: the tension between reason and experience. In this tension, reason may even tend toward rationalism, experience toward mysticism, but this tension is always there. It gives the visionary input and the determination and commitment. On the other side, however, it provides critical scrutiny and restraint. We are true American theologians if we keep inspired as well as critical, if we stay reasonable believers.

On October 6, 1957, Thornton Wilder received the Peace Prize of the Association of German Publishers and Booksellers in the Paulskirche in Frankfurt on Main. The Paulskirche in Frankfurt is considered to be the cradle of German parliamentary democracy because here the first freely elected national assembly met. It was, therefore, apt that Thornton Wilder entitled his address "Kultur in einer Demokratie," "Culture in a Democracy." The address was in German, beautifully presented by the author. I heard the address on the radio. It was at the time when I was about to conclude my career, first as minister and now as trade-school teacher, and was reflecting on my new career as university teacher, which was to start in a few weeks. Thornton Wilder's address set me going. The direction and assignment I heard from him is something I feel still committed to and have shared with you tonight.²

---

2. Amos Wilder, Thornton's brother, was present when I gave the original address. Amos, although retired, had been a very helpful friend and colleague during my days at Harvard Divinity School. We had many good exchanges that had started several years before my coming to Harvard during various visits of Amos and his wife Kathleen to the meetings of the "Alte Marburger," the circle of former students of Rudolf Bultmann, of which I had been the executive secretary for a while. Amos had been a source of encouragement and inspiration for me from the first time we met in Jugenheim, Germany. With my farewell address I wanted to thank him as well as his brother. In both persons, I wanted to thank all American colleagues who went with me to Frankfurt ἐν πνεύματι, in the spirit. I want to thank Amos very personally, too, because he has been such a friend.

2

SOCIOECONOMIC REASONS FOR THE "DIVINE MAN" AS PROPAGANDISTIC PATTERN

1. THE SITUATION OF THE CITIES

We are accustomed to look at ancient history most of all as being defined and represented by "great men." These figures of old are commonly identified as kings. They and their empires stand in the eyes of modern people as the major content of the ancient world. Cities and their and personalities come into view only secondarily at best. Such perspective does injustice to the ancient reality, in particular to the entity that formed much of later history, including our own: the urban world of Greece and Rome. This will be demonstrated in the following essay. Its focus will be on something that still appears to be the motivation and backbone of urban consciousness: competition, performance, and achievement.

The fourth century B.C.E. is commonly seen as the period of the final decline of the Greek *polis,* that is, of the Greek city not only as state but as an institution. However, the many scholars who share this view are only the latest victims of the propaganda of the Athenian imperialism of Pericles' time, usually presented as the classical period of Greek culture The very fact that several hundred "Greek" cities were founded in Asia, Africa, and even Europe during the next three hundred years would speak against that scholarly assumption and put it into the area of fairy

---

* This essay appeared first in Elisabeth Schüssler Fiorenza, ed., *Aspects of Religious Propaganda in Judaism and Early Christianity* (Notre Dame, Ind.: University of Notre Dame Press, 1976). This book published papers presented at a conference under the same theme, a conference Elisabeth Schüssler Fiorenza had organized and chaired.

tales. Moreover, Roman cities were another version of the Greek city. Athenian imperialism had claimed that Athens was the one and only real city, but it had done so at the expense of many other cities it had subjugated. They were brutally forced to pay the price for what we now call classical Greece, namely, Athens' fame economically, socially, and culturally. At best they were reduced to satellites and were not allowed to become or to remain cities like Athens.

The Greek city as a form of life did not collapse during the fourth century. The struggles taking place between 430 and 330 simply reflect the birth pangs of the Greek city coming to its true mission as a center of trade, industry, and culture. They were labor pains preparing for the explosive spread of cities under Alexander the Great and his successors. Such an expansion would be unthinkable without assuming that the Greeks were ready for it and had prepared for it by a hundred years of hard work and experience.

The Greek city had come to realize that it could not be a state. In that role it had proven to be a costly and unwieldy instrument, practically an unworkable one. The imperialism, first of Athens and then of Sparta, Thebes, and Syracuse, had shown that in each case the "state" had killed the "city," turned it into a rather parochial phenomenon. The cities, most of all Athens during the classical period, could not have survived on their own. They needed the resources of other cities, which they freely exploited, and they were heavily dependent on the energy of immigrants, traders, craftsmen, artisans, and the like from other cities, even of philosophers such as Aristotle. Although these strangers contributed enormously to the well-being and fame of the "host" city, they were not integrated and duly respected. In Athens these "immigrants" were denied citizenship by a law that Pericles himself had introduced in 451 that allowed citizenship only to one whose father and mother had been citizens of Attica before. The Greek city encouraged specialization of skills and functions, and the discovery of the individual was only a philosophical accompaniment of the economic fact of this growing specialization, which showed also in the arts. The cities burst with diversified energy, but they could not handle it through the instruments and institutions of the collective consciousness of the archaic period. Nor was the Athenian democracy an answer. It left out many immigrants and denizens despite heavy dependency upon them, and it methodically disrespected other cities.

The cities encouraged not only skill but also extreme, even monumental accomplishments by individuals, but the cities could not handle the individual greatness that they elicited and produced. Everywhere the divine was seen and presented in individual human form; the society called for great individuals who reflected in their work the divine and thus rose by definition above the ordinary. But when these individuals did excel they were punished, exiled, or executed. While the city as culture created "divine men," the city as state could not handle them. In Athens, for instance, Themistocles, Kimon, Phidias, Alcibiades, Thucydides, and many more were exiled; Miltiades and Socrates were killed.

This tendency to remove extraordinary persons was a perverted recognition of the fact that these persons (by the very instigation of the society in which they lived) rose above their native or host city and transcended into an urban culture at large—the Hellenistic culture, a thoroughly urban culture of a universal kind with the Greek language as its instrument of communication. This culture already existed many decades before Alexander, although in the disguise of the imperialistic as well as parochial city-states. Trade had already turned into world trade. A world currency was in the making. The need for world traffic by sea and land was seen and partly responded to by the Persians. Lifestyles and cultural expressions had become similar. Ideologically, the idea of one world and of one humankind became conceptualized. The need for a universal humanism dawned on the philosophers slowly. To describe all this as decomposition and disintegration seems to me highly inappropriate, and those modern scholars who judge the period before Alexander in this fashion are too quickly following the party line of certain critics who happened to live at that time, with Thucydides as their most influential spokesperson.

2. THE ROLE OF RELIGION

The common claim that religion broke up in those days again reflects more contemporary party opinions than historical fact. It is certain that the Homeric religion did not survive very well, but there was a rather positive and constructive reason for this. Homeric religion was basically feudal and could not provide the necessary infrastructure for the urban society, that is, a society calling for interaction of cities and their citizens and experimenting with the oneness of the world and humankind in praxis and in theory.

The Homeric religious potential had been finally destroyed by Athens' attempt to usurp the pan-Hellenic piety of the Persian wars. Pericles' attempt to unify Greek culture and religion under Athenian leadership did not succeed because it proved to be an imperialistic program.

The humanizing of gods had not been foreign to Homeric religion, but in the fifth and fourth centuries the kinship between gods and humans became more consciously emphasized. It found expression in epic, lyric, drama, sculpture, and painting and then especially in philosophy. Despite the continuation of other more archaic forms of religion, the urban society concentrated on this more aesthetic form of religion. The ancient gods on the whole remained associated with their traditional locales. They stretched only reluctantly beyond that (mostly via *interpretatio Graeca*, a Greek interpretation and integration of foreign phenomena). The new humanistic religion, however, found its base easily beyond the confines of the native city. It conquered the world.

It is noteworthy that Dionysus, who still had a sort of human (i.e., heroic) past and was understood as the most mobile god, received increased attention in the period described. Euripides offered his services to Dionysus, the missionary, in his rather propagandistic play the *Bacchae*, composed not in Athens but at the royal court of Macedonia. Just as Heracles had expressed the cultural aspirations of the Greek colonists between 750 and 550, so Dionysus accompanied the explosive expansion from 330 onward. Alexander the Great himself took Heracles, the alleged ancestor of his house, as his guide and protector as he moved beyond the border of his father's empire, first to the north and then into Asia and Africa. Dionysus was also seen as precursor, guardian, and model for Alexander's invasion of Asia, either by the young king himself or by his admirers immediately after his death.[1]

The third hero who caught general attention at that time was Asclepius. He later was transformed into a full god, but he was still seen as someone who knew of the predicaments of the human race, through his own fate and that of his sons. He became the healer-god of the Hellenistic

---

1. The question of whether Alexander had already deified himself or how much so is of no importance to our subject. What are the sources? How did such deification happen? How was it supposed to be understood? What were the interests behind it? How could it find belief among educated and uneducated alike? The book by Erwin Mederer, *Die Alexanderlegende bei den ältesten Alexanderhistorikern* (Würzburger Studien, 8; Würzburg: Triltsch, 1936) demonstrates that even the oldest sources, including contemporary ones, must have spoken of miraculous events and circumstances in Alexander's life. The issue of Alexander's deification is discussed in all major biographies of Alexander (e.g., William W. Tarn, *Alexander the Great* [Boston: Beacon, 1948]; Ulrich Wilcken, *Alexander the Great* [trans. G. C. Richards; New York: Norton, 1967]). For Alexander and Heracles, see Andrew R. Anderson, "Heracles and His Successors," *HSCP* 39 (1928): 7–58. Regarding the enduring admiration that Alexander received, which often lead to imitation, see Margarete Bieber, *The Portraits of Alexander the Great* (Lancaster, Pa.: Lancaster Press, 1949), repr. from *Proceedings of the American Philosophical Society* 93 (1949): 373–427; Alfred Heuss, "Alexander der Große und die politische Ideologie des Altertums," in idem, *Gesammelte Schriften in 3 Bänden* (Stuttgart: Steiner, 1995), 1:147–86, repr. from *Antike und Abendland* 4 (1954): 65–104; and Friedrich Pfister, "Alexander der Grosse. Die Geschichte seines Ruhms im Lichte seiner Beinamen," *Historia* 13 (1964): 37–79.

age, and his importance was still growing in the Roman imperial period. The successful oracular and medical practices at his temples were major factors in the ancient world's belief in the reality of miracles.

Of major importance for the growing urban society were the diversified availability and swift mobility of the divine. The cities realized that they could not afford to remain self-contained. They needed to be open for the extraordinary, whatever it was and wherever it came from. They needed to let people come and go, to stir up energy, and to invite talent. The imperialistic failure taught the city that openness was the best protection because it best served the interest in a free flow of resources, human resources as well as material and ideal goods. These cities lived on and for greatness, and they invited extraordinary, "divine," achievements.[2] Already the architectural appearance of the city was prestigious, and most of the other expressions of city life followed suit. The most economic way of utilizing the necessary talent was to share it on a wide geographical scale.

The ancient city-state was quite dependent on lavish voluntary contributions by its well-to-do people to cover the expensive outlays that the monumental achievements of the city demanded. Enforced contributions from conquered cities were supposed to alleviate that later, yet when this turned out to be a failure, the cities again had to look for benefactors. Taxation would not have been sufficient. While to various degrees voluntary benefactors were still found in their own midst, a great portion of support was expected from the outside. Mother cities occasionally helped, but substantial help frequently came from the strong men of those days, generals and, most of all, kings, especially after Alexander.

It may surprise modern people to learn that even in America today cities and towns do not possess the degree of freedom from state and central governments that the Hellenistic cities had. Even in Ptolemaic Egypt the most centralized system in the Hellenistic world, the city of Alexandria, had a relatively high degree of independence. It is surprising how many central governments in the Hellenistic and Roman world minded their own business, which was that of the royal court, the central bureaucracy, the military, and foreign affairs. There was, of course, always the temptation to interfere with the cities for extra revenue, better control of trade, and political correction. The cities' openness made them vulnerable. However, one way for cities to check those temptations was to lure sovereigns and other strong and rich men into some beneficial action and

---

2. The transparency between the divine and the human makes it impossible to look for linguistic demarcation or other distinctions. Where the extraordinary is experienced, the divine is felt; see below note 15.

then by vote of the people to acknowledge them through statements, acts, and even monuments of public gratitude, the gifts of the benefactor (χάρις) being responded to in the εὐχαριστία of the people. The expressed gratefulness of cities amounted to at least an increase in reputation for the strong man.

Anything, matter or action, that could be considered beneficial to the city could be counted here: the alleviation of financial burdens (tributes and taxes), financial contributions, rendering of commodities, providing of public buildings or streets, and so forth. The stronger the benefactor, the more he could also be counted on for interference against internal and external adversaries by way of protective force. The most spectacular actions of that kind were the acts of military deliverance from oppression; the restitution of the city's autonomy and original rights, with granting of new rights, usually issued after that. In these cases of emergency protection the cities were most willing to vote recognition of this act as a divine act, perhaps even to establish cultic worship in gratitude for it.

This worship might vary from occasional to perennial cultic exercises, the erection of statues in temples and elsewhere, the building of temples, institution of games, naming of month, after benefactors, and so on. Cultic honors were the most dramatic and public form of the recognition of "divine men" in the ancient world. Whether or not this worship related at all to the dynastic worship requested by the Hellenistic monarchs is still much debated. In any case, dynastic worship seems of little importance for our topic. The cult of benefactors in Hellenistic cities had much more impact on ordinary life, and it was more intricately related to expressions and forms of urban life.

3. THE ROLE OF "DIVINE MEN"

We have already seen that the borderline between the human and the divine was rather fluid in those days.[3] It was a matter of taste as well as of political sensitivity and shrewdness to single out certain actions as dramatic and extraordinary enough to justify gratitude in the form of cultic worship. The establishment of worship implied a degree of commitment, which could prove embarrassing in the case of a change of policy or even a shift of political power and sovereigns.

---

3. Documentation in Christian Habicht, *Gottmenschentum und griechische Städte* (2nd ed.; (Zetemata 14; Munich: Beck, 1970); Stephen C. Mott, "The Greek Benefactor and Deliverance from Moral Distress" (Ph.D. diss., Harvard University, 1971).

But against Habicht I would hold that the growing transparency between divine and human actions and between clearly extraordinary deeds and more ordinary assistance applied not only to monarchs or, at best, major generals. If there was any distinction between the beneficial deeds of rulers and those of other people it did not last very long. Mott has shown more definitely than Habicht that cultic honor as response to acts of benevolence could be conferred on lesser people than kings, such as generals, statesmen, or administrators. Acts 14:7–13 (18) gives a good example. In this narrative a healing miracle exercised in Lystra by Barnabas and Paul makes people of the town discover in them Zeus and Hermes. The priest of Zeus is about to bring them sacrifices. The humorous tone of the story betrays the narrator's belittling criticism. However, the pattern is clear. Another New Testament equivalent for this public recognition of "divine" visitation is found in the so-called *Chorschlüsse* in miracle stories of the Synoptic Gospels: the praise of the miracle worker by the people who were present at the miracle or who were informed about it.[4] Although we do not see in these stories that the city's official political machinery acts by way of voting, we frequently see that the public of the village or the town reacts in a honorific manner.

The miracle worker is not made divine by that acclamation any more than the voting of cultic honors confers deity on the benefactor so honored. Rather, the vote or the simple acclamation states that the public has experienced divine action through a benefactor, perhaps even a divine visitation. This is not an expression of abstract interest in divine essence but only the pragmatic question of the demonstration of divine power and its public recognition and ratification. The fact that this public recognition became an established feature of miracle stories, both on the level of folklore and of popular literature, speaks for its firm ground in public life and expectation.

The question of the origin and meaning of the concept of the "divine man" must be seen in the context of the wholly urbanized system of Hellenistic culture.[5] It cannot be treated as a separate issue. It is also an

---

4. See Rudolf Bultmann, *History of the Synoptic Tradition* (trans. John Marsh; New York: Harper & Row, 1963), 225–26. In reacting to these miracles people do not confer divine titles upon Jesus, but this does not mean that they do not acclaim divine visitation brought through Jesus (his divine beneficial acts).

5. Examples of the phenomenon of the "divine man" (θεῖος ἀνήρ) are found in Habicht, *Gottmenschentum und griechische Städte*, and Mott, "Greek Benefactor," as well as in my book, *The Opponents of Paul in 2 Corinthians* (Philadelphia: Fortress, 1986), which also discusses the theological background and superstructure of the phenomenon. In the article on υἱὸς θεοῦ in *TWNT* 8:334–40 and 355–57, Peter Wülfing von Martitz and Eduard Schweizer are methodologically insufficient because they limit the question of the existence or nonexistence of the

important segment in the complex infrastructure of cultic, religious, philosophical, artistic, and trade associations so characteristic of Hellenistic urban life. These groups created many additional connections to people of other cities, which bore on the public life of a city.

This urban infrastructure provided and guaranteed the flow of resources relating to the health, wealth, and vitality of each city. Each hoped for as many extraordinary contributions as possible, especially from outside sources, because all cities lived close to the limits of their means, if not beyond them. Every city hoped for an increase in reputation in order to attract more attention, which in turn meant the chance for more contributions, gifts, talents, trade, and so forth. In this context we can define the "divine man" pattern as an ideological expression (1) of the cities' dependence on extraordinary contributions and (2) of the fact that essential contributions came from outside. This could also imply (3) mobility as a necessary element of the "divine man" pattern.

4. FOREIGN RELATIONS

Thus far I have spoken more or less about the relationship of cities to one another and to governmental institutions. What about religion? The infrastructure of beneficial relationships described above supplemented and often even replaced the relationship to local deities as benefactors. In former times, the local gods and cults provided a major source of well-being for the city, not only spiritually but also materially. As public religion changed, the role of the gods changed as well. A deity now could be of real help if he or she attracted attention from the outside. This had been true already in classical Greece, but there (e.g., in Athens) imperialistic measures brought about these outside attentions, by means of military and economic force. Now more voluntary means were looked for.

Even foreign cults and new religions gained the eyes, ears, and, finally, hearts of Hellenistic citizens because they proved to be of benefit for the public as well as for the individual. The most sensational example of the fact that foreign cults were introduced for the well-being of a city was the transfer of cult objects and priests of the cult of the Great Mother

---

religious and cultural phenomenon to the occurrence of the terms "divine man" and "son of God." This is some kind of Platonic, that is, ontological reverence for the definite term. The term itself is identified with the reality it relates to. Where the term does not exist, the reality implied does not exist either. This terminological Platonism, which is symptomatic for the *TWNT* of Gerhard Kittel, is still found in studies like that of William Holladay.

from Asia Minor to Rome during the time of the Second Punic War. However, this was by no means the only instance of that kind of public recognition. The most consequential case of public recognition of a "foreign" religion was that of Christianity under Constantine.

This meant an open acknowledgment that the persecution of Christians had done damage to the state and its people and that the acceptance of Christianity would be for the common good. The Christian apologists had worked toward this goal of public recognition for the sake of the state's and of humanity's well-being, and the Christian apologists had only imitated the idea, intent, and technique of the Jewish apologists. Most missionary religions meant well for the public—at least in the understanding of the missionary—in their venture, which was usually somewhat inaccurately described as "apologetic."[6] The works of Jewish apologists, the Acts of Luke, and the Pastoral Epistles are good demonstrations of that spirit. The activities of Apollonius of Tyana and of Alexander of Abonuteichus present impressive examples as well, the first especially with respect to the advice he is supposed to have given to the cities of Asia Minor, the latter with respect to Abonuteichus and the neighboring country. For us today the questions of an individual or personal nature and of personal choice dominate in the discussion of religion. In the ancient world, especially in the time of Hellenism, the collective and societal issues were the first considerations in most missionary activities. Having reviewed the primary evidence over and over again, it appears to me that the individualistic and privatistic character of the so-called missionary religions has been unjustifiably overemphasized. The *Letter of Aristeas,* the Acts of the Apostles, and *The Golden Ass* by Apuleius, here especially the eleventh book, are only a few of many documents to demonstrate missionary interest in the well-being of all, where the propagated religion is proposed as the major instrument for bringing this about and for serving the best interests of the individual as well.

The practice and success of the propaganda of these foreign or new cults show how they wanted to be "of help." As soon as it was possible for them, professional and especially "lay" missionaries established cult-related associations of their religious persuasion. These functioned as

---

6. See the discussion of the problem of Jewish "apologetic" missionaries and their Christian (and pagan) counterpart in Georgi, *Opponents of Paul in 2 Corinthians.* Paul and the majority of gnostic missionaries represented quite different options of missionary philosophy. One could say that they were less *eudaimonistic.* However, Paul showed strong concern for the human race, and even the Gnostics often retained a curious interest in a sane world, although in the beyond.

clubs for compatriots and fellow believers in the same city. The Island of Delos, for instance, gives ample evidence for that.[7] As a foreign cult was introduced by a professional missionary or by a merchant, sailor, or traveler, the principal issue was not personal religious satisfaction. The foreign cult worked as protective and supportive agent for the migrant person or alien resident and eventually for his or her compatriots and fellow believers. The respect for the new god or cult was good for the health of the host city as well, because it helped to avoid divine wrath and made trade and other religions prosper. In many cases these cults then attracted the attention of natives, not only when full-time missionaries worked toward that goal but often also when "lay" people or part-time missionaries were the only ones responsible for the existence and appearance of their own religion in town. Again the Island of Delos provides evidence. Many cults that flourished in Rome, not the least of which was Christianity itself, seem to have been introduced there in this fashion. The exotic nature of the new or foreign religion, the peculiar traditions and customs, the extraordinary promises and experiences were the major means of stimulating curiosity and, finally, loyalty among the natives. Again, the extraordinary offer from the outside was seen as something that made private and public life flourish.

The sixth satire of Juvenal gives us an idea of the diversity of these cults and of their attractiveness. The cults of Cybele, Isis, and the Jews are mentioned, along with those of magi and astrologers. The different means used were first and foremost customary to the cult. However, Juvenal indicates that there was some extra effort displayed in order to attract attention, namely, some more aggressive propaganda. Here extraordinary acts can be assumed, demonstrations of divine power. Juvenal criticizes the social phenomenon represented by these propagating cults. He castigates their upward mobility, their interest in gaining access to the social establishment. It is part of Juvenal's polemic to make it appear as a matter of an individualistic interest, wholly perverted. For example, he attempts to make female curiosity paramountly responsible for this inroad of foreign cults into the Roman society. This gives him a chance for facetious ridicule of the development. The interest Caesar showed in Isis, for instance, proves Juvenal to be wrong. Caesar's interest was certainly not just a matter of individual and private religiosity. The concern of the Serapis religion for the public is also well known. In my study of Paul's opponents I have mentioned that even the mystery

---

7. See the material collected on Delos by Philippe Bruneau, *Recherches sur les cultes de Dèlos a l'epoque Hellènistique et a l'epoque impériale* (Bibliothèque des écoles françaises d'Athènes et de Rome 217; Paris: Boccard, 1970).

religions showed a tendency to relate to public life.[8] There is sufficient indication that other mystery religions imitated the Eleusis mysteries in order that they might promise at least as substantial a contribution to the vitality of the host society as the prototype had given.

But there was also the possibility in these missionary movements of upsetting society. I am thinking of their potential as expressions of the underground. The embodiment of the divine power in human beings could be seen as means of defying the given social structure. The structure of the Dionysiac mysteries in Rome in 186 was sufficiently different from established Roman social values and structures to make the Roman authorities fear the growth of a state within a state, leading to sedition and revolution.[9] Women were not only emancipated in this cult but were in the leadership position. Slaves were fully recognized also, and there was no outside control and domestication, as there have been in Eleusis, through the machinery of the state. Integrating the cult into Athenian society, for instance, neutralized the effect of allowing slaves into the Eleusinian mysteries. Although many more traces of an underground trend among religious groups in the Hellenistic period could be mentioned, I shall limit myself to two further examples.

In the gnostic movement, especially in its Christian form, women were fully liberated, and all social distinctions were relinquished.[10] With the complete bedeviling of procreation in the radical gnostic groups and with sexual abstinence as a powerful tool, population zero (in its most literal sense) was the goal, which promised the most drastic and efficient liberation from the evils of this world.[11] Being empowered by the divine was felt to be the decisive stage toward liberation, with deification as the end. It promised a degree of world-defying ecstasy that made all normal experiences of excitement meaningless and therefore nonexistent.[12]

---

8. Georgi, *Opponents of Paul in 2 Corinthians*, 163–64.

9. Livy 39.8–18; *CIL* 1:196; *ILS* 18. On the issue of the "Bacchanalia," see Dieter Georgi, "Analyse des Liviusberichts über den Bacchanalienskandal," in *Unterwegs für die Volkskirche: Festschrift Dieter Stoodt zum 60. Geburtstag* (ed. Wilhelm-Ludwig Federlin and Edmund Weber; Frankfurt am Main: Lang, 1987), 191–207.

10. Cf., for instance, the hierarchical, antiwomen, and pro-establishment orientation of the polemics of the Pastoral Epistle against the Gnostics.

11. See the description of gnostic attitudes in Hans Jonas, *Gnosis und spätantiker Geist* (2nd ed.; Göttingen: Vandenhoeck & Ruprecht, 1954), 140–251, esp. 214ff.; idem, *The Gnostic Religion* (Boston: Beacon, 1958), 241–89. The paradigm that the *Acts of Thomas* offer for this revolutionary attitude has been all too frequently overlooked. The original gnostic documents discovered in Nag Hamadi have not altered our view of gnostic ethics as expressed in Jonas's description.

12. But even gnostic movements as much as other underground religions were ready to compromise when a chance of becoming established religion or even state religion occurred.

Another example of religious underground propaganda survives in popular literature, namely, in Hellenistic romances. Martin Braun has emphasized that properly.[13] Braun shows that in some of the romance literature motifs of the social and political establishment were usurped and then associated with traditional heroes of local lore. But traditional figures (and values) of the oppressed could be associated with established heroes of the ruling class too, thus converting them into camouflaged spokesmen for the identity and liberation of the oppressed. In the Alexander romance,[14] a collection of quite different Alexander traditions, the first part deals with the relationship of Alexander and Nectanebus, the pharaoh of the fourth century who mysteriously disappeared and whose reappearance was prophesied by some Egyptian prophets. The tradition, which the Alexander romance uses, makes Alexander the natural son of Nectanebus and thus an Egyptian prince. Father and son possess supernatural powers, especially in the original tradition, somewhat belittled by Pseudo-Callisthenes. Alexander's first major activity is the conquest of the Mediterranean and the return to Egypt with the founding of Alexandria as climax. Here in the tradition Pseudo-Callisthenes used for the first part of his romance, Egyptians forcefully revised history, thus expressing the hope for a radical reversal of Hellenistic society.

Such eschatological elements in religious propaganda would not necessarily upset the established urban society because the Hellenistic city itself in all its excessive and turbulent life was a utopia in stone, and therefore many forms of eschatological excitement were a rather natural accompaniment of the common way of urban life. However, the reversal of all societal conditions, as can be seen in the examples described, could be a threat. Alexander was welcome as long as he appeared in propaganda and lore as successor to Heracles and imitator of Dionysus, as a divine warrior and even as a son of god, a divine man in the superlative. But as an Egyptian prince he reversed history, and that was not permissible. If the oppressed and ridiculed, the common people, saw in him not only the reservoir but also the representation of the heroic and divine, that smelled of revolution. The present text of the Alexander romance has

---

The most striking example of this, besides that of Mani's relations to Shapur I, is the Christian religion.

13. Martin Braun, *History and Romance in Graeco-Oriental Literature* (Oxford: Blackwell, 1938).

14. The oldest extant version is by Pseudo-Callisthenes. For the text, see Wilhelm Kroll, *Historia Alexandri Magni* (2nd ed.; Berlin: Weidmann, 1958). For the translation of Kroll's text into English, see Elizabeth Hazelton Haight, *The Life of Alexander of Macedon* (New York: Longman, Green, 1955). The most comprehensive study is that Reinhold Merkelbach, *Die Quellen des griechischen Alexanderromans* (Zetemata 9; Munich: Beck, 1954).

tried its best to correct these dangerous trends in order to make the lore readable to Hellenistic readers at large,[15] but the strands of underground opposition and reversal were present under the surface of a large segment of popular religion. Still, the Hellenistic ghettos never broke out—and Christianity missed its chance too. Constantine meant the end to any serious attempt at radically correcting the urban society. Instead, the urban society became increasingly pushed aside. Christianity as "state religion" became a rural religion.

---

15. A good example for this rather superficial compromise is the present version of chapter 34 of the first book of Pseudo-Callisthenes, which tries to rationalize why the Macedonians overcame the Egyptians with all their skill. This is done in the face of the oracle of the return of the pharaoh and the presentation of Alexander as Sesonchosis redivivus. The names of Sesonchosis and Nectanebus are becoming confused.

3

WHO IS THE TRUE PROPHET?

1. INTRODUCTION

In the previous chapter and in the preface I have already hinted at the fact that the climate of ancient urbanization had a heavy eschatological dimension. However, the understanding of the last things and their light on contemporary life was not necessarily associated with the city. Urban eschatology indeed was later. Initially, ancient eschatology essentially was of a rural character, as already the notion of paradise shows. The paradise is literally a garden. In the following essay I present the curious contrast between two different prophets, both heavily involved in thinking and speaking about the future of the world: the writer of the last book of the New Testament, John, and the Roman poet Horace. The social image the writer of the book of Revelation gives to the new and final world is that of the city. The Roman poet and prophet instead sings of the idyllized countryside as the place of the good world to come and thus returns to the more traditional form of eschatology. The dramatic dimensions of these visions are increased by the opposite origins of both prophets. John most probably came from Palestine and wrote his portrait about a future grandiose megalopolis when he was banished, a victim of

---

* The first form of this essay was given at the 1984 meeting of the Society of Biblical Literature in Chicago. A revised and enlarged form was prepared for the Festschrift for Krister Stendahl in *HTR* 79 (1986): 100–26; repr. as *Christians among Jews and Gentiles: Essays in Honor of Krister Stendahl on His Sixty-Fifth Birthday* (ed. George W. E. Nickelsburg and George W. MacRae; Philadelphia: Fortress, 1986), 100–26. The choice for the particular topic with its strong religio-historical and social-historical perspectives was honoring the common predecessor of Stendahl and myself as Frothingham Professor at Harvard University, also Stendahl's predecessor as editor of *Harvard Theological Review*, Arthur Darby Nock.

Roman oppression on a desolate island. Horace gave words to his poetic voice about the idyllic future around and in the world capital, the center of ancient urbanity. Whom of the two would the future verify? What may first strike us in Horace as a complete contradiction to our situation may not be without modern parallels after all.

Krister Stendahl and the colleagues assembled around him during his tenure at Harvard Divinity School contributed to the fact that the history of religion approach has taken a sure foothold in New Testament studies in the United States. In the countries of its origin this approach has gone into sad decline, even in the homeland of the "history of religion school." A major part of the heritage of that school has been the refusal further to abuse biblical studies for apologetic reasons lest one make the biblical environment merely a negative foil to the claim of superiority for the experience and message of Jesus and the primitive church. The attack on Christian triumphalism in *exegesis* and the insistence on the integrity of the historically particular, indeed of the peculiar, have been one of Krister Stendahl's hermeneutical contributions to the exegetical pursuit.

Stendahl has helped me to realize the need for fairness to the dead, to acknowledge the original excitement, challenge, and tribulation of the dialogue of two thousand years ago, and not to make it a mere extension of our own interests and agitations. The participants in that dialogue of old are not copies of us but have an integrity of their own, their identity being often vastly different from that of their alleged heirs. The fact that many of the dead in the New Testament tradition and its "Christian," Jewish, and pagan environment have no heirs is not to be held against them.[1]

A history of religion approach appears most necessary vis-à-vis the concept of eschatology because no other concept has been so misused in biblical studies in recent decades. The history of religion school, in discovering the eschatological aspects of Jewish and early Christian thought and literature, experienced this as a shocking encounter with strange phenomena. Meanwhile "eschatological" has become a household word in biblical studies, a term that now denotes what is peculiarly and uniquely Christian, *our* property, as it were, *us* over against *them, us* being early and modern Christians together, *them* being all others, including post–first-century Jews. Moreover, "eschatological" has also become synonymous with what is amaterial, apolitical, and frequently "dialectical," but now in a sense neither Hegel nor Marx would have associated with it,

---

1. The challenge Krister has brought to us, his colleagues, can be condensed in the famous phrase of Tacitus: *sine ira et studio*. Tacitus and Stendahl prove that this methodological ideal does not diminish adrenaline.

namely, *neutral*. Thus an adjustment of our focus on eschatological texts of New Testament times appears to be in order. The inclusion of some unexpected worldly material will be of help, for part of the reason for the apologetic triumphalism abuse of the "eschatological" has been the isolation of the biblical connection from its "pagan" and "apocryphal," even its diaspora, environment, contrary to the history of religion school's branching out and its subsequent discovery of strange bedfellows.

It is rather curious that students of the New Testament, particularly those making eschatology a battle cry, never mention certain highly eschatological texts contemporary with Jesus and Paul—namely, Roman texts—despite the fact that they reflect the origin and consequences of a rather lively propaganda in New Testament times, a propaganda that extended far beyond Italy. The only text some will mention here is Virgil's *Eclogue* 4, and then only to say that the poem is a strange and curious text, rather foreign in its environment; in addition, since no one really knows how to interpret this alienum the text is dropped again. However, Virgil's *Eclogue* 4 is not a strange and singular bird but rather the expression of a much more general and pervasive mood, ranging from Cicero's *Somnium Scipionis* to the poems of Statius.[2] The fact that Rev 13 describes the Caesar religion as a prophetic one deserves more attention.[3]

I would like to single out an "official" Roman text and its context, a text written by one of the major contributors to the Augustan cultural renaissance but also, besides Virgil and Augustus himself, the major theologian/prophet of the budding Caesar religion, the prophetic religion John of Patmos attacks. I am speaking of the *Carmen saeculare* of Horace. This poem is relatively contemporary with the New Testament. It originated at a time when the gospel according to Augustus had the world spellbound. Because there is not space here to produce a detailed textual analysis of that ode,[4] I will limit myself to certain observations

---

2. Besides the texts of Horace mentioned below and Virgil's *Ecl.* 4, there are other texts of Virgil that have eschatological overtones, not just the *Nekyia*, the descent into Hades in the sixth book, or the description of the divine shield in lines 626–728 of the eighth book of the *Aeneid*, but many more passages of this famous epic. Among the *Eclogues*, the first, fifth, sixth, and ninth should be mentioned too, as well as certain passages of the *Georgica* (e.g., 1.24–42, 498–514; 2.136–176, 458–541; 3.1–49; 4.315–558). The two fragmentary *Eclogues* of the Einsiedeln Manuscript, the Caesar *Eclogues* of Calpurnius Piso, and the Caesar poems of Statius are further examples of Roman eschatology in New Testament times.

3. The Harvard Th.D. dissertation of Steven Scherrer, "Revelation 13 as a Historical Source for the Imperial Cult under Domitian" (1979), presents excellent material for this comparison.

4. See in particular the commentary on Horace by Adolf Kiessling *Q. Horatius Flaccus Werke* (rev. by Richard Heinze; 10th ed.; Berlin: Weidmann, 1960), 1.466–83 (on odes and

and considerations that are relevant for understanding eschatology in New Testament times

2. THE *CARMEN SAECULARE* OF HORACE

The *Carmen saeculare* was commissioned for the official celebration of the secular games, the official jubilee for the founding of the republic.[5] This was not an annual affair but was meant only for the end of a *saeculum*.[6] The origin as well as further occurrences of the games are a matter of dispute.[7] The length of a *saeculum* was not firmly established and was open to local variety and political manipulation. The date of the games certainly fell in the province of political expediency and was therefore easy prey for convenient adjustments. Major occurrences and catastrophes, like the outbreak of the civil war, could also influence the calendar. The games were supposed to propitiate for past sins.[8]

Since Octavian understood himself as the savior of the republic, a celebration of the turn (revolution) of a *saeculum* as centenary of the initial republic fit well into his program. He had the secular games, long overdue,

---

epodes). See also the epilogue to this volume by Erich Burck, with a detailed and annotated bibliography (569–647). Important also is Eduard Fraenkel *Horace* (Oxford: Oxford University Press, 1957). On pages 467–70 Kiessling gives the text of the oracle and of the records for and of the respective games. Relevant texts are also found in Viktor Ehrenberg and Arnold Hugh Martin Jones, *Documents Illustrating the Reigns of Augustus and Tiberius* (2nd ed.; Oxford: Clarendon, 1955), nos. 30–32 (60–61) See also n. 11 below.

5. On the secular games, see further Martin Nilsson, "Saeculares ludi" PW 1.A.2:1696–1720; Lily Ross Taylor, "New Light on the History of the Secular Games," *AJP* 55 (1934): 101–20; Ronald Syme, *The Roman Revolution* (Oxford: Oxford University Press, 1952), 84, 218, 443–44; Franz Altheim, *A History of Roman Religion* (New York: Dutton, 1938), 72, 287–91, 353, 382, 390, 394–407, 442, 458–60; Kurt Latte, *Römische Religionsgeschichte* (Handbuch der Altertumswissenschaften; Munich: Beck, 1960), 248, 298–300; Robert E. A. Palmer, *Roman Religion and Roman Empire: Five Essays* (Philadelphia: University of Pennsylvania Press, 1974), 102–8; J. Gagé, "Beobachtungen zum Carmen Saeculare des Horaz," in *Wege zu Horaz* (ed. Hans Oppermann; 2nd ed.; Wege der Forschung 99; Darmstadt: Wissenschaftliche Buchgesellschaft, 1980), 14–36. These authors give more primary data and secondary literature.

6. The idea of a *saeculum* and its use as an instrument for dividing epochs cultically and institutionally seem to have come from the Etruscans. The lengths of these periods were and still are matters of debate. Prodigies played a role. On the concept and the debates see n. 4 above and Gerhard Radke "Saeculum," *KlPauly* 4:1492–94, here also further bibliography and further evidence about the games.

7. Different opinions concerning age and further occurrences of these games in Taylor, "New Light"; Latte, *Römische Religionsgeschichte,* 246, esp. n. 4, new considerations in Palmer, *Roman Religion and Roman Empire.*

8. This is the opinion of Latte, *Römische Religionsgeschichte,* 248 n. 3.

very carefully prepared.⁹ Most probably he planned them immediately after the decisive battle of Actium but then delayed them for political reasons.¹⁰ Like his politics in general, his final arrangement showed respect for tradition together with conscious modifications. In fact, his reform of the secular games "veränderte ihren Charakter völlig, indem sie den Akzent von der Sühnung der Vergangenheit auf den Beginn einer neuen Epoche verlegte."¹¹

The relationship of the *Carmen saeculare* to the games has been a matter of dispute since the discovery of the records of the games and Theodor Mommsen's commentary on them.¹² However, it seems certain that Horace's poem played a liturgically important role, that it "einen einzigartig wirksamen Ritus darstellte, die Götter gnädig zu stimmen."¹³ In *Ode* 4.6, which is contemporary with this "centennial song," Horace describes the situation of origin of the festival hymn. Here he defines his own mission as inspired by Apollo.¹⁴ Horace dedicates this ode as well as the *Carmen saeculare* to the Delphic god who has a temple on the Palatine Mount.¹⁵ The poet of the ode, "Parcus deorum cultor et infrequens,"¹⁶ takes the gods not as a mere foil of poetic hyperbole. Gods for him are a presence laden with power, as his ode "Bacchum in remotis carmina

---

9. On these preparations see, e.g., ibid. 298–300.

10. So, with good arguments, Harold Mattingly, "Virgil's Golden Age Sixth Aeneid and Fourth Eclogue," *Classical Review* 48 (1934): 161–65.

11. Latte, *Römische Religionsgeschichte*, 248. This official eschatological concept of the new age as political reality is presented in a fascinating way in the famous letter of the proconsul of the province of Asia and in accompanying decrees on the new calendar. A copy was found in Priene, then also in Apamea, Eumeneia, and Dorylaeum (*OGIS* 458 and *SEG* 4:490, reprinted in Ehrenberg and Jones, *Documents*, no. 98 [81–83]; see also the inscription from Halicarnassus *IBM* 4 1 n. 894; Ehrenberg and Jones, *Documents*, no. 98a [83–84]). A translation of the text of this inscription is given below.

12. For the text of the official records of the Augustan games, see *CIL* 6:32323 = *ILS*, 5050; and Theodor Mommsen's commentary on them in *Ephemeris epigraphica* 8 (1891): 225–309. Also important is his "Die Akten zu dem Säkulargedicht des Horaz," in idem, *Reden und Aufsätze* (Berlin: Weidmann, 1905). See also above n. 3.

13. Gagé, "Beobachtungen zum Carmen Saeculare des Horaz," 33. This observation appears correct, although some of Gagé's hypotheses concerning models for Horace, i.e., earlier "carmina," may be debatable. In any case, the festival song contributed to the efficacy of the rites. Hellenistic religion in general and Roman religion in particular kept the ancient conviction that the word, here the poem, is magically effective. The idea of Horace's poem as a mere melodramatic accompaniment of the festivities, intended only for aesthetic enjoyment, is a typically modern thought, foreign to the ancient mind.

14. "T'was Phoebus lent me inspiration, Phoebus the art of song, and gave me the name of poet" (lines 29–30). All quotes of texts and translations are from LCL.

15. Also to the sister of Apollo, Diana/Artemis.

16. "I, a chary and infrequent worshipper of the gods" (1ine 34).

rupibus vidi docentem" also demonstrates.[17] Viktor Pöschl has described the bacchantic inspiration of Horace in an essay that is also instructive for the student of the New Testament.[18] In his discussion of this ode Pöschl observes a certain phenomenon of composition that is important for the *Carmen saeculare*: "Der Mythos als Gipfel und Zusammenfassung des Ganzen erscheint auch sonst gelegentlich in Horazgedichten."[19]

It speaks for Horace's high degree of self-estimation that he calls himself *vates*, as does Virgil.[20] It is most probable that these poets follow the opinion of Varro concerning the meaning of the Latin term. This antiquarian, so important for Augustan reform, had assumed a false etymology and claimed that *vates* originally meant the poet.[21] Virgil and Horace both took this term to mean the inspired singers of ancient times, but then they used the term to refer to themselves, thus putting their own function and importance on the same level as the bards of old.[22]

The poet belongs to the sphere of the extraordinary, the miraculous. According to the ode "Non usitata nec tenui ferar,"[23] the poet is more successful than Icarus because he has turned into a heavenly bird, has

---

17. "Bacchus I saw on distant crags ... teaching hymns" (2.19).
18. "Dichtung und dionysische Verzauberung in der Horazode III 25," repr. as "c. 3,25; Quo me Bacche," in Viktor Pöschl, *Horazische Lyrik: Interpretationen* (Heidelberg: Winter, 1970), 164–78. Plato already knows the tradition about Dionysiac ecstasy of the poet, which likens him to the Maenads. In New Testament times, this idea was still present, as Philo shows. See Hans Leisegang, *Der Heilige Geist* (Leipzig: Teubner, 1919), 126–231, 236–37; Hans Lewy, *Sobria Ebrietas* (ZNW 9; Berlin: de Gruyter, 1929), 3–72; Hans Jonas, *Gnosis und spätantiker Geist* (2nd ed.; Göttingen: Vandenhoeck & Ruprecht, 1954), 2:92–107. Philo proves that Judaism had also become acquainted with this idea.
19. "Dichtung und dionysische Verzauberung," 169 n. 2. Since the second century B.C.E., a movement toward remythicizing was much stronger than the tendency toward rationalization, religious uncertainty, or even decomposition. Some of the most impressive examples were apocalypticism, Gnosticism, and Neopythagorean philosophy. As Lucretius's poem shows, even Epicurean philosophy, so important for Horace, was not untouched by this mythicizing tendency. In *Horaz und die Politik* (2nd ed.; Sitzungsberichte der Heidelberger Akademie der Wissenschaften, Phil.-hist. Kl; Heidelberg: Winter, 1963), Pöschl writes: "Horaz bedient sich der Formeln und Symbole der früheren Poesie—sie umgestaltend und steigernd—, um seiner Aussage grössere Würde und Monumentalität zu geben, wobei auch der römische Glaube an die Autorität des Vorbildes hineinspielt, und, was für die Entwicklung römischer Poesie und Rhetorik besonders wichtig ist und einer Untersuchung wert wäre, die römische Überzeugung von der magischen Kraft geprägter Formen" (16).
20. In *Ode* 4.6.44 and frequently elsewhere.
21. See on this esp. Hellfried Dahlmann, "Vates," *Philologus* 97 (1948): 337–53; also Dietrich Wachsmuth, "Vates," *KlPauly* 5:1146–47.
22. In the *Augustus Epistle* (*Ep.* 2.1.18–49[89]) Horace scolds those who would like to admit and appreciate only the old poets and show contempt for the modern ones.
23. "On no common or feeble opinion shall I soar in double form through the liquid air" (2.20).

turned immortal during his lifetime, and his immortal song has made funeral songs unnecessary.[24] According to Horace's *Augustus Epistle*, the poet is not merely an educator of youth and comforter of the poor and the sick but also effective in prayer.[25] In these lines from the letter to Augustus the "song" means first of all the *Carmen saeculare*, but it also stands for the poetry of the singer in general. His word is powerful, not only among humans but also among the gods. It has a relationship to prayer, magically invoking the gods, imploring and interceding for the purpose of winning the good and averting the bad.[26] In short, the divine and the human meet on the territory of the song.[27] Bringing this about is the function of the poet as *vates*.[28] His mission thus gains soteriological dimensions. Horace utilizes here the associations of *vates* during his time, namely, that of seer and magician.[29]

The glorification of the *princeps* and of the time of Augustus is not mere courtly poetry. Horace sees it as the immediate fulfillment of a heavenly order and as the execution of divine inspiration. The motif of

---

24. "Let dirges be absent from what you falsely deem my death, and unseemly show of grief and lamentation! Restrain all clamor and forgo the idle tribute of a tomb" (lines 21–24). Of the miraculous inspiration of the poet I have spoken before. Horace also narrates a wondrous preservation during his early youth (*Ode* 3.4; see below) as well as a rescue from the attack of a wolf (*Ode* 1.22). On these and other miraculous events, and on the idea of the miraculous in Horace, see E. Zinn, "Erlebnis und Dichtung bei Horaz," in Oppermann, *Wege zu Horaz*, 369–88, and esp. the enumeration of Horace's accounts of wondrous events in his life (377). Zinn says of the poet (based on *Ode* 1.22): "So kann er aus Faktum und Deutung die Konsequenz einer entschlossenen Bereitschaft ziehn: immer und überall dem Beklemmenden und Drohenden standzuhalten und liebender Dichter, dichtend Liebender zu bleiben" (383). Zinn writes (based on the research of Otto Weinreich): "Bei Horaz erscheint keine Religiosität einer reinen Innerlichkeit, sondern die Fülle einzelner sacra als Konkretionen des Göttlichen, das eben an den konkreten. faktischen Rettungen und Gaben, die man ihm verdankt, als übermenschlich, als göttlich erfahren wird" (686). I agree with Zinn (here and in his study "Aporos Soteria," in Oppermann, *Wege zu Horaz*, 220–57, esp. 247 n. 37) against Pöschl that Horace does not want to express himself merely figuratively but that he has concrete experiences in view. I would, however, like to stay away from using the term "Faktizität."
25. *Ep.* 2.1.126–138.
26. "Their chorus [that of the boys and girls at the centenary] asks for aid and feels the presence of the gods, calls for showers from heaven, winning favour with the prayers he [the *vates* mentioned before] has taught, averts disease, drives away the dreaded dangers, gains peace and a season rich in fruit" (*Ep.* 2.1.134–137). Here the poet gives a more general description of his function as *vates*.
27. Cf. the *presentia numina sentit* in the passage just quoted and then the following lines: "Song wins grace [*carmine placantur*] with the gods above, song wins it with the gods below" (Ep. 2.1.137–138).
28. "Vatem ni Musa dedisset" (*Ep.* 2.1.133).
29. On this association, see Altheim, *History of Roman Religion*, 381–93.

ecstatic rapture, comparable to the "sweet" danger of the communion of the poet with Dionysus,[30] alludes to the situation at the composition of his song in honor of Augustus. As the poet wants to put the Caesar among the gods he does not speak as courtly sycophant but as peer, as one who himself belongs to the immortal ones.[31] In fact, it is the power of the poet's word that places the Augustus among the gods.

When people discuss the relationship of Horace to Augustus they often overlook this proud self-estimation of the singer. In the fourth Roman ode (3.4) the divine protection of Horace and of Augustus are put side by side.[32] Horace sees both in the context of the mythical triumph of divine wisdom and moderate rest. The immediate miraculous experiences of the poet are extensively described; those of Caesar are only hinted at (37–40). The narrative of the wondrous events of Horace's life is steeped in the light of eschatological myth: of paradise, in the case of the protection of the boy (9–20); of demonic terror at the ends of the earth; of hope for future preservation (29–35). In between Horace mentions the miracle of rescue during the battle of Philippi but also the wonders of protection from a falling tree and from the waves of the sea (25–28). The Muses with whom the poet is in intimate conversation throughout his work give rest to the Caesar and his troops. They give counsel, too, and through whom but the poet, so divinely saved and thus adorned? Imperial campaign, rest, and poetic counsel to the Caesar then are put into the context of the primordial myth of the rebellion of the Titans and Jupiter's miraculous victory over them (42–80). The recurrence of the mythical past in the end time is a major tenet of apocalyptic thought.

This ode proves how closely related personal quietude, idyll, and world peace are for Horace. Peace is not merely seen as political status but is put into the light of cosmic processes. Election, inspiration, experience, and linguistic magic all are personal realizations of this cosmic process. The ode to Maecenas[33] shows in an impressive manner that for

---

30. *Ode* 3.25. "Whither, O Bacchus, dost thou hurry me, o'erflowing with thy power? Into what groves or grottoes am I swiftly driven in fresh inspiration [*velox menu nova*]? In what caves shall I be heard planning to set amid the stars, and in Jove's council, peerless Caesar's immortal glory? I will sing of a noble exploit, recent, as yet untold by other lips" (25.1–8).

31. In *Ode* 1.2 Horace speaks of Augustus as a savior who has come down from heaven. See Ernst Doblhofer, *Die Augustuspanegyrik des Horaz in formalhistorischer Sicht* (Heidelberg: Winter, 1966), 113–14. On the deification of Augustus in this song, see also Pöschl, *Horazische Lyrik*, 165–67.

32. "Descende caelo" ("Descend from heaven!").

33. *Ode* 3.29, "Tyrrhena regum progenies" ("Scion of Tuscan kings").

Horace the experiences of rest and of composed serenity are divine gifts, miracles indeed, when they happen during hopeless situations. They are comparable, yes superior, to the military and administrative securing of the empire (the business of Maecenas).[34]

The political and the private for Horace are not two separate spheres, as Viktor Pöschl claims in his essay "Horaz und die Politik"; rather, they constantly interconnect. The ode to Maecenas demonstrates this. In this poem, which is so private in one way, Horace also gives political counsel to his patron. These suggestions are summarized in the μηδὲν ἀγάν.[35] Horace wants to be an exemplary Roman in this connection of the political, the religious, and the private. He hopes to restore old civic virtues in contrast to the individualistic tendencies of the previous decades. Horace sees different roles or functions in each of these areas, but they do intersect. Interpreters have exposed the work of Horace again and again to questions about personal conviction and consistency, but these questions are conditioned by an image of personality as developed in the nineteenth century, an image unknown to people of the first century B.C.E. or the first century C.E. Even today this concept of personality is not a realistic one. It is still an everyday experience that the same persons play different roles and serve various functions at the same time. In compliance with such roles and functions, they follow varying requirements, often expressing themselves in different, even contradictory, utterances and behaviors. Even in all his various statements Horace appears to be more consistent and unified than many modern academicians are.

The *Epistle to the Pisones*, usually called *Ars poetica* and written about the same time as the *Carmen saeculare*,[36] shows the opposition Horace feels to something like pure poetry. Poetry for Horace transcends mere private satisfaction or the enjoyment of aesthetically minded small audiences.

---

34. See Zinn, "Aporos Soteria," 246, about the miraculous aspect of the protection of the poet in the last two stanzas of the poem Zinn says, "Es ist derselbe Mensch, der seinen Besitz—wenn das Schicksal es will—gelassen preisgibt, und dessen innerer Unanfechtbarkeit auch von aussen, von Natur und Gottheit her, Schutz und Rettung erwidert. Indem Horaz dies Geschehen fur sich selbst im Indikativ fester Zuversicht prophezeien kann, verbindet sich in den Schlussversen des Gedichtes eine äusserste Selbstbescheidung mit äusserster Selbsterhöhung—das schlichte Abtun aller 'indifferentia' mit der 'Anmassung' eines Bewusstseins der Auserwähltheit." On the interpretation of the ode, see also Pöschl, *Horazische Lyrik*, 198–245.

35. In his interpretation of *Ode* 1.37 ("Nunc et bibendum") Pöschl (*Horazische Lyrik*, 78) rightly says, "Wieder klingt die für Rom so charakteristische Verflechtung des politischen und des religiösen, des privaten und des öffentlichen Bereiches an."

36. Extensive discussion of this epistle and its date can be found in Carl Becker, *Das Spätwerk des Horaz* (Göttingen: Vandenhoeck & Ruprecht, 1963), 64–112, 232–37. See also 246–47 on its relationship to the *Carmen saeculare*.

Poetry is an ethical, a political task. Indeed, according to lines 391–407 it has the function of creating and maintaining culture.

In the *Augustus Epistle* (2.1), one of, if not the last, works of Horace, poetry is described as an essential instrument of political education. Thus the attention that great men of politics pay to great men of the word is quite appropriate. Poetry and military-administrative achievements are different expressions of wisdom and, therefore, should appreciate each other.[37] The beginning of this poem sees the *princeps*, the semigods, and the singers as colleagues. All are θεῖοι ἄνδρες.[38] The poet has the advantage that fame and name, that is, the real divine eternity of the *princeps* and other divine men, depend on the poet's reporting and eternalizing them.

Even the sixteenth epode, in which Horace contemplates surrendering Rome, must not be read as an escapist poem.[39] On the contrary, it is a political sermon.[40] The chaos prevailing in the Roman Empire at the end

---

37. Future research will have to study further the relationship between the various forms of interest in wisdom in the Hellenistic world. The connection between Jewish and Hellenistic eschatology discussed in this essay seems to be but one part of the connection.

38. On the θεῖος ἀνήρ, see Dieter Georgi, *The Opponents of Paul in 2 Corinthians* (Philadelphia: Fortress, 1986), esp. the epilogue with reference to further literature. On the socioeconomic dimensions, see idem, "Socioeconomic Reasons for the 'Divine Man' as a Propagandistic Pattern," ch. 2 above. The development of the Hellenistic θεῖος ἀνήρ concept in Jewish missionary theology and its successful integration into worldwide missionary practice added to the attraction of the concept for Roman theologians and practitioners of the first century B.C.E. The Jewish missionaries proved the potential of the concept. Its interplay of tradition, law/morality, plurality, purpose, competition, and merit showed success, provided motivation, and promised control. Any radical democracy (grass roots–oriented and participatory) was feared as anarchy, but a consensus structure was needed that transcended the capital, Rome, and was able to stimulate local activities and loyalties beyond the confines of Roman citizenship, military force, and administration. Caesar's attitude toward the Jews had ingratiated them and set the pattern for the future. Collaboration was the consequence. Even the Jewish *Sibylline Oracles* did not propagate fundamental opposition. Hellenistic-Jewish missionary theology on the whole appreciated the Augustan reform, thus providing a trans-Italian support structure that helped to tie the provinces to Rome.

39. In *Der junge Horaz und die Politik* (Heidelberg: Winter, 1971), Doris Ableitinger-Grünberger sees in the sixteenth epode a decisive turning away from political life for Horace. She emphasizes even more strongly than Pöschl a polarity between Horace's life and poetry on the one hand and the political world on the other. Even in the late Horace she sees at most an approximation towards a certain sacred synthesis which intends the propitiation of the political sphere, but never a real exchange. She claims that Augustus is praised for giving the possibility of existence to the sphere of the poet within the real world. Her ideas of reality and spirituality would seem to be foreign to Horace.

40. The outline of the poem imitates the form of a speech in the people's assembly introducing a motion. So Richard Cornelius Kukula, *Römische Säkularpoesie* (Leipzig: Teubner, 1911), 13–14.

of the 40s and beginning of the 30s was tremendous, as was the corresponding loss of hope. The later savior of the republic, Octavian, was in his early twenties. Rome was about to commit suicide. On the surface it appears as if Horace completely concurred with the many predictions of doom circulating at the time.[41] However, the reference to certain catastrophe serves as a foil for the banner of bright hope that the poet raises.[42] He calls for emigration across the sea. The closing of the epode alludes to the migrations and colonizations of the epic period but does not mention directly the most logical example, that of the flight of Aeneas. The reference to the Phoceans (line 17), who fled Persian rule, indicates that Horace is led by the idea of emigration for political and religious reasons.[43] The isolation of a *melior pars* (line 39) shows a familiarity with thoughts of contemporary sectarian circles that cherished the motif of emigration. Naturally, this idea of emigration associates easily with the expectations of eschatological doom and salvation.[44]

Epode 16 betrays acquaintance with Jewish motifs, especially those of an eschatological nature.[45] They can be traced back to biblical prophecy, which Horace probably knew by way of Jewish missionary propaganda.[46]

---

41. On this see Latte, *Römische Religionsgeschichte*, 288–89.

42. The majority of interpreters rightly think that the sixteenth epode is not ironic and the projected voyage not a journey into a fool's paradise, as Kukula has claimed. See, e.g., Ableitinger-Grünberger, *Der junge Horaz*.

43. On the motif of emigration, see Harald Fuchs, *Der geistige Widerstand gegen Rom in der antiken Welt* (2nd ed.; Berlin de Gruyter, 1964), 9–13.

44. The Essenes (at least their radical community in Qumran) are well known for an ideology of world flight and a corresponding organized isolation, as are the Therapeutae and Hermetic groups.

45. See, e.g., Isidore Lévy, *Horace, le Deutéronome el l'Évangile de Marc: Études horatiennes* (Brussels, 1937), 147–52. Franz Dornseiff, *Verschmähtes zu Vergil, Horaz und Properz* (Berichte über die Verhandlungen der sächsischen Akademie der Wissenschaften zu Leipzig. Phil.-hist. Kl. 97.6; Berlin: Akademie Verlag, 1951), esp. 44–63 (on Virgil's *Ecl.* 4), 57–60 (on the connections between Horace's *Epod.* 16 and the *Sibylline Oracles*), 64–72 (on Jewish elements in Horace's satires), 72–91 (on relations between Horace's odes, Virgil, and the LXX), 97–104 (on the Jewish influence on the fourth book of odes); Rudolf Hanslick. "Die Religiosität des Horaz," *Das Altertum* 1 (1955): 230–40, esp. 238 (on the influence of Jewish messianic ideas on Ode 1.2); Ableitinger-Grünberger, *Der junge Horaz*, 16–17, 67, 73–79. See also the more general discussion of analogies between Roman and Israelite-Jewish ideas in Otto Seel, *Römertum und Latinität* (Stuttgart: Klett, 1964), 103–37, 167–88.

46. Dornseiff (*Verschmähtes zu Vergil, Horaz und Properz*, 60–62) has drawn attention to the similarity of the passages in Jer 9:1–2 and 8:1–2 (not 8:17, as printed) to *Epod.* 16.1–14, esp. 16.13 and 14. Dornseiff has argued that Horace's father was at least a proselyte, if not a born Jew, and that the son knew the LXX and the *Sibylline Oracles* of Jewish origin (65). The resemblances of Jewish motifs in Horace given by Dornseiff (see previous note) are often striking indeed. Although this specific biographical argument seems unwarranted, the acquaintance with Jewish missionary activity and its theology appears evident, and thus

This Jewish missionary theology contained a vivid eschatology, found, among other places, in the Jewish *Sibylline Oracles*.[47] The Sibyl(s) and the Sibylline books were not an originally Jewish phenomenon, but the Jewish (and then Christian) literature in question picked up on the popularity of the Sibyl and of collections of Sibylline oracles throughout the Mediterranean world. Their popularity did not rest on their mild language. On the contrary, heavy amounts of dirge and gore together with cryptic language added to the attraction of these oracles.

The many oracles going under the name of individual sibyls or of *the* Sibyl (the majority not extant) were of varying origins, character, and authenticity. In the majority, *ecstatic* prophetic and oracular phenomena were described with such terms. The official Roman Sibylline books of legendary origin were *ritual* prescriptions and regulations. According to Dionysius of Halicarnassus (*Ant. rom.* 4.62.6) they were destroyed in the fire of the temple of Jupiter on the capitol in 83 B.C.E. Then a curious decision was made to restore this collection by "carrying together (oracles) from many places" (εἰσὶ συμφόρητοι [χρησμοί]ἐκ πολλῶν τοιούτων), that is, from all over the Mediterranean world, including the Near East. This was accomplished not only by official delegates but also by private persons who offered what they claimed were transcripts. The obvious expectation was that from all of that mass of material (with apparent ἐμπεποιημένοι [χρησμοί] τοῖς Σιβυλλείοις [χρησμοῖς]) one could restore the authentic ones. As to tendency the new collection followed the more common notion of the Sibyl and her oracles as being outright prophetic, although the new oracles (established, stored, and thus made secret, on the capitol starting from 76 B.C.E.) were also consulted by the appropriate institution of interpreters (the *quindecimviri*) on ritual matters, such as the secular games. The reinstitution of the Roman Sibylline books did not stop their further edition, nor the circulation of their sources, nor the production and circulation of new oracles. This is clearly demonstrated by the many quotes and the history of tradition of the *Sibylline Oracles*. Tacitus (*Ann.*

---

also an indirect familiarity with biblical motifs. On this Jewish propaganda, see Georgi, *Opponents of Paul*, 41–60, 69–151, 174–217, esp. 148–51.

47. On the *Sibylline Oracles* as part of that propaganda and of that eschatology, see Georgi, *Opponents of Paul*. John Collins has given good arguments (*The Sibylline Oracles of Egyptian Judaism* [SBLDS 13] Missoula, Mont.: Scholars Press, 1974) for dating and locating major portions of the third and fifth books of the *Sibylline Oracles*, the major Jewish parts of the whole collection, but he does not deal sufficiently with the missionary aspects of these Jewish oracles, which are, in my opinion, of primary importance even in the fifth book. The extant Jewish *Sibylline Oracles*, remainders of a larger corpus, thrived among many competitors. On the interest in such literature, particularly in Rome and among Romans of the late republic and the early principate, see further Gerhard Radke, "Sibyllen," *KlPauly* 5:158–61.

6.12) attests that under Augustus many of such oracles circulated *(multa varia sub nomine celebri vulgabantur)*. Augustus felt compelled to order all Sibylline oracles known to the public to be delivered to the urban praetor up to a set deadline, after which any private ownership would become illegal. He concluded his own sifting and collating of oracles and editing of the Sibylline books with their transfer to the temple of Apollo on the Palatine (Suetonius, *Aug.* 31.1). Under Caligula even official attempts were still made—though unsuccessfully—to add new Sibylline books to the canon of 76 B.C.E. Following Franz Dornseiff,[48] Moses Hadas compares two passages, one of Horace, one of the Jewish Sibyl.[49]

> *Already a second generation* is being ground to pieces by *civil war,* and Rome through her own strength is loitering. The savage conqueror shall stand, alas' upon the *ashes* of our city, and the *horseman shall trample it with clattering hoof,* and (impious to behold) shall scatter wantonly Quirinus' bones that now are sheltered from the wind and sun.[50]

> Upon thee, Italy, no warfare of foreign foes shall come, but *bloodshed* lamentable and *of long continuance* shall ravish thee, thou famous land, for thy shamelessness. And thou, stretched prone among the burning *ashes,* shall slay thyself, in thy improvident heart. Thou shall be no mother of good men, but a *nurse of wild beasts.*[51]

On the one hand there is the great mass, the *indocilis grex* (the "unconvertable crowd"). On the other, there is the *melior pars* (the "better part"), the two forming the *omnis exsecrata civitas* (the "entire self-condemning state").[52] This is reminiscent of the division of Israel by the prophets into the just and the unjust, particularly of the motif of the holy remnant. Like the prophets, Horace addresses the entire people, but he expects only the truly pious to follow his call.[53]

---

48. See above, n. 45.
49. *Hellenistic Culture: Fusion and Diffusion* (New York: Norton, 1972), 242.
50. Horace, *Epod.* 16. I have italicized parallels between this and the following quotation.
51. *Sib. Or.* 3.464–469 from the translation of H. N. Bate, *The Sibylline Oracles: Books III–V* (New York Macmillan, 1918).
52. Horace, *Ep.* 16.36–37. On *exsecrata* as "unter Selbstverwünschung schwören" ("swearing by cursing oneself," not "cursed"), see Ableitinger-Grunberger, *Der junge Horaz,* 37–40.
53. On *pius* and *pietas,* so important for the later Augustan reform, see Latte, *Römische Religionsgeschichte,* 39–40, 238–39; Theodor Ulrich, *Pietas (pius) als politischer Begriff im römischen Staate bis zum Tode des Kaisers Commodus* (Historische Untersuchungen 6; Breslau: Marcus, 1930); H. D. Weiss, "Piety in Latin Writers in Early Christian Times" (Ph. D. diss., Duke University, 1964).

The proposed voyage will go to the isles of the blessed, the Greek Elysion, an individualized golden age.[54] Traditionally this eschatological place is accessible for common mortals only after death, but heroes may reach it before they die (that is, they become immortal). Horace realizes this eschatological concept, but not, as expected, in the manner of Hellenistic utopian literature, where, in attempts to realize eschatology, the islands of the blessed had become the place for institutions, laws, customs, offices, peoples, or societies. It was an anticipation of the return of the golden age in the collective sense of that motif.[55] This is all the more surprising since Horace does not stick to the traditional concepts of the Elysion, although he uses some key words.[56] The idyll described in lines 43-62 resembles the notion of peaceful paradise returned as found in biblical prophecy and translated into sermons and treatises of Jewish missionary theology.[57] However, this Jewish theology has visions of an exemplary society, too. Thus Horace wants to border on such utopian thoughts, including their pacifist tendencies, without committing himself to any social concreteness. He commits only his will to utilize the heroic, immortalizing dimensions of the Elysian concept in order to undergird the call to immediate political action. Those following Horace's appeal, that is, the morally sound, who still have political courage, are promised the place of immortal heroes *now*. The other utopian dimensions remain just beyond the horizon.[58]

Horace tries to influence the sociopolitical reality with a dialectic blend of prophetic criticism and hope in the concept of flight (*fuga*, 66) The desperate situation makes him concentrate on the critical side of this dialectic. This can be interpreted in the sense of critical distance, but not

---

54. "Let us seek the Fields, the Happy Fields, and the Islands of the Blest" (lines 41-42).

55. On utopian literature, see Hans Volkmann, "Utopia," *KlPauly* 5:1083-84. Unfortunately, Volkmann does not acknowledge the indebtedness of Roman literature of the first centuries B.C.E and C.E. to Greek and Hellenistic utopian thought. See also Robert von Pohlmann, *Die Geschichte der sozialen Frage und des Sozialismus* (3rd ed.; Munich: Beck, 1925); Reimar Muller, *Die epikureische Gesellschaftstheorie* (2nd ed.; Schriften zur Geschichte und Kultur der Antike 5; Berlin: Akademie Verlag, 1974); idem, "Zur sozialen Utopie im Hellenismus," in *Die Rolle der Volksmassen in der Geschichte der vorkapitalistischen Gesellschaftsformationen* (Veröffentlichungen des ZIAGA der Akademie der Wissenschaften der DDR 7; Berlin: Akademie Verlag, 1975), 277; idem, "Sozialutopien der Antike," *Das Altertum* 23 (1977): 227.

56. The concepts *divites insulae* and *arva beata* are found together in Pindar's second Olympian Ode (55-83) and Hesiod's *Erga* (167-170).

57. On the description of a future of bliss in missionary texts of Hellenistic Judaism, see Georgi, *Opponents of Paul*, index under "eschatology." The most extensive representations are in Philo, *Praem.* 79-126, 152-172.

58. Horace shares this "teasing" approach to the symbolic-allegorical with the eschatological one of Jewish missionary theology, as Philo's *De praemiis et poenis* shows so well.

in the sense of resigning to inner emigration. The poet sees himself as the head of another emigration to a mythical west, like the founder of Rome, Aeneas. A threat also resides in the poet's suggested flight; namely, the remaining republic will lack the creative word of the poet-prophet and the morally sound core of the people who follow him. Rome, alas Italy, will be doomed like Troy. Its only future will be with the emigrants in another Rome, another Italy.

Rome, torn asunder by the strife of civil war, has turned into an incarnation of the myth of the catastrophic end of the Iron Age, just at the threshold of the return to the new age. Horace presents a mythicized form of the move away from the city, here radicalized into a move away from Italy altogether. The civil war seems to have proven the end of a civilization sold on urbanization. This had led to an extreme overpopulation in major cities, especially in Rome, with devastating consequences for the labor and housing market. Mass employment was never contemplated. This dilemma was covered up by the provision of inexpensive or gratuitous grain for the "plebs." This "dole" had turned into an expensive but successful instrument of demagoguery because it created an impression of leisure among the masses, a resemblance of the freedom of the Roman nobility. Thus it distinguished the recipients of the gift of grain, the *annona,* from social peers elsewhere. Demagogues in the political competition and conflict would promise more such material leisure and nobility in exchange for votes and other support. This made the city all the more attractive, and the social pressure of people migrating to the city increased, along with the potential for social and political unrest.

Horace suggested flight as an extreme form of remedy: countermigration, flight from the city instead of from the land. This would decrease the overpopulation in the city and thus the economic pressure and revolutionary potential there. Horace shows no awareness that his call to the west gave some ideological support to the practices of richer people who had started to invest heavily outside of Italy. Their interest in better financial returns could not be backed with the excuse of the catastrophic situation in the capital and in Italy. Horace, out of despair for reasons of dramatizing his criticisms of the state of affairs in Rome and in Italy at large, would propose an extreme version of that move to the open country, a migration where the vision of the unknown world would provide more certainty than the chaotic reality of the doomed city.

At the fringe of the dialectic message of *Epod.* 16 stands the hint of an impossible possibility (lines 25–34):[59] the emigrants swear not to return

---

59 Horace uses here the stylistic element of accumulating impossibilities (ἀδύνατα). See on this esp. Ernest Dutoit, *Le thème de l'Adynaton dans la poesie antique* (Paris: Bude, 1936).

unless both inanimate and animate natures change in a revolutionary fashion. The cosmic changes described in the oath of those who have been exiled bear eschatological traits and thus concur with the eschatological nature of the goal of the proposed voyage. The enumeration of impossibilities appears to be more than a means of rhetorical style. The conditions for the return expressed in the oath play with the idea of a greater miracle than the voyage to the land of the blessed could be the restoration of the republic. Horace can predict this only in eschatological cosmic dimensions. The return of Rome will be an event that will shake and move the world.[60]

The *Carmen saeculare* celebrates the miracle that occurred in the meantime: the salvation of the republic. The impossible had happened. The hope expressed in the *Carmen* is no doubt miraculous but present, indeed fulfilled. The confidence about the realization of what has been desperately expected before is concrete, and the materialism of the expectation indicates the degree of reality. There are many eschatological themes: the eschatological language of *Urzeit-Endzeit,* the ideal of the miraculous return of the golden age and paradise, even the ideal of the eschatological savior—in line with the heroes of old.[61] All this is embedded in a prophetic framework with reference to the Sibyl at the start of the poem and with the conjuration of the divine prophet and protector of the seers, Apollo, in the beginning and at the end. Reference to the prediction is found at the end as well.[62] There is also the prophetic role of the *vates,* the poet himself.

Ableitinger-Grünberger (*Der junge Horaz,* 40–42) has shown that Horace has formed the "adynata" in an original way.

60. The correspondence between Horace's *Epod.* 16 and Virgil's *Ecl.* 4 is one of the more dramatic occurrences in world literature. Scholars differ as to who presupposes and criticizes whom. I follow those who take *Epod.* 16 to be the earlier poem, with Virgil's *Ecl.* 4 opposing his friend's skepticism. Virgil says that the taking to the sea can be at most an interlude (lines 31–37). The impossible, in fact, has already happened: the Iron Age has ended and the golden age is beginning. This interpretation stands in contradiction to that of, among others, Dornseiff (*Verschmähtes zu Vergil, Horaz und Properz,* 63), Hadas (*Hellenistic Culture,* 243), and Becker (*Das Spätwerk des Horaz,* 314). Dornseiff bases his argument in part on some other correspondences with Virgil in the entire work of Horace. But the two friends were in dialogue, and that dialogue was mutually influential, at least until the death of Virgil. The golden age hoped for is that of peace, the new age of the eschatological hope of Jewish missionary theology. Virgil's confidence will prove to be in line with economic, social, and political development.

61. Jewish eschatology of missionary persuasion was attractive to Romans not only because of its inherited soteriological and cosmological breadth and depth but also because of its utopian dimension with a clear interest in using propaganda to influence present structures of social consent.

62. Christian theologians and scores of other critics throughout the centuries take exception to the "materialistic" interests expressed in Horace's and similar statements. Their

The recently enacted marital legislation of Augustus at first glance may not appear to be an appropriate subject for a poem of eschatological orientation (lines 13–24).[63] Our readiness to take the ordinary political allusion of Horace seriously is dimmed further by our hindsight: we know of the ultimate lack of success of this legislative measure of Augustus. For the author and the audience of the song, however, the marital legislation of Augustus is a new and impressive symbol of Augustus's efforts to reverse the catastrophe of moral and physical decay, the suicide of the republic. It is a sign that far-ranging change is on its way and its duration is secured.[64] The poem prays for stability, prosperity, and peace with impressive language.[65] The hearer receives sufficient indication that these things are not bloodless dreams but present reality[66] and that the *Carmen* prays for their increase.

The longest single portion of the song (lines 37–52) invokes the tradition that was only alluded to in *Epod.* 16, that of Aeneas. At the time of origin of the secular song this tradition was not yet codified in the public consciousness. The epic of Horace's friend, Virgil, was not yet public property,[67] but the tradition was already part of public education, especially since Augustus had started to take an active interest in this Trojan hero.[68] Horace mentions only briefly the flight of the great man from Troy and his subsequent adventures, including those in Italy. He uses the divine interference in these experiences as examples for his own prayer, which asks for further divine actions to improve the education of youth and the security of old age.[69]

Then, in lines 49–52 (60), Aeneas suddenly turns into a contemporary figure that brings about worldwide peace through weapons, threat, and

---

religious integrity is doubted. However, this criticism only proves that Christians have used eschatology to dematerialize and thus deconcretize the hope for change.

63. Using his tribunal power Augustus had initiated in 18 B.C.E. the *Lex Julia de maritandis ordinibus* legalizing marriages between freeborn citizens and people freed from slavery (senators, however, were excluded from this liberalized practice), thus rewarding marriage and childrearing and discouraging abstention from marriage and childbirth, and the *Lex Julia de adulteriis coercendis* making adultery a public crime.

64. The existence and return of the *saeculum*, as such already an eschatological good, depend on this (lines 21–24).

65. Esp. in lines 19–32, 57–60, and 65–68.

66. See, besides the references to the marital legislation, the double *iam* ("already") in lines 53 and 57.

67. The *Aeneid* was published after Virgil's death (19 B.C.E.) against the expressed will of the poet but by the request of Augustus.

68. Augustus suggested the topic of the *Aeneid* to Virgil.

69. See lines 45–46, obviously connected with lines 33–36. The third recipient of the beneficial assistance of the gods, proven in history, is the entire progeny of Romulus, all of the Roman people (47–48).

persuasion. The miraculous heroic past has become present epiphany in the activity of Augustus. In Aeneas, the Caesar himself has entered the scene. We hear that the age-old virtues of *pietas, pax, honor,* and *virtus* have returned. In the same breath *copia* is mentioned as a quality of similar value; it also experiences a return. It is not just a certain good but a basic value that guarantees the salvation and duration of the commonwealth.[70] Thus it is not surprising that in the end the song prays not merely for general audition but also for growth of the might and fortune of Rome and Latium (lines 65–68).

The *Carmen saeculare* describes the perfection of the endtime in rural colors. The tones of pastoral idyll as we know them from Virgil's *Ecl.* 4 resound in Horace. Although this style fits within the genre of the bucolic poem of Virgil, it is hardly expected in the *Carmen* of Horace. Neither can it be said that eschatological writing requires rural expression. Biblical and Jewish eschatology can work with urban images, as the prophecies concerning Zion prove.

Horace does not even offer any harmonization between the rural and the urban image as found in the end of Ezekiel or in Pseudo-Aristeas. In these, the harmonization is not a secondary accommodation but an acknowledgment of an important socioeconomic problem in antiquity. The antithesis and conflict between urban and rural grew into heavy exploitation of the countryside by the cities during the Hellenistic period. Thus the harmonization in some of the eschatological predictions promised a coming reconciliation of social adversaries and thus the miraculous resolution of a dilemma that history had been unable to solve.

However, in the *Carmen saeculare* Horace does not mention the urban world at all. This is striking in a festival song that praises the achievements and blessings of the principate of Augustus, one of the major city builders of the ancient world, and that celebrates the largest city of the age. One of the most important achievements of Augustus was the restoration and improvement of the city of Rome, not merely politically and morally but also architecturally. In addition, the Augustan reform had brought about a worldwide improvement of urban life, including an increase in the number of cities and of the size of many existing ones. Thus the silence of the *Carmen saeculare* on urban life is quite surprising. The traditional interest of Romans in soil and agriculture is not a sufficient explanation. During the time of Augustus the city of Rome had lost direct contact with the life of farmers and shepherds. In the Hellenistic

---

70. One is reminded of the southern panel on the eastern side of the altar of Pax Augusta, erected some four years later, where Italy is depicted as a goddess in the midst of signs of agrarian plenty and peace.

world in general and especially in Roman society, *the* city, particularly the city, the *urbs absoluta,* Rome, had become the central symbol.

There are socioeconomic and political reasons for this silence on the city and emphasis on the countryside in Horace's secular song. These reasons also explain the preference for the idyllic in the preceding works of the two main theologians of Augustus, with Virgil initially being more optimistic than Horace was. Although Augustus was the first citizen of the city of Rome and although he actively improved the image of this city, he still established his own base and his prosperity through Egyptian soil. Under him Egypt grew into a gigantic agricultural domain for the principate. However, what developed fully under Augustus had begun before. The trends of Hellenistic society and economy had moved from the direction of worldwide urbanization to that of ruralization.[71] The Romans followed this trend. Augustus built in part on the extraordinary position that agriculture held in Roman tradition, which he wanted to restore. However, the restoration of the rural world would not have happened if the socioeconomic situation had not been ready for it.

Rome's ideology and social structure had remained basically agrarian. Noble and rural, piety and soil, were always related, if not synonymous. Migration to the countryside for the purpose of fanning could create a counterweight to the explosive urbanization, reviving old strategies and their potential for social stability and control.

The land issue had been a major element of the Roman civil war. The popular party, that of the Gracchi, of Caesar, and later of Augustus, had taken up the banner of the plight of the ever-increasing urban masses. Their impoverishment was supposed to be helped by distribution of public land, and this was to relieve the socioeconomic and political pressures of overpopulation on Rome. But during the civil war the Gracchic reforms were only partially realized, and the population of the city continued to grow, with devastating consequences for the labor and housing markets.

---

71. Or, as one might call it, paganization, using the Latin term *pagan*, which denotes persons living in a *pagus* (rural country), the hinterland from an urban, "educated," point of view. The *pagans* happened to be more conservative, holding on to their inherited religion. Thus the term later became synonymous with non-Christian But the irony of history wills that the move of the church toward power sharing in the state coincided with the church's increasing missionary success in the countryside. The phenomenon of the massive return first of the Roman elite and then of others to the countryside is also the topic of the book by Werner Raith, *Das verlassene Imperium: Über das Aussteigen des römischen Volkes aus der Geschichte* (Berlin: Wagenbach, 1982). However, my perception of the character and dimension of the phenomenon and my explanation differ from Raith's.

Despite the distribution of land since Tiberius Gracchus and the settlement of veterans in rural areas in the subsequent century, there was, nevertheless, an increasing hesitation among the masses to leave the city. The socioeconomic development of farming moved away from small farms toward large estates aimed at maximizing profits. Worked and administered by slaves, these estates had turned into centers for the production of profitable goods, starting with a limited number of profitable agricultural products but soon taking advantage of the presence of resources and cheap labor to produce other wares.[72]

Thus, since the end of the first century B.C.E. property in the open country promised to be a better investment of capital with a growing rate of productivity and profit, at least in the case of large agricultural plants. The Ptolemaic system, with its controls and monopolies, had prepared the way for this economic development. Although Augustus provided for the free distribution of wheat to more than 300,000 citizens of Rome, his profit from relatively little expenditure in the Nile Valley was tremendous. The principle that worked in rural estates and plants also proved to be a better basis for the expensive, long-distance sea trade, which was essential to the economic structure of the empire.[73] This trade needed major capital backing, without which it could not survive. It was too expensive and too risky for short-term financing, but, literally, in the long run, it could pay off.

Meanwhile, the social pressure on the city had not yet diminished; on the contrary, the big cities, especially Rome, still attracted many lower-class people, and the slave-operated estates were driving farmers away and not attracting free laborers. Therefore, a concerted effort was necessary to allay realistic fears among the lower classes regarding their situation on the land. In addition, more landowners needed to be moved

---

72. E.g., brick, pottery, glass, and even metal. Agriculturally the big estates would concentrate on whatever proved to give the highest financial yield given local circumstances. In Italy this would mean wine, fruit (particularly figs), and oil. In some suitable areas space was also devoted to the large-scale raising of cattle, sheep, pigs, and poultry.

73. Land routes were too expensive for long-distance trading because horsepower could not yet be economically "harnessed" in the literal sense of the word. Ox power was too slow, clumsy, and costly. On sea routes much space was preempted by grain imported to Italy, especially to Rome, not just from Sicily, but from Africa, Egypt, and as far away as the Black Sea. The remaining freight space could be more profitably used to transport luxuries for the well-to-do. This transportation factor is one of the reasons for the lack of interest in mass production in the city. It would have required extensive systems of distribution, particularly for long-distance conveyance. The provision of inexpensive or gratuitous grain to the masses, though expensive to those responsible, was maintained because it proved to be more beneficial politically (cf. chapter 7, 103–34).

to care for their rural estates personally instead of relying on slaves. This would work against the disastrous effects of investment in estates outside of Italy and of absentee ownership of land. Having wealthy Romans invest more in Italian estates and be physically present would create confidence among the smaller farmers because of the shared Roman consensus-structure. An invocation of the old Roman virtues, particularly of thriftiness, could induce restraint in the consumption of luxuries among the rich, thus reducing social envy and improving the catastrophically negative balance of trade.

If more lower-class free people moved to the countryside, landlords might also be attracted to invest still more in their estates because they could count on a better labor market. City people might be attracted to work as farm hands, which would tempt small farmers to forego economic risks and turn their plots over to the landlords and take up tenancy as a safer way of farming. This would help the landowners, since slavery was becoming increasingly expensive.

Augustus was more a symptom than a cause. He stood for the acceleration of an economic and social momentum that later developed into an avalanche: the rise of the owners of the *latifundiae* ("large estates") into the position of essential and decisive producers and prompters and carriers of trade. The flight from the city would eventually end in the dethroning of Rome as the capital city. The centralizing efforts of the Caesars of the first and second centuries were futile attempts to create a counterweight. They helped neither the empire nor society at large but aided the deurbanizing decentralization because they tended to make ever-larger parts of the empire imperial domains. This turned increasingly larger portions of the populace into an imperial clientele with other investors, proprietors, and producers imitating and competing. Virgil and Horace express the eschatological dimensions of this growing development: the capitalism of the suburbs and of the rural estates as realized eschatology.[74]

---

74. Augustus, the Augustan religion, and all that helped them became pacesetters of an economy and society that turned away from the city, of a flight to the countryside. The centralizing efforts of the Caesars of the first century were not really of an economic nature in this respect but a mere passing stage in a contrary development. The Caesars themselves boycotted their centralizing measures by their own private economic activities, arrangements, and establishments. As it turned out, the development that Virgil and Horace promoted and supported did not happen for the sake of the city of Rome. It did not strengthen the situation of small and moderate farmers either, but of the rich, particularly those willing to invest. The political theology expressed in the poems of Virgil, Horace, and those sharing their opinion in the end gave encouragement and good conscience to the leading class for leaving the cities to the masses, thus turning them into sources of cheap labor for the future heirs of the big country estates, the coming centers of economy and society.

Idyllic elements appear early, too, in the eschatology of Jewish missionary theology. Although this theology and its practice initially were heavily if not entirely urban, from the start it tended to relate happiness to nature.[75] Whereas initially reconciliation with the urban was contemplated, this interest later receded into the background. In the *Sibylline Oracles* the positive urban dimension does not go beyond abstract references to Jerusalem as the center of the world. In Philo's *De praemiis et poenis* the rural aspects of the future world described prevail. Philo proves elsewhere that he is acquainted with handbooks on agriculture,[76] typical reading for the well-to-do who wanted to establish or improve their investments in rural estates.[77] Jewish missionary theology proved to be in line with socioeconomic development. Thus its eschatology, constructively utopian through its biblical heritage, became supportive for the trends highlighted in Roman theological literature,[78] active efforts in social collaboration.

3. THE BOOK OF REVELATION OF JOHN OF PATMOS

I want to turn now to an author who, toward the end of the first century, had to suffer under the consequences of the confusing trends and policies that the principate and the Caesar religion stood for: John, the author of the book of Revelation. Whereas in the case of Horace's work the religious and theological sides have not been taken seriously by its interpreters, in the case of John's visions the opposite is true: John's revelation is interpreted at the expense of its relationship to the real life of its addressees. In both cases the interpreters claim a distancing of the respective author from political reality, particularly with respect to social and economic dimensions and consequences.

The work of John has gained the attention of critical exegetes only recently, although it deserved it long ago, given its historical and theological importance. The Revelation of John presupposes the genre and

---

75. Georgi, *Opponents of Paul*, 129–32, 143–46, 149.
76. *De agricultura* and *Plant.* 152–172.
77. See the handbooks of Cato and Columella.
78. It is interesting that the Gospel of Mark and the work of Luke, both pro-Roman, show growth of the idyllic element. The trend toward the development of Christianity as a separate entity from its start coincides with the interest to come to an accord with socioeconomic tendencies of the leading forces of society. The fact that Mark and Luke both have certain ascetic aspects would not interfere with their acceptability in leading circles, since the official Roman ideology stressed a certain degree of discipline, promoting not only social but also economic control.

theology of apocalyptic literature, but it pursues interests contrary to apocalypticism. The author does not use a pseudonym but mentions his name, John. The historical situation of the addressees thus is not veiled and transcended by a legendary past but is spoken to directly and concretely in the addresses to the seven churches. The format of the heavenly letter, basic for John's work, is known to apocalypticism, but John has radically modified it through the concrete addresses in the first three chapters and the utilization of the form of the Pauline epistolary prescript (1:4–6).

Because of their interest in calculable prediction of final events, apocalypses usually provide their readers with coded but verifiable information about past and present events as a basis for their eschatological projection. However, the continuous delay of the predicted eschaton made adjustments and revisions necessary time and again. This became one of the essential traditional and historical reasons for the literary peculiarity of apocalypses, which present themselves more or less as comprehensive and often contradictory compilations of various apocalyptic sketches and fragments. John imitates this literary peculiarity of apocalypses skillfully, but he uses it to establish a compositional scheme that Victorinus of Pettau described long ago and Günther Bornkamm and Adela Yarbro Collins have recently rediscovered.[79] The author presents in several series a similar sequence of eschatological visions.[80] Each new series is slightly more extensive than the previous one, has a two-part key

---

79. Günther Bornkamm, "Die Komposition der apokalyptischen Visionen in der Offenbarung Johannis," in idem, *Studien zu Antike und Urchristentum* (3rd ed.; Munich: Kaiser, 1969), 204–22; Adela Yarbro Collins, *The Combat Myth in the Book of Revelation* (HDR 9; Missoula, Mont.: Scholars Press, 1976). Collins's study has also blazed new trails for understanding the theology and religious context of the book. She has enlarged this in further stimulating studies that are contained or at least reflected in her *Crisis and Catharsis: The Power of the Apocalypse* (Philadelphia: Westminster, 1984). She sees the views of John not as directly politically involved as I do, although she shows well the social orientation of the book's perception of reality and its message to its situation. More emphasis on the political concerns of John is found in Elisabeth Schüssler Fiorenza, "Religion und Politik in der Offenbarung des Johannes," in *Exegetische Randbemerkungen: Schülerfestschrift für Rudolf Schnackenburg zum 60. Geburtstag* (Würzburg: Echter, 1974), 261–71, and in "Visionary Rhetoric and Social-Political Situation" in her *The Book of Revelation: Justice and Judgment* (Philadelphia: Fortress, 1985), 181–203. All the other essays in that volume provide further enlightenment for our understanding of John. My own views on some major aspects of the Apocalypse of John can be found in "John's 'Heavenly' Jerusalem" (161–86 below).

80. In *Combat Myth* Collins shows that John presents the same arrangement of the sequence of persecution, judgment, and triumph five times: in Rev 6 and 7; 8–11 (without 10:1–11:12); 12:1–15:4; 16:4–19:10; and 20:1–21:8. She proves that there are other, even more intricate correspondences and that there are interludes in this complex of 6:1–22:5 as well.

vision precede it, dresses the whole collation of visions into a letter format with seven addressees,[81] and, finally, adds a preface (1:1–3). In the several parts of the epistolary introduction many of the formal and material elements of the main body are already touched upon.[82] By way of his recapitulation scheme John prevents his readers from abusing his visions as objectifying means for defining their privileged place in salvation history and for setting the clock for the end of time. John's concept of history is different, and so is his understanding of the character of the church's situation within it.

John shows himself to be sufficiently acquainted with apocalyptic hermeneutics, particularly as it concerns the integration of tradition and symbolism. John is conscious of the creative dimension of language and literary composition. The peculiar Greek style of the book is not an expression of linguistic incompetence or barbarism but proves to be an original creation of a singular language with its own rather consistent grammar, syntax, and vocabulary.[83] John uses this language not, as apocalypticism does, in order to create another supernatural reality but in order to get hold of historical reality with the help of prophetic magic. Nowhere in the New Testament do we find a similarly rich collection of heavenly statements. One can even speak of a heavenly authorship of the book, and John is of the conviction that the finished work is holy writ word for word. The heavenly sphere, which the seer invokes by his word, is not another world but the concrete basis for the historical reality of congregations as they witness to Jesus in their Sunday worship and in their confession. John's work is anything but the product of an esoteric quietist piety. Here a prophetic consciousness that has a hold on historical reality expresses itself. It is ready to call into question the claim of "official" reality that considers itself able to create and control everyone. John challenges the Roman state, in particular the principate. According to Rev 13 and 17 John sees in the gigantic machinery of the *Imperium Romanum* the demonstration of a prophetic religion fascinating the world. In addition, Rev 13, 17, and 18 testify to the correctness of the analysis of Horace

---

81. The two key chapters are 4 and 5; the epistolary frame is 1:4–3:22 and 22:6.

82. A few examples include (1) macarisms (lacking in apocalyptic literature, with one or two exceptions, rather surprising considering the sapiential development of apocalypticism since Daniel), which occur in Rev 1:3; 14:13; 16:15; 19:9; 20:6; (2) Παντοκράτωρ as a title in 1:8; 4:8; 15:3; 16:7, 14; 19:6, 15; 21:22; (3) the motif of the heavenly temple in 3:12; 7:15; 11:1–2, 19; 14:15, 17; 15:5–6, 8; 16:1, 17; 21:22; (4) the white garments in 3:4–5, 18; 4:4; 6:11; 7:9, 13; 19:14; and (5) the book of life in 3:5; 13:8; 17:8; 20:12, 15; 21:27.

83. On the language of Revelation and its internal regularity, see esp. R. H. Charles, *A Critical and Exegetical Commentary on the Revelation of St. John* (ICC; Edinburgh T&T Clark, 1920), 1:cxvii–clix, under the significant heading "A Short Grammar of the Apocalypse."

given above, namely, that the political ideology of the principate possessed religious integrity, relevance, and attraction. John is aware of the eschatological dimension of the intentions and actions of the principate, although he protests them. For him the Caesar religion is the cult and theology of the devil that apes the authentic eschatological conviction, that which is caused by Jesus. It speaks for John's prophetic consciousness, his confidence in having a hold on reality, that he dares to make such anachronistic claims about the imitation of the Jesus faith by the Caesar religion. At the same time the power and persuasiveness of the Augustan religion finds an indirect testimony in John's polemics. John can describe it appropriately only by using high-powered categories. The seer feels himself in a dramatic competition with the prophet(s) of the Caesar religion, people such as Horace and Virgil and lesser ones. The religion they represent and propagate is a world religion, the religion of a world empire. Therefore the battle with them has to be seen in cosmic proportions.

There is a long section in Revelation that at first sight seems to be entirely foreign to the rest of the work. It appears to be too secular. I am speaking of chapter 18. It contains the great lament about the fall of Babylon (18:9–20), the mourning of the allies of the city (18:9–10), the wailing of the merchants (18:11–17), and, finally, the dirge of the captains and sailors (18:17b–20). There is no doubt that the seer had found a model for this threnody in Ezek 26–27, the lament about the fall of Tyre. There the loss of the trade center on the east coast of the Mediterranean is described in a very concrete and technically precise fashion. But there are sufficient differences, which suggests that Ezekiel had prompted John to look at the reality of his own days in the same realistic fashion.

John also has people lament the loss of a center of world trade.[84] That center in John's days was Rome, not a port in the strict sense of the word but through its harbor, Ostia, connected with the sea. The commerce of Rome depended on long-distance trading. It was indeed ship related. Since the Second Punic War Rome had quite consciously turned to the sea, and shortly before Revelation was written Ostia had experienced major improvements. The elegy in Rev 18 correctly recognizes the fact previously mentioned that Roman trade had turned particularly to exotic luxury goods as primary freight, in addition, of course, to grain.

---

84. Ernst Lohmeyer's commentary on the text (*Die Offenbarung des Johannes* [2nd ed.; HNT 16; Tübingen: Mohr Siebeck, 1953], 151) misses the point: "Die Waren sind die des Transithandels einer orientalischen Stadt, aber sie passen nicht zur Kennzeichnung Roms. Zudem war Rom niemals in irgendeinem hervorragenden Masse Handels- oder gar Seestadt, sondern verdankt seinen Ruhm rein seiner politischen Bedeutung."

The recognition of Rome as a center of world trade in the book of Revelation is a new idea in early Christian literature and has no parallels in Jewish apocalypses. The prediction of the decline of Rome as a center of world trade, expressed in the prophetic perfect, proves John to be quite realistic, at least as much as Horace during his own time. John proves even more clairvoyant with respect to future developments in Rome. The subsequent decades brought about an economic decline of Rome. During the end of the first century Rome experienced an essential reduction of its central commercial role. Certain provincial cities and ports such as Ephesus gained renewed or entirely new influence on industry and world trade and tried to increase their importance at the expense of Rome.

With respect to the rural situation, Revelation takes a position entirely opposite to that of the *Carmen saeculare*. Despite his attack on Rome, John confirms urban life at the end of his book in a truly monstrous fashion. The future world is portrayed as one huge city, and this as Babylon redeemed.[85] This is not a simple reflection of the importance Jerusalem had for biblical and Jewish eschatology.[86] The new Jerusalem of Revelation has nothing to do with the topography of either Jerusalem or Zion.[87] It is also astonishing to note how the issue of Jerusalem as city is subordinated in *4 Ezra* and *2 Baruch*, documents contemporary with Revelation. There the new world is not described as an urban world. Neither *1 Enoch* nor the Qumran writings emphasize the urban dimensions of Jerusalem in their eschatological predictions, only the sacred, the temple.

Revelation reflects the post-Easter decision of the majority of the Jesus movement for the city. Stephen and his friends apparently had concentrated on this already. It is even more unambiguous with Paul. His independent missionary strategy is directed toward major trade centers, particularly harbors—places connected with world trade. The missionary strategy of the early church has to be seen in the context of the competition that the cities of the Hellenistic world carried on with the city of Rome. In this competition the ports of western Asia Minor were especially successful, among them the addressees of the Revelation of John.

---

85. On the seer's concept of Jerusalem as Babylon redeemed, see "John's 'Heavenly' Jerusalem," 161–86 below.

86. The most elaborate discussion on the comparability of John's visions of the heavenly Jerusalem with biblical and Jewish tradition is found in Charles, *Critical and Exegetical Commentary*, 1:144–80, 200–111. For Qumran material on the new Jerusalem, see esp. Dominique Barthélemy and J. T. Milik, *Qumran Cave 1* (DJD 1; Oxford: Clarendon, 1955), 134–35; Maurice Baillet, J. T. Milik, and Roland de Vaux, *Les "petites grottes" de Qumrân* (DJD 3; Oxford: Clarendon, 1962), 84–90, 184–93, 211–302.

87. On the topography of John's heavenly Jerusalem, see "John's 'Heavenly' Jerusalem," 161–86 below.

But John stands in the shadow of Paul, whose epistolary form he uses. Paul had paid particular attention to the most important place of industry and trade on the coast of Asia Minor, Ephesus. Of all his various stays in Hellenistic cities during his independent missionary activity, the one in Ephesus was the longest: two and a half years.[88] Moreover, the importance of Ephesus grew continuously. John addresses this city in his first circular letter.

The concentration of missionaries of the early church on the east reflects the growing importance of this part of the Mediterranean. The period in which John is writing is informed by a return to ethnic values and groups, among others Greeks and Jews, but all of this still under the universal umbrella of Hellenism. This growing self-confidence of the provinces found manifold expressions, including philosophical and religious ones as well. Apollonius of Tyana, Dio Chrysostom, Plutarch, and the Pharisees are examples of this—not necessarily always in opposition to Rome. Missionizing religious groups such as the Jesus groups helped to increase this self-confidence.

As regards the foreseeing of this immediate future, John proved to be superior to Horace. He saw the deterioration of Rome ahead of time, particularly the decline of its previously dominant role in world trade. However, as to the predictions of the predominance of the rural, Horace seems to have been more reality bound, truer to the future. John, on the other hand, was wrong in his prediction of complete urbanization and the final victory over the Caesar. The Caesar finally co-opted the church, and the church of Jesus Christ became basically a rural religion and remains so today. Was this a final triumph of Virgil and Horace over Paul and John?

---

88. Dieter Georgi, *Remembering the Poor: The History of Paul's Collection for Jerusalem* (Nashville: Abingdon, 1992).

4

THE URBAN ADVENTURE OF THE EARLY CHURCH

1. JOHN'S UNIVERSAL URBAN VISION

We have already seen that voices exist in the New Testament that profess an affirmation of an urban mission of those who confess Jesus as the Christ. We found also a definite readiness to concretely work out such a commitment. It has become clear too that such readiness was not uncritical. However, the exercise of such constructive critical consciousness happened in a rather explosive fashion. Nature and potential of such astonishing historical ventures and changes are explored in the following essay. It necessarily ends with a first critical comparison of the original phase of the early church and the later phases that show an increasing distance to the initial urban adventure. This comparison will be picked up again and strengthened as the discussion in the book goes on.

The New Testament ends with the utopian projection of a city that is approximately 2,500 kilometers long, 2,500 kilometers wide, and 2,500 kilometers high. This city would embrace an area that reached from the Persian Gulf in the east to the Adriatic Coast in the west, from Sevastopol in the north to Mecca in the south. This city would be larger than the entire Mediterranean. On the map of North America, it would reach from New York to the Rocky Mountains and from Montreal to Florida. The whole area covered would be identical with the extension of the empire of Alexander the Great ranging from Greece to Afghanistan. The additional peculiarity of John's cosmopolis is the fact

---

* This essay is a revised version of the inaugural lecture at San Francisco Theological Seminary in San Anselmo at the end of the winter term 1967.

that it also stretches as far into the sky as it is wide and long. Only the astronauts would have reached beyond the height of this massive cube whose portrait concludes the "Christian" Bible. It is obvious that the book of Revelation wants to describe the entire world with this image of the cosmopolis Jerusalem. The cubic format is chosen because the cube is a perfect body. In other words, an ideally ordered world is being described here.

However, this future world is identified with a city that has no outside, no separate countryside beyond its walls. The new world in its entirety is projected as a city. In this vision, the ultimate world of peace and salvation includes the paradise, yet it is not identified with rural life. It is not painted with idyllic colors. This is rather different from our contemporary liberal wildlife nostalgia. It is even more surprising that this future world reminds one neither of the real Jerusalem nor of Ezechiel's prophetic portrait of the future Jerusalem. The new Jerusalem has all the traces of Babylon, the prototype of the sinful world, the primordial manifestation of the equation of sin and hubris. This is all the more remarkable because in previous chapters John had described Babylon as the epitome of evil, had identified it with the capital of the Roman Empire, with Rome. This implies that at the end of his book John wants to present God and the Lamb as architects and mayors of a new Babel. At the end of days, the New Testament blesses neither the countryside, peasants, nor nomads but urban civilization. In the end, Babylon has come to life again, identified with the heavenly, the new world. That is the conclusive message of the New Testament.

2. ORIGIN OF THE URBAN VISION IN THE EARLY CHURCH

This certainly is not a consistent continuation of all of the preceding New Testament. One major element of the New Testament in particular represents a diametric contradiction to this final image of John: the teaching of Jesus. Primarily the parables intimate that Jesus' thinking and teaching—as far as we can reconstruct it at all—seems to have been oriented toward the small town and the surrounding countryside. This is not surprising, since Jesus appears to have been a citizen of a small town, namely, Capernaum. His disciples, too, seem to have come from rural or small-town milieus. There are no indications that the city of Jerusalem was of any importance for the teaching of Jesus, neither the present nor the heavenly Jerusalem. Even Jesus' last journey to Jerusalem does not present a difference. The best and most simple explanation for that trip was that Jesus and his disciples wanted to join the annual Passover pilgrimage to the holy city.¹ For the disciples, the arrest and death of Jesus contributed nothing positive to Jerusalem. At least the male disciples seem to have flown after the arrest of Jesus, with all probability to their home region, Galilee.

Shortly after arriving there, some of them seem to have had visions of Jesus resurrected. Other such visions occurred to women disciples who had remained in Jerusalem. The reports of the visions to the women intimate that they had been earlier than those to male disciples in Galilee. These Jerusalem appearances of the women may have occurred even earlier than those the male disciples experienced in Galilee. Important for our deliberation is that the women stayed in the city of the crucifixion and burial of Jesus whereas the men fled, and only a few of them returned, Peter and eleven more, all of them together "the Twelve."²

Why some remained in the city of the arrest and murder of Jesus and others returned to it needs to be explained. Apparently, extraordinary experiences were the cause. These experiences also explain the major change in estimation of the city of Jerusalem, entailing a new attitude to urban reality. People conditioned by the countryside and small towns took up residence in a large city. This change was even more remarkable because it happened in clear contrast to Jesus' earthly career. He had sanctified Galilee by his origin and presence. Those disciples who remained in Jerusalem and those who decided to return there did this also in opposition to the decision of those who remained in Galilee.³ In the interpretation of these people, the post-Easter Jesus had chosen Galilee again, not Jerusalem. In the *Gospel of Thomas*, the geographical situation is Galilee, and the authority speaking is that of the "living Jesus," clearly a post-Easter figure of transhuman proportions.

---

1. The passion predictions, of course, want to integrate this journey into God's saving plan and make it the result of Jesus' conscious decision. Yet these announcements breathe the air of later rationalizations of the church, trying to put the career of Jesus under a higher rationale. This legendarizing is even more the case with our present Gospels, who extend that higher rationalization to the entire narration of Jesus' public career—making Jesus' planning and decision coincide with the plan of God, clearly a legendarizing tendency.

2. There is no reason to assume that only these twelve or thirteen men had such visionary experiences in Galilee or that all disciples returned to Jerusalem. The greater probability is that other people had experiences in Galilee as well, yet they remained there. Literary complexes such as the *Gospel of Thomas*, the Sayings Source (Q), and the peculiarly Matthean material are the strongest pieces of evidence for such post-Easter experiences and developments in Galilee itself. The *Gospel of Thomas* is at least as old, if not older, than our other Gospels. On the whole issue of Jerusalem and Galilee experiences and developments, especially the conflicts between Peter and the twelve and the women, see pages 58–60 below.

3. See the previous note.

We should not overlook the fact that remaining in or returning to Jerusalem implied the risk of extreme social insecurity. We can assume that all disciples of Jesus, female or male, had been Galileans, with the center of their lives, family, profession, and the like in Galilee, with no background or resources in Jerusalem. This social point of departure was difficult enough, but it became even harder to bear when pressure from the Jerusalem authorities started, of which Luke's Acts give a highly legendarized yet not entirely implausible account. The Acts of the Apostles present the authority of the resurrected one as the reason for the disciples' continued residence in Jerusalem. He orders the disciples to remain in the capital of Judea until the Feast of Pentecost. This coincides with the observations mentioned above, although it cannot be established with certainty that the Twelve were already among those who experienced the Pentecost following Good Friday and Easter in Jerusalem.

The concentration on Jerusalem after Easter did not rest on the authority of the earthly Jesus, at least on the basis of our limited knowledge about him. Those disciples, women and men, who chose the murderous city did so despite their Galilean origin and their experiences with Jesus in that region. They did not depend on the historical Jesus for that. There is no positive assessment of Jerusalem in the surviving Jesus material nor any preparation for the Easter experiences and their consequences. The decision of certain disciples to choose Jerusalem as the center of their future operation rested on a new authority expressing itself in their visionary experiences and auditions that they claimed to have received. This new authority was interpreted as active heavenly power that had appeared among them. The Easter witnesses interpreted this new ruling authority in their midst with prophetic force through the adoption of various titles stemming from biblical and Jewish eschatology. These titles had received additional apocalyptic flavor already.[4]

The various titles of royal or prophetic messiah or of Son of Man that the visionaries gave to the resurrected Jesus show that biblical and Jewish eschatology, popular in those days, were utilized in order to interpret the nature and role of the exalted master. Prophetic inspiration must have occurred and assisted in this interpretative process. In such prophetic experiences, the interpretative designation was expressed in

---

4. The difference in the employment of titles used to explain the new authority of Jesus exalted most probably is due to the preferences of different groups and their prophets. The development of post-Easter Christology did not happen without debate and conflict.

the name, that is, in the authority of the risen master himself speaking through the prophet.[5]

Jewish apocalyptic thought certainly provided arguments for looking at Jerusalem as an eschatological basis. Already in preexilic and postexilic eschatology a strongly mythicized understanding of Jerusalem appears. Jerusalem is seen as the exalted center of Israel and the world at large. Isaiah, Micah, and Ezekiel present Jerusalem as the navel of the world. Heaven and earth meet at this place. Jerusalem is described as the city that puts an end to all other cities, not by way of incorporation but through subordination. The remainder of the world is declassed socially, a society of metics! How much this centralist view is meant to be literally hierarchical, not only metaphorically, can be seen in the fact that only Zion, that is, the temple mountain, is important in these prophecies, not Jerusalem in general. This tendency to overrate the temple was already quite old. With respect to Solomon, the tradition especially and almost exclusively recorded that he was the builder of the temple. Other achievements that had been nearly as important for the history of Israel are not at all mentioned, such as the grandiose improvement and enlargement of the composition of Jerusalem as a whole.

The Babylonian destruction of Jerusalem was not able to put an end to the hope in a renewal and aggrandizement of Jerusalem, in particular of the temple, because already before the exile the ideas of heavenly models for the temple and its parts had originated. They were linked with an elevation of temple and city into mythical proportions, and they were projected into an eschatological future.

Deutero-Isaiah, the great grandfather of apocalypticism and Gnosticism, is especially important in this line of mythical projections. The prophet can perceive of Zion only as product of an eschatological miracle and as a marvelous entity itself, not as work made with hands from hewn and burned bricks, not as conceived by a human architect and constructed by human builders. This transposition of the actual Jerusalem and its temple into the heavenly and even into the primordial world continued in the later development of theological thought, despite the rebuilding of the earthly Jerusalem and temple. The profanation of the temple by Antiochus IV gave new fuel to such speculations.

The tendency to overemphasize the temple again shows itself in the Qumran *Temple Scroll*. It is remarkable and important, however, that even

---

5. For more on this, see Dieter Georgi, "The Early Church: Internal Jewish Migration or New Religion?" *HTR* 81 (1995): 35–66. An abbreviated version of this essay in *HTR* appeared under the title "Was the Early Church Jewish?" *BRev* 17/6 (2001): 33–37, 51–52.

in the most dualistic drafts of Jerusalem and its temple the relationship to actual geography was never completely lost. This is proven, for instance, by the Ethiopic *Enoch* and the Syriac *Baruch*. Despite all heavenly glory, the heavenly city remains a renewed Jerusalem. In the New Testament, Paul gives evidence for that as well. Despite his radically dualistic image of the heavenly Jerusalem in Gal 4—there amended by polemics against the earthly Jerusalem—Paul demonstrates in the same letter an astounding respect for the present Jerusalem. He continues to hold Jerusalem in high esteem, as the organization and execution of the collection shows. All this is important for an understanding of the decision of those circles of Easter witnesses who chose Jerusalem as their locale.

The Easter witnesses wanted to occupy and hold Jerusalem. They saw themselves as God's down payment for his future worldwide activity that would take its departure from Mount Zion, that is, from the eschatologically converted Mount Sinai. Jerusalem was seen as the place of God's final *parousia* and as the dwelling place of God's renewed people, to which all people from abroad, Jews and Gentiles, would direct their pilgrimage: the Jews in order to live in Jerusalem itself, the others because they wanted to camp around the city. This concrete decision of the disciples for Jerusalem was rewarded by an ecstatic mass vision on Pentecost.

Everyone who had gotten to know the real Jerusalem had learned to affirm the role of Jerusalem as one city among others. Jerusalem had become a Hellenistic city—even without a gymnasium. Remarkable testimonies to that can be found in the cemeteries of Jerusalem. Innumerable Hellenistic symbols have been found there on Jewish graves. The Maccabees and Hasmoneans had turned Jerusalem into a Hellenistic royal residence, and this Hellenization had increased since the appearance of the Romans. The Jerusalem temple achieved almost the rank of another world miracle when Herod renovated it. Principles of Hellenistic architecture were used with grandiose results.

However, for the first Easter witnesses, the situation and perspective were initially different. Their eschatological fundamentalism, reawakened and reinforced by their visionary experiences, initially did not have a worldwide urban orientation. They looked at Jerusalem from a rural and small-town perspective. In this view, the holy city received enlarged dimensions. It was seen in an eschatological light.

However, as they remained in the city and proclaimed their conviction, they met people who represented the Hellenistic urban culture at large. For them, Jerusalem was a center of pilgrimage that attracted Jews from all over the world. It would not be astonishing at all that Hellenistic Jews living in Jerusalem and supporting and serving the pilgrim industry were fascinated and attracted by ecstatic visionaries as we must presuppose them among the Easter witnesses. There is some reason to assume that the connection of such curious Hellenistic Jews with the Jesus circle in Jerusalem was made by the women leaders of this circle. The story about the ministry to (more probably *of*) the widows, the ministry of the deacons, and the ministry of the Twelve in Acts is a slightly veiled report about a leadership conflict in Jerusalem between the "widows," in fact, independent women like the various Maries of the Easter stories, the mother of Jesus among them, the Seven from the newly won Hellenistic Jews, and the Twelve under the leadership of Peter. None of them was ministered to as the present version of Acts 6 claims for the "widows." They all were ministers (of the word). It is Luke who in the beginning of the narrative gives the meaning "serving/ being served at tables" to the term *minister/ministry*. However, he uses the same term in the subsequent text for the preaching office of Peter and the other eleven, and what Luke then says about the activity of the Seven has nothing to do with charitable service. Stephen and Philip preach in an inspired fashion like the Twelve.

It seems that, in the tradition Luke found and worked over, the widows,[6] the original women leaders of the church, suggested that the newly won Hellenistic Jews organize additional leadership among themselves, that is, establish the Seven as additional leaders. The Twelve, who seem already to have conspired against the women leadership, used this moment for open revolt, insisting on their older rights, their alleged closeness to the dead master during his lifetime. This revolt was unknowingly assisted by the Jewish authorities who found the proclamation of Stephen and his friends blasphemous against God and Moses (i.e., the Torah; Acts 6:11). Stephen was convicted and executed, his friends driven out of Jerusalem, and with them most probably most of the women leaders. The Twelve remained unpersecuted and usurped the leadership of the Jesus community in Jerusalem.

3. THE SPREAD OF THE URBAN ORIENTATION OF THE EARLY CHURCH

The consequence was that the Hellenistic-Jewish followers of Christ, and with them the original women leaders, went from the city of Jerusalem into the urban culture of the Mediterranean, including the large cities such as Antioch. These "Hellenists" did not get involved in a

---

6. In Greek, not only women whose husbands had died but also frequently independent women.

theology that was oriented on Palestinian eschatology. They made their own experiences with the Easter conviction. They broke through the barriers of apocalyptic literalism. They started to look at Jesus, the elevated Christ, as the decisive figure in world history and began to express that in their own Hellenistic-Jewish terminology.[7] In their newly acquired spiritual perspective, these Easter witnesses saw in their spirit-guided interpretation of the scriptures of Israel an identity between God and Jesus, the Christ. Jesus, the Christ, interpreted himself to them as the κύριος, the translation for the Tetragrammaton in the Septuagint: Jesus as Yahweh, the Lord not only of Israel but also the master of the entire world. This had been most probably the cause for the accusation of Stephen for blasphemy and thus for his conviction, execution, and the subsequent expulsion of all like-minded people from Jerusalem.

The first Easter witnesses used their eagerness about being the "holy ones," that is, the avant-garde and the bridgehead of God's own coming, in order to evolve a radical degree of obedience to God's will, that is, to the law. Worldwide missionary activity was initially excluded. One was oriented in a concentric and centripetal fashion around Jerusalem. The Hellenistic-Jewish Easter witnesses instead claimed that Jesus, the Lord, as God's representative, had begun his rulership over the world. Therefore, in following thinking and activity well-known in synagogues of the Diaspora, they said farewell to a particularistic understanding of the Torah as for Jews only. They saw in Jesus, the Christ and Son of God, God's wisdom, righteousness, sanctification, and redemption for the entire world (as a Hellenistic-Jewish formula of the early church says that Paul quotes in 1 Cor 1:30). The activity of the Hellenistic-Jewish adherents of the Jerusalem Christ community demonstrated that for them Jerusalem was not the one and only city that put an end to all other cities. Instead, for them Jerusalem became a city among other cities, the first of all Hellenistic cities. They demanded the Hellenistic urban society for Jesus, for the κύριος of the world.

Wolfgang Schrage convincingly argued some time ago in an article on the origin of the use of the term ἐκκλησία in the early church that it must have been the first Hellenistic-Jewish adherents of the Christ witness who introduced this term into the language of the early church.[8] Schrage shows that this term cannot have been taken from the LXX and cannot mean the *qāhāl* of the biblical people of God. The concept comes

---

7. There is some intimation in Luke's legendary report of the death of Stephen (Acts 7:56) that the latter had interpreted the apocalyptic figure of the Son of Man in a Hellenistic-Jewish way, similar to the Christology of the Wisdom of Solomon.

8. Wolfgang Schrage, "Ekklesia und Synagoge," *ZTK* 60 (1963): 178–202.

from normal secular Greek. It means the assembly of the free citizens of a city as it could be found in any Hellenistic city—even in Roman times—that was recognized as a full and free city. The ἐκκλησία was the basis of the self-governance of such places. Schrage emphasizes that the Hellenistic-Jewish novices in the church used a secular term, thus avoiding as a self-definition an established religious term such as *synagogue* or *thiasos* or any other concept that would have been identified with an existing religious association.[9] However, would not the addition of θεοῦ intimate religious connotation? It would, yet not in contradistinction to the original secular and political use of the term ἐκκλησία. The absolute usage of the term ἐκκλησία is frequent in the New Testament, and nowhere is there a trace of any definition of congregations as ἐκκλησία of Yahweh. Only once do we find the term ἐκκλησίαι Χριστοῦ (Rom 16:16), and it is significant that it occurs in the plural here.

It is not without reason that the term ἐκκλησία appears especially in passages that deal with universal matters. The densest usage of the term is found in 1 Cor 14. In this text in particular Paul argues that the character of the Christ congregation should be an open assembly and emphatically refuses the idea of the church being a religious ghetto. The worldliness of the Christ community, the individual congregation or church, is described in this chapter in an impressive fashion, if looked at from the perspective of history of religion. Paul here makes οἰκοδομή (constructive building) and νοῦς (reason) almost synonymous. He uses their combination as a decisive criterion for defining the integrity and authenticity of the worship service of the ἐκκλησία in Corinth. This speaks for an anticultic aspiration of these services—at least in Paul's eyes and as the intention of his organization. Worship service of such a community that confesses Jesus as world ruler becomes, in the words of Ernst Käsemann, "worship service in the everyday of the world."

There is every reason to assume that the adoption of the secular term ἐκκλησία with its special reference to the political institution of the people's assembly in urban situations had a political connotation as well. This was not a pet idea of Paul's but had been a very early decision by important representatives of the Easter witness. It was a decision for the worldwide urban society and for the urban as well as political character of the Christ community, locally and ecumenically. The choice to take the existence of the adherence to the early church as a secular and urban form of communal organization could be understood

---

9. I doubt that the adoption of the term had any anti-Jewish connotation, since Jewish scriptures were used extensively.

by everyone. Those outside must have recognized it as a challenge, and with all probability those who chose that term meant it as such. The challenge would read as the claim that these new communities would be the most authentic representatives of urban freedom and communal self-determination and would as such be the real models of the universal Hellenistic culture.

Such claim for a particular, a local or subcultural, expression of Hellenistic culture as the best representation of the whole culture that others should heed and imitate was quite common in Hellenism, indeed an essential mark of Hellenistic self-understanding and consciousness, in each case combined with a missionary zeal. It had been made not only by Athenians and other original Greek communities but by the Etruscans, Hannibal, the Hellenizers in the Jerusalem before the Maccabean revolt as well as their Maccabean and Hasmonean opponents, by the Jews in the Diaspora, the representatives of the Scipio family, by Augustus, Hadrian, and so forth. That means that even the Romans understood themselves as the most authentic representatives of Hellenistic civilization and interpreted their imperialist expansion as a world mission, as their successful attempt to spread their understanding of the Hellenistic world culture around the Mediterranean and beyond.

Even the Jewish consciousness of the Maccabees, reported in 1 and 2 Maccabees, was not Hellenized later on. Rather, it was Hellenistic from the start. Their engagement for the heritage of the fathers, for the battle cry νόμοι πάτριοι, was thoroughly Hellenistic and was nothing else than the legal claim of proper recognition of the right of each particular subculture within the universal culture, a claim that Alexander had raised to the structural principle of his world empire. His successors did not move away from that principle, not even the Ptolemies, relatively the most absolutist of the "diadochs," the "successors." Antiochus IV and the Maccabees were rivals in a typically Hellenistic legal battle.

The circle of Stephen and all those converted by them to the Christ conviction demonstrated the same dialectical attitude that could be found everywhere in the surrounding culture. This peculiar urban consciousness present everywhere in the Mediterranean and the Middle East also expresses itself in the addresses of the Pauline letters: "Paul to the people's assembly of God that is situated in...." We have here the same dialectical blend of unity and difference as it presented itself in each individual city and its local assembly, proud of its local particularity and with a sense of mission. At the same time, they shared with other cities a common style, a common idea. From this sense of belonging to a larger, ecumenical culture, local patriotism got its major impetus, namely, to be a proper and authentic incorporation of the whole, indeed, to be its best and inimitable representation.

4. THE URBAN NATURE OF THE ORGANIZATIONAL STRUCTURE OF THE EARLY CHURCH

This leads to an explanation of an initially confusing peculiarity of the structure of the life of the Christ community as a whole, that is, in the entire Mediterranean: the independence of the different congregations from one another together with strong intracommunal relations. The linkage was not provided by a central and elevated umbrella organization, something like a church government. Instead, an infrastructure of active relations and communications between the congregations caused and maintained unity. It is obvious that this organizational arrangement contradicts everything we know of modern organizations, models we are accustomed to and consider to be the only effective ones. Our mentality believes in centrality and leadership and organization from the top down. Most Christian churches perpetuate this pattern. They cling to it even more than secular organizations, which are slowly rediscovering the advantage of decentralization over vertical and pyramidal structures.

Hellenistic antiquity provides successful counterexamples to such centralist ideology, and so do Judaism and the early church, including their missionary activities. Here we find horizontal structures and activities, not only on a small and local level. Even huge arrangements are structured this way, such as the Jewish Diaspora. It reached from at least Parthia to the Western Mediterranean, a distance greater than most modern states cover. The Roman Empire provides the best and most prominent example for such basically horizontal structure. It grew relatively the most during the hundred years of civil war. It is significant that this happened after the Romans had started to emulate Hellenistic thought and practice.

The organization of the early Christ congregations, in particular the Pauline ones, is anything but a product of eschatological fever dreams or of an unworldly enthusiasm. It mirrors the successful organizational principles described, principles that kept the Hellenistic world together, especially including its Roman version, the empire as a confederation of cities and their people's assemblies.

The young Christ-oriented churches adopted this form of organization and radicalized it. The change that can be identified with the name of Stephen was a turn of the early church to the urban, indeed an orientation toward the metropolitan culture of the Mediterranean. This also helps to explain individual elements of Paul's public activity. He and other missionaries of the early church concentrated their work on the cities of the Hellenistic world. This is even true for the beginning of Paul's mission for Jesus as the Christ. He says in Gal 1:17 that he began in Arabia. This is the Nabatean Arabia that extended from the Negev toward Damascus and environs, a thoroughly Hellenized kingdom. This "Arabic" episode of Paul's missionary activity seems to have been concentrated on Damascus.

There is only one case in Paul's missionary career when he worked in rural areas and small-town environments: his activity in the province Galatia, on the Anatolian plains. Paul was forced to remain here most probably because of an eye disease, yet even in his relationship to the Galatians Paul does not do without an essential instrument of urban culture, the letter as means of communication. In addition, there are other urban elements. There is, for instance, the universal perspective, starting with the first chapter and continuing throughout. The reference to the schooling of Paul in Judaism (1:14) can be mentioned as an urban aspect in this context. Naturally, the Jerusalem conference as a meeting and exchange between representatives of two large cities, that is, of their churches, is an urban event (2:1–11), as are the issues of the Antiochene incident in Gal 2:11–14 (21). The points of departure of this conference—the conflicts, discussions, negotiations, and conclusions—are varieties of the problems and models of conflict resolution and organization in the infrastructure of intraurban relations of Hellenistic culture. The treaty of Jerusalem, something like a constitutional agreement, is the most prominent expression of this. As reported by Paul in Gal 2, the disputes in Jerusalem and in Antioch intimate that the differentiation in terms of ethnic and subcultural distinctions and associations—characteristic for the sociocultural composition of Hellenistic cities and their interrelations with other cities—was utilized in the attempts to reconcile different styles of different groupings.

Galatians 3:28 is an immediate parallel to the universalism of the Hellenistic urban culture, the disappearance of all ethnic, racial, religious, and class distinctions but also a growing emancipation of women. The legal questions mentioned in Gal 3 and 4 revolve heavily around the issue that was particularly interesting in the cities: liberty from slavery. We then have in Gal 4 the reference to the free heavenly city as the common link of all those who adhere to the Christ. It is interesting that the city here is not looked at as an architectural phenomenon but as an idea of a certain kind of human community, again a peculiar side of Hellenistic urban thinking.

5. THE PAULINE CHURCHES AS SYMPTOMS AND PARADIGMS

It must be by now obvious that I cannot look at Paul as an extraordinary figure but rather as representative for the historical and theological peculiarity of the Hellenistic Christ community. This does not exclude the acknowledgement of certain modifications due to Paul but includes them. However, Paul can no longer be seen as the only inventor of theology and organization that were operative in his congregations and showed in his letters. His co-workers and his congregations contributed to communal life and theological exchange on Paul's mission field. Paul depended on their suggestions and cooperation, which extended beyond the limits of individual congregations. Protestantism has taken over this hero worship from the Middle Ages, especially from the late Renaissance. It has been further cultivated by the adoption of the romantic cult of the genius, pervasive in nineteenth-century Protestantism and still going strong today.

As already stated, the Pauline congregations strongly embodied the concept of the confederation of cities as a Hellenistic form of expression of pluralistic unity. Just as within the confederation of cities a sense of equity within and between cities could be achieved and thus a worldwide balance, so Paul argues in 2 Cor 8—within the context of the administration of the collection for Jerusalem—for the necessity of equity within and between the Christ communities. He does so with the use of the Greek term for equity, ἰσότης. Already relations to the Pauline teaching of justification can be found in the immediate context of 2 Cor 8. I have discussed this in my book on the collection of Paul for Jerusalem. If one adds the debate in 2 Cor 9, the fragment of a letter that was written shortly after the fragment in 2 Cor 8, one can see that Paul here quite consciously blurs the border between the righteousness of God and that of humans. Righteousness clearly is not only a status but also a behavior. The eschatological aspect of righteousness known from other Pauline passages is not minimized here, yet it does not prevent Paul from speaking about presuppositions, circumstances, and consequences of human activity. In so doing, he also uses terms and thoughts of proverbial wisdom and of popular philosophy.

Since Plato righteousness has been identified with the function that was appropriated to each person. This included the enabling and realization of such "properties." Equity and balance were the consequences of concrete righteousness. Therefore, righteousness was essentially a political and social term referring to the urban community. Only within this context was it a legal and juridical term as well. In the first universalistic exuberance of early Hellenistic times, the term *righteousness* lost its connection with political life. It was completely individualized. Later on the term again caught up with political reality. Righteousness now was related to a concrete historical community. The concept was now associated with the idea of the (theatrical) role. Even more concretely than under Plato, righteousness was now the ability to recognize the role and task that was assigned to each person. It was part of righteousness to understand the relationship of the individual role to the roles and tasks of others and of the community as a whole. Righteousness became the ability and action of recognizing as well as of realizing these roles in context in an appropriate way and to take care that others could take up and execute their personal roles as well. The well-known motto of the Hohenzollern "suum cuique" originally came from Stoic philosophy and meant the distribution and assignment of the role appropriate for each and everyone.

This "suum cuique" can be spoken of indeed in connection with the Pauline interpretation of the body-of-Christ idea in 1 Cor 12. Whereas the first part of the discussion of this motif (12:12–13), uses the gnostic myth, the latter part (12:14–26) utilizes the Stoic conception of organism. The emphasis on the differentiation of functions different people have and on the mutual relationship of these functions stems from the discussions of middle Stoicism. This means, too, that the Pauline description of communal life corresponds to the developed Stoic notion of δικαιοσύνη, although this term does not appear in 1 Cor 12. In reality, Paul takes the Christ community to be a manifestation of righteousness just as the Stoic philosopher Panaitius thought of the political community. This is clearly an urban perspective.

In 2 Cor 9—again not without precedence in the politically oriented philosophy of middle Stoicism—Paul personifies the intracommunal relations with the term δικαιοσύνη, which is supposed to be related to the life of the individual congregation. The individual Hellenistic city, especially the larger ones, consisted of individual sub-ommunities that communicated with one another, and such was also the case on the level of the Christ-ecumene as well, or, Stoically formulated, on the level of the κοσμόπολις

This observation is able to explain the rather curious thesis of Paul in Rom 14:17: "For the kingship of God is not eating and drinking but righteousness, and peace, and joy in the Holy Spirit." If the terms *righteousness, peace,* and *joy* that are associated here with the term βασιλεία were to be understood from an apocalyptic background, as is often argued, then the unambiguous emphasis of Paul on the presence of this kingship or kingdom would make no sense. What one would then rather expect is a radical orientation toward the future. Seen within the context of middle Stoicism, the text makes more sense. Righteousness, peace, and joy are well able to describe content and goal within a political and social setting that understands itself as the rule of freedom.

It is obvious that the common understanding of Paul's concepts of ecclesial organization and political power as hierarchical arrangements is wrong. So is the denunciation of any democratic or enthusiastic elements in Paul's texts as allegedly unrealistic and utopian. Of course, Paul is a utopian, but the utopian references of Paul, for instance in Galatians, to the universal character of the church and to the heavenly Jerusalem do not have a Disney world in mind. Both passages express the conception of complete freedom as it was developed on the basis of the Greek and Hellenistic city.

I concur with Lewis Mumford that the city of antiquity was a utopia formed in stone. This was especially so in the case of the Greek and Hellenistic city together with its Roman variety. In Paul, the motifs of the heavenly Jerusalem and of the pilgrimage of the peoples are alive, but they have been transformed. The eschatological process that these concepts relate to is already under way. The peoples are already on the road. In addition, the sequence is turned around. First the Gentiles come to Jerusalem, primarily symbolized by the collection. Then, when all Gentiles are converted, the Lord will take his place on Mount Zion and will turn to the Jews in the entire world and save all of them. The references to Jerusalem are in part quite concrete geographical references, and partly they relate to Jerusalem as an idea. Particularly here the motif of the heavenly Jerusalem is important. In this motif and its use by Paul, Hellenistic and Roman thoughts meet as they are developed under the impression of Cynic-Stoic popular philosophy as well as modified under the influence of Gnosticism.

We face here the conception of a turnover of the world order, of its hierarchy of values, its realization of freedom, a freedom more radical than the Greeks had conceived of. It means a complete surrender of all differences in society, of gender, race, social status, ethnic, cultural, and political belonging. The discussion in 1 Corinthians proves that Paul is more radical than Stoics and Gnostics because, in distinction to them, he attacks all forms and traces of elitist thought. He radicalizes the functionalism of the concept of the role of the person in society, and he translates the concept of equity into that of equality and of equivalence. This is another example for the fact that the Christ community integrated and radicalized the principles of urban culture in a critical fashion.

I could continue with these examples. It would be interesting to study the influence of urban thinking on the Pauline school and on the Epistle to the Hebrews. It is also almost impossible to talk about this theme without an extensive discussion of Luke either, for Luke considers the authentic "Christian" as the proper citizen (cf. the image of Paul in Acts). It would also be fascinating to pursue the development from Luke to Constantine. Such a study would show that the growing Christian church remained an urban religion until the invasion of the Germans. Then the people from the backwoods took power, and Christianity turned into a rural and small-town religion and has remained so until today. There is no consciousness in the contemporary church of really belonging to the city as to a universal phenomenon. This is one of the major reasons that our cities are not much more than proliferating and sprawling villages.

The image of the new city in Rev 21 and 22 poses several critical questions for the modern world.

- ✦ Is the often-heard thesis of the urbanization of the world more than a slogan?
- ✦ Is such a development seen as a nightmare or as something positive, constructive?
- ✦ Can the concept of the city be separated from all centralist and hierarchical elements, including the hierarchy of values?
- ✦ Is a city thinkable without a temple and with God and the Christ as citizens?
- ✦ Is it possible to really imagine the city as a city, that is, the city not as a conglomerate of fortresses and prisons but as a communication in flesh and in stone, as a city in which the major elements of life are the streets and plazas, not the houses as little castles?

5

THE HOUR OF THE GOSPEL: JESUS AND CAESAR

1. INTRODUCTION

Time was of the essence with respect to eschatology, yet it was time entirely in the province and authority of the divine. This appeared to contradict completely the understanding of time as advanced in urban quarters of antiquity. For since ancient times the city, contrary to the countryside, gave itself the appearance of manipulating time as much as it manipulated space. The rural world instead confessed to its being governed by time, most of all the seasons but also other phenomena of the calendar. Punctuating time by defining certain moments in a pointed fashion were major instruments in this urban manipulation of time. The early church had its peculiar way of dealing with this issue of "timing." Time is of the essence for modern urban life. The issue of time is intimately related to our understanding of the urban situation in many different ways. Whereas farm and village life are conditioned by the seasons, urban life seems to depend completely on calendar and clock. These are needed in production, trade, and services offered in town, already in planning and building the town, as well as in later repairing and restoring it. Urban cultural life entails partly going with the clock, partly

---

* Initially this was a paper given in the context of a lecture series of the School of Protestant Theology of the Johann Wolfgang Goethe University in Frankfurt on the issue of time. The papers were published under the title *Religion und Gestaltung der Zeit* (ed. Dieter Georgi, Hans-Günter Heimbrock, and Michael Moxter; Kampen: Pharos, 1994), 52–68.

defying it. What about religion? The following essay gives some New Testament perspectives in the cultural situation of the early church.[1]

One can say that cities are time set in concrete, steel, and asphalt. Time has been turned into a major instrument and commodity of economy and commerce, a tool for all administrations, municipal as well as industrial. And the instrument has turned itself into a constitutional factor as well as into a whip, a dictating force. Urban life in all its forms is dictated by innumerable clocks and watches, ever more precise, with continuous increase of speed, haste, measurability, accountability, and control. Time differences around the globe are supposed to matter no more—as little as day or night. Jet lag is an unfortunate deficiency, a leftover of unenlightened times. We are working on it. But is this dictate of the chronometer our true reality? Are our cities really "under the watch"? Fundamental for the following essay is a thesis of the Harvard philosopher Josiah Royce.[2]

---

1. The phrase "the hour of the gospel" is, in this form, not a quote from the New Testament. It combines tendencies of the Pauline understanding of the gospel with the Gospel of John's understanding of time, in particular of the hour. Both terms denote phenomena of announcement. Time and space limitations forbid a discussion here of John's understanding of time.

2. Josiah Royce, *The Problem of Christianity* (ed. Jessie A. Mann; Chicago: Regnery, 1968), a series of lectures given in 1913. The thesis mentioned above is presented by Royce especially in the lectures 9 ("The Community and the Time Process") and 14 ("The Doctrine of Signs"). In the latter, Royce says, "Time ... expresses a System of essentially social relations. The present interprets the past to the future. At each moment of time, the results of the whole world's history up to that moment are, so to speak, summed up and passed over to the future for its new deeds of creation and interpretation" (344). On 348, Royce states even more emphatically: "Past time and future time are known solely through interpretations. Past time we regard as real because we view our memories as signs which need and possess their interpretations. Our expectations are interpreted to our future selves by our present deeds. Therefore we regard our expectations as signs of a future." For Royce, this is a demonstration of the reality of the spirit and of authentic community. In fact, only through this interpretation is reality created, and this is done in and through the community, a "community of interpretation." This understanding of time has an essential advantage over against our allegedly objective, pretentiously scientific relationship to time. In the latter, we face a fundamental contradiction: in measured time, the present is nothing but an essentially abstract, concretely ungraspable moment of transition from a more or less infinite past to a more or less infinite future. On the other side, there is the cultural as well as scientific tendency to take this present as the more or less infinite tableau of synchronic observations of an infinite number of observers, their experiences, and even of the contemporary assessment and evaluation of all of that. It is allegedly the present time of the so-called neutral observer, a mythical phenomenon if ever there was one. But this chimera has all the power of interpretation, so our societies presume and expect. This understanding of the present of the neutral observer is all too easily identified as a milestone of modernity. Oftentimes it is attempted to lend this factually fleeting present more material dimension by its severance from past and future, most recently even by way of a coup declaring it as postmodernity.

He claims that true time is time interpreted. Royce developed this thesis before the First World War in an elaborate discussion of the Gospel of John and the letters of Paul, using in this philosophical meditation the concept of the body of Christ as a major hermeneutical tool.[3]

The phrase "the hour of the gospel" means such interpreted time, pointed time, not clock time. The two names that follow in the title of the paper, Jesus and Caesar, have much to do with our definition of time, even with our chronology and thus with our measurement of time.[4] In the theme of this essay there is also some tension, not only between both names but also between them and the "hour of the gospel." This also means that the discussion of the relationship between measured and interpreted time will carry through this entire discussion. It will become clear that there are historical and theological arguments for the thesis that our predominant notion of time, so-called objective time, is determined by the more subjective time. The philosopher mentioned has given philosophical reasons for assuming this order of importance.

2. JESUS AND CAESAR IN RELATIONSHIP TO CHRONOLOGY

2.1. JESUS

Jesus determines our chronology in its crude structure: our calendar years are related to the birth of Jesus, calculated according to the (assumed

---

3. The thesis that is the basis for this essay actually became manifest during the time of its first oral delivery. It happened during the climax of the Gulf War. One may still remember that many television stations blended a running clock into their reports from the military theater in the Gulf region. The time indicated by the clock promised objectivity, although it was belied by the true time of the reported events, for the clock showed the station's local time, not the local time of the actual events. The promised objectivity was even more contradicted by the commentaries that penetrated the new reports themselves, yet still more by the many accompanying programs in which Mr. and Ms. Anybody were presented as experts. The censoring engaged in by both warring parties and their camouflaging of propaganda as information stood together in a colorful association. There was an alliance of sorts between the enemies. This alliance occurred in the living rooms, of which both parties knew that they were the real battlefields where the military decision was in fact going to take place—in front of the television screens.

4. This essay is also a contribution to the subject "history of chronology." There is a rich literature on this theme. Particularly helpful is Elias J. Bickerman, *Chronology of the Ancient World* (Ithaca, N.Y.: Cornell University Press, 1982). Of the other literature mentioned, Friedrich Karl Ginzel, *Handbuch der mathematischen und technischen Chronologie, das Zeitrechnungswesen der Völker* (3 vols.; Leipzig: Hinrichs, 1906–14); and Hans Lietzmann, *Zeitrechnung der römischen Kaiserzeit, des Mittelalters und der Neuzeit für die Jahre 1–2000 n. Chr.* (4th ed.; Berlin: de Gruyter, 1984), are important.

date of) his birth. Whether this date is correct or whether Jesus was born earlier or later—rather earlier than later—is unimportant for our deliberation. In any case, the original point of reference is the birth of Jesus. The calculation that stands behind our calendar years goes back to the monk Dionysius Exiguus, who in the sixth century received a papal commission to set up a table for the more precise calculation of the date of Easter. In this table, he introduced the counting of the years after the incarnation of Jesus (*ab incarnatione domini*). The original purpose of our calendar years is the same as that of our counting of hours, namely, to provide a more exact liturgical practice.[5]

It is interesting to note that for Dionysius Exiguus the point of reference for the birth of Jesus Christ was the foundation of the city of Rome, which he dated 753 years before the birth of Jesus.[6] With this he continued the customary Roman chronological counting *ab urbe condita*, that is, since the foundation of Rome. This remained the custom even in Christendom for counting the time prior to the birth of Jesus Christ, and this custom prevailed even until the high days of Enlightenment, that is, deep into the eighteenth century. This is all the more interesting since the French Jesuit scholar Denise Petavius had already proposed in the seventeenth century to count the time before the birth of Christ just as we are presently accustomed to, that is, in an ascending negative sequence in mirror fashion to the time after Christ's birth. In the nineteenth century one can still find even among well-known historians, beside the counting of the years before the birth of Christ now customary for us, the count *ab urbe condita* as well. In addition, even in those days the medieval custom of counting according to the Jewish chronology can be found (postulating the creation 3,761 years before the birth of Christ).[7]

---

5. Bruno Krusch, *Die Entstehung unserer heutigen Zeitrechnung* (vol. 2 of *Studien zur christlich-mittelalterlichen Chronologie*; Leipzig: Veit, 1937), 63–87.

6. This positive orientation along the Roman basic date in Orthodox and Roman Catholic churches stands, from the very beginning, in an interesting contradiction to the synchronous opposition to the Diocletian chronology. Fundamental for this is the distinction between good and bad Romans; Diocletian, as the fanatic persecutor of Christians, belongs to the latter.

7. So, for instance, still Karl von Rotteck, *Allgemeine Geschichte vom Anfang der historischen Kenntniß bis auf unsere Zeiten* (14th ed.; Braunschweig: Westermann, 1840). Rotteck follows Petavius in the historical integration of individual events. However, he organizes them into a chronology that is based on a world creation date. This he infers from a conservative harmonization and computation of biblical dates. At the same time, he gives a timetable in which counting "before the birth of Christ" is included.

2.2. Caesar

With these observations the Roman influence on our chronology and our understanding of time has already become evident. The Roman impact on our chronology is more intensive than the Christian one. The Christian influence on our calendar is exhausted by the counting of our years according to the birth of Christ and by the dating of the high festivals, Christmas, Easter, and Pentecost. The names of the months stand entirely under Roman auspices. And here we are also in the sphere of influence of the second person mentioned in the title of the essay: Julius Caesar. Jesus and Christianity have left no traces in the names of our months—or in the days of the week. We will have to ask why not.[8]

The Latin character of our calendar is most obvious in the names of the last four months, which are formed after the Latin numerals from seven to ten (*septem* to *decem*). In particular, the peculiarity, maintained for more than two thousand years, that our twelve-month calendar ends with the tenth month preserves a conscious decision of Julius Caesar, namely, to move the beginning of the year from the first of March to the first of January. For reasons of political ideology, Caesar adopted with this change the old legendary tradition about the original royal calendar of the Romans (with January and February as the first months). The result of Caesar's reform of the calendar was a consistent orientation toward the solar year. This meant a prolongation of the year and a complete change of the arrangement of leap years.[9] Further below I shall have more to say

---

8. On the week, see Bickerman, Bickerman, *Chronology of the Ancient World*, 58–61. The names of the days of the week in our calendar are all of pagan (Germanic) origin. The major exception in the German calendar, contrary to the English calendar, is Saturday, in German the "Samstag," the "Sabbathday" (the other exception is the censorship felt necessary of the highest god Wodan, expressed in "Mittwoch"). This resembles the practice of the Jews and also of Paul to see the week as a stretch of time between two Sabbaths. In 1 Cor 16:2, the first reference to Sunday in the literature of the church, this day has no name of its own. Paul does not use the Greek name for the week despite addressing the letter to a Greco-Roman town. Instead, he uses the Jewish term for week, *sabbata*, literally the interval between two Sabbaths, more precisely the period from the day after the Sabbath day (the later "Christian" Sunday) to the next Sabbath. The meeting of the Christ community on the day after Sabbath is easily explained as a display of pragmatism. One wanted to give the members of the synagogue community the chance to participate in the Christ community service as well; by not having to decide between the two services, competition and conflict were avoided, thus allowing for an inclusive approach. For Paul, Sunday is not singled out as a special holiday yet. By the way, it should not be overlooked that in the first century the reduction of the week to seven days was not the only possibility; an expansion would also have been possible. The Romans, for instance, had an eight-day week in New Testament times.

9. This reform of the calendar was enacted in 46 B.C.E.

about that. The final product of that reform is even today called the Julian calendar. It still is the constitutive element of our contemporary calendar. The so-called calendar reform of Pope Gregor during the time of Reformation was nothing but a marginal change.[10]

Julius Caesar left his name in the calendar as well. The month that originally was called Quintilis, the fifth, was the month of Caesar's birth, and after his death it was named Julius, July. Since the death of his adoptive son, the new Caesar Octavianus Augustus, occurred in the sixth month, the Sextilis, this month was named August after the honorary title of Octavian Augustus. Thus, to the present day the two first Caesars stand in our calendar side by side and make pagan Latinity an essential element of our conscious and unconscious measurement of time. Jesus, on the other hand, does not manifest himself in our calendar by name. Even Easter and Christmas are merely secondarily associated with the story of Jesus and the year of the church. Originally they were pagan and Jewish festal days.

3. COMPARISON OF THE HISTORICAL PERSONALITIES OF JESUS AND CAESAR

Are Caesar and Jesus—aside from their stronger or lesser influence on our chronology—comparable at all? Concerning their way of life and their social status, not at all. They were no precise contemporaries either; this not only because of the relative temporal and spatial distance between them but also because of the fact that their different social statuses made their experienced time quite different. Here was Caesar, the statesman, the military figure, the rhetor, and author. He intentionally shaped not only his own time as he lived it, in a very clever fashion, but he took his posthistory in his hands in advance. This he did not only in

---

10. The Julian calendar in its Gregorian modification was introduced slowly and not everywhere at once, yet it was resisted at the beginning. My forebear Georg Mylius (Müller), Lutheran pastor in Augsburg, preached in 1584 against the initiation of the Gregorian calendar by the Catholic magistrate. He condemned this ordinance as a papist measure. In response to this public criticism, the magistrate expelled Mylius and his family from the city. Mylius was anything but an ignoramus. He later was made professor of theology, first at Jena, then at Wittenberg. In the Eastern Orthodox Church the Julian calendar is still in effect. Due to the irregularity of the beginning of the Caesarean year and the inconsistency of the Gregorian reform, the introduction and use of the reformed calendar did not guarantee the same beginning of the year in all countries. In England, the year began on 25 March until 1752, and in the American colonies of Britain the introduction of 1 January as the first day of the year had to wait even longer.

his political work that lasted beyond him but also in his writings, which "scripturalize" his experiences, especially in the famous *commentarii*, of which every student of Latin knows, at least in form of the *Gallic War*.

On the other side is Jesus, who showed no interest in "scripturalizing" his proclamation or experiences, although he could read and knew Jewish scriptures and most probably knew how to write. On the contrary, in his case a remarkable concentration and limitation to immediate orality was manifest. Yet in this phenomenon there is a peculiar formal similarity between both personalities, a similarity that relates to our main theme: both Julius Caesar and Jesus of Nazareth were interested in a demonstrative fashion in spontaneous and immediate momentousness, in form as well as in subject matter, in the concise and gripping expression, the aphoristic and epigrammatic. In the case of Julius Caesar it is demonstrated, for instance, by the famous statement: "veni, vidi, vici." In the case of Jesus we could mention, for instance, Luke 10:18: "I saw Satan fall from heaven like a bolt of lightning."[11]

Comparability existed between Julius Caesar and Jesus of Nazareth in particular with respect to the ends of their lives. In both cases it was a violent death. And then there are the interpretations that color not only their lives but determine and shape their posthistory as well. Here they become especially important for our main question. In both cases, that which was common to both of them, their type of death, came as an addendum to their lives, to the time they had themselves shaped and experienced. Even in the case of Caesar, who had tried actively to influence his posthistory, the violent end of his life created radical irritations and shifts, unanticipated by the ingenious manipulator. This was even more the case with Jesus, whose sudden death as a criminal—tried, convicted, and executed by the Roman power, with which he had never had direct contact—defied all anticipation, if there ever was such at all. In both the cases of Jesus and of Caesar, their deaths became essential interpretative elements in their posthistories.

Their memorials, the remembrance of the signs they had left, grew into something more than mere remembered time because of their very deaths and the events following their demise. They became interpreted time itself. Death changed into a sign of its own: it became more than an interpretative element directed toward understanding the past (as its ending); it gained an interpretative direction toward the future as well. One of the oldest interpretative motifs of both, the

---

11. Not only in the individual parts of the Our Father and in the Beatitudes do we have this concise language. The longest expression of Jesus preserved is the parable of the Prodigal Son—actually more the parable of the Prodigal Father.

mutinous murder of Caesar and of the judicial murder of Jesus, is that of martyrdom.

4. COMPARISON BETWEEN JESUS AND CAESAR WITH RESPECT TO THE ENDS OF THEIR LIVES

4.1. Caesar

In the various descriptions of the Ides of March, the shock and uncertainty that the death of Caesar caused for murderers, friends, the whole senate, and the people as well show through. The reports differ greatly in details, especially concerning the opening of Caesar's testament, the attitude and actions of Antony, and in particular his speech.[12] In his testament Caesar had with all probability ordained tremendous gifts to all members of the plebs. Caesar's gardens on the Tiber were opened to the masses, and between 150 and 300 sestercias—depending on the various reports—were stipulated for every citizen, roughly the equivalent of ten to twenty days' wages. Whatever the details and the exact wording of the speech may have been, Marc Antony built on these extremely generous favors of the murdered leader and manipulated and moved the masses. Caesar's charity and his interest in the common weal were dramatically contrasted with the drastic presentation of his bloody corpse, effectively supporting Antony's arguments. The antithesis between the good intentions of the martyred person and the malintentions of his treacherous assassination was infinitely enlarged by such tactics, further increased by Antony's mention of the dead dictator's past and intended future beneficial deeds for some of his murderers. In the public obsequies, Marc Antony no doubt skillfully used the contrast of the butchered corpse with the insistence on the victim's continuous concern for others—a drastic witness of the "for us/for you all"—in his effort to move the audience against the assassins. Shakespeare in his *Julius Caesar* picked this up in the sarcastic scansion: "and Brutus was an honorable man."

In this context it is not unimportant to note that the idea of martyrdom had found expansion and appreciation in the Rome of the first century B.C.E. The violent end of life of many persons in past and present found new consideration under this perspective, first in the party of the

---

12. The most extensive descriptions of the reasons for the revolt against Caesar are found in Plutarch's *Caesar* (57–69), *Brutus* (7–21), and *Antonius* (11–15). They are not without contradiction and cannot be easily harmonized. According to Plutarch's *Caesar* (58), the calendar reform was a major argument against Caesar and one of the possible reasons for his murder.

populares and then also among the *optimati*. For instance, Livy's history, which belongs among the restorative ventures of Augustus, presents many examples of the growing popularity of the martyr motif, now expanded into the past.

We even find reports that certain persons of the contemporary period took their own deaths into their hands with conscious use of the martyr ideology. Intent on turning their own deaths into a propitiating event, they either committed suicide or ordered their subordinates or slaves to kill them. This was certainly an extreme form of consciously shaped time. In this active interpretation, not only the present and the past time were in view, but they also provided an anticipatory grasp of the future.[13]

4.2. Jesus

In the case of Jesus, there is an early interpretation of his death on the cross as a martyr's death. Paul, for example, quotes in Rom 3:24–25 a tradition that leans toward Jewish martyrdom. It describes the death of Jesus similarly to 4 Maccabees where the death of Jewish martyrs under the violent rule of Antiochus IV is presented as propitiation that God had provided.[14] The propitiating event as presented in Rom 3 is meant for the past sins of only the pagans who recently joined the church. Thus the death of Jesus has turned into a temporal division between two periods, that of God's forbearance in the past and righteousness in the present.

5. COMPARISON OF THE INCREASED MYTHIFICATION OF CAESAR(S) AND JESUS (CHRIST)—THE SUPERTEMPORAL?

5.1. Caesar

The transcending of the deaths of our two theme figures goes even further, however, for Marc Antony and the other adherents of Julius Caesar did not consider him a normal human being. For them, he was of divine origin and had proven in his life that he was a god. Now the gods had taken him up into their midst. Julius became *divus Julius*, the divine Julius. In his person and his life, eternity had shown into human time.

---

13. Dieter Georgi, *Theocracy in Paul's Praxis and Theory* (trans. David E. Green; Minneapolis: Fortress, 1991).
14. Ibid., 94–95.

His adoptive son Octavian increased this interpretation of the memory of Julius Caesar. Octavian put into the center of the new imperial ideology the thesis that Caesar's life meant the beginning of a new age, indeed a new religion. Yet this renewal at the same time was remembering in a pointed sense: restoration and completion of the republic that the civil wars had corrupted.

5.2. Augustus

Octavian continued and completed what his adoptive father had begun. This continuation and completion received a new name: Caesar. The addition of the name Caesar to his own name (and that of his successors) was more than the consequence of his adoption by Julius Caesar, also more than merely a sign of the continuation and completion of the work and intention of the original Caesar. It became an identification with the divine genius of the first Caesar. In fact, the name Caesar (pronounced in Latin as it was spelled in Greek: Kaisar) turned into an institution, an expression of divine providence and potency, the beginning of a happy future not only for the new bearer of the name and for his successors but also for the restored republic. A new era had begun, an epoch that needed to be seen under transworldly, under eschatological auspices. The golden age, return and fulfillment of the happy primordial age, was recognized and called for religious formation. The Caesar religion was born.[15]

In this new situation, the activity of the new Caesar, that is Octavian, did not stand back but was able to modify and correct the work of his adoptive father, even to improve on it. Octavian, or as he wanted to be called, *Imperator Caesar divi filius Augustus*,[16] brought about what Julius Caesar had not been able to achieve: global peace, the greatest miracle of the first century B.C.E. and the first century C.E.—for the people of that time certainly a greater miracle than the resurrection of Jesus Christ. Thus the new Caesar received another name, Augustus, the exalted one, and this, like the name Caesar, became a political and religious institution.

---

15. The *Res gestae* of Augustus found in Ancyra contain, in a condensed form, the eschatological proclamation of salvation promised and administered by this religion. I have dealt with this text in two different studies (Georgi, *Theocracy in Paul's Praxis and Theory*, 84–85; idem, "Legal Dimensions of Money and Theological Conequences," 117–21 below).

16. "Supreme Commander, Caesar, Son of the Divine, the August."

5.3. The Calendar

In all ancient religions, the calendar played an essential role in religious, public, and private life. The cultic life could not be thought of without the calendar. All this was especially true for Roman culture and religion, but even more so for the Jewish religion in the first centuries B.C.E. and C.E. The importance of certain days, especially of public feast days, the *fasti* and the *feriae,* was increased by the superstitious concern of the Romans with respect to certain favorable or fateful moments and their portents. The calendar reform of Caesar that I have referred to brought to an end the almost chaotic confusion that had previously characterized the chronological situation in Rome.

This calendaric chaos had been caused by intercalations in the lunar calendar that made it lean toward the solar year. The lunar orientation befitted a basically rural society. An urban society needed a more precise temporal arrangement such as the solar orientation could provide. Yet for a long time the Romans hesitated to give up the agrarian constitution of their society and with it the arrangements as to the measurement of time. The priests, the pontifices, had the task of arranging for adjustments by ordaining the intercalations. They did this in an arbitrary manner, which increased the difficulties. These caused a growing confusion, and in the year 46 B.C.E., the year of Caesar's calendar reform, a divergence from the solar year of ninety days had been accrued. For a religion like the Roman one, this had catastrophic consequences. It was geared toward exact chronological order as essential for the well-being of state, society, and private life. This order depended on the particular value of certain days and of calendaric arrangements. If that dependability was shaken or became even questionable, chaos was at hand, creating not only anxiety but also a threat to the whole society.

Caesar's reform of the calendar, adapting it to the solar year and providing fixed intercalations no longer dependent on arbitrary priestly decisions, meant a marked improvement, a relief, and indeed a liberation. What was demonstrated by this reform of the calendar was the final wedding of two phenomena that in any case had been intimately related in the Roman state, namely, religion and administration. Administration as religion and religion as administration—this became an essential part of Roman life, indeed, of Roman consciousness, a religious impetus that continues to this very day in the various entities that succeeded and imitated the Roman state.

5.4. The gospel in the Caear religion

In this calendar, meant to be lasting, the dedication of certain days also played an important role. This was caused not only by the maintenance of memorial days sanctified by tradition, but new festal days were established as well, sometimes of an extraordinary nature and thus for the nonce, sometimes intended for repetition. The days of feasting that were celebrated only once were essentially days of penitence. New holidays that were to be repeated usually were joyful days. These festivities needed to be announced and organized, and not only the first time. In such cases, time was announced as well as interpreted.[17] Such announcement was a prophetic act, although its was done mostly by normal officers and clerks executing the decision of the people's assembly and/or the senate.[18]

Into this category also belong the famous minutes of the debate of the provincial diet of the province Asia, as they took place in the coastal town of Priene during the time of the principate of Augustus.[19] This diet passed a law announcing and establishing a festal day and its continuous repetition and defined them as gospel(s), εὐαγγέλια.

A letter of the procurator Paullus Fabius Maximus introduces the decision to the diet of the province. This letter is quoted in the beginning of the inscription of the decision of the diet.[20]

---

17. Public announcements of dates and periods were common among the Romans. These announcements always had a cultic nature as well and were associated with cultic ceremonies. The term *calendae* is characteristic for that. It comes from the verb *calare*. Each month it is publicly announced (*calo* "I call,") by the high priest, who at the same time decrees whether the period to the next *nonae* will be five or seven days. The first *calendae* of the year were even more prominent, and the announcement was solemnized accordingly. This makes the emphasis on the issue of beginning in the following Priene inscription more understandable. It is not a matter of course. The "calendar" is not yet an abstract given; it is still set and defined by rituals at the *calendae*. These Roman habits and performances found the understanding of non-Roman people and institutions because they had their own ways of setting time and times as well.

18. The prophet (*vates*) is able to invoke past and future time. The heralds of the gospel of the Caesar religion, beginning with its first theologians Virgil and Horace, know themselves in this role.

19. This text is found in *OGIS* 458. A corrected version is found in *SEG* 4:490. The language mirrors the complexities of a legal document, even more complicated by the baroque style of adulation of the Caesar. In my presentation of the translation I have attempted to reflect the organization of the text in the graphic presentation.

20. The letter of the procurator and the motion of the diet were both bilingual and were found in fragmented form elsewhere, too. The best-preserved version is that which was dug up in Priene.

It is hard to say whether the birthday of the most divine Caesar (Augustus) is to be observed more as an event of joy or of salvation, (still) we justifiably consider it the equivalent for the beginning of all things, (equivalent) if not in reality then rather in usefulness (since) he (the Caesar) has brought into full shape everything that had decayed and had been corrupted. He has given a new face to the universe, (the universe) which was all too ready to fall into perdition, had not the Caesar—the common good luck for all of humanity—been born. Therefore everyone may look to this day as the beginning of his own life, too, even of his own physical existence. It means the end and the limit of any feeling of being burdened now that he (the Caesar) has been born.[21]

[Further,] since one could take from no other day luckier occasions for the common weal and one's own benefit than (from) the one that is lucky for everyone; since it so happens that the date of his start of office is the same for all the cities in (the province of) Asia;[22]

(it happens namely also) together with the revelation according to a divine decision, that the order (of time) was shaped beforehand (in this way) that there was an opportunity for the honoring of Augustus;

since it is difficult <to say thanks> for such great beneficial deeds in a suitable manner, except we would think up a completely (new) way of (response);

since humans celebrate the common birthday much more easily if an enjoyment for each with respect to the beginning is added,

—therefore, it appears appropriate to me that all citizens have one and the same new year's day, the birthday of the most divine Caesar, and that all (officers and clerks) enter the office on that (day) which is the ninth day before the *calendae* of October.[23]

Therefore, it was resolved by the Greeks of the province of Asia upon the motion of the high priest Apollonius from Azani, the son of Menophilos:

whereas the providence that orders all of human life (in a divine fashion) has <demonstrated> zeal and concern and has conferred upon life the most perfect <good> as ornament (by the fact) that it brought forth the Augustus whom it filled with (divine) power of virtue[24] for his

---

21. The subject of the subordinate clause is not quite clear. It could be the Caesar, but it could be the individual, that is, each and everyone.

22. The coincidence of the birthday of Augustus and of the beginning of the year in western Asia Minor is intentional. This could happen because in that area the Macedonian-Hellenistic calendar was still in effect.

23. That is, 23 September.

24. Greek ἀρετή, Latin *virtue*. In both languages the term meant much more than our modern moralistic understanding of "virtue." It was almost more in line with the recent electronic and futuristic development of the term that grew out of one meaning of the adjective *virtual* and, even more, of the adverb *virtually*. The initial sense of "not quite" then stretched to something unreal, (merely) imagined, another reality. ἀρετή and *virtus*

beneficial activity among humanity as it gave us and our successors a savior who brought the war to rest but organized peace,

and whereas Caesar <had appeared> and surpassed the hopes of those who anticipated the <running fire of the good news[25]>, not only surpassing those who had been benefactors before but leaving no hope either for the following ones of ever overcoming him, and the running fire of the good news[26] which by his efforts went forth into the world had taken its start (with the) <birthday> of the god,

and whereas it was resolved by (the province of) Asia in Smyrna under <the high priest> Leukius Volkakius Fullus, when Papi<as> was the scribe, that <a wreath> <as a witness> should be (given) for him who would find the greatest honors for the god,

Paullus Fabius Maximus, the procurator of the province who had been sent through the right hand of Caesar and (his) will to the province <for (its) salvation>, has devised with his own inventiveness benefits for the province the grandeur of which nobody is able to express <sufficiently>, and he invented for the honoring of the Augustus what to this day has been unknown <to the Greeks> (namely) that from his <birth> (on) the time for the (individual and common) way of life (bios) would begin.[27]

Good news (gospel) here is not so much a certain content but continuous constantly renewed announcement of things happening, itself a dynamic event, indeed understood as a lively process. This announcement is in its repetition continuous communal reinterpretation of the memory of the past, full of hope for the future. Through this interpretation, the future receives its impetus and its face—not only the future of the political community but also the future of all those who live in it. Their personal biography, too, is affected by the commonly shared salvation event.

5.5. The Gospel of Paul

5.5.1. The First Epistle to the Thessalonians

This letter corresponds to the understanding of gospel and preaching of the gospel in Paul, already found in his first preserved letter, 1 Thessalonians.

---

addressed the miraculous power proper to the gods as it expressed itself in miraculous deeds. Thus, the term could describe the miracles themselves as well.

25. This renders the plural εὐαγγελία in this context best.

26. Here εὐαγγελία again.

27. Then follows the motion that, on the basis of what had been said, the beginning of the year should be celebrated in all cities of the province on the ninth day prior to the *calendae* of October, that is, on Augustus's birthday.

Here the term *gospel* already appears in the first chapter. Here, too, the announcement, the proclamation (i.e., the gospel) goes hand in hand with powerful and joyful things, namely, the divine power, the Holy Spirit, and confidence. Lacking is the atmosphere of feasts and festivals transcending the everyday experience. The latter we find in the context of the birthday of Augustus. In the Pauline proclamation of the gospel, the concern is with the "praxis of faith,"[28] the drudgery of love, and the endurance of hope" (1:3), all of them phenomena of daily life, and pointedly so.

However, Paul is interested in the announcement of the new time, and this in conscious competition with the gospel of the Caesar, so prominent in Asia Minor and around the Aegean Sea. The encounter with this competing gospel shows again in 1 Thess 4:13–18 and 5:1–11.[29] For reasons of space, I limit myself to the second text, which in any case contributes more to the understanding of time than the former.[30]

In 1 Thess 5:1–11, it is noteworthy that time is not defined by terminal fixation but by the opposite: incalculability. "The day of the Lord comes like a thief in the night" (5:2). Wengst has correctly shown that the phrase following in 5:3a, "peace and security," is a slogan of Roman imperial propaganda.[31] Contrary to that, Paul implies in his argument that times and moments in the context of Christ are quite different from the time that was politically fixed by the Caesar, administered worldwide by his officers; the Christ's time is not militarily protected. It is not the time that, according to contemporary Roman ideology, guarantees the peace and the security of the empire.

The allegedly firm and stable imperial offer of salvation was in reality weak. It was continuously threatened by rebellion and overthrow, which would turn the promise into perdition (5:3b). Paul saw as the real cause behind this insecurity the incalculable onset of the day of judgment, the "Day of the Lord." In contrast to the salvific and festal dates of the Romans, which fixed the official time calendarically, Paul saw the day of the Lord in its incalculability as an illumination for the congregation. The

---

28. I have here used the traditional translation of the Greek term πίστις. In my essay "Legal Dimensions of Money" I have shown that the translation "loyalty" meets the Pauline intention much better. In that essay I argue that all Pauline letters can be fully understood only if they are read as a continuous debate with the Caesar religion.

29. My *Theocracy in Paul's Praxis and Theory* argues that the authentic letters of Paul known to us can only be understood in full if read as a continuous debate with the Caesar religion.

30. In *Theocracy in Paul's Praxis and Theory*, 25–27, I give an interpretation of 1 Thess 4:13–18. On pages 27–31 I deal with the following pericope 5:1–11, too.

31. Klaus Wengst, *Pax Romana: Anspruch und Wiklichkeit. Efrahrungen und Wahrnehmungen des Friedens bei Jesus und im Urchristentum* (Munich: Kaiser, 1986), 97–100).

congregation has its basic existence in the daytime, as "children of light" (5:4–5). It does not pretend that its time, its present and its future, is precisely defined, contrary to apocalyptic circles and the Caesar religion. These claimed that their time, now and to come, was precisely determined and that they had precise knowledge of it. The Christ community, instead, takes the incalculability of its time in a positive manner; its time has a new quality, no longer that of waiting but that of being awake and of acting in an attentive and sober way (5:5–6).[32] It would not be uninteresting for our theme if we could analyze the gnostic terminology that has entered the light symbolism of 5:5–7, for in Gnosticism belonging to light is an indication that one is freed from the measuring and controlling force of the up and down of day and night, light and darkness, and thereby the prison of time at large. A precise analysis of this aspect would, however, go beyond the frame of this essay.[33]

Another remaining variant of the theme of time needs analysis, not as elaborate as the pursuit of the gnostic issue. I have 1 Thess 5:8 in mind: "Let us do as those who belong to death, be sober and put on the breast armor that consists of trust and love,[34] and as helmet, the hope for rescue." Paul alludes here to Isa 59:17, and the following verse 9 makes clear that Paul has read this allusion in the context of the issue of judgment ("wrath of God"). The biblical text speaks of God making things right at the end of days. He does it himself through his personal interference as divine warrior:

> And Yahweh saw it and did not like it that right existed no longer and that nobody was there, and he was astonished that nobody stepped in. Then his own arm and salvation helped him. It was his support. He put on righteousness as armor and the helmet of salvation. He put on the helmet of salvation upon his head; he put on retribution as garment. He wound zeal around like a topcoat. He punished his adversaries with his wrath. And he meted out retribution to his enemies.[35]

---

32. The text says, "For you are all the children of light and the children of the day. We do not belong to the night and not to darkness. Therefore, let us not sleep like the other ones, but let us wake and be sober."

33. I have dealt with this aspect extensively in Georgi, *Theocracy in Paul's Praxis and Theory*, 29–30.

34. On the translation of πίστις, see note 28 above.

35. Translation of Claus Westermann, *Das Buch Jesaja: Kap 40–66* (Göttingen: Vandenhoeck & Ruprecht, 1966). Military engagements played an essential role in the cultures of the ancient Middle East and in the Mediterranean as marks of temporal processes and of public life in its political, social, and legal aspects. In the holy-war motif this was most dramatically present. The warring activity of the gods was seen behind theogony and cosmogony. It was transferred to the basic events that constituted and endangered the tribal origins and

The successive Roman civil wars and their end, the victory at Actium, were already looked at by contemporaries—even more by the later generations who had been influenced by the Augustan reform of public religion—as events that went beyond the agents responsible at the time, even transcending the human realm and involving the world of gods and demons as well. Even those who took a negative view of Augustus's policies did not deny that, although they might interpret it negatively, as something demonic. A reading of Virgil or Horace gives plenty of evidence. The demonizing of Julius Caesar and the heroification of Cato in the "Pharsalia" of Lucan give evidence for the fact that even the opposition needed to invoke the superhuman in order to interpret the change. Ordinary political and military aspects did not suffice. Divine or demonic engagement needed to be taken into account. But whereas in the classical concept of holy war, and in its Roman application to the turn of the ages during the times of Julius Caesar and Augustus, the divine and its great human counterparts had all the attention, it is completely opposite in 1 Thess 5:8. The congregation and its members take over the role of the gods and human heroes, namely, that of turning the ages. Moroever, they achieve this not by means of violence and triumph but though the everyday features mentioned in the beginning of the letter: faith, love, and hope. Judging by the following sentences, this very democratizing imitation and continuation of the holy-warrior action of Yahweh expresses itself constructively in mutual "paraclesis," a typical Pauline blend of encouragement and exhortation. In this, the sharing of concrete imaginative experience and creative activity absorb and reconcile past, present, and future. A deep cut, deeper than the one between day and night, has caused this: the death of Jesus Christ. It has ended the world of darkness as a world dominated by antagonism. It has brought about a world of the

---

developments and the religions. It was carried over into prophetic and later also apocalyptic eschatology, used there for the description of the transworldly processes that terminated this world and gave birth to a new order. Impressive are the various statements of Frank Moore Cross, *Canaanite Myth and Hebrew Epic* (Cambridge: Harvard University Press, 1973), index under "Divine Warrior," esp. 91, 111–55. Here the relationship between biblical texts and Middle Eastern myth is described extensively. Important are the works of Cross's students: Patrick Miller, *The Divine Warrior in Early Israel* (Cambridge: Harvard University Press, 1973); and Paul D. Hanson, *The Dawn of Apocalyptic* (Philadelphia: Fortress, 1975). J. Alberto Soggin ("Krieg II. Altes Testament," *TRE* 20:19–25) has not taken these mythological, syncretistic, and cultic sides of the motif seriously enough, not only with respect to its early history but also with respect to its influence on the history of development and redaction of the traditions that worked with that theologumenon. The Middle Eastern and Mediterranean context of this motif remained alive and effective into Hellenistic and Roman times. Soggin and also Harald Hegermann ("Krieg III. Neues Testament," *TRE* 20:25–28) have overlooked that completely.

"for" and "together." In Paul's understanding and preaching, God's interference in worldly affairs, which Isa 59 could only describe in mythical terms as eschatological judgmental action, becomes constructive and clarifying life in and with Christ and for the community—as much a political model as a political protest against anything aggressive, allegedly creative, but in reality destructive.

5.5.2. The Epistle to the Galatians

Galatians 4:4 belongs into this context of ideological-social dispute with the understanding of time in the Caesar religion and also with its socioeconomic environment. This text is a birthday statement as well. Like the statements about the birthday of Augustus, it eyes universal world order and new-world time as well. Yet here it is Jesus, not the Caesar, who is meant with the description of being godsend and defining and determining the present and future world: "When the fullness of time came, God sent his son, originating from a young woman, that is, originating under the law, in order that he could emancipate those who are under the law and they could receive the sonship."

Talking about the fullness of time is eschatological, indeed apocalyptic language.[36] This resembles the practice of the Caesar religion that uses eschatological language as well, not even shying away from the apocalyptic dimension. In these political eschatological texts, there is a sound of fate, and that dimension of fate reverberates in Gal 4:4 as well: God's intervention is dependent on the development of time. In 4:4 as well as already in 4:2—where the issues are majority age and economy in the literal sense, namely, the managing of the household—the reference point is a certain limit, set within the frame of a social order like the law of the world, not an arbitrary setting. The reference is to a certain terminal point for that interference. In the entire context, time and law are synonymous, as much as social order and world order. The world order does

---

36. Heinrich Schlier, *Der Brief an die Galater* (KEK 7; Göttingen: Vandenhoeck & Ruprecht, 1962), quotes in his commentary as a parallel for this passage the following texts from *4 Ezra* 4:36 and 37: "For he has weighed the Aion with the scale. He has measured the hours with the measurement.... He does not disturb nor wake them up until the indicated measure is fulfilled"; 6:18: "The ... will be when I come, and will approach when the grace of peace is full, and the Aion of evil is sealed (perfected)"; and 11:44: "Then the Most High looked at his times, and behold, they had come to an end, and his Aions were full." In all these apocalyptic texts God is presented more as observer of the processes of time hinted at. That implies that in apocalypticism the God of Israel comes under the dictate of the God Aion, understood as fate. The only thing left for God to do in such a situation is to measure the fullness of time.

not merely mean the Jewish law and the Jewish religious world; rather, it refers to the law of the world in general. This identification is put into a satirizing caricature that sketches the world and its law as being playthings of the demonic powers (the rule of antigodly elementary forces, reflecting the elements of matter—constituted and governed by the law—as much as the elements of the alphabet in which the law and the laws are written throughout the world). This demonic world order is further satirized by embedding it into the frame of reference of education, the pride of Hellenistic and Roman civilization, its pedagogy taken as the distinctive mark over against barbaric socialization. This satirical sarcastic polemic addresses the attempt of the Hellenistic culture of combining world order and education. In the first century, Romans as well as Hellenistic Jews had completely adopted this equation. The criticism of law in Gal 3 does not limit itself to internal Jewish issues. It is manifest and comprehensive criticism of society at large.[37]

The relationship of Gal 4:4 to 4:3 presupposes a direct connection of law and time, not only in the sense of a realm of time set by law but also in the wider sense of identification of time and law. For Paul, existence under the law here is the negative counterpart to the phenomenon described in 4:5: "in order that he emancipate those who are under the law and they receive the sonship." The subjugation of the son under the law is the end, better said, the threshold, of law and time. The term *plērōma* ("fullness") in Gal 4:4 is understood as negative, not as positive, which is frequent in Gnosticism.[38] The Galatians passage equates the fullness of time with the gnostic understanding of the present evil world.[39]

The entire context makes it clear that Paul does not want to speak in a way that would be removed from everyday life, in a "religious" fashion that would be more or less immaterial. A critical understanding of social order runs through the entire argumentation. Paul presupposes in this argumentation that time and law are identical. Essential for such identification is a negative definition of time: description of situation and circumstance of enslavement under the law. By the fact that the son subjugates himself to this condition, that is, also to this enslavement by time, he creates a threshold phenomenon. Although as an otherworldly figure he does not belong to this world and its time, he undergoes the time-bound tortures of this worldly life. Thereby he undercuts the rule of time and brings about liberation. This is all mythological language, yet

---

37. See further Georgi, *Theocracy in Paul's Praxis and Theory*, 33–46.
38. Evidence in Kurt Rudolph, *Die Gnosis* (2nd ed.; Göttingen: Vandenhoeck & Ruprecht, 1980), index under "Pleroma."
39. Evidence in ibid., 98.

through this wording concrete perspicuity is achieved with respect to the negative as well as to the positive dimension of existence, that of slavery and that of freedom.

Galatians 4:4 and 5 do not speak of the death of Jesus, only of the fact that the divine child had become human, a motif that already in Greek mythology was known as a liberation motif.[40] It appears as the motif of the miraculous child in the Caesar religion too. The Priene inscription I quoted above gives evidence that the birthday of Augustus could be understood as a liberating event of salvation. It is not without interest that the negative side of the experience described in Gal 4 is reported of a later Caesar, namely, Claudius, a contemporary of Paul. Claudius, according to the report of Suetonius, complained about having been surrendered to pedagogues who had used the stick and caned him again and again and that this had gone on even beyond the normal time—all due to his mother's spitefulness (Suetonius, *Claud.* 13.)

In Gal 4:6 and 7, liberty is described as the result of attaining majority age. It is defined as being gifted by the spirit. This inspiration is anything but a sign of belonging to the social elite, even less a sign of oneself being divine, demigod or god. On the contrary, freedom of the spirit, full legal age, is presented as the true humanness—living out the everyday frailty, the stumbling and stuttering limitation of human existence.[41] So for Paul the true sign of spiritual being is to live not only like the human being

---

40. That the birth of a child means the renewal of world and humanity is sung also in Virgil's famous *Ecl.* 4, a gospel text of the Caesar religion. I have quoted here the title of a chapter of the book of Eduard Norden (*Die Geburt des Kindes: Geschichte einer religiösen Idee* [Darmstadt: Wissenschaftliche Buchgesellschaft, 1969], 46–50), where Norden puts this very eclogue under this perspective. Norden's book is still relevant today. There are other myths and legends of birth, too, in the Orient, in Egypt, Greece, and the Hellenistic-Roman world that one could use in this context. The Hellenistic-Roman versions often presuppose and develop those of earlier East-Mediterranean cultures. Considering the importance of Augustus's birthday, the decree of the diet of the province Asia mentioned above gains a much higher weight for New Testament exegesis and theology than scholars to this day have conceded to this religious-historical and sociohistorical phenomenon.

41. The text says, "Since you are sons, God sent the spirit of his son into our hears and (that spirit) cries 'Abba, Father!' Therefore, you are no longer slave but son, but if son, then also heir." Ernst Käsemann ("Der gottesdienstliche Schrei nach der Freiheit," in idem, *Paulinische Perspektiven* [Tübingen: Mohr Siebeck, 1969], 211–36) has brought this text into direct relationship with the more expanded parallel text in Rom 8:16. He has concluded from the manifest use of inspiration language in both texts that Paul in both cases ironically treats this phenomenon of alleged spiritual exaltation and exclusion, commonly judged as extraordinary in Jewish and pagan circles and those of the early church. According to Paul, none of that pretension is valid; instead, such experiences are normal, everyday occurrences, childlike, as it were. They illuminate the weakness of humans, even, and even more in the context of spiritual gifts. Thus, Paul presents a rather critical anthropology here.

Jesus of Nazareth but also like Jesus as the son of God—a truly contrasting model to the supermen, the Caesars.

In Gal 4:8–10 a warning is sounded about relapsing into slavery under the legal order dominating the world. This enslaving order is described as the concern about the timing of certain days and certain months, especially distinguished moments and years. There has been much puzzlement as to how this could have been meant. Jewish legal piety does not provide the right parallels, is actually foreign to what is described here. The discussions in this essay point to a different, more relevant solution: what is referred to are the religion and the piety around the Caesar cult. Here the rather superstitious respect and reverence for time measurement were essential for religious order and practice. In fact, official interpretation turned such respect and reverence into basic constituents of the salvific nature of the Caesar religion, of which the state administration was a natural element; it was an accompaniment of religion and vice versa. Liberation and the experience of freedom under Roman rule were promises basically associated with such time-related combination of law and order.

Against this, Paul sets the announcement of the Jesus gospel in the daily life of people. In his eyes, this gospel enables the realization of new, open time within normal human relationships that permit humanness as the experience of real freedom. In human exchange and mutuality, the gospel helps to create togetherness through interpretative remembrance of God's saving deeds, Christ's presence, and the lives of their friends, dead or alive. This sharing opens up the future reciprocally and communally, in solidarity that respects personal integrity.[42]

5.5.3. 2 Corinthians and Romans

The preceding explanation corresponds to the discussion in 2 Cor 6: 2, a text that deals with time as well: "Now is the pleasant time, now is the day of salvation!" Here, Paul picks up the promises of Deutero-Isaiah

---

42. Verses 10 and following of Gal 4 elaborate the concretization of the law that Paul is against. He describes it as the superstitious fear of a time filled by belief in demons and idolatry. Therefore, it breathes constantly new life into a continuous and differentiated chain of powers. Here time is mythicized again with a demonic meaning. Paul, instead, thinks of a time that we can face with confidence, time under the reconciling, justifying, and creative grace. In this, there is more than merely a new chance for the individual in the ever-new today, that is, more than Bultmann conceded for the Pauline understanding of time. Time justified and reconciled is time communally experienced and formed, neither threatening nor covered up, neither bought nor sold, especially not time sold out. No, it is time that is communally fulfilled.

of the creative, covenant-constituting mission of the servant of the Lord and of the people and also of their miraculous chance to create things anew. In quoting Deutero-Isaiah, Paul declares these promises authentic for now and sees them in the process of realization. The prophetic promises materialize through the help of Paul's mission (*diakonia*), in which the process anticipated by the Old Testament prophet is realized in the dialectic of Paul's and others' everyday experience. Only here, in everyday life, is the new time to be found, in all its resistance and despite countless adverse circumstances. The arrival of the new, the golden age, is manifest in the light of ordinary day. The golden age's limitations are the agents of the revolution of time.

Romans 13:11–14 continues the discussion about fulfilling the biblical command of loving one's neighbor (Lev 19:18), a concern common in Jewish circles of the time. Paul had picked up this debate in 12:9, in the context of the reflection on corporate existence that had started in 12:3. In 12:9 he had spoken of love as gift and action, ordinary action—as Paul had demonstrated in his previous letters, most of all in 1 Cor 13. In Rom 13:1 he had embedded into this interweaving of communal existence and neighborly love an older Hellenistic-Jewish tradition of the proper respect for magistrates. It is quite obvious that Paul sees this relationship to the phenomenon of organized society as an acute experience of the world of law. Romans 13:11 states this clearly and declares neighborly love as the fulfillment of the law, that is, in the form of Roman law as well as in the form of Torah. Knowledge of the fact that love toward neighbors and also toward foreigners (Lev 19:34 in wording similar to 19:18) represent the fullness (more than the fulfillment) of the law establishes a new understanding of time, indeed the new age itself. We have already noted that this idea of an efficacious announcing of time corresponds to ancient, in particular Roman, practice under the Caesars, a time that was announced (in form of feasts and the like) and whose announcements were associated with an institutional interpretation by the announcing agency. This proclamation worked also for the benefit of such an institution.[43] The new proclaimed time is and will be the time of the empire, the province, the municipality, and the community. Paul adopts this understanding of the announcement of time. The time described in 13:1–14 is time that is publicly charged, is time interpreted anew. As in the Roman context this openly declared *tempus* naturally turns into the expression of communal consciousness, emotion, and experience. Communal as well as

---

43. The text says, "And since we know the point in time, when the hour is here for rising, because salvation is closer than we had thought. The night has moved ahead; the day has come near."

personal sentiment and understanding enter into that and are reshaped as well. Contrary to the practice of the Roman Empire, this process of adoption, integration, and re-creation is not initiated, formed, controlled, and administered from above, and it is not publicly represented by a priestly, administrative, and military machinery, nor is it under the dubious protection of such public forces. Instead, it is brought about and formed democratically.[44]

In order to understand Paul's train of thought, it is necessary to consider the importance of prophets in antiquity with respect to the announcement and interpretation of time. Paul is a prophet; as such he can announce time. He does it not as a religious genius but as instigator, mouthpiece, and integrator of the corporate community. He is not the leader but a part of that community. Romans 12 had invoked the corporate nature of the Christ resurrected and alive as and in the community, and it had made that corporate reality the context of all subsequent ethical deliberations and suggestions. Thereby conscious and active similarity and solidarity of all community members found its paramount constitutional expression, in modern terms its "corporate identity," in a corporate personality.

Paul's Christ is not another world in the beyond of that corporate identity but is that corporation himself. The "we" and the "he" are together, intimately related and interdependent. Through that corporate identity, the Christ is the Lord, not merely of the congregation, the church local and universal, but of the universe. In all the Epistle to the Romans, from the beginning to the end, this Lord is set as the critical counterpart of the Caesars, their religion, their ideology, their political activity. The time Paul is talking about is less the time left for waiting for the future coming of the Lord, more the time of the imaginative communal shaping of the interval. Paul is merely the loudspeaker of the communal enactment of such corporate consciousness.

6. Conclusion

It seems to be a curious phenomenon that Christianity victorious has conquered almost everything with the exception of the calendar. Jesus as well as the Christ and Christianity are left out of the calendar. The

---

44. Therefore the following adhortative subjunctive in the first person plural, "Let us put down the works of darkness and let us put on the weapons of light." Here we move again, as in 1 Thess 5, in the world of symbols of the holy war, also here translated into democratic relations.

Christian feasts of Easter and Pentecost are not fixed elements of the calendar but movable dates, whereas the date of Christmas is grafted on a solidly pagan festal day. Thus the Christian tradition and experience does not really influence, even less determine, the calendar, its months, or its days. But could that not be a faint remembrance of the critical openness and freedom vis-à-vis measured and fixed time that I have described above? This critical stance is apparent not only in Paul's letters but is also found in other New Testament texts, especially in John's Gospel and in the book of Revelation. Perhaps this curious phenomenon retains an element of understanding that the prophetic spirit is present and effective in the Christ community, announcing and thus establishing time ever anew? At the same time, the congregation is actively opening and shaping that space of time as expression of their freedom, bringing into this process all the ideas, experiments, and results of their spiritual power of imagination as they are present in the active understanding and formation of their daily life.

Returning to the current observations on time as presented by the media, the above reflections on ancient texts seem to advise us to resist interpretations forced on us by television gurus and the powers behind them. Instead, their advice would be to establish a communal exchange about our understandings and to thereby come to independent interpretations that can offer all of us a liberated future with real hope.

6

ON PAUL'S IMAGE OF THE HUMAN

1. SOME GENERAL OBSERVATIONS

Hellenistic civilization took up the Greek promise of forming a liberated humanity, now no longer limited to people of Greek origin but offered to humankind at large, more precisely to all those who were ready to expose themselves to Hellenistic education. The Romans adopted this claim. Thus, the formation of the human, as individual person and as social being, was one of the major objectives of the Greco-Roman world, and the cities were supposed to be the training centers for that transformed humanity. In the cities the educated were supposed to relate to the political, social, and religious structures as independent as well as responsible beings. This claim of the culture implied the smooth interplay of various dialectical relations. Often enough they turned into clear antitheses if not outright conflicts and often enough perverted the assertion of freedom. The following essay will demonstrate how Paul in his anthropological reflection attacks these dehumanizing tendencies that were essentially linked with the individualized concept of humans. The cause of it in Paul's eyes was the association of the idea of personhood with competitiveness and achievement-orientation. Paul shows that this individualism threatened the communal dimension, allegedly a major element of Greco-Roman urban life as well.

---

* This paper, originally a radio address, treats an issue as Paul elaborates it in urban contexts, epistles, which were written to new Christ communities in two capitals of Roman provinces in Greece, of Macedonia and of Achaia.

2. Judging Persons

2.1. In General

If one is required to judge a person nowadays, one feels compelled to make a distinction between person and issue. This distinction, no doubt, often helps to humanize the situation, such as when an unacceptable issue is represented by a sympathetic person. If, on the other hand, a wretched advocate represents a good cause, the distinction between person and issue can also result in a considerable increase in objectivity.

There is no doubt that this way of judging people, practiced especially in the middle class, has essentially Protestant roots and even indirectly refers to Paul. In fact, many Pauline exegetes consider this practice an adequate interpretation of Paul's intentions. Paul, indeed, passionately advocates the thesis that one is not vindicated through her or his works but through faith.[1] This does suggest a differentiation between internal and external or, better said, between personal and objective. Many of the bourgeois philosophies originating from Germany, and in certain respects even Marxism, have up until recent times cultivated and reinforced this way of judging. A further result of this kind of thinking is that it is customary in the Western world to make a distinction between a person and her or his position.

2.2. The Issue in 1 Thessalonians

However, already the oldest extant text by Paul prevents making him responsible for the idea of distinction between person and issue. I am thinking of his first letter to the Thessalonians, the oldest Pauline epistle still available to us. Here Paul gives thanks for the good reception that the gospel has encountered in Thessalonica. Faith, hope, and love did not remain only the proclamation of the gospel but became concrete patterns for the Thessalonians' daily life. The words of the gospel turned into work, care, and patience. Paul's preaching really caught on. It did not remain mere sermonizing. The proclamation bore fruit in abundance. Paul sees the cause for this revolutionary change of the Thessalonian Christ community's lives in their willingness to accept him as he arrived in Thessalonica: unsightly, outcast, and persecuted. They were willing to

---

1. The term "faith," customary in the translation of Paul's letters, is very questionable. "Loyalty" and "trust" express Paul's intention much better. See 83 n. 28 above, 119 below.

identify him with his message. Precisely in considering Paul's person, they believed the word proclaimed in the name of the strange god that lets his messengers be chased around the world by their fellow humans. They accepted that through this kind of reception this god nevertheless challenged and revolutionized the world and humankind, precisely by means of the witness of such outcast persons. With Paul, they themselves forewent all obvious signs of the great and overpowering. In this active renunciation they experienced a change of circumstances and of themselves, which they clearly noticed, at the latest when the surrounding society banished them. This happened within a few weeks.

Paul praises the Thessalonians for not taking offense at him and for even going so far as to identify his curious manner of appearance with the nature of the issue he represented, even accepting his manner of appearance for themselves. The experience of the finiteness of everything human showed the Thessalonians that the seemingly unshakably stable order of the surrounding world in reality had seams.

The seemingly invincible world order in its oppressive uniformity and benumbing size revealed itself as brittle to eyes sharpened by trust in and sympathy with Paul's message. In the cracks, the power of a new world at work showed itself, a world not determined by overpowering order and subordination, not by anger and fear, but by peace and solidarity between all.

The Thessalonians understood that the message of the strange god that puts himself on a par with a hanged man means both the end of the world and a turning point toward something new. They realized that the turning point in the world's history had arrived and that the change would not start in the palaces and offices but on the streets among common people. This realization made the Thessalonians newly interested in the world around them and created a sense of responsibility for their neighbors.

The Thessalonians reacted to Paul's preaching quite positively. This made Paul realize that the surrounding society had no choice but to speak about this living faith of the Thessalonians. He further sees the Thessalonians on the verge of enlarging the community of those who believe in the world's turning point in Jesus and who try to experiment in comprehending the new world through mutual trust.

However, Paul has to keep the Thessalonians from considering each loss of a member of their community as a continual disruption of the community. As Paul sees it, because the future belongs to the crucified Jesus, his community also has a future. To the degree in which the members of the congregation receive their spiritual force from the community, they will also be integrated together with their personal history as living voices in the community of the future, even after their death.

I see in these statements about human future Paul's tendency to lead away from being spellbound by individual hopes of salvation and of the future and to direct the attention of everyone to the future of the community. We will later see that Paul does not define community in terms of the individual, as we moderns do, but understands the individual as part of the community. Paul has not parted with the Old Testament's concept of the reality of God's people as an entity in time and space, as especially Middle-European Protestantism believed he did, but has, in fact, adopted it. Certainly, he modified the concept of God's people, but these modifications do not mean dilutions but, on the contrary, radicalizations.

For when Paul in 1 Thessalonians ends his statements about hope with words from Isa 59:17, he has stretched the meaning of the prophet's statement in a downright blasphemous manner. In Paul's use of the text, what is said in Isaiah about God's intervention at the end of time is now applied to the activity of the members of the congregation themselves. Paul says: "Let us—that is, all those who belong to the Christ community—who belong to the day, put on the breastplate of trust and of love and the helmet of hope for salvation" (1 Thess 5:8). The First Testament text instead drastically reports God's own definitive intervention to right the wrong in God's people and states: "And he—the Lord—put on righteousness as a breastplate and placed the helmet of salvation upon his head and cast around (himself) the cloak of judgement and the robe as one who would pay back reproach as revenge to the enemies." According to Paul's use of the biblical text, it is the Christ community's own activity that actively represents the role of the divinity in the above scriptural text; the Christ community enacts authentic judgment that establishes justice. That is, this recovery of justice begins within the Christ community. The Isaiah text, however, has as its real objective the outside world. Through his quotation of the biblical prediction and its application to the Christ community, Paul thus stresses that within and through the Christ community an efficacious provocation of its environment occurs. The administration of justice by the powerful is the target of the challenge. The powerful are those alluded to in the beginning of the passage. They are the ones who, according to 1 Thess 5:3, falsely announce "peace" and "security," slogans of the Caesar religion, which do not lead to the "gaining of liberation" (5:9) but only to "destruction" (5:3). As the "justice" and "righteousness" of the text from Isa 59 are reinstated in the Christ community, the world with its different values is put on trial. The world's weapons are wrath and terror, whereas the Christ community offers the gain of liberation through trust, love, and hope (1 Thess 5:8–9).

The congregation's manner of existence reflects the apostle's characteristics, and the latter in turn are molded by the unique fate of Jesus, including his posthistory. Paul is touched that the Thessalonians believe him specifically because his appearance mirrors the singular style and content of his message. Therefore it is only natural that he describes the Thessalonians' coming to faith as an imitation of his lifestyle. This imitation also shows itself in that the Thessalonians began proclaiming the Christ message themselves and began to organize themselves independently of their founder, who had had to leave them. They started to govern themselves. Timothy and Paul were no longer leaders but turned into advisors and consultants. As the lordship of Christ (5:9) is demonstrated by his dying for others (5:10), mutual encouragement and constructive empowerment (5:11) maintain his community.[2]

3. PERSONHOOD AND ROLE-PLAYING

3.1. The Role of Jesus Christ

Contrary to the modern custom of differentiating between person and issue described in the beginning, it is self-evident for Paul and his community members that one can recognize the content of the proclamation, the crucified Christ, in the appearance of the proclaimer. Therefore this image of humanity also further communicates itself to the public, changing and activating the latter. Paul's image of humans cannot be separated from his image of Christ nor from his concept of his own ministry. However, since all these notions are also directly related to the idea of an active congregation—and that means with the concepts of God's people and humanity—it is impossible to misunderstand the close relationship of person, vocation, and Christ expressed in Paul's ministry in the sense of a religious or cultic superhumanness.

The fate of Christ molded the apostle, and the latter, thereby coalesced with the message, communicates in an effective way with his listeners. These in turn immediately express their solidarity with this chain of events and with each other and integrate humankind into the new world through their living manifestation of faith. Consequently, it is not a coincidence that the Pauline Epistles fail to help if one tries to use them as a manual on specific theological issues, as if certain parts of the letters addressed themselves more or less exclusively to specific themes. No matter whether one asks about Paul's idea of Christ, his apostle concept, his ethics, his image of humans, or anything else, the question should

---

2. The passage 5:12–24 hints that the character of this community was democratic, guided by the spirit. The members became independent by respecting one another.

always be addressed to the whole correspondence—and we have only a fragmentary documentation of Paul's continual reciprocal conversation with his communities and with their and his situations. Equally interesting in this rather lively dialogue is how and what statements are made.

3.2. The Concept of Life as Playing a Role in the New Testament

Although in Paul's writing person and issue are fused in this way in style and content, he did not invent this procedure but rather adopted it from others. It is familiar to us from recent literature of today, particularly of the theater, and especially the popular philosophers of Paul's time were masters of this technique of constant reciprocal relation of person and issue, which also included the listener in a lively manner. I must refrain from going into the philosophical aspects of this method in detail, but I do not want to omit mentioning the often-recurring one that has, since the very beginning, gained decisive importance for the "Christian" image of humanity, yes, even for the doctrines of Christ and of God. What we want to look at now directly concerns the meaning and use of the term *person*. This term originally referred to the mask that the actor wore and therefore also the role that he or she played on the stage. We would do more justice to the New Testament and early church if we kept in mind this correlation between person and theater and realized that equating individual and person as a matter of course is a dubious if not disastrous confusion of ideas. What I will try to elaborate in the following as the concept of person is something quite different from the modern idea of the individual, whose distinguishing characteristic is specifically being distinct from the community, who is interested in identity and being true to oneself, and who actually can gain only an at best stunted relationship to history. This concept of individual has to leave the world in the hands of an order based on violence, either howling with the pack or washing one's hands in innocence.

Hellenistic popular philosophy conceives of humanity and especially of the exemplary human, the philosopher, as an actor designated by the gods to play a role. The drastic-realistic way in which the popular philosophers demonstrate this proves that they fall back on the theater of the poor of the time, mime, which nowadays is unjustly looked down on as mere farce. Hellenistic and, even more, Roman rulers appreciated this expression of public opinion, not just as a safety valve for the people's anger but indeed also as expression of the truth about man in her and his social conditions. This truth was acted by the mimes, these forebears of Brecht and Beckett, but also of Shakespeare. By means of their dramatic imitation of everyday behavior, the mimes produced laughter that was supposed to tear the spectators away from their daily routine for at least a moment, literally causing them to laugh tears. In the most famous examples of mime, especially in Herondas, the spectators are brought to laugh so much by drastically acting out the conventional that they have to notice sooner or later that they have been enticed away from the self-evidence of their conventions. They have already begun to laugh about themselves as well as about the notion that life and society can only be organized their way. For example, when Herondas lets a brothel keeper claim damages for one of his protégés in the style of the elaborate judicial speech and invoke the holiest traditions of the city state, the ensuing laughter sooner or later addresses the eternalness of the city-state and its laws.

To speak of life as a play and of a person's life as a role therefore means understanding and sociocritically judging man on the basis of his and her actions in their historical and social contexts. The truth about man becomes evident in her and his social relationships, especially where the abyss of laughter opens up. Here the procedure of mime and the dialectic of popular philosophy help the listener to gain distance to the role. Engaging acting becomes temporary or, in philosophy, permanent liberation from the role.

3.3. Paul's Use of Life as Role-Playing

Paul radicalizes the idea of life as a role. He sees God and Christ giving themselves up to ridicule. In 1 Corinthians, Paul says: "Since through wisdom the world did not recognize God in his wisdom, it pleased God to save through foolishness of the proclamation those who trust in it," and further, "we proclaim Christ as crucified, for Jews, a scandal, for Gentiles, foolishness; yet for those called, Jews as well as Greeks, the Christ as God's power and God's wisdom" (1:21, 23–24). Because such is the case with God and Christ, Paul can also find his own justification only in surrendering to the ridicule of the crowd. He succinctly expresses this in the same epistle as follows: "God has depicted us, the apostles, as the least ones, as condemned to death, because we became a spectacle [θέατρον] for the world, for angels, and for humans" (4:9).

This way of thinking and acting has found its most sublime expression in the so-called fool's speech in 2 Cor 11 and 12. Attacked and ridiculed by competing preachers specifically because of his all but impressive appearance, Paul submits to the challenge of their spiritual boasting. The other side's self-praise is expression of spiritual arrogance and self-confidence. Paul, on the other hand, plays the role of a fool in the mime theater (2 Cor 11:2–4). More precisely, he plays the role of the bridegroom's friend who has recommended and introduced the bride to the groom, that is, the role of a typical braggart. The young woman has in the meantime cuckolded the groom, and now the friend has made a fool of himself. True to the style of the mime theater, the bridegroom's friend justifies himself by means of exaggerated bragging and defamation of the swindlers, that is, the bride's lovers. All this of course must incite the laughter of the audience, which has already been informed of the decisive fiasco, the bride's affairs. While Paul himself plays the bridegroom's friend, he presents Christ as the bridegroom, the Corinthian congregation as the bride, and the opponents as the adulterous lovers of the bride.

In his boasting and scolding Paul only strengthens the misunderstanding between the pretensions of the Christ community and the achievements of his opponents, on the one hand, and his own comportment, on the other hand. Paul appears more and more as a loser and thereby deliberately holds himself up to ridicule. In exactly this way, however, Paul more and more underlines the seriousness of his ridiculousness in an at first imperceptible progress; finally he insinuates more and more that his fool's role is that of the crucified Christ himself (11:2–4). In the all too human appearance of Paul, one is confronted with nothing less than the revelation of the Lord of the world: "My power is mighty in the weak" (2 Cor 12:9). Thus the laughter of the opponents and their followers turns itself more and more against their own principles of faith and thereby against themselves. The crown of thorns is indeed the crown of the fool's king. He justifies the fools who believe in him as the only world revolutionary, but the only sign of this justification is the fool's cap. Paul feels that those who believe in Christ must risk the ridicule that comes with expecting a world revolution in the realm of the habitual monotony of everyday life and of trivial things. Real fools are only those who are able to play their role without any reservations. They can fully engage themselves in the game called life. When the laughter of the crowd surges around and spills over them, they know they are really where it is at. They then know that the stage is beginning to grow into a world theater that will also engage those who still think they are mere spectators.

4. CONCLUSION

One may perhaps object that this essay spoke too much about Paul and too little about humans in general. In Paul's understanding, however, speaking about the messenger means speaking about Christ and humans, even about the world. One may criticize that nothing was heard about sin and redemption and more about laughter, but the laughter meant was the kind that criticizes as well as liberates. Sin and righteousness, death and life, law and gospel, servitude and liberation, God, the world, and humans—they all become part of the action when one engages oneself on the stage called life. May it be left to further reflection why the "Christian" West has time and again shown a preference for the role of the fool, a role that reappears again and again in literature and arts up to this day. As a representative for many others, I would like to mention William Faulkner; I consider him one of the greatest interpreters of the Pauline concept of justification and would very much recommend him for further study. His works are full of foolish characters with Christlike traits. The most moving is that of Benjamin in *The Sound and the Fury.*

7
LEGAL DIMENSIONS OF MONEY AND THEOLOGICAL CONSEQUENCES

1. INTRODUCTION

Reading the New Testament's discussions on humans and humaneness with an awareness of the urban context of its authors and readers sharpens the eye not only for the social aspects of the documents but also for their discussions of economic and, in particular, monetary issues. The concentration of trade and finances had been an essential element of cities since their beginning. That increased in Hellenistic times, strengthened even more by the Romans. The Greco-Roman period was also a time of a heightened awareness of the legal dimensions of money. It is not customary to look for that in the New Testament. False understanding of the spiritual nature of New Testament documents has blinded the eyes for these very mundane elements of the founding documents of the early church. Paul will tell us again that labor and remuneration are essential issues of an urban theology. The renewed observation of the material nature of Pauline spirituality will help us to rediscover the major contribution that these reflections of old can make to our knowledge about the critical aspects of the range of social life in the cities of antiquity—and of today. These observations make it mandatory to include the legal aspects of money and also of economy and trade into these reflections as well.

---

* This is an enlarged form of a paper I gave to the New Testament doctoral seminar of Harvard Divinity School on 12 March 1997. I gave this lecture in honor of James Luther Adams, my old colleague and friend from Cambridge, who inspired me to the pursuits of which this paper is one result.

The last two decades of biblical scholarship have been surrendered to a hypertrophic concern for methodology, something like a methodological messianism, with little relevance for anyone in other theological disciplines. It is high time that we return to exercising the major tool of biblical scholarship, the continuous dialectic of question and observation, analysis and synthesis, a conjunction of disciplined historical and theological curiosity, as it were. Methods are merely ancillary to this, supportive as well as critical, but not productive as such, let alone creative. My Lutheran socialization had immunized me against the assumption of any positive legal questions in the Bible. This changed drastically in my first semesters with Ernst Käsemann in Mainz. In the Gospel of Mark I learned to see the conclusions of miracle stories as ratifying acclamations without which the miracle would have no reality. Prophetic statements became legal adjudications having even creative force. The poetic pieces of the book of Revelation turned into legal affirmations. These are just a few examples of a process during which I learned to raise questions and make observations, which a certain socialization had prevented me to ask and to see. This kind of prevention is not found in Lutheranism alone but was and is common in all of Protestantism. Ernst Käsemann had become interested in legal matters through his own New Testament teacher Eric Peterson, whose "magnum opus" *Eis Theos* has unfortunately turned into a classic nobody reads any longer. Peterson, who later converted to Catholicism, was, despite being a professor of New Testament, able to relate to many other disciplines, something I as well have tried to do as much as possible.

I would be entirely misunderstood if anyone would assume that the raising of legal questions were my main concern. However, for today I shall concentrate on legal issues, but not on these alone. The title of my essay indicates that I shall do what Käsemann never did, nor any other of my teachers, and rarely a colleague. I shall interrelate legal and economic questions and observations and connect them with matters of religion and theology.

Here I should insert a note of gratitude to my friend Elisabeth Schüssler-Fiorenza. In the mid-1970s she asked me to give a paper on propaganda and mission in the Hellenistic-Roman world at a conference she had organized at the University of Notre Dame. My topic was the "divine man" motif on which I had done a good deal of work before. While preparing that paper, I realized that I could not deal with that topic without assessing its socioeconomic dimensions, something I had been onto before but not yet consciously. Therefore, I must give credit to Elisabeth for being a successful midwife to one of my mental babies, a baby now grown to some independence. The final title of that paper was "Socioeconomic Reasons for the Divine Man as Propagandistic Pattern."[1]

Discussion of economics or socioeconomics in biblical studies is marginal at best. The wider theological circles are not any better. In most theological quarters, even the discussion of law limits itself to the biblical and Jewish Torah,[2] more often in a negative than in a positive sense. That limitation is even truer with matters of economy. I do not know of any theology that takes the interplay of law, economy, and religion seriously. The fact that Frankfurt is my hometown has certainly influenced my line of questioning. Frankfurt is the birthplace of a lawyer called Johann Wolfgang Goethe, who happened to become Germany's greatest poet. Frankfurt is also the banking center of Europe. Its two nicknames are "Bankfurt" and "Mainhattan," a takeoff on the river Main, on which Frankfurt is situated.

2. THE ORIGIN OF MONEY

In the English translation of my book on the collection,[3] I have given considerable but not exhaustive attention to the relationship between money and law in antiquity. I shall begin with a sketch of the origin of money. It is an abbreviated and adjusted form of the presentation in the afterword of *Remembering the Poor*. It will give an illustration of the basic triangular relationship between religion, money, and law that the present essay is about.

I follow the sociohistorical arguments of the historian and sociologist Gunnar Heinsohn from Bremen. He opposes the common theory that money originated in the interest of easing barter. According to this theory, manageable and identifiable coined metal replaced the heaviness and clumsiness of animal and other material values used in barter. That is, coins were introduced as countervalue—so the theory of Aristotle and his many students, including most modern economists. This theory requires that the origin of money be trade, trade of quite large proportions.

In addition, this theory does not explain why money was from the very beginning heavily related to legal issues and to religion. Heinsohn argues convincingly that the interplay of numerical and legal abstraction was basic to the character and role of money from the start. The barter-to-

---

1. It is included on pages 11–23 of this collection of essays.
2. With very little recognition and even less knowledge of the halakah.
3. *Remembering the Poor: The History of Paul's Collection for Jerusalem* (Nashville: Abingdon, 1992).

money concept cannot explain that. Even if Heinsohn should be incorrect in his view of the historical evolution of money, the fact remains that money, law, and property were interrelated from the beginning; trade was a secondary phenomenon.

Heinsohn's suggestion is that the societies in central Greece that invented money had come out of major catastrophes. After near annihilation, these societies reorganized themselves. A major step in this reorganization was the equal distribution of all common land as private property to all free grown-up males. In this theory, the origin of private property is interrelated with the beginning of patriarchy in the sense we now understand it. These private owners did not isolate themselves on their property; they congregated in cities instead. Cities provided the physical, social, and legal locales for the discussions, agreements, and arrangements made; this was the origin of the city-state.

As the idea and practice of private property was born, the concern for its protection originated as well. It rested on three pillars. Divine protection was the first pillar that guarded property, money, and trade. The next pillar can be inscribed with the term νόμος. Its etymology gives us a clue as to the creative milieu of that term. Νόμος comes from the verb νέμω, which means "distribute." This verb relates to another noun, νομή "grazing ground," which also means "distribution." The question is whether this is not the prior meaning of that term. In any case, law was concerned with the arrangements of dividing land into private properties. Law regulated these arrangements and also the problems—and their proper resolution—that grew out of the basic agreements. The third pillar of the protective arrangement consisted of the twin activities lending and borrowing and was the major reason for the invention of money.

Property was first used for the purpose of providing sustenance for the family of the patriarch, where the term *family* is meant in the biological as well as social sense. The efforts of the family's labor were meant for this sustenance, yet the yield of that labor frequently exceeded the needs of the family. What should they do with the surplus? Using it for the purpose of lending gave additional protection. What could be demanded as collateral? Initially, when only minor borrowing occurred, physical goods could do as securities, just like in a modern pawnshop. Larger collateral could not be stored or used so easily. It became necessary to translate lending power into something that was literally more bearable. It needed to be standardized in value, too. Such were the most prominent reasons for the creation of money in the form of coined valuable metal. Now it was easy to assess and agree upon credit, security, and interest that the lender would give and demand and that the borrower would receive and pay. Credit would be the value of trust asked and given. Interest would be the gain hoped for through the rendering of this service.

There was one additional advantage to monetary arrangements of securities, something the parable of the Rich Fool in the Gospel of Luke presupposes: what to do when the harvest is much bigger than expected. The rich fool thinks of building new and larger barns. That would be a costly affair, not only in terms of money but also in terms of time. Having the gains converted into something more easily storable and certainly more durable, such as coined metal, would make much more sense. Storing coins was less expensive than storing grain.

The notions of trust, credit, security, obligations, debit, fees, and interest bring me back to the first pillar mentioned, divine protection. Temple priests could provide witnesses and sanctions for monetary transactions in the names of their gods. Trust represented by the temple and its priests became quite real in terms of testifying, depositing, crediting, contracting, trading of debts, and collecting of interest. The obligations were traded beyond the original parties and provided profit for the temple and further traders involved. Thus, the temple became a bank, and money became a handy abstraction.

This trading and business of credits and debits never would have developed without coined money. The gods and the cities guaranteed the value of the money through the symbols they provided and impressed on the coins. That guarantee and protection were not merely ideal but had a physical side to it, and this in double form. One was the actual metal value of the coin; the other was the financial power of the temple, not merely expressed in the form of the valuable metal the temple had stored in its vaults but also in the form of the written debits and obligations the temple held; and divine wrath had general oversight. We gain good insight into the Jerusalem temple as one of the major banks of the Mediterranean in 1 and, especially, 2 Maccabees, including a story of divine oversight and interference, activities that ancient people would expect from divine banking control, security, and trust.[4]

---

4. Part of my argument is that the interplay of economic, legal, and religious issues was essential to the cultural environment of Paul's time and was not lost on him. This can be seen on the basis of certain exceptions he made. In my book on the collection for Jerusalem, I have shown that he left out three elements of the pattern described and reaffirmed by Augustus, see "Is There Justification in Money? A Historical and Theological Meditation on the Financial Aspects of Justification by Christ," pages 283–307 below. There was first the tax aspect of the collection, related to temple and sacrifice. Paul never mentioned the Jerusalem temple. Contrary to common assumption, Paul never connected his Christology with the Israelite temple sacrifices either. The reason for this was that Paul was intent on the motif of spiritual sacrifice, which had become relatively common in much of the Mediterranean. The second point was Paul's avoidance of the whole imagery of borrowing and lending, indebtedness and obligation—one of the pillars of protection of the ancient economy. It is important to

It needs to be stated that most ancient temples were public phenomena; most of them were built and maintained by cities and other higher institutions. The yields of financial transactions of temples were not necessary for maintenance; public money was used for that, directly spent or acquired through taxes.

Time forbids intensive further investigation of the subsequent evolution of the Mediterranean monetary system. Extensive descriptions of these developments can be found in the studies of Heichelheim and of Rostoftzeff on ancient economic history, in particular the Hellenistic and Roman forms. It was a history of refinements, including the invention of checks. This did not change the basic patterns described above. Religion, by definition, was always in the picture, too.

3. TEXTUAL DISCUSSIONS

3.1. General Remarks

The approach I will take in the second part of this essay is to use some of Paul's texts in order to show how people of his time interrelated money and law.

A major result of my paper on the socioeconomic reasons for the "divine man" as propagandistic pattern was the discovery of the nature of the Hellenistic-Roman world as a performance-oriented market society. In the afterword of the English translation of my book on the collection, I have worked this out further, but I deal with the issue of remuneration only marginally, not much more extensively than I do in my book on the opponents of Paul.

Now I want to carry this further. It is well known that the market was in the middle of the cities and towns of the Mediterranean.[5] These

---

note that the bourgeois mind since its inception in the eleventh century and until today continues to claim, in contradiction to the texts, that the motifs of sin as guilt and of consequential indebtedness are fundamental elements of Paul's doctrine of justification. The tendency to see Paul's doctrine in this way has increased since the Reformation. The third omission was in the area of the private and the self. In Hellenistic-Roman economy, this dimension had developed further. The true individual was defined as the smallest indivisible entity that could own property, private property. Bourgeoisie, in particular Protestant bourgeoisie, has reintroduced the individual as a basic concept, that is, the self in private pursuits and engagements, allegedly defined by its will and its decisions. See below 221–54 and 323–36.

[5] This remained the case through much of the Middle Ages. The market lost its physical dimension as urban center in the fifteenth and sixteenth centuries and turned more

markets were not given to commercial business alone. Spiritual goods were traded as much as material ones. Communication in many different forms occurred there; even legislation and adjudication happened on the market or at least close by. Temples and other sacred objects were an essential part of the market, too. They represented the presence of the supraterrestrial. Thus, all three pillars of protection I mentioned earlier were found on and around the Mediterranean market.

Temples and other public buildings were rather costly outlays. Their financial costs, public or private, were usually tremendous. For ancient people, this was not only a sentimental demonstration but also a prudent investment, not unrelated to the character and stability of the economy. Such investment served the protective function of religion and the stability of economy and society. Investing in such costly structures meant supporting the main character of that society through a demonstration of extraordinary power or, better said, of the power of the extraordinary, whether of the gods or of persons of semidivine status. This kind of investment was similar to maintaining modern armies with their costly playthings, less meant for fighting than for showing off.

However, this does not suffice to explain the presence of temples and other sacred objects on the Mediterranean marketplace. The first and most important purpose of sacred objects around the market was to demonstrate and secure the support and control that the gods rendered to business and the people in the market. Since all ancient gods had a local as well as a general side, they usually were not worshiped at one place alone but also elsewhere. Therefore, their worship provided a translocal infrastructure protecting trade and traders, missionaries, philosophers, and other people presenting their goods on the world market.

Investment in urban grandeur was one of the most important services these communities expected from their citizens, especially from those who wanted to be considered relevant and respected. Rich people had to prove their indebtedness to their native or chosen communities through such giving, in return indebting the communities to them as well. Such public service was called λειτουργία, civic assistance to a wide variety of the needs of the city and its citizens. It resulted in a cyclical interplay of giving and thanksgiving. Yet the ancient eye would already see the gift of the sponsor, his or her *leitourgia,* as a result of being showered with presents by the city and its gods. The cycle of gift and thanksgiving was characteristic for Hellenistic-Roman society at large, the grease, so to

---

and more into an abstraction as an accompaniment to the development and growth of modern capitalism.

speak, that kept the wheels of society turning. It was good for market, business, and community. There was an interplay of gift/service and needs. This cyclical relationship did not work on the lateral level alone. It also had a vertical side. It applied to the relationship between deities and humans as well. This interplay of giving and thanksgiving was not sentimental; it was legal.

I now move to a discussion of certain particular texts. First I discuss passages that relate to remuneration: 1 Cor 9; 2 Cor 2:17; 11:7–21; 12:11–18; Phil 4:10–19; and Rom 4:1–12.[6] Then I deal with the convention in Jerusalem as a constitutional event, mostly dealing with Gal 2.

3.2. 1 Corinthians 9

Let us look first at 1 Cor 9. That chapter is usually read merely as a discussion of the rights of the apostle or apostles, with particular emphasis on Paul's understanding of his rights. It is seen as an example of the spiritual approach I spoke about.[7] However, the whole chapter can only be understood if it is read with the eyes of people who are a full part of Hellenistic-Roman society and its economy, money, and market.[8] This is demonstrated by the very first line of the chapter and sealed by its conclusion. That is, 1 Cor 9 begins with a question formulated in a general manner: "Am I not free?" picking up a slogan of all citizens of cities of the Eastern and the Western Mediterranean in the first century, all of them claiming to be free, free citizens. The chapter ends with references to the stadium, one of the prides of any Hellenistic city, not only as an architectural pearl but as the place where free citizens compete, a demonstration

---

6. I can give only a glance at 2 Cor 2:16 and 2 Cor 11 and 12.

7. We are partly under this misconception because we depend heavily on ancient historians who were either upper or upper middle-class people and thus socialized in the values of leisure people. The other part of our misconception, especially with respect to reading the New Testament, is the Protestant religious disinterest in the material side of the New Testament, especially with respect to the issues of labor and work, bulldozed over by a misunderstood doctrine of justification by faith alone and its polemic against works. This has been supported further by the general tendency of Christian exegesis and theology to this day to set the Bible apart, in particular the New Testament, to claim that it deals merely with the spiritual, isolating the spiritual from the material.

8. The term *chapter* is, of course, an anachronistic one, often entirely misleading. No biblical author wrote in chapters and verses. The division of the documents into chapters occurred as late as the Middle Ages. Luther did not know of verses. They were introduced in the middle of the sixteenth century. In the case of 1 Cor 9, however, the later separation into chapters works well; what is now called the ninth chapter is indeed one major unit of thought.

of the agonistic nature of the city and of urban society at large. The athletic competition is taken as a paradigm for the nature of society at large and its economy, too.

The questions introducing 1 Cor 9 are original. The formulation "Am I not free?" was too general and too worldly for many readers. Thus early copyists already put this phrase, this question, that is, behind the question relating to apostleship. So they changed the rather general and worldly nature of the beginning of that chapter into the "proper" theological tone.[9] There is no reason to doubt the authenticity of this series of questions. The difficulty this tenor provided for copyists and translators proves the character of these questions as the more difficult reading and thus confirms the probability that they were the original version.

The freedom talked about in the first question is not the spiritual freedom of the apostle. That would indeed have required a reversal of the questions.[10] Instead, freedom is introduced here as a general phenomenon that everyone would know about and understand, not only Jesus believers. Paul starts the chapter with a cultural and a legal given.[11]

The general notion of freedom Paul starts out with is not just that of intent and mission. It is also the freedom to work and to have success and recognition going with it. There is a seal to such success, in Paul's case the existence of a community he founded through his work. In 1 Cor 9:3 Paul speaks of those who judge him. That is again formulated in a very general fashion. It refers to the other side of the competitive society

---

9. The Jerusalem Bible translation does not change the sequence of questions. However, it tries to achieve the same, namely, the easing of the general, worldly tone of that beginning, by changing the questions into statements; the clear intent is to arrive at a more purely theological message. In addition, this translation embellishes the first sentence slightly in order to give it a more religious ring: "I, personally, am free." This turns the first sentence into a thesis and the subsequent statements into supportive arguments or explanations. The intent is clear and also found in many commentaries, namely, to join the first and the second statement in order to create the appearance that Paul is not talking about freedom in general but about freedom in relation to his apostleship, religious freedom, so to speak.

10. Just as some copyists tried to arrange it.

11. The chapter is about the freedom that society knows about, in particular also a Roman colony such as Corinth, which was not identical with the ancient city by the same name and at the same location. This had been completely destroyed by the Romans in 146 B.C.E. One hundred years later the Romans themselves had refounded and rebuilt it. More precisely, Caesar initiated this refounding and rebuilding enterprise shortly before his murder, and his nephew and successor, Augustus, completed it. Its legal status was that of a Roman military colony, intended first and foremost for both Italian and other veterans of the Roman army. However, during the more than one hundred years before Paul came to this city, its natural position between the Adriatic Sea and the Aegean Sea had turned it again into a major port, actually a double port, with harbors at both seas, a major trading place with industry to support it. This had attracted inhabitants from all over the world.

I have been talking about. The competition was constantly assessed and judged, not by particular people but by everyone. In 9:4 we have an interesting synonym of the concept "free" the chapter started out with. The term I have in mind is ἐξουσία. That means an active authority, an authority to act, to act out the freedom one has to do things or to leave them. This authority here is described first of all in a rather materialistic fashion as the right to eat and to drink (9:4), then also as the right to make decisions, to move and to settle, here associated with continuous heterosexual companionship.[12]

Paul makes an important distinction in 9:6 that is only superficially between working and not working. However, since Paul contrasts himself and Barnabas with the missionaries mentioned before, he cannot have in mind the contrast between work and leisure. The other missionaries are active as well, but their work is not an ἐργάζεσθαι. This Greek term specifically means working for wages, that is, in a contractual relationship. The work of the other missionaries mentioned is not contractual, yet it is also work paid for. Money earned this way, Paul points out, is legally earned, too; rightly paid and received, it is something like an honorarium, as we would say today.

In the next verse Paul assures us with various examples that, however acquired, this money is earned money.[13] Not every kind of worker can expect to be paid with money for his work. The fact that Paul uses the soldier's profession as an example is interesting because in case of war armies live off of the spoils of their warfare. This is an interesting aspect of this example in that, according to Paul, a job cannot merely be remunerated by a salary but must also be remunerated by extra gains. This is underlined further by the image of the use of fruits of property and labor in the examples of the vineyard and the flock. The idea of remuneration implies, therefore, that a working relationship must provide livelihood,

---

12. This reminds me of some ancient philosophers who were on the road with their wives, but also of Aquila and Priscilla, who moved from Rome to Corinth and then to Ephesus, combining their concern for their profession with missionary interests, the shop functioning also as a recruiting and meeting place.

13. Of Paul we know that he worked for money, besides his preaching and organizing activities, which he did for free. This he states in 1 Cor 9 and in other related passages. He does not tell us what his profession was. Luke speaks of tentmaking, whatever that was, and he makes Priscilla and Aquila colleagues in the same profession. There is some chance that Paul, instead of going directly from Saloniki to Rome, took a detour to Corinth because, according to Luke, he had learned that Priscilla and Aquila had fled from Rome to Corinth. Paul seems to have been eager to learn from them what had happened in Rome. However, the other reason most probably was that they had been able to set up shop in Corinth and that Paul was interested in working his trade in their shop

not in the form of the bare minimum but clearly in a profitable way. Remuneration of whatever kind is interpreted as spoil and harvest, that is, clearly with an element of plenty in it, comparable to what we nowadays call profit. Although Paul and his time clearly knew of a vast variety of labor and of division of labor, for Paul and his readers there is no distinction between labor and profit. This is a clear contradiction to the modern differentiation between gains from labor and gains from stock.

Paul introduces in another important perspective 9:8–14, not only that work deserves its reward, and that in abundance, but also that the right to earn entails an exercise of power of those serving over those served. That presumes that earning money in whatever way turns people who earn into power figures.

It is obvious that in 9:9 Paul uses a text from Deut 25:4 in a highly allegorical manner.[14] He wants to make it work as scriptural proof of the remuneration of spiritual service. The allegorical nature of that argument usually makes people blind as to the worldliness and humor of such use of scriptures. The oxen stand for the apostle and other like-minded people. The text could not be more materialistic. Again, abundance and the absence of measuring are the criteria for the remuneration of the work done. The other scripture quote that Paul adds remains in the realm of agriculture but speaks of humans, plowman and thresher, instead of animals. The hope factor is added, but not to make things more immaterial or more uncertain. Rather, the hope spoken about is a certain expectation, hope that one can bank on. It is a highly material hope, no eschatology of the sweet by-and-by . This material dimension is maintained in the next verse as well. The rule, material goods—and that is mainly money here— for spiritual goods, services, or the like, is referred to as a general, legal rule, not as something peculiarly Christian. This general and rather worldly tone is continued in 9:13, speaking about temples and their priests. Paul may have in mind the Jerusalem temple in particular, yet what he says here is true for all temples and priests in the Mediterranean. The dominical saying, quoted here, that preaching the gospel is worth a monetary reward is as worldly a statement as any, in fact more a proverbial sentence.[15]

It is important to note that Paul brings in the issue of right or rights. We can assume that, since his contemporaries understood his previous argument about remuneration, they also understood the association of the intimate relation of labor and wages with rights. This is a necessary

---

14. To this day it has remained the scriptural proof of ministers' salaries, a text also used in 1 Tim 5:18.

15. Is it really an authentic Jesus saying?

accompaniment to the starting and leading term of the chapter, that of freedom. Remuneration is not only a basic right but a major demonstration of personal freedom.

Still, we should not overlook the point that Paul wants to make in this chapter. As far as his own mission is concerned, he yields his right of expecting and receiving remuneration. He takes his mission as his obligation, free of charge to the addressees and recipients. Paul insists that this is a personal exception and is his free choice.

3.3. 2 Corinthians 2:17; 11:7–21; 12:11–18

I can present only a sketch of the points in 2 Cor 2:17; 11:7–21; and 12:11–18 that relate to our subject of remuneration. Here we see this issue heavily associated with competition within a market-oriented society. Jesus-oriented missionaries had invaded Corinth and tried to turn the congregation away from Paul.[16] Their message and their practice were quite competitive, achievement and market oriented. For them, the missionary situation was a competitive one, with many different religions, Jewish and non-Jewish, competing for attention. They carried this competitive spirit into the church as well. They saw Paul's refusal to compete as a concession of his spiritual weakness. For them, spiritual power manifested itself objectively in miracles. They looked back at biblical miracles and understood themselves as coming out of an old tradition, celebrating signs and wonders, continued in Judaism. They viewed Jesus as the peak of that biblical and Jewish past, the greatest "divine man," proven by a miraculous life. They wanted to continue that line of spiritual achievers through their message and their actions. Their objectified success was verified in letters of recommendation, and new achievements that even unbelievers could not deny confirmed their success in the market and in the congregations.

It is interesting that Paul denounces them in 2 Cor 2:17 as peddlers in or of the word of God. He denounces them as selling the message for a price and within a competitive setting. This means that the images of selling and buying were applicable to their approach and reception and were a negative aspect for Paul, but neither for them nor for most of their public. Looking for and granting monetary appreciation appear to have been considered natural. Remuneration was considered a reward for

---

16. The text is part of a larger fragment that Paul wrote to the Corinthian congregation. That fragment reaches from 2:14 to 6:13 and is continued in 7:2–4. Only the address and the final greeting of the original letter seem to be missing here.

spiritual achievement in such competition. This is even more obvious in the texts cited above from 2 Cor 11 and 12.[17] By accepting payment, these spiritual achievers also showed appreciation of those paying.

In 2 Cor 11:7–21 Paul shows us that the Corinthians' and Paul's opponents saw a further advantage in the audience's payment for spiritual achievements.[18] The decision to pay or not gave the payer the right to judge and assess and to pay accordingly. The monetary reward acknowledged and encouraged the performer, thus giving a material and a sentimental reason for continuing to perform the abilities given and for even increasing their audience and success. These missionary activists knew that producer and seller depended on the customers, and vice versa, and both sides condemned Paul's refusal, so contrary to society's rules, as injustice.[19]

Paul compares his practice of refusing pay for his work with parental care. Obviously Paul here changes the social context. He moves from the open market, also present in 1 Cor 9, to the family. Paul follows the line of reasoning that care without pay is a matter of course in a family, the natural sign of true appreciation and love. It is love without looking for reward. However, the opponents of Paul and their Corinthian admirers upheld a view of economics not different from Aristotle's, nor the one predominant today, for that matter.[20] Aristotle (and his school) found it possible to discuss matters of production, reproduction, property, goods,

---

17. These chapters stem from a different fragment, consisting of 2 Cor 10–13, again without a beginning and perhaps without an end. Both fragments were probably relatively short, and their ends were broken off, as easily happens with the beginnings and endings of papyrus documents. In Paul's eyes, the attitude of the Corinthians toward him denounced God's not retaliating for the complete lack of appreciation that he had received from his creatures. Instead, God gratuitously demonstrated his appreciation, his love, by sending his Son and allowing him to be crucified by unappreciative humans. Even then, God did not respond in kind. He did not turn the resurrection of Jesus into a curse and judgment of thankless humanity but offered the resurrection of Jesus as the beginning of a new life, indeed, of a new world. The final reference of Paul to God in 13:11 comprises all of that. The hermeneutical question arises as to how cross and resurrection relate to a theological understanding of money, its use, and circulation.

18. Although Paul expresses himself in the parodistic style of the fool's speech, he is dead serious in his underlying message.

19. Just as today, even the poorer citizens of a rich city or country proudly identify with their city or country if they see it put down by an outsider. In Paul's fool speech there is also a deeper level of irony that actually turns the tables on the mocking audience, makes those initially laughing at last laugh at themselves and their principles.

20. The tractate *On Economics* ascribed to Aristotle may not be authentic in its entirety, but its basic material and intention seem to go back to the philosopher. Later generations of the Aristotelian school seem to have revised it.

trade, management, profit, and revenues in the confines of the "household," Greek οἰκονομία, the management of the house. Here the house is much more than the nuclear family. As an "economic" unit it is comparable to the state, of which it is the smallest constitutive part. The difference is in size and in the kind of management ruling. Only the "family" is ruled as a "monarchy," with the father at the top and from thereon downwards. For the author of the treaty on economics this is clearly an advantage over the state that is ruled by many. There is affection in Aristotle's family, but respect and discipline are more important. Attachment is a welcome accompaniment, yet stability and gain are more central and weightier. Aristotle's family is a producing and trading firm. Xenophon shares this view. In this conception, the individual household also provided the model and the criteria for the market at large.[21] It is quite obvious that Paul's concept of parent-children relations is quite different from Aristotle's and Xenophon's views of the nature and purpose of the family.

We are presently witnessing a fatal consequence of this early Hellenistic view of equivalence between the economic functioning of individual households and larger entities such as municipalities, states, and nations. I am thinking of the battle cry of conservatives in all Western nations today, the push for a balanced budget. The 1996 Nobel laureate in economics, the Columbia University economist William Vickrey, has attacked these ideological slogans as a fatal fallacy for a long time, recently in an online publication.[22] Vickrey argues in this text that it is completely unreasonable to read a national budget like the family budget. Not only the size is different but also the kind. The municipal,

---

21. The modern term *economics* is the transliteration of the Greek term οἰκονομία. Modern political and economic institutions still build on and move around their respective "households."

22. "Fifteen Fatal Fallacies of Financial Fundamentalism: A Disquisition on Demand Side Economics" (online: http://www.columbia.edu/dlc/wp/econ/vickrey.html). Major ideas of Vickrey on this topic are already found in his presidential address, "Today's Task for Economists," to the American Economic Association, printed in the edition of Vickrey's essays, edited by Richard Arnott et al. under the title *Public Economics: Selected Papers by William Vickrey* (Cambridge: Cambridge University Press, 1994), 432–53. Vickrey felt indebted to the U.S.-American economist Henry George (1839–97), who in his major work *Progress and Poverty* (1879) had identified private ownership of land as the cause of social demise. He demanded the elimination of private ownership of land or at least its indirect removal by way of confiscation of the gain made on land through a unified tax (single tax). His economic theory is at the base of what is called "Georgism." Although important for the development of American economic theory, George's theories were more influential in Britain and in Germany (land reform). Vickrey died on a trip to a meeting of a conference of contemporary Georgists.

state, or federal budget is in no way comparable to an individual or family budget, where there is a concern for balancing the checkbook. If balancing would be done on all larger levels of the economy, there would be a radical reduction in the building and buying of houses. Banks would make no sense any longer, let alone stock markets. Corporations could not exceed the size of the grocery store around the corner.

3.4. Philippians 4:10–19

I have already dealt with this text in my book on the collection of Paul, but I have gained new insights on this, not the least through the dissertation of my student, Dr. Lukas Bormann, on the church in Philippi.[23] This text from Philippians is particularly important for our assessment of the contemporary situation of Paul and his congregations. From the Philippian and the Corinthian correspondence, we know that the Philippians were the only congregation that Paul allowed to support him monetarily, but even that happened only with hesitation, as the chosen passage intimates.[24]

Community and participation are the major points Paul wants to make. With this, he invokes the issue of client-patron relations. This issue is quite important first of all for the city of Philippi. Philippi carried the name of the father of Alexander the Great. Since the days of the decisive defeat of the murderers of Caesar in the battles of Philippi by Mark Antony and Augustus, this Macedonian town had been made a Roman city. It had become a colony of Roman military veterans, similar to Corinth. However, contrary to Corinth, Philippi remained primarily such a colony of veterans. Lukas Bormann has shown how much the Philippian correspondence worked with the sociohistorical background of Philippi. Bormann demonstrates that Paul uses perspectives and criteria of that social situation as he addresses this congregation. Paul works primarily with the concept of the patron-client relationship, common in all Mediterranean armies since Alexander. In the Roman army, its usage had increased since the times of Marius and Sulla, even more since Caesar, Pompey, Marc Antony, and Augustus. Through the Caesar religion,

---

23. Lukas Bormann, *Philippi: Stadt und Christengemeinde zur Zeit des Paulus*, (NovTSup 78; Leiden: Brill, 1995).

24. Again, this passage from Philippians is a fragment, as much as the present Epistle to the Philippians is a collection of fragmentary letters of Paul to the Philippians, too. Our fragment starts in 4:10 with only an address missing, and it stops in 4:20 with a proper ending. The present conclusion of Philippians belongs to another letter.

Augustus advanced the idea of patron relationship as being fundamental to society. In the *Res gestae divi Augusti,* it is obvious that Augustus understands himself as a patron, with the entire Mediterranean world as his clientele. Thus emphasizing the clientele idea, the Roman military and its veterans demonstrated the major relationship that was at the heart of the entire society and its economy.

This can be illustrated by the wider meaning and bearing of the well-known phrase already mentioned, the *do ut des* principle. It is usually associated with Roman religion, yet one finds its variations in Hellenistic-Roman society and culture at large as well. It is frequently taken as summarizing the manipulative, if not outright devious and corrupt, nature of pagan religion. Protestant theologians are particularly adamant about this accusation. This objection allegedly defends the sovereignty of God—in and of itself a rather questionable concept of God—or, in a derived fashion, of any governing authority. The objection evolved out of the medieval idea of *aseitas,* meaning the self-sufficiency and basic self-justification of God—and of any other authority derived from God and claiming sovereignty.

The ancient notion of *do ut des,* in whatever religious variation, allowed for relations of mutuality, reciprocity, interrelationship, and interdependence between deity and human. It did so individually and collectively.[25]

I have to refrain from dealing with other terms of the text that also relate intimately to Paul's contemporary society and stay with the clientele idea. Now I have to point to the terms of participation in 4:14 and 15. They relate to the clientele system in particular, presupposing and intimating these patron-client relations, here in the form of participation and sharing, mutual giving and reciprocity. There is also a give and take and its reversal. There is further the additional religious dimension, not only in general but also in particular in 4:18, where the monetary gift is interpreted as a spiritual sacrifice. All this is not particularly Pauline but

---

25. In my book on the collection I have dealt with this mutual and reciprocal relation by giving examples that are linguistically prominent, too. I have shown that the idea of a cyclical relationship occurs in the interplay between divine χάρις (grace, gift) and human αὐχαριστία (thanksgiving, gratitude), divine δόξα (splendor, glory) and human δοξολογία (giving splendor, glorification). This has been shown convincingly in a study by George Henry Boobyer, written under Martin Dibelius, *"Thanksgiving" and the "Glory of God in Paul"* (Borna-Leipzig: Noske, 1928). This cyclical notion is found also in Judaism and in the New Testament, not the least in Paul (e.g., 2 Cor 4:15). In this kind of religion, there is no place for an isolated deity, as little as for an isolated humanity. For this form of religion gracelessness as well as ingratitude are ends to life altogether. This is certainly a warmer understanding of religion than the belief in a removed, omnipresent, omniscient, and omnipotent deity, high and above in the beyond. It is, moreover, an interesting ecological proposition. For the synonymy of ingratitude with sin, chaos, and death, see Rom 1:21 within its context.

part of general thinking. The recipient of a gift, even if that recipient is a patron as Paul, is to a degree an instrument within a divine cycle that keeps heaven and earth together and society alive.

We have already encountered this idea of a cosmic cycle that also affects monetary exchange. The idea of clientele fits well into this concept. The patron-client relationship is not only a one-way street of giving and receiving but also a relationship of mutual sharing, participation, and interdependence.

In the ancient clientele system, especially in its Hellenistic-Roman form, clients were certainly dependent on their patrons, but they could move to another if they did not find sufficient appreciation from their previous one, and if the new one would accept them. Since the number of clients and their means and skills would increase the fame and claim of their patrons, the patrons had to keep their clients happy. They had to share with them and care for a good climate among the clients, too.

We all know that the Romans were masters of the "divide and conquer" principle. However, it is rarely said that there also existed, particularly in the Roman clientele system a "divide and conquer" from below, fed by the fact that patrons could never be entirely sure of their clients. The patrons could distribute monetary gifts, jobs, titles, influence, and similar advantages and thus endear and indebt their clients. This was not enough. In addition, they also needed to prove loyalty and trust to their clients. Only if the clients were sure of the trust and loyalty of their patrons would they show such loyalty and trust themselves. The Greek term for loyalty and trust is πίστις, the translation of which we have unjustifiably limited to the meaning "faith." Considering monetary exchange in this context of clientele relationship gives a very direct feeling for the interplay of cash and creed.[26]

3.5. ROMANS 4:1–12

The last text that I am going to discuss under the subject of remuneration, Rom 4:1–12, in particular its beginning, will add some

---

26. It needs to be mentioned in passing that Augustus made great and successful efforts to have an almost-forgotten Roman goddess, "Fides" (who stood for contractual trust), worshiped again. He turned her into one of the main goddesses of the Caesar religion. This relates to the *Res gestae divi Augusti*, too. The claim of this document that the whole Roman realm was a place distinguished by *fides* (Greek πίστις) and among others by *iustitia* (Greek δικαιοσύνη) too, could be read in Greek by Paul and others on the outside of every Augustus temple in any major city. The two terms mentioned happen to be the two lead terms of Paul's Epistle to the Romans.

interesting notes to Paul's understanding of the relationship of labor and wages, again based on general assumptions that Paul shared with contemporary society. The larger passage speaks about Abraham's relationship to Jews and Gentiles and vice versa. The introductory remarks in 4:2 and following relate to working for wages and to leisure. This discussion is again based on general societal presuppositions of the first century concerning the relationship of money and society, just as in the discussion in 1 Cor 9. I am thinking most of all of Rom 4:4 and 5. Whoever works for monetary gain counts on the fact that wages are not given as a favor, that is, in gracious condescension or with a similar attitude. Instead, it is expected and given according to the rate of indebtedness that accumulates according to time, energy, resources, and imagination invested and shown by the worker. This reference to wage as an indebtedness of the employer is an interesting one, certainly true today also, but not so often expressed in this kind of language. Employers on various levels have always tended to give their payments to employees a touch of grace. This is an attitude that Paul condemns outright, and Paul's opinion concerning the relationship of money and labor reflects that of contemporary society.

Verse 5 speaks of someone not working for wages; Paul is here thinking of the leisure person. This is confirmed by the continuation of the argument to David, the king, who, in ancient perception, was by definition a leisure person. The context interrelates the concepts of, on the one hand, gain and leisure and, on the other hand, justification by trust, faith, or loyalty.

The interrelationship and interaction between justification and the concrete formation of life has been misunderstood or even forgotten in church and theology. The reason for this was and is that the term *faith* has unduly received center stage in Christian religion, already in its Roman Catholic form and even more so in Protestantism. With respect to Paul, it must be questioned whether the terms *faith* and *belief* or *believing* are in view at all. I have already stated that everything speaks in favor of using the combination of the terms "trust" and "loyalty" when translating the Greek term πίστις in Paul's letters. In Paul's understanding of the Abraham story, trust and justification go together. Justification is not dependent on a set of beliefs. There are other Pauline passages that demonstrate that this trust is another expression for loyalty. This loyalty is not understood as a one-way concept, from the subject to the sovereign. It is a two-way affair, with the divine loyalty, in fact, preceding and causing human loyalty.

Romans 4 states in its beginning that all are justified who trust God on the basis of his trust and loyalty, not on a foundation of working for wages, and therefore leisure persons such as David, that is, as all kings—

forgiven sinners as they are, just like all of us.[27] Justification creates royal beings, an idea that stands at the beginning of Anglo-Saxon democracy since the Reformation, in particular since the Puritans. In the ancient world, even more than in the Middle Ages, the very power of rulers and their standing were based on their confidence that the deity had entrusted them and continued to trust them. The necessary complement to this was that their subjects trusted in this trust relationship that made and sustained a king. Missing trust was the cause of the infighting common in royal families, of the many rebellions of trusted underlings, even of revolutions. These phenomena are well known with respect to the Hellenistic-Roman era, and this issue related back to the clientele format I spoke about in discussing Phil 4.

In a biblical context these relations are adaptations and a modernization of the ancient covenant idea, too. In this covenantal form, they also entered the Presbyterian Reformation, particularly in its Puritan variety, and thereby Anglo-Saxon democracy. In that covenantal sense, we also have to read the inscription on the dollar bill: "In God we trust."

3.6. Concluding Remarks on Remuneration

I now want to raise some concluding questions concerning remuneration. Paul would not consider it improper to understand payment as recognition of performance—just as the market did in his time. This has remained so to this day and should not be disclaimed for sentimental reasons. We must rediscover these dimensions of legality and mutuality relating to religion as well as to money. For Paul and for his contemporaries, legality and mutuality were easily associable with monetary and religious relations.

These relationships also included an understanding of the rights of the employee, as a matter of course, of divine and human legal relations, and, indeed, of interdependence. In the eyes of Paul and many people of his time, these issues were not something that had to be fought for, that had to be pulled out of the teeth of the employers, so to speak, but could be counted on and taken for granted. There was also the idea of mutual indebtedness, sharing, and interdependence, evident in the context of the clientele system. This included the concepts of loyalty and trust, not as one-way phenomena but as essential elements of a two-way street.

---

27. Rom 4:7 and 8, one of the few references of Paul to forgiveness of sins.

Paul's refusal of remuneration stands paradigmatically for another indebtedness, that to the giver of all gifts, certainly a challenge to the concept of property and dues. The knowledge that divine gifts and blessings were not merely the topping of human cunning but stood at the base of all human endeavor, this knowledge made all endeavors equal, no matter what the costs or what the price. They were all expressions of the continuance of gifts from on high. The ancient understanding of spiritual services as being comparable to other work and being integrated into the market society in many different ways entails a demythologizing message for our days that lifts the unnatural barrier between theological and economic deliberations.

3.7. Galatians 2: The Jerusalem Convention

I suggest that we define the meeting we are talking about as the Jerusalem convention. We have two reports about it: in Acts 15 and in Gal 2. They have two major features in common. One is the fact of a meeting in Jerusalem between representatives of the churches of Jerusalem and those of Antioch. The other feature is a main topic of the negotiations themselves, the full integration of Gentile converts into the church, a proposition brought forth by the delegates from Antioch.[28]

Both reports, that in Acts 15 and that in Gal 2, have been qualified by different scholars as being tendentious and, therefore, as less reliable than the other one. The more conservative scholars tend to go more for the reliability of the narrative in Acts, particularly with respect to its main points, the subordination of the congregation in Antioch to that in Jerusalem.[29]

The more liberal scholars opt for the report in Gal 2 as being more reliable. They judge that the story in Acts 15 is completely in agreement with Luke's overall tendency to portray the early church as being a centralized organization where the Twelve had and maintained leadership and control. I happen to agree with this liberal line of critical argument, not the least because Paul was a participant in the meeting. It is to be noticed further that his report in Gal 2 was not made to the Galatian

---

28. An alleged third report, seen by some scholars at the end of Acts 11, has nothing to do with the subjects spoken about by Luke as well as by Paul in Gal 2 and Acts 15.

29. The other main point in this conservative appreciation of the report in Acts is Luke's claim that the turmoil about the integration of Gentiles was caused not from within the church but from outside. Conservative scholars also have the tendency to consider the Pauline report as all too colored and as fabricated in his own favor concerning his importance and independence.

Jesus-believers alone but through them also to the opponents. Therefore, Paul could not stray too far in his account of the actual events, since the other participants remembered them. The opposition he fought in the Epistle to the Galatians had direct connections to the church in Jerusalem. They would immediately attack anything in his report in Gal 2 that contradicted the facts of the conference and that would put the so-called Jerusalem authorities in a wrong light, and such a contradiction would be communicated back to Galatia. As a consequence, Paul's trustworthiness with the Galatians would deteriorate even more. On the other hand, Paul's narration needed to be brief and to the point. He could presuppose shared knowledge and merely needed to bring in his perspective—but in a situation that had changed considerably.

Already the appearance of Peter as a missionary in Antioch proved that the situation had changed.[30] Paul's report is not historically correct here insofar as it identifies Peter almost completely with the mission to the Jews, a development of later days.[31] The fact that both Barnabas and Paul were equal delegates of Antioch at the convention is not consistently upheld in Paul's report either.[32]

However, some liberal colleagues go too far when they discount the report in Acts completely. Here as well as elsewhere in Acts a selective approach is appropriate. There is a good deal of information in Acts that does not agree with Luke's tendency, often even contradicts it. For instance, the leading role that Luke has James, the brother of Jesus, take in the Jerusalem convention does not fit Luke's concept of the Twelve. This picture of the role of James at the convention agrees with Paul, who also makes James the first of the three leading figures. Luke does not deal with that contradiction, and this bypassing is his usual way of easing difficulties. Luke indirectly also supports the Pauline narrative with respect to the role of the congregations of Antioch and Jerusalem. In both texts the communal assembly can expect reasonable presentation of the cases affecting the community, and the assembly has to give consent and thus legitimacy. The leaders can prepare and present issues, but they do not have the final decisive power; this is with the assembly. In this respect, Luke complements what Paul does not state at the end of his story of the convention. Although he had spoken of the role of the assembly before,

---

30. Paul relates that incident in Gal 2:11–14.

31. The beginnings of that development are reported in the story of the incident in Antioch in Gal 2:11–14.

32. Here Paul occasionally tends to speak of himself alone as if he were the only missionary to the Gentiles. This reflects the situation in the independent Pauline churches founded after the Antioch incident and Paul's separation from Antioch.

Paul fails to mention it at the end. This is amazing because the emphasis on the importance of the assembly would agree with Paul's ecclesiology in general. He must have forgotten this point in his report of the meeting in Jerusalem due to his interest in hastening to tell of his compliance with the agreements reached.

There is the question of the dependence or independence of the Antiochene congregation and, connected to that, whether the collection was meant and stipulated as a tax to be paid to the Jerusalem church. The conservative view takes the trip of Antioch delegates to Jerusalem as an indication of that dependence. The collection is seen in the same light. It is interpreted by conservative exegetes as a tax that the Jerusalem church has been authorized to levy; the collection is seen as comparable to the annual temple tax Diaspora Jews paid to the temple in Jerusalem.

Luke's silence here supports Paul because any notion of a tax character associated with the collection would have supported Luke's idea of the hierarchical nature and organization of the early church. Neither Paul's report about the convention in Jerusalem nor any of his later descriptions of his efforts to collect money for Jerusalem would support the notion of the collection as a tax. Tax language is absent, and the most basic elements of any tax are lacking as well: the idea and provisions of and for repetition and continuance.

Paul indicates that the convention had legal dimensions, especially the final agreement. However, he makes it quite clear that the agreement was a treaty among equals, between the churches of Jerusalem and Antioch: James, Peter, and John were the representatives of the Jerusalem church, while Paul and Barnabas, and perhaps Titus, represented the Antioch church.

Luke states in Acts 15:22 that at the end of the convention the apostles (here clearly the Twelve plus James) and the Jerusalem congregation arrived at an agreement imposed by the Jerusalem side, the so-called "apostolic decree."[33] Radical critics have even denied that this document

---

33. In Luke's report, they agree to send a delegation to the church in Antioch. The writing following in Luke's narrative in 15:23–29, the so-called apostolic decree, is presented by Luke as a missive that expresses the superiority of the leaders of the Jerusalem church and sets this against a subordination of the congregation in Antioch and of Barnabas and Paul. This cannot be true to fact, for nothing of that is in the treaty that Paul reports, although merely fragmentarily, in Gal 2:9 and 10. Luke, on the other hand, leaves out the treaty completely because it speaks against his tendency of stressing the superiority of Jerusalem and of the subordination of the other churches. Luke has no interest either in telling anything of the collection for Jerusalem because it disagrees with his concept of the church as a whole, and it works against his notion of the dependency of the Pauline congregations on Paul and, through Paul, on Jerusalem.

was written during Paul's lifetime.[34] However, in Paul's report on the convention, there is a phrase that can be best explained as a veiled reference to the decree, but as something that did not concern him because it was not part of the Jerusalem negotiations and conclusions but of later origin, without his participation or agreement. I am thinking of 2:6, where Paul argues that no additional regulation was agreed upon. This is best explained as a veiled reference to a later agreement negotiated between Antioch and Jerusalem after Paul had left Antioch in disgust. This agreement could have been more or less substantially equal to the content of the "apostolic decree," although without the latter's introduction and its imposition of the superiority of Jerusalem.

Four main issues were discussed and negotiated in Jerusalem: (1) the independence of the church in Antioch as to organization and mission; (2) Antioch's independence as to its gospel, that is, its theology; (3) the future relationship between Jerusalem and Antioch; and (4) the role of biblical, Jewish, and Jesus-related tradition in the whole church, focusing on, but not at all limited to, the issue of circumcision.

The issues debated were fundamental enough to make this meeting a constitutional conference. The result was, in fact, the first constitution of the church of Jesus Christ. Unfortunately, its complete text has been lost. Paul condensed his report of it into two brief, fragmentary sentences, in Gal 2:9 and 10, where he clearly presents the two main points of the document lost to us. Without the complete document, his sketch has become cryptic for the modern reader. The reason for Paul's brevity is obvious. He can presuppose his readers' knowledge of the document. He is not writing a church history but a letter addressing a highly critical situation in some or all of the churches he had founded in the province of Galatia. There, the Jerusalem meeting and its conclusion served as major points of contention. Paul's communication therefore needed to be pointed and concise.

Luke, the historian, who represents the ecclesial ideology of the church that later won out, intimates the reason for suppressing and forgetting this constitution. It endorsed the legal independence of two churches from each other. They agreed to disagree. They established that the unity of the church was not guaranteed by hierarchical arrangements or offices but by preaching the gospel in different colors and applications, yet in mutual respect and love. The legal nature of the Jerusalem

---

34. It is true that Paul never mentions it directly. Not true is what Luke alleges later: that Paul introduced this decree as a basic rule in all of his congregations. Paul never refers to it in his letters, although it would have been relevant, for instance, in the discussion of the meat issue in 1 Cor 8 and 10.

convention goes beyond the issue of dependence or independence of the Antioch church and that of integration of the uncircumcised. The more liberal scholars vote for independence, the more conservative for dependence. However, the terminology used by Paul in introducing the sketch of the agreement goes further: "James, Peter, and John gave us the right hand of fellowship." This is contractual language and is a constitutional arrangement.[35]

As to perspectives and criteria, I have learned a little more about Gal 2 than my book on the collection reveals.[36] My stress on the two terms *constitution* and *covenant* intimates the change and, I believe, the improvement of my understanding. With respect to the integration of the uncircumcised into the church at Antioch, the convention is usually seen as the beginning of the Gentile church at large, grudgingly agreed to by the people of Jerusalem. Most exegetes and theologians consider the latter a disappearing species.[37] In this interpretation, the primary and most important aspect of the issue of independence (i.e., the equality of the two congregations) is overlooked. Here are two communities negotiating and agreeing on the same legal footing, not only concerning their past and present but also their future, and not only regarding their immediate precincts but the whole world. Thus, the achieved constitution meant a global covenant.[38]

---

35. Evidence and arguments for this and for the fact that the following sketch entails the two main points of the agreement can be found in my *Remembering the Poor*, 31–42. But in terms of the issue of the Jerusalem agreement and the conclusions about its constitutional relevance, the above discussion goes further.

36. Ibid., 31–32.

37. This impression has a history that starts, with all probability, in Antioch. The Antiochene church, its satellite congregations, and the Gentile churches in general apparently increasingly disregarded the Jerusalem church, the Jewish-Christian church in general, and thus the Jerusalem constitution. They achieved this through a mixed approached, partly still visible in the New Testament and other documents of the early church, a mixture of respect for the initial phase of the Jerusalem church, neglect for the development of that congregation and its sphere of influence, and denunciation of their later phase, that of Jewish Christianity since the second century, as being heretical. This attitude robbed the Torah observants of the "Jerusalem way" that Paul had respected in acknowledging their claim to be equal constituents of the church. The epigones of James, Peter, and John were denied any continuation of their constitutional rights in the church. This meant the abolition of the Jerusalem constitution but also neglect of Paul's warning against Gentile arrogance in Rom 11:16–24, where the Gentile church is put potentially under Paul's curse. At the latest since the convention of Nicea, the victorious Gentile church has lost Paul's consent and blessing, is under his curse.

38. This is easily overlooked because, as already stated, the present text has the inclination to put Peter and Paul up front. There are however still sufficient traces of the original situation when, together with others, Peter and Paul were both merely delegates of their

There are still further hints of legal and economic aspects of the relationship between the Jerusalem church and the Diaspora churches represented by the Antioch congregation, issues that relate to the lasting integrity of the Jerusalem church.

In early Judaism[39] the title "the poor" implied the meaning "the hidden, oppressed, and persecuted repository covenant, the future co-rulers of God who, though for now harassed by the old eon, nevertheless constitute the true representatives of God's chosen, eschatological people."[40] Through the adoption of this claim, the Jerusalem church made a confession with their lives, even at their own physical expense.[41] There was also a temporal side to this. With the title "the poor" was meant "the essential dignity" of the congregation in Jerusalem, understood under the perspective of the end of time having come about and of the new age nearing. The title intimated knowledge of revolutionary changes waiting in the wing. There is the probable connection with the tradition of the Lord's Supper, in particular its emphasis on remembering (e.g., 1 Cor 11).[42] It was recognized in the Jerusalem constitution of the church that the Jesus people who remained in Jerusalem were not marginal to biblical and Jewish tradition and hope but were at its center. Obedience to the Torah was considered by the Jerusalem congregation that Paul knew as something essential for the basic function of tradition. The relationship to Jesus and the early post-Easter proclamation were not the only issues that mattered.[43]

---

respective congregations; Barnabas and Titus, in the case of Antioch, James and John, in the case of Jerusalem. The "I," the "I and Barnabas," as well as the "we" in the Pauline text stand not only for the Antiochene delegation but for all of the Antiochene church they represent. The same is true for the persons from Jerusalem. They represent the church of Jerusalem as its delegates.

39. The collection was meant as the founding of a revolution to come. A well-known parallel is the famous motion of the Roman tribune Tiberius Gracchus to fund a revolutionary increase of rightful proprietors in Rome with the help of the inheritance of the Attalides.

40. This is how I explain the meaning of the early Jewish use of "the poor" in *Remembering the Poor*, 34.

41. I have dealt with this extensively in ibid., 33–42.

42. Whether the particular concept "Jesus as the poor one," later stated by Paul in 2 Cor 8:9, already played a role at the Jerusalem conference is hard to decide. I would doubt it. A more probable connection exists with the tradition of the Lord's Supper, in particular with its emphasis on remembering (e.g., 1 Cor 11:24 and 25).

43. On pages 36 and 37 of *Remembering the Poor* I have shown that the biblical background of "remembering the poor" points to the prophetic prediction that at the end of time there will be a pilgrimage of the people, that is, of the Gentiles, to Jerusalem, bringing not only the Jews dispersed with them but also the pagan riches. In my book I also emphasize the importance that these global and eschatological, indeed, utopian dimensions of poverty have for religion and economy. As the Jerusalem constitution was drawn up with this

The term "the poor" also invoked covenantal solidarity: that of God with the poor, and that of the poor with God. Thus, the use of the term by the Jerusalem church also had a symbolic side, the physical recognition of the confessed linkage of the Jerusalem church to the biblical and Jewish tradition.[44] Therefore, the result of the convention and its conclusion at Jerusalem in 48 C.E. was an interesting blend of legal, economic, and sociopolitical aspects. Discussion and final agreement were about much more than circumcision and mission fields. At issue were the continuance and meaning of the biblical covenant. At the same time, something was brought into consideration that Greek, Hellenistic, and Roman civilizations were quite knowledgeable and practical about: the metropolitan status of certain larger cities. The expression and concept of μητρόπολις were developed within the context of Greek colonization; the "mother cities" sent out colonists into the larger Mediterranean and into the Black Sea for the purpose of founding colonies, not in the modern but in the ancient sense. These colonies were daughter towns and cities that would not only trade with the mother city but also represent her particular culture in the new land.[45]

Thus, the treaty of Jerusalem established not only mutual recognition and respect of the churches of Antioch and of Jerusalem but also their spheres of influence, each representing a certain way of life and a theology going with it. The Jerusalem way was basically Torah-oriented, including the practice of circumcision and certainly also respect for the purity laws, not only in their biblical but also in their Jewish understanding. Conversion to this way of life and theology, despite being Christ-oriented, would follow the usual requirements for Jewish proselytes, in case the converts were pagans.

The Antioch way was not directly Torah-oriented. That meant it did not require its converts or members to heed the ordinances of the Torah,

---

worldwide perspective, with past, present, and future in mind, the Mediterranean society and economy were not ignored. They were the wider context that all the participants of the conference were aware of.

44. This association with the biblical and Jewish tradition was manifest also in Jesus' own life, as far as we know it, and in the past connection also of Jesus' disciples with that tradition.

45. Contrary to modern colonialism, even the indigenous inhabitants of these Greek colonies could eventually acquire citizenship if they went through the institution of *paideia*, i.e. education, which the daughter city established in the spirit of the mother city. This interest in particulars did not exclude but, instead, included respect for the Greek culture at large, later the Hellenistic and then the Roman culture. So Greek culture was already multicolored, and thus the recognition of differences was part of the common heritage that all the various entities respected. This remained so and even increased in Hellenistic and Roman culture.

in particular that of the biblical and Jewish purity laws and regulations. Neither was it necessary to follow the requirements of the Jerusalem temple cult. This meant that the Torah was not rejected altogether, but its meaning was transformed into that of a moral and theological authority. Hellenistic Judaism had prepared the way for this kind of transformation.

In the case of the Antioch incident, sketched in Gal 2:11–13, Peter decided to join the Antiochene way when he came from Jerusalem to Antioch for a longer visit. The persons sent by Jesus' brother James decided to remain with the Jerusalem way when they came to Antioch. This did not create any trouble. The difficulty started when Peter decided to join the James people, that is, join their purity style, which set him apart from the Gentile members of the congregation. Barnabas and other Jewish members of the congregation joined him. Paul says that Peter's reason was fear of the James people, most probably because he feared their investigation. This cannot have been the reason for Barnabas and the others. Hospitality and temporary fellowship seem to have been the considerations. This could have been the case with Peter as well. For Paul, these reasons were not sufficient to override the Jerusalem accord as stated. In Paul's judgment, respect for the visitors and the Torah turned into disrespect for the members of the congregation in Antioch and their agreed-upon rule of life and their theology.

The angry speech in Gal 2:14b–21 was most probably not completely identical with the speech Paul actually gave at the time, indicated but abbreviated and updated to meet the present situation and the understanding of the Galatians. Paul denounced the back and forth of Peter and the others, but he did not criticize the James people. The theological language Paul uses in this speech intimates that he is giving more than a moral exhortation. The idea of a definite way of life, the language of justification and solidarity, the terminology of building, of choice and of separation, the concept of incorporation—all speak for a covenantal perspective.[46] Put in the light of the metropolitan perspective, this takes on

---

46. Thus, the story of the Antioch incident in Gal 2:11–21 enlightens us further as to the meaning of the first part of the Jerusalem agreements. The provision was that newly founded communities would follow either of the two ways, usually the way to which the founding missionary was committed. This would correspond to the practice in the larger Mediterranean with respect to its subcultures. Certain communities in their subcultural style would still reflect their relations to their founding mother cities. The activities of the so-called "Hellenists" in Jerusalem according to 1 and 2 Maccabees demonstrated another possibility, namely, that a community, here Jerusalem, could adopt a mother city, here Antioch, and her way of life. In very large cities such as Alexandria, Rome, or Antioch there were actually different subcommunities, called πολιτεύματα, that would live according to the mother culture or city they related to, such as Jews, Syrians, and others. In the Antiochene

new meaning. This covenantal perspective remains at issue in view in most of Paul's passages that deal with the collection.

I already mentioned that, for the biblical and Jewish mind, remembrance was a major element of covenantal thinking and practice. All covenants that the Bible tells about have a memorial part. This relates to the past not only passively but also actively, making memory a major stimulus of present and future activity. This remembering related to events as well as to people. The mutual recognition of differences included the respect for different histories and for cultural differences, in which religion always played a major role. The Jerusalem convention proved that for the persons and communities involved the differences could not be overcome by sentiment alone. Legal, indeed, constitutional agreements and concrete consequences were necessary. This is the background of Paul's dispute with Peter in Antioch.

The conclusion of a covenant of constitutional importance in Jerusalem demonstrated that the monetary dimension was of more than a charitable nature, something other than a sentimental, moral, and educational effort. It had something like cultural dimension and effect, yet under a legal perspective. The phrase "remembering the poor" certainly had a present and a future tense to it. It meant a concern for the "poor ones" in the sense of really impoverished people. That concern was supposed to express itself now and tomorrow. Was it meant to have a revolutionary dimension? For Paul it definitely had. It meant a new, a modular community.

The surrounding society of New Testament times was aware that by giving money or other contributions to persons, institutions, or issues four things were achieved: (1) a beneficial effect for the recipient(s) of the gift, resulting in grateful acclamation in public; (2) a beneficial effect for the benefactor in terms of his or her social, and even more his or her legal and political, status in public; (3) an improvement of the cultural climate, to which often belonged a respect that transcended the present time and was directed to past and future, all of which resulted in (4) a benefit for the economy. The costly concern that expressed itself in beneficial deeds

---

conflict, Paul represents a literal interpretation of the Jerusalem accord. According to this understanding, a congregation would have to stick to the way of life and theology once adopted. Individual Jesus believers entering an established congregation would have to choose whether they wanted to adopt the particular lifestyle of the congregation visited or whether they wanted to follow the lifestyle of their previous denomination. The latter would mean that one either conducted one's way separate of the larger congregation but with different provisions and in a different style, a side-table arrangement, so to speak, or that one founded a new congregation.

created a spirit of general trust in which people could feel at home and without which no economy can survive, let alone flourish.[47]

4. THEOLOGICAL CONSEQUENCES

The last part of my essay deals with the theological consequences of the questions raised and the observations made thus far. Occasionally I have already made suggestions as I went along. I shall limit myself to some exemplary hints, mainly concerning the doctrine of God.

The first and most obvious issue is the need to reconsider the character and function of the law in religion and theology. Luther's doctrine of law and gospel will not do any longer—if it ever really did. Theology in all its branches needs to rediscover and elaborate the positive dimensions of law, its constructive and prophetic character. In addition, we must also learn to appreciate the many hints in the New Testament that the Jewish understanding of the Torah in the first century C.E. was not isolationist but also related to human law at large. All of this is much more than an ethical matter.

The theological mind must become aware that law and economy connect in the biblical world and outside of it. Adam Smith is usually taken as the whipping boy of theological and common Christian criticism of capitalism. This overlooks the fact that Smith was also the author of *The Theory of Moral Sentiment*.[48] Smith's *An Inquiry into the Nature and Causes of the Wealth of Nations* did not invent greed as the motor of economy.[49] Smith in the *Wealth of Nations* tried to harness the blatant exploitative capitalism of the robber barons of his day. For this purpose, he applied concepts of enlightened Scottish Presbyterianism. It is obvious that the idea of the self-regulating character of the market and its beneficial end is an application of the Presbyterian doctrine of providence and theodicy. It

---

47. It is clear that not all members experienced these cultural and economic blessings, indeed relatively few. But the number who believed in these possibilities was very high—as the growth of the cities proved. And promises were something critics could take up in their challenge of society and make part of their own pledge to achieve a fulfillment of promises that the governing powers were withholding or destroying for their own benefit. The early church belongs into this category of critics and radical reformers.

48. First edition, London, 1759; sixth edition 1790; this edition edited by D. D. Raphael and A. L. Macfie (vol. 1 of the *Glasgow Edition of the Works and Correspondence of Adam Smith*; Oxford: Oxford University Press; Indianapolis: Liberty Classics, 1976).

49. First edition, London, 1776; fifth edition, 1789; now vol. 2 in the Glasgow edition cited in n. 48, edited by R. H. Campbell, A. S. Skinner, and W. B. Todd (Oxford: Oxford University Press, 1976).

is also typical for this enlightened Calvinism that the concept of reason is introduced as the proper accompaniment of divine providence, working in and through the market. Of course, Smith does not say this openly. He wants to meet the capitalists on their own terrain, the market. However, the translation of greed into enlightened self-interest cannot be explained directly from philosophical presuppositions. It has some theological background. Why have in the area of theology only ethicists dialogued with Smith? The state of the discussion of the nature and role of the law in New Testament studies is part of the explanation.

The next point I want to make relates to the issue of power. Protestant theology is still tempted to interpret God's power as absolute power, restrained merely by love. Feminist critique of patriarchy has shown that love can be a higher form of despotism, not restraining but enhancing the violent dimensions of power. It has to be noted that issues of freedom and human rights, so important for Paul, as we saw in 1 Cor 9, have at best entered ethical and anthropological deliberations, for instance in the context of free will. They have not invaded the thinking and speaking about God in any depth.

Ancient philosophers and also Jewish theologians such as Philo tried to move out of that entanglement by putting the idea of God into the world of complete abstraction, far above the daily fray of gods truly worshiped. Christian theologians have taken that attitude further, and Protestant theologians have refined these abstractions even more. Modern theology has continued to do this. It is claimed that this abstraction into the beyond is the best answer to the present multireligious situation as well. However, such confrontation with a multifarious religious context is not as new as is often claimed. The Hellenistic-Roman environment of Judaism and the New Testament presented a climate not that different. Recognizing that a great number of religions were at the time in competition with one another also implied that the various gods confessed and prayed to were in a competitive relation. By acknowledging this also for the Christian religion today within our contemporary multireligious world, we put the Christian deity into the same situation. Christian theologians would do better to integrate this into their reflections about God than try to come up with higher abstractions, with ensuing generalizations that are irrelevant to anyone confessing or praying.

The medieval concept of *aseitas dei,* that is, the self-sufficiency and self-justification of God, is still predominant in Protestant theology. This medieval concept, by the way, is also the source of the modern understanding of sovereignty, in politics as well as in theology. Much of what is written, preached and taught about the understanding of God reminds one of "Big Brother" in Orwell's *1984.*

The interplay of power, grandeur, investment, and achievement that is characteristic for Hellenistic-Roman society, its economy, and its legal dimensions has been discussed in my book *The Opponents of Paul in 2 Corinthians*, in the essay on the "divine man" already mentioned, and in *Theocracy in Paul's Practice and Theory*. I have given hints how this can be integrated into theology and Christology. The proximity of medieval cathedrals and abject, even deadly poverty in the cities of the Middle Ages gives an example of how disastrous the alliance of a certain power-obsessed theology and monetary and cultural investment can become.

In a systematic arrangement of my essay, now would be the place for talking about competition as well as about solidarity within the understanding not only of the church or of the Christ but also of God. However, there is not enough room left to discuss the relevance of the concept of competition to our understanding of God.[50] There have been considerable attempts to use the idea of solidarity in theology at large. Much of it remained on the moralistic and sentimental side. The legal and economic dimensions of sharing authority, power, impoverishment, suffering, costs, and benefits have remained underdeveloped in theological thought. The idea of God profiting from sticking to his creation still appears blasphemous to us, despite Judaism's and the early church's unabashed interrelation of divine grace and thanksgiving in a rather synergistic fashion, following the cyclical relation of χάρις and εὐχαριστία in the Hellenistic-Roman society discussed earlier. Paul can even equalize grace and a sum of money, shared with God as well as humans. Here the biblical suggestions about a close relationship of solidarity, justice, promise, and justification need to be worked out further, including their relationship to the culture, economy, and laws of their environment. The biblical dialogue with surrounding religions and cultures can give innumerable examples for that.

The concept of covenant stands close by. Our democratic forebears learned from the Bible that the covenant cannot be concrete enough. Legal, social, and economic dimensions need to be included. Where has

---

50. The idea of competition was common in the society and economy of New Testament times, also in religion. There were definitely also some positive legal aspects to this. Contrary to that expressed in the Bible, the modern theological understanding of God is far removed from such earthly patterns. The First Testament already sees the God of Israel in competition with other gods. An example would be a text such as Isa 40:12-26. Here Israel's God and its religion are clearly set in competition with other religions and their gods. Marduk or Isis could make statements like that, too. There are many other similar texts. The evolution of biblical-Jewish angelology also fits into this pattern. Another good example is 1 Cor 8:4–6.

the covenant of Jerusalem or of the Scottish Covenanters or of the New England Puritans gone? Following the spirit of the biblical understanding of covenant, Massachusetts called itself a commonwealth, an ingenious translation of the Latin term *res publica*.[51] This does not imply "public matters" alone. The addition of welfare does not suffice either. Common wealth proper is included, too, and long before the Communist Manifesto. In consequence, a certain clash follows, namely, between common wealth and profit. Commonwealth and covenant, two basics, especially in Massachusetts, imply a beneficial atmosphere of and for all. Is this part of our theological agenda for tomorrow?

Some ideas could be gained from the environment of the New Testament, where the idea and practice of money consciously and concretely related to an atmosphere of general benefit, an atmosphere caused not merely by filtering down profits but actively created by the gods and others who possess wealth. How, in dealing with personal and public consciousness, do we engender the idea that profit makes sense only if it stays close to the commonwealth in its double meaning?

Two terms, closely related to the interplay of economy and law, reveal the sorry state of present affairs. I am thinking of the terms *private* and *interest*. Who thinks of the etymology of these terms anymore? *Privatus* is the "one who is robbed," robbed of all communal relations. Interest comes from *interesse*, which means engaged presence. In order to recover some of the original meaning of these terms in our present situation, theology has a lot to do. Public consciousness has to be changed again; the wrong direction common consciousness took in the late Middle Ages when the modern monetary system and capitalism developed on the British Isles has to be corrected. A major force in that change of public consciousness was the new meaning mendicant monks gave to *res* and *realitas*. They appeared at first sight to be rather abstract philosophical terms, yet in fact they were ideas with quite concrete and disastrous consequences. We have to move beyond that alleged "realism."

---

51. The use of this term, borrowed from the Puritan Revolution in Britain, to designate a state in the United States, is not limited to Massachusetts but is found also in the cases of Kentucky, Pennsylvania, and Virginia.

8

LIVING WITH CHAOS: MEDITATIONS ON PAUL'S ETHICS

Speaking about legal issues, the ancient world had an understanding of the close relationship of law and prophecy, not only in Israel and Judea and the worldwide synagogue. The legal and the visionary would not necessarily exclude each other; on the contrary, they were closely interrelated everywhere, and not only in prehistoric times. It remained a fact even after prophets had left their initial location, the countryside, and entered the cities. Isaiah, Jeremiah, and Ezekiel are the most prominent of these urban prophets in Israel. In chapter 3 of this book I have described the importance that people such as Virgil and Horace had for the Caesar religion and the culture of the Roman Empire. I have emphasized that these theologians were prophets and poets alike, and they were urban residents when they envisioned and wrote their poetry. As they helped to shape future cultural consciousness they described in their dreams not merely the revival of the Roman ethos of the past but projected a new ethos as well. *Lex* and *leges* were basic for such a prophetic ethos. They demonstrated that ethical and legal perceptions and pronouncements easily associated with visionary perspectives and creative anticipations. This was common in the Mediterranean and in Near and Middle East, most prominently among Jews and Romans. In the following essay I argue that Paul's ethics belongs into this kind of prophecy too, clearly urban prophecy. As all good prophecy, Israelite, Jewish or pagan, it had a critical, indeed a challenging, dimension.

1. LAW AND CHAOS

The world in which we live is conditioned by laws, norms, and principles. Legitimacy and order are major concerns. Social and political spheres are governed by such considerations, as are the fields of education and of religion. The concepts of law and order dominate in particular the modern sciences. Ideological bases and presuppositions and social and political consequences of the use of the concept of law in the context of natural and behavioral sciences have not yet really been analyzed and debated. Paul's thesis that the law is a murderer (2 Cor 3:6) and that "Christ is the end of the law" (Rom 10:4) sounds strange within this modern context, where there are not only many more laws than at the time of the First or Second Testament but where laws have also become much more domineering.

Usually the radicality of the statement just quoted is softened. However, the claim that Rom 10:4 speaks only of Christ's fulfillment of the law is shattered by the antitheses and polarities within the text and its context. Furthermore, this softening has no basis elsewhere in Paul's other letters either: Gal 3:2; 2 Cor 3, and all of Romans—especially Rom 10—are all of the same critical nature. We do not have merely polemical overstatements here, since Rom 10:4 is not directed against any particular opponents. It is also incorrect to argue that Paul's statements merely meant the law of the First Testament—as misunderstood by Paul's Jewish contemporaries—and that they could not be applied to law in general. Paul does not want to limit his discussion to contemporary abuse, misunderstanding, or a certain party opinion. Paul means the law of Moses as such. Yet from the Epistle to the Galatians, particularly chapter 3, we learn that the law for him is not limited to a certain religious community. It relates to all human beings and to the world at large before the coming of Jesus the Christ. It is the law that governs history and the world.

Paul understands the law as universally treacherous, as a deceiving and deluding power that enslaves and murders the human race. Whereas this power pretends to order and to protect, it in reality creates chaos and kills. Paul is not convinced of the old and durable doctrine that the law is a power that protects the human race on an island of order, the creation, against the surrounding, ever-threatening primordial chaos. Paul's argument in the first three chapters of Romans, for instance, proves convincingly that the law, in his opinion, does not protect against chaos but that it leads into chaos, even more, that the law causes chaos.

For Paul, the proclamation of Jesus Christ is a proclamation against the law. It is curious that in its two-thousand-year history Christian ethics was hardly ever developed on the basis of Paul's thesis that Christ is the end of the law and that the law is a murderer. Almost any attempt to take up this idea and to relate it to church, society, and world has been very quickly suppressed in its roots, often in a bloody fashion, especially by "Christian" authorities under the influence of allegedly "Christian" tradition.

In order better to understand what Paul means when he speaks of Christ as the end of the law, we have to see that Paul refers in the context of Rom 10:4 to the biblical book of Deuteronomy. Paul reads there in 30:12–14 that God's commandment is neither hidden nor stored away in heaven nor in the sea's abyss. There is no need for any great effort to search for it. It is close, in the mouth and in the heart of the people of Israel. The Israelites can carry out the commandments of God right now.

This particular biblical passage had posed riddles for Jewish exegetes for hundreds of years before Paul, and still during his lifetime. The claims of Deuteronomy seemed not to have come true in the history of Israel. If the commandment of the Lord was so close, why was it not obeyed? Why had Israel fallen so often for unbelief and apostasy and, therefore, experienced judgment after judgment?

The most important solution that exegetes found was based on the distinction already made by the book of Deuteronomy, the distinction between the spoken and the written (codified) word of God. Many exegetes of old were of the opinion that the written word was the closer one. They saw it as the more accessible one and, therefore, as the true center of Israel.

However, there was also an important exegetical tradition in Judaism that stated the opposite, namely, that the unwritten word, the oral communication of God, was the center of Jewish faith. These exegetes saw the written word as a mere reflection of the unwritten one. Scripture, therefore, required special insight and art in order to grasp God's live communication behind the letter and to make it understandable. The oral word behind the written word was most often identified with God's wisdom.

Paul is influenced by this second exegetical tradition, but he breaks with the common agreement that the law/commandment was to be seen as the concept that connected the two words. Paul follows a suggestion he found in the book of Deuteronomy that identifies God's word as the living word. Whereas for Deuteronomy this is the book of the law, Paul concludes, on the contrary, from this statement about the living word of God in Deuteronomy that only the written word is the law. The living word, instead, is the oral word, and that is the Christ, who for Paul was preexistent already. For Paul, only Christ, like the living word of God in Deuteronomy, is close, namely, in the form of the word of preaching and in the confession of faith. This Christ as the living word of God has terminated the epoch of the written word, the law. The Christ event has revealed that the law hindered true understanding and destroyed the people of God.

In these exegetical deliberations of Paul, the experience of the early church's worship is presupposed and used. There the conviction ruled that the living Christ was present and spoke himself. He presented himself through the mouths of the many prophets in the exegesis of scriptures, in hymns, creeds, and acclamations. The Christ himself was the creative source behind the many sayings of the Lord and of the Jesus stories. Christ was experienced as present, especially in the Eucharist, as host, Lord, and brother as much as the sacramental gift, as the one who communicated himself and his action to the people. Thus the word of God, that is, the Christ communicating himself, was truly near. It/he challenged and provoked the congregation continuously as they assembled for worship. The word created and maintained this congregation. It stimulated their imagination and their actions. Therefore, the congregation had every reason to identify this creative force with the word of the creator of heaven and earth.

The problem people had with the law can be well illustrated by a moving scene of the early Paul Newman movie *Cool Hand Luke*. Here the police in the schoolhouse of his old village, a building where worship had apparently also taken place, have found Luke, the inmate, who has escaped prison (i.e., the law). Luke is besieged by the powers of law enforcement. He opens a window and says to the waiting policemen and prison guards, "Gentlemen, I believe there is a communication problem," and the deadly bullets cut him down. The Pauline church and many others understood the law as the power that clogs communication and oppresses the administrators and enforcers of the law as much as the remainder of humankind.

2. LAW AS CREATIVE PROPHETIC FORCE

The opening of the window as well as the spoken word, they do it, so Paul would say with respect to Jesus Christ, the model for the *Cool Hand Luke* of the movie. The opening of the window and the spoken word, they blow away the terrifying spell of the murderous law. But what about guns and bullets? The execution of Jesus has taken place. The person who had stepped forward in order to start communication was killed—but that did it, that broke the spell, that created a worldwide community of hope and engaging power. Christlike characteristics exist in abundance all over the world and have always existed, but there was the one seemingly unfortunate accident that started the new move, that had these worldwide reactions, which then started changing everything else.

In pursuing the ethical consequences of this, we can follow the outline of Paul's Epistle to the Romans. There the presentation of ethical questions in the second part of the letter, that is, Rom 12–15, is merely the other side of the Pauline idea of the importance of the Christ event for all of humankind as expressed in the first part of the epistle (Rom 1–11). One could describe the intentions of the first part of Romans as a reflection on the new light that history and humankind have received from the Christ. The second part of Romans speaks about the bodily aspects of this new revelation, the physical and corporate dimensions. As Paul speaks of the body of Christ, he first of all thinks of collective bodies, only secondarily of bodies of single persons. The collective bodies he refers to in the first place are small corporations, namely, the individual congregations. The global aspect of the body of Christ is only secondary. For Paul, personal ethics is only possible under this collective, this corporate perspective. Nowadays we are only slowly rediscovering that ethics is something else than the dichotomy of institutionalized collective moral systems on the one hand and individualized I-Thou relationships on the other. In Paul's congregations, every member realizes that there is no polarity between the corporate and the single person but a dialectic relationship of mutual integration. Each person is conscious that her or his life is caused and influenced by relationships that are beyond her or his control, namely, the relationships within the single congregation and also the relationships between the congregations of the church at large. Paul makes no attempt to channel or control these transpersonal relationships, to force them into an institutionalized value system comparable to medieval or Victorian morals or Puritan ethics. On the contrary, in the Pauline churches each one and all together help nurture a continuous imaginative and practical exchange of ethical experiences, insights, and suggestions and support the mutual communication of the living word.[1] Paul understands his ethical deliberations as competing with the initiatory rites of pagan and Jewish Hellenism. The Pauline exhortations can be called docket material for the liturgy of the early church. In other words, ethics is communal worship for Paul, the celebration of the new creation.

In texts such as Rom 12 and 1 Cor 14, the worship of Jesus believers is described as an enterprise that causes spiritual transformation and new rational insight at the same time. The experience is colorful, inspired and inspiring, and critical as well as sharing and participatory. The ecstatic excitement is as present as the sober responsibility for new and old members of the congregation and for the life of the community as a whole. The life of the community, the congregation, is by no means understood as an established phenomenon, regulated and objectifiable, but as a collective

---

1. Congregation and church function as markets and fairs with strong influences from ethical ideas and practices from outside the church, Jewish as well as pagan. They are looked at, integrated, and exchanged with great liberality.

experiment. The Pauline term *edification,* which must be mentioned here, does not mean the emotional private experience of an individual that one would gain from a religious speech or action; rather, edification means collective experimentation in a communal lifestyle, a lifestyle that incorporates and represents tendencies that reach into an unforeseeable future. The prophetic element in Pauline worship, and that means in Paul's ethics, should not be overlooked. Prophets are constitutive for Pauline worship, and it is expected from everyone that she or he become a prophet. Isaiah, Jeremiah, Ezekiel, and the other biblical prophets are all shown to be relevant and democratized. There are no aristocrats. All members are, like the prophets of old, viziers, ministers, and foreign secretaries in the divine court. The local worship is for Paul and his congregations an essential part of the meeting of the divine government, taking place not in outer space but here and now.

Christ's prophets possess the ability to uncover what the world, what people are all about. The prophets really bring home what makes sense in ordinary life. Is this cheap evangelism? Certainly nothing of the kind we have today. Already the great number of prophets then present in every worship service would speak against such comparison. There was no soul-searching either. Whoever was hit by the prophets' communications personally lost interest in her or his own identity, turned away from herself or himself and turned toward the center of the community and with it to everyone around. The prophetic proclamation led them and made them recognize that the community was placed at the heart of creation itself. The new creation pulsated and flourished. "God is truly in your midst!" was the confession Paul hoped for from persons at the margin of the congregation and even from outsiders, according to 1 Cor 14:25. This, for Paul, would be the acclamation and ratification of the authenticity of the church's worship.

We are accustomed to identify prophets with grandiose schemes, but small change is the currency of revolutions. We see in Paul's letters that the prophetic challenge within his congregations breaks down the barriers of legal and moral systems and the rigidity and frustration that go with them. Neither pride nor despair survives. Instead, we find an unlimited number of suggestions for a new lifestyle. Ethics for Paul and his communities is the domain of prophetic happenings every Sunday, but this ethics appears in the form of dozens, even hundreds, of suggestive remarks.[2] The prophets of the Christ faith are to a degree like the popular

---

2. The Jesus believers make liberal use of the storehouses of ethical insight of earlier centuries.

ethicists, the migrant philosophers, the hippies of the ancient world: they break up the rigid systems of early philosophies and of general morals into bits and pieces and organize the parts into new, colorful patterns. Pauline ethics possesses even more kaleidoscopic characters than Cynic-Stoic popular philosophy. We may presume that the prophets in the congregations founded by Paul used their communications as kaleidoscopes, too. An unlimited number of new, colorful variations were produced from the fragments of past and common ethical insights. This occurred in order to expand expectation and courage among the members of the congregations. They were to be encouraged to become active prophets themselves.

If we compare the style and content of the many exhortations in the Pauline letters, the unsystematic character and the associative force is as overwhelming as the range of variations.[3] No exhortation repeats the previous one. There is no general organizing principle except variety itself. There is a suggestive style already mentioned that calls for an unlimited number of variations and additions.

All exhortations hint at a certain direction. The suggestive power aims at the future. In these innumerable suggestions, deliberations, and encouragements the new creation is projected and anticipated. The prophets in the Pauline congregations, including the founder, are continuously in the process of sketching the Day of the Lord in ever-new variations, the future Day of the Lord in the present one. These sketches are of an impressionistic kind because they do not want to overwhelm the single member of the congregation, let alone oppress her or him; they want to suggest, eliciting creative imagination, confidence, and courage.

These prophets of the early church are not interested in monumental pictures of paradise, neither the past nor the coming one. These pictures would only be repressive. The style and tendency of these sketches are instead pragmatic. I am inclined to call Paul's ethics utopian or pragmatically utopian. In his eyes, the prophets (including himself) suggest a lifestyle that anticipates the future, in which freedom will take its course.

Compared with our ethics defined by negations and prohibitions and our judgmental style of preaching, the exhortations of Paul surprise because of their almost complete absence of negations. The interest is not in what is wrong or in what ought not to be; on the contrary, there is concern for positive suggestions. This is the different sense of direction showing in Paul's ethics: the encouragement for freedom expressing itself

---

3. On occasions, there is a limit. In 1 Corinthians, especially in chapter 5, Paul sometimes shows but a limited degree of tolerance.

in proposals intended to excite, not with irrational excitement but with an excitement that awakens attentive reason, clear imagination, and courageous action. It is an encouragement for freedom that means a developed sensitivity for one's actual situation and surrounding and for one's contemporaries. The inspiration of all members of the congregation, their initiative, and their activity—these nurture this utopian pragmatism. A good deal of Paul's ethics is empowerment. Thereby the congregation is guarded against the possibility of turning into a passive and numb mass that would suffer manipulation and turn into a totalitarian instrument against others.

Reason and imagination create tact, too. One is able to empathize with others, even with those who are not members of the congregation or the church at large. In fact, the ability of these outsiders to understand what is going on in the congregation becomes the decisive measure for the Christ believers' constructive contribution to the community.

There is criticism in this community. If a prophet seemed to discover that the urge into the future and the sense for the freedom of the congregation are overlooked or even forgotten, he or she would speak up. This is what Paul does in 1 Corinthians, his extended prophetic contribution to the worship service of the congregation. However, this criticism is open for discussion. Often enough, prophet stands against prophet, and Paul, too, is not beyond the reach of the public scrutiny of the whole assembly. There is no superceding tribunal, and there is no judge on earth to adjudicate this. Paul tells people that they should not rely on the future judgment. Even in the case of the fornicator of 1 Cor 5 Paul expects that the spirit in the fornicator, his belonging to the community, would be the turning force in the divine judgment. This heavenly force would lead to his acquittal. Thus, the suggested excommunication of the culprit, in fact, would be merely temporary.[4] Therefore even the apostle, the founder of the congregation, has only one vote. Paul's discussion of the case in 1 Cor 5:1–5 appears too severe for modern liberal taste, yet even there Paul proves that the ethics that he suggests to the Corinthians as well as to all his congregations remains constructive. The prevailing tendency of church discipline in his congregations is not the exclusion of someone from the people of God. Instead, it is the continuous attempt to keep the member in the body of the community through all dissent and rupture.

---

4. 1 Cor 5:5. However, Paul does not and cannot decree such excommunication. He can only suggest it through the statement in the letter referred to. This expressed wish is merely a proxy to be communicated in the assembly of the congregation in Corinth. Whether the assembly will go along with Paul or decide by majority vote against him will have to be discovered. In the final tally Paul's proxy will count as only one vote.

The Pauline community does not know a complete severance from the community of salvation, even less one that would be forever binding and that the final judgment would have to abide by. The Lord who is identified with the dialogue ruling the community makes the dialogue itself the constructive disciplining tool, the weight being with positive concepts and attitudes.

3. THE LIFESTYLE OF THE PAULINE CHURCHES

Thus, the Pauline congregations are actively engaged in an open lifestyle, open to the future, open to others and to their insights, and open to suggestions from outside. The congregation is not defined by its borders but by its center. No esoteric theory is leading it but rather an imaginative use of common sense—a very British community, it appears to me. In fact, both the Pauline congregation and British society have Stoic influence in common. Paul exhorts his people to look around with critical imagination and to trace values that could be used creatively and constructively within the context of the Christ faith. We find syncretism and eclecticism right in the center of Pauline ethics. The historical diversity of people assembled for worship is fully recognized, the differences of their origins as much as the differences of their actual situations. However, origins and situations are not petrified. Paul teaches his communities not to capitulate before the power of strong ideological or social forces that would come from outside. He makes them ready to listen to the outside, but such listening is neither subordination nor cynical relativism or even skepticism.

The open style described means, on the contrary, a truly critical dialogue with the world, be it Jewish or pagan. The freedom to recognize, acknowledge, and integrate contributions of unbelievers implies the lack of respect for the alleged exclusiveness, completeness, and perfection of the value systems from which these contributions stem. This critical and selective attitude toward systems is borne by the conviction that Christ is the end of the law.

The world as constituted by the law, whether the law of Moses, of the philosophers, of Alexander, of Caesar, or of Nero, this world of the law is not taken seriously. Since the law has found its end, it no longer has any right or power over people. This is demonstrated by the attitude with which Paul and his communities look at Jewish and pagan culture as a treasure house of values. It can be exploited by people who are liberated from the law's oppression. They can use it as they want—for constructive purposes. Their context is now the dialogue within the congregation of Jesus Christ and the exchange of that community with the world.

This picture of the early church appears to be anarchic, and if ever there was an anarchist, it was Paul. But in which sense? In the ordinary sense of the term *an-archist,* that is, without *arche,* without a ruling head and without a mediating structure, an anarchist who does not acknowledge any centralized, vertical, hierarchic value system together with its structure of leadership and central control. Even Christ cannot be seen as the tip of a pyramid, in this case the church, because in Paul's authentic letters Christ is not the head of the church. Christ and his body are identical instead. Christ is the people.

Does this not invite chaos? In a way, yes; it is conscious living with chaos. Is it chaos in the eyes of Paul, too? No, for him chaos is in those entities that promise to protect against chaos. For Paul, chaos is the suicidal and destructive cycle of law and legalistic behavior that destroys persons, groups, and societies again and again.

This chaos created and maintained by law and order has lost its terror since Christ was killed by the law. This law is quoted in Gal 3:13, which speaks of the curse of the law, primarily the Torah. However, the law Paul is speaking about in Gal 3 and 4 goes beyond the Jewish one. It also comprises the rules that govern the Mediterranean at the time, that is, Roman law. In Paul's eyes, Jesus has died by force of the chaos power that is within all law. This killing of God's agent has, according to Paul, been a deadly blow that the law administered against itself. Therefore, now the following rule is true: wherever there is the Christ, there is new creation. It does not need any protection from the outside. This new creation is no longer a pretentious island claiming to be outside of chaos and protecting from it. It is, instead, within the turbulence of human beings trying to organize and regulate their relationships, small as well as large. This new creation is ready to experiment with the unlimited imagination of divine providence inspiring humans. Paul's ethics shows no trust in institutions and systems; rather, it shows trust in God and in people.

Therefore, even laws can be interpreted anew. They can be demythologized. They can be stripped of their undue claims and promises. This way they can be understood in a creative way, namely, as reasonable human suggestions and arrangements. They can suggest; they can be creative. Arrangements thus made can be measured according to the quality of the future that they are able to open. And they are measured according to the number of people whom they are able constructively to integrate, that is, not merely as subordinate, obedient subjects or objects but as active and creative persons. In the form of this constructive potential, the law can turn into a prophetic category, an open and opening outline for the communal life of tomorrow, imaginative anticipation and visionary empowerment.

Thus, an ethic oriented on Jesus as the Christ can produce arrangements that are formed around prophetic proposals, the ever-renewed sketches of pragmatic utopia uttered by Christ's common prophets. If one reads Paul carefully enough, one can discover a community of faith that is called to be a pragmatic model of its own proclamation of the new creation, a community that offers itself to the consciousness of everyone and to life in general. This community is fundamentally disloyal vis-à-vis every ideology or system but is, for the sake of solidarity with all people, a determined avant-garde that publicly calls for general subversion. The church of Jesus Christ incorporated by God into the bringing about of his new creation has no time to swing beyond the world nor any time to be satisfied with its own importance and achievement. The church of God pulsates with life and is efficient because it is the community that is ready for a daily reformation out of its very midst.

9

WHY WAS PAUL KILLED? THE EPISTLE TO THE ROMANS AS A DOCUMENT OF RESISTANCE

1. INTRODUCTORY OBSERVATIONS

The ancient world knew of rural rebellions, and not only the biblical and intertestamental traditions give examples for the countryside as basis for intended larger revolutions. On the whole, however, the urban environment was more common as a seedbet of rebellions, especially when they intended to challenge given power structures. Such seditious efforts by definition needed a more refined conspiratorial preparation. Scholars of antiquity, however, have spent little time and effort researching those more secretive ventures. With very few exceptions, not much has been done to explore the dimensions of resistance to Roman rule within the empire beyond the phenomena of outright rebellion. Not only the term *resistance* but also related concepts such as *opposition, conspiracy, plot, cabal,*

---

* This paper was given at the Mid-Atlantic and Eastern-Lake Regional meetings of the Society of Biblical Literature and at Union Theological Seminary. This paper presupposes that Paul was tried, convicted, and executed in Rome, with all probability in 62 C.E. Our oldest sources do not state directly and clearly that Paul was forcibly killed. The so-called Deutero-Pauline epistles, Colossians and Ephesians, 2 Thessalonians, the Pastoral Epistles, and the book of Acts were all written in the name of Paul after Paul's death. These documents camouflage Paul's end in indirect language. That is significant. It proves that the form of Paul's death was something unusual, if not embarrassing or even endangering to his school and his congregations. In addition, Revelation and *1 Clement* also hint at Paul's death. These documents speak of Paul's end in a veiled fashion, in particular Colossians, Acts, and *1 Clement*. The early church could and would not invent the idea of Paul's death being carried out by the state. It would have embarrassed, even endangered them. If Paul's forcible end would have had any trace of innocence, the documents mentioned, especially Colossians, Acts, and *1 Clement*, would have elaborated on that.

and *intrigue* are hard to find in the relevant dictionaries, lexica, and encyclopedias. The Caesar religion with its claim of being a force, indeed the form of liberation and salvation, guarded this assertion with jealousy. Suspicion of counterclaims and of plotting activities that would spread such asseverations was rampant and had its instruments in public and secret police and their many agents, informers, and spies. Claudius's active dealings with Jews in Rome, with Druids in Gaul, but also with the Attis cult and with the Eleusine mysteries prove that the Caesar was interested in getting and keeping popular religions under control, if necessary by repression. State activities, however, tended to remain below the level of outright persecution. Interference with the activities of leading figures offered itself as a clever measure of discipline. The holders of political power were conscious of the explosive mix of "outsiders," extraneous people who congregated in the *insulae*, the living quarters of the big cities, most of all of the capital Rome. The satirist Juvenal, around the turn of the century, proves that there were reasons for the suspicion of communication lines between the *insulae* and the living quarters of the rich and influential. One of the supporters of Paul in the Roman veterans' colony Corinth was the treasurer of that city, Erastus, certainly a Roman citizen, a person with means and influence.

2. THE PROBLEMS OF ASSOCIATING PAUL AND RESISTANCE

Professors and students of theology in the Western world do their work completely unaware of the fact that the study and teaching of theology could imply the danger of getting jailed, shot, decapitated, or hanged.[1] Yet as I came to the United States, I learned that studying, teaching, and doing theology can become dangerous. This was drastically demonstrated to me by the fate of two of my former students at Harvard Divinity School. Both got into trouble with the Ku Klux Klan trying to apply what they had learned in Cambridge, Massachusetts. One was shot dead in bright daylight in North Carolina; the other, after various threats on his life, was driven out of his parish and his home state West Virginia, with the state police telling him that they were no longer able to protect him. South of the latitude of North Africa, people are much more aware of such possibilities.[2] Urban environments are not

---

1. The first form of this chapter was written in New York when I was Dietrich Bonhoeffer research-exchange scholar. So this start with a Bonhoeffer point is appropriate.

2. My Frankfurt students experienced a drastic illustration of the danger of engaged theology when we learned that the president of the university of San Salvador was shot together with his compadres and confreres a week after he had delivered a lecture in my class.

safer than the countryside. On the contrary, Paul's letter to the Romans gives major suggestions concerning resistance in an urban environment.

However, the common understanding of Paul's Epistle to the Romans, entertained for almost two millennia, would take anything but this document as a demonstration of resistance. It is especially the beginning of the chapter 13 that informs the understanding of this document as advertising obedience to the state, if not conformity. I shall demonstrate that, in reality, the text speaks for the opposite. Indeed, it was Paul's Epistle to the Romans that caused his death. Under the cover of a code, this letter took on the Caesar religion, and thereby the Caesar. This attack of the Caesar provided the grounds for Paul's conviction and execution. Paul's being killed cannot be explained any other way.

In order to make you understand my thesis, I have to presuppose that the Caesar cult generated veneration that was much more extensive than would be expected from an official cult. This cult, with temples, sacrifices, festal days, and all other cultic implements, was meticulously maintained by ordained Augustan priests. It served not only the Caesars but also the city of Rome and its people, the entire empire, and people living within it. It maintained the welfare of the universe. The range of its purpose made this cult an interesting object for those living in the empire, fascinating indeed. This did not happen against the intention of the Caesars, on the contrary. Thus the Caesar cult became the nucleus of the Caesar religion. It became the expression of the religious reverence as shown and exercised by the Roman nobility and the army but also by the entire Roman population. It transcended even the boundaries of Roman citizenship. Philo's panegyric about Julius Caesar, Augustus, and Tiberius in his tractate *Legatio ad Gaium* is a prominent example of an admiration the Caesars enjoyed among noncitizens. The threshold to religious reverence is slight. Revelation 13, 17, and 18 give a differentiated portrait of the veneration the people of the Roman Empire gave to the beast. The beast is the Caesar as origin and object of the religion that the Romans established and nourished. The people's worship is not portrayed as enforced. It is described as a blend of planned temptation and voluntary consent.

I shall approach the subject of my essay in three steps. The first and major part will show how and why the Epistle to the Romans turned into a coded letter for me. I shall sketch what the code was and how it worked. The second part will give some samples of the decoded message. I shall show that it is a message of resistance. I shall limit myself to a selection from Rom 1–8. There is more of that to be found in my book *Theocracy in Paul's Practice and Theology.* In that book I have hinted at the nature of the letter as a coded message. This coded dimension I shall work out in this chapter a little more. The consequences of coding and unencoding in the letter to the Romans will be shown as well.

3. CODE LANGUAGE?

The term *code* has received tremendous use in recent times. This has not helped the precision of its understanding. On the contrary, the range of meanings and, therefore, also of imprecision has increased in geometrical proportions. Biological, medical, and computer language have contributed greatly to the growth in imprecision. Structuralism and literary criticism have added to the confusion in the area of literature.

I shall use the term *code* in the old-fashioned sense of encrypted language, as it is known from the world of military and other intelligence and from the world of diplomacy. Encoded language in the sense of implied coding also exists in literature. Allegories, allegorizing, and allegorical interpretation work with encryption and decipherment of methods and ideas in ways comparable to the coding and decoding used in military and diplomatic communication and intelligence.

This process of encoding and decoding, encrypting and deciphering expressed itself already in Roman times, and still does, in basically two ways. The first basic method was and is that of scrambling and unscrambling, with various forms of mathematics used as a basis for burying and unburying the real message. In literature close to the New Testament, gematria and magical language were of that kind. The other basic approach in coding and decoding presented and presents a surface text in a seemingly intelligible fashion, yet at the same kind entailing and communicating a hidden message. The encoded text had or has to look at the same time sufficiently innocent to the uninitiated eye as it betrays to the initiated eye that it wants to be read as an encoded text.

Espionage and intelligence are no modern invention, nor are secret messages. They existed in the ancient world since early times already. Aeneas Tacticus, the earliest known writer on military matters, reports on many different forms of secret communication. This was in the fourth century B.C.E. Cryptograms and cryptology were already advanced then. Egyptians and Mesopotamians had used it, and smaller powers as well. The methods of encrypting and decrypting were not used in the strict military contexts alone. They were found in diplomatic situations as well. Gematria is an example for the technique of cryptograms. Such communication always had to anticipate discovery. The written message had to present a definite intelligibility that would not cause the suspicion of the uninvited discoverer. That made the scribbling down of numbers a good cover. In case of longer texts, enciphering by marking individual letters according to a certain system also known to the expected reader was common. However, it was not all too safe, since the marking was visible to the unexpected reader, too, putting both message and bearer under suspicion.

I do not know of any surviving unmarked text that functioned as such a secretive message. They must have existed. However, since the codes and code books are lost, we cannot begin to decode. Allegories, allegorizing of texts, and allegorical interpretations are, however, such phenomena that have survived. I am certain that "bona fide" allegories preceded allegorizing practices and allegorical interpretations. Allegorizing and allegorical interpretation can offer clues about the connection between the idea of allegory and the maintenance of power and power games through encoding and decoding written communications of greater length. I have to refrain from discussing this further. It would take too long. Apocalyptic and gnostic texts prove that people dissenting and resisting power had learned to use the methods of allegorizing and allegorical interpretation. They present us with encoded messages of resistance waiting to be decoded. Allegorizing and allegorical interpretation were not at the whim of anyone for any message that one should like. They were very method-conscious. Conscious contradiction, intentional riddle, and forced puzzlement were essential indicators, either brought into the text, in the case of intended allegory, or found or presupposed in a text, in the case of allegorical interpretation. There was always the distinction between a surface text, either intentionally puzzlesome or believed to be puzzlesome, and giving away hidden clues as to decoding.

Paul learned these techniques of hiding and unveiling in the apocalyptic and gnostic environment of Jewish wisdom, his theological and organizational training ground.

4. A NEW LOOK AT ROMANS 13 AND ITS CONTEXT

Let me go back to my own story of discovery of the encoded character of Paul's Epistle to the Romans. Observations made on Rom 13:1–7 were at the base of the insights that I will present here. This appears strange because the exhortation of these verses about the proper relationship to political authorities seems to imply subordination under the governing authorities. This rather common assumption has been applied to the epistle at large as well. Many of the "God arguments" in Romans have been used in support of a basically hierarchical orientation, especially the description of the divine will as entirely arbitrary in chapter 9. Autocratic political structures often enough have been justified by such authoritarian interpretation of Paul's longest writing.

The curious alliance of Martin Dibelius, Heinrich Schlier, Julius Schniewind, and Karl Barth before and during the Nazi period arrived at an ambivalent opinion on the meaning of Rom 13:1–7. The *exousiai* here were seen as powers, and they were related to the powers in 1 Cor 2:8 and Col 1:16; 2:9–15. History of religion gave reason to introduce cosmic dimensions to these powers. Yet through this mix of texts one felt entitled to add the earthly side to this as well. This meant that the earthly powers were seen in a double light or potential. Their authority was of a cosmic, an angelic nature. That nature could go two ways: the true one would be working as God's beneficial instrument; the false one was the inclination toward the demonic. Ernst Käsemann blew the whistle on this ingenious interpretation. He placed the meaning of the passage into the context of the theology of Hellenistic Judaism, but not of a gnostic type. Käsemann argued for the independence of Rom 13:1–7 from its preceding and following contexts. He argued against any ideologizing and mythicizing of this overused text. These demythologizing tendencies had found expression in August Strobel's exegesis of Rom 13 as well. Strobel stressed the similarity of the terminology of this pericope to contemporary political and administrative language.

This was the point of departure of my own exegesis. It gained profile during the fight against German rearmament, especially nuclear armament. The governing Christian democrats advocated the return of German armed forces and their equipment with the most recent arsenal of mass destruction. In support of this, they used Rom 13, thus construing the reestablishment and rearmament of German forces to be required by divine will as supposedly expressed in that Pauline text.

I belonged to a group of theologians and lay people who upheld the critical tradition of the confessing church of the Third Reich. We attacked the ideological and theological motivation and justification of the conservative, if not reactionary, call for German arms. We likened the situation to that of 1933 and 1934, the time of the origin of the Barmen Confession. Thus in 1957–58 we prepared an update of the Barmen Confession, this with another false theology of the state in view, a theology that justified the use of absolute, unrestrained power in case of global confrontation. This is the autobiographical origin of the exegetical view presented here.

At that time, however, I did not yet think of codes or of Romans as a document of resistance. I merely responded and objected to a highly charged reactionary interpretation of Rom 13. I provided exegetical arguments for my group in our attempt to arrive at something like Barmen II, now in 1958 to be formulated in a confessional assembly of critical church people in Frankfurt on Main, my hometown.

Following Käsemann and Strobel, I assumed that the text presents Hellenistic-Jewish theological ideas about the relationship to contemporary political authorities, an exhortation of people to respect these powers in the name of God. This critical exegesis blew away the mythological steam of these authorities, a steam that in conservative interpretation had gained thermonuclear proportions. In these critical reflections, two observations struck and irritated me. Käsemann had uncovered the isolation of that passage from its context, theologically and formally. Strobel had related the terminology to political and administrative language of the time. However, Strobel did not sufficiently realize that the political and administrative situation had considerably changed at the time of the writing of Romans. Käsemann had fallen short of defining the isolation of this passage from its context.

Compared with all of Rom 12 and 13, the first seven verses of chapter 13 are the best-structured ones. This is all the more striking since the context follows very much the tendency of Pauline paraenesis toward an associative style, in particular, toward catchword association. There are also obvious terminological differences between Rom 13:1–7 and the remainder of Romans and the authentic letters of Paul in general. Despite Paul's interest in the power issue, even in something like a theology of power, there is no linkage of any thought of Rom 13:1–7 to that, especially not in any christological and pneumatological sense. The theology expressed is Hellenistic-Jewish indeed, not Jesus related at all.

Having observed these differences, the dimensions of Strobel's observations became even more striking for me. The administrative situation he presupposed was not that of the time of origin of Romans. It was the late Hellenistic and early Roman period, especially that of the Eastern Mediterranean, in particular around the Aegean Sea, not the period of the principate, and certainly not in the West.

This irritation of mine was topped by the fact that I did not find in Rom 13:1–7, although being in an epistle addressed to people living in the capital of the Roman Empire, any reference to Rome itself or to the princeps. In other words, in form and content Rom 13:1–7 turned out to be entirely anachronistic, curiously oblivious of the contemporary situation at large and of that of the city of Rome in the middle of the first century in particular.

My conclusion was that the seven verses were a brief "diatribe" formulated in the context of the Eastern-Mediterranean synagogue in times well before Caesar and that they betrayed a certain idealization of the Roman political structure. This, in fact, had no concept of political power in a hierarchical sense but claimed full authority for each individual magistrate, thereby establishing and maintaining a system of checks and balances unknown before.

Given my state of mind in 1957 and 1958, I interpreted this integration of the anachronistic text and its nonmention of Rome or Caesar as a challenge to the princeps and to Rome and its imperialism. My knowledge of the Caesar religion at that time was still limited. Therefore, it played merely a subordinated part.

At the back of my mind was the notion of ambivalence introduced by the alliance described, between Dibelius, Schlier, Schniewind, and Barth. There is certainly some striking ambiguity in this text, although not of the kind these scholars assumed. The real ambivalence is that caused by the integration of that curious traditional text into the Epistle to the Romans context; this causes an apparent anachronism.

5. NEW OBSERVATIONS ON ROMANS 1–7

The next in my series of discoveries that led to my present position on Romans concerned the initial quote of a traditional formula in Rom 1:3 and 4. As in some of Paul's other epistles, this traditional formula serves as a basic text that is to be interpreted in and by the following writing. It is obvious that these two verses present a two-stage setup for entering the royal throne. The first step is that of the designation, that is, the formal election of the future king, the crown prince, as it were. The second step is that of enthronement. This two-step pattern represents the legal frame of the installation of a king in Israel according to the biblical tradition. The election and designation of the future king was the duty of the prophet. Then in due time the person designated would be enthroned. This constitutional protocol entailed dangers for the reigning king and the country. We see it in the case of young David. This two-step arrangement prevented Saul from establishing his own dynasty and threw the country into civil war. Samuel had interfered with Saul. Similar turbulences happened later in the northern kingdom of Israel again and again. David and Nathan prevented such future turbulences for the south by means of a ploy. Nathan provided a prophetic selection and designation once and for all. Through this prophecy of Nathan, the first son of the present king would always be the king designate.

The creedal tradition quoted by Paul in Rom 1:3 and 4 applies this two-stage pattern to the figure of Jesus. The pattern is reset: stage one, the designation of the king, refers to the birth and lifetime of Jesus of Nazareth. A claim of Davidic lineage is made, as also found in part of the Gospel tradition. Stage two is identified with the afterlife of Jesus, the Christ, with the resurrection functioning as the act of enthronement. This latter point uses a concept found in other New Testament traditions as well. Here the resurrection event is seen as a promotion of Jesus' status and rank. Since the formula quoted by Paul in Rom 1:3 and 4 speaks of Jesus' lifetime as not yet messianic or royal, not only in appearance but also by law, this formula cannot be reconciled with our present Gospels. The formula does not reflect Pauline theology either. Indeed, its Christology flies in the face of a clear interest of Paul in a preexistence-based

Christology. Why, therefore, does Paul present such a text, even use it as a basic text? A text that runs counter to his own Christology? A text with a clear interest in protocol?

Here a curious coincidence occurred to me as I read and reread Romans. Romans with its initial quote was written roughly a year after Nero had become princeps and Caesar. Prior to that accession, an official, a legal event had occurred: Claudius's ascent to heaven and into divine position and glory, decreed by the senate. Suspicion and mockery immediately shrouded the legality of this occurrence. The suspicion was that this death had not been natural but forced, a suspicion that turned out to be correct. The mockery was done by none less than Seneca, who lampooned Claudius's ascent to heaven in his tract *Apocolocynthosis*, the "pumpkinification" of Claudius. This had an indirect effect on the assessment of the legality of Nero's accession to the principate.

I started to wonder whether Paul's choice of the formula might not entail a hidden message related to the Caesar religion, casting a critical eye on the events in Rome of a few months ago and still discussed in the population, certainly also in the Roman congregation Paul addresses.

Paul does not provide any direct statement in this direction, but perhaps the quotation of such a dated formula as a basic text is the first indirect clue that Paul gives, a coded mark intended to alert the reader. It could instigate bewilderment among the Roman recipients, making them wonder about legality and legitimacy, making them question whether the forthcoming letter would have something to do with matters of Caesar reverence and the current local discussion in Rome about it.

This suspicion gained further weight for me when I read the poems of the so-called Einsiedeln Papyrus. It contains fragments of eclogues, pastoral poems written in the form of the famous eclogues of Virgil. The person that the eclogues of the Einsiedeln Papyrus present as being better than Virgil is Nero himself. These pastoral poems must have been written around the time of Nero's accession to the principate in 54 C.E. They are contemporary with Paul's letter to the Romans, only a few months earlier. They reflect the hopes people had about this new Caesar, even people in the East. These eclogues praise Nero as the bringer of the golden age, as a real savior figure.

This additional information gave new force to other observations of mine, namely, that Paul must have known the record of the deeds of Augustus, the *Res gestae divi Augusti*. In this rather theological text, composed by Augustus himself and found everywhere in the empire on the outside of the Augustus temples for everyone to read in Greek,[3] the

---

3. Whereas the original Latin text was written on the inside of the temples.

terms *dikaiosyne* and *pistis* are found, likewise lead terms of Paul's Epistle to the Romans.

The Caesar religion also knew the term *euangelion,* found in the theme of the Epistle to the Romans that Paul gives in 1:16 and 17. The famous Priene inscription understands the saving message about Augustus's coming into the world as *euangelia.* This proves that the term was used in the Caesar religion as well. The person whom this inscription praised is also affirmed as savior.[4] This gives the theme of Romans and the letter an altogether very political ring.

A third traditional text quoted by Paul brought me over the hump, as it were, in my approach to the relevance of the Caesar religion for understanding Romans. Preparing for a lecture on Romans, I reflected again on Rom 3:24–26, among other passages.[5]

Sam Williams has shown that this text is related to the martyrology of 4 Maccabees and its Greek and Hellenistic counterparts of propitiation through personal martyrdom of noble people. The martyrology of the ancient church was based on a well-developed Jewish martyrology. This again was not isolated; it was connected with a growing reverence for martyrs in the pagan world, too. Socrates had been a famous martyr. Marc Antony and Octavius had interpreted Caesar's death as a martyr's death. Livy, contributing with his historical work very much to Augustan theology, gave moving portrayals of the noble death of a good number of Roman forebears. They witnessed to the grandeur of Rome and the values Rome stood for.

The present context of the formula quoted in Rom 3:24–26 shows that Paul has great difficulties integrating this traditional formula about the propitiating effect of the martyr's death of Jesus into his own theology. It contradicts Paul's concepts of liberation, justification, solidarity, and reconciliation. Why does Paul undergo these difficulties? It made sense if it helped to draw in the Caesar religion with its stated interest in the beneficial effect of the Roman martyrs, especially of Julius Caesar, on the *res publica,* the common weal of the Roman people.

Another stunning text is Rom 7. It must have bewildered the ancient readers already that this text written by a Jew and dealing excessively

---

4. The plural gave the "good news" an even more active voice than the term had in and of itself. I translated the plural as "the good news like a brushfire."

5. Sam Williams had shown how much this traditional text relates to Greek and Hellenistic thought. With these observations he strengthened the links with the thought world behind 4 Maccabees. I had my doubts about Williams's conviction that there existed even a textual relationship between the formula in Rom 3 and 4 Maccabees, but 4 Maccabees stands for the wider background of this text that Paul quotes.

with law does not mention anything peculiar to the Torah. The only legal reference made in the beginning of the chapter (7:1–3) is to marriage law, more in a Hellenistic or Roman understanding. As to the general understanding of this chapter, especially 7:7–24, I still follow the reading of Bultmann and Kümmel, namely, that Paul does not speak here about himself as a person, but that the "I" is a general human I.

As to the meaning of this chapter, my own interpretation in *Theocracy in Paul's Practice and Theology* builds very much on that of the philosopher Josiah Royce, who, in my opinion, has convincingly shown that Paul speaks here of the experience of human society. There are many more features of the surface text that must have stunned or bewildered the members of the Roman congregation addressed: the contradiction between the total condemnation in 1:18–3:20, including that of the Jews on the one side, and on the other side the salvation of all in chapter 11, and this after the Jews had received further bad treatment from 9:6–33; 10:21; and 11:7–15. These contradictions are furthered by the invocation of Paul's solidarity with all Jews in 9:1–5; 10:1–6; and 11:1. In this context, it needs to be mentioned that Paul in 1:18–22 and 2:14–15 pretty much follows Hellenistic-Jewish theology, and in 2:17–24 he characterizes and caricaturizes the proud Diaspora Jews in particular.

I could mention, too, the rather triumphant picture that Paul gives of his world mission in 15:14–22, a triumphalism that reminds one of the triumphalism of the opponents Paul has so severely criticized in the polemical fragments of 2 Corinthians, and this despite the chance that some of these opponents, who had left Corinth, could meanwhile be in Rome and thus amongst the readers. This glorious self-description recalls the Alexander saga, which was quite popular and revived by the Romans, especially by Caesar and Augustus for the Caesar religion.

These examples, bewildering on the surface, are not complete. However, they may suffice to show why my surface reading of Romans ran into more than enough stumbling blocks. Reading them more and more with the eyes of people of the first century, I had to assume that they had the same experience, most probably even stronger than I. My own suspicion had one advantage over the readers because I knew what they could not have known yet: that Paul had never seen Rome as a free man but only as a prisoner of the Caesar and that the court of the Caesar had tried, convicted, and executed him. What was the reason for this conviction and execution? Paul's behavior in Jerusalem could not have bothered the Roman court. Rather, *1 Clement* gives us the clue. In alluding to Paul's death, it puts all of Paul's message that led to his death into one word: *dikaiosyne,* the theme word of Romans.

Let me cut short the discussion of discovering the code. The surface text of Romans contains a good deal of polemic. This polemic speaks in language known to Hellenistic Jews but is directed against them, not against Palestinian Jews, nor against temple, priests, scribes, or Pharisees. This polemic is, however, inconsistent; it contradicts itself as I have shown. The text gives clues that the Caesar is in view. As soon as we see that as the underlying address of the polemic and see the Caesar religion as the real counterfoil of the positive message, everything falls into place. This brings me to the second part of this essay, the message of the letter in light of resistance to the Caesar religion.

6. ROMANS AS A LETTER OF RESISTANCE

The *hyponoia* of the text of Romans, its underlying real meaning is that Paul wants to introduce the letter as a basis for discussion with the Roman Jesus-believers after his arrival there. The decoded message, the underlying *hyponoia*, is the following.

I shall limit myself to a sketch of the first chapters. Contrary to the belief of Caesar Claudius, he had no right to claim the heavens as reward for his saving deeds to the world, nor had Nero brought the golden age. The letter is supposed to give the reasons why this can be properly said about Jesus, that he is deservedly the world ruler and savior. His "good news" brings what was promised and boasted of in the *Res gestae divi Augusti*, the report of the successes of Augustus set inside and outside the temples of Augustus all over the empire. The place where *dikaiosyne* and *pistis* prevail is not the *Imperium Romanum*; rather, they are spread by missionaries such as Paul and realized in the churches.

The terms *dikaiosyne* and *pistis*, in Paul's use, do not mean "righteousness" and "faith" but "solidarity" and "trusting loyalty." The world is not governed by Roman *pietas*, since all humans are godless. The world is moral chaos, contrary to Roman claims and their Hellenistic-Jewish admirers. No law can change that. Law, even the glorified Roman law, brings and sustains chaos. The opposite can only be brought about by solidarity and trusting loyalty. This last point is the message of Rom 3:21–31. Not Caesar's death but Jesus' death brought about the solidarity and freedom hoped for not only in Jewish quarters but also in the world at large. Jesus' solidarity and trusting loyalty reflected God's own. It was not limited to a certain biographical period but became through Jesus' resurrection collective reality, collective consciousness. Within this atmosphere of solidarity, loyalty, and trust, law comes into its own. In Rom 4 Abraham is presented as the counterimage to Aeneas. Abraham is truly the father of the world and of all peoples. In Rom 5 Jesus as the live image of loyalty is contrasted not only with Adam but also with the Caesar. It is his death for the godless, for a truly uncivilized world, that has brought solidarity to life and has caused worldwide reconciliation, an achievement the Caesars claim for themselves. Chapter 6 admonishes readers to make up their minds and decide where they want to belong, to the world of Roman justice or to that of God's solidarity. The pride in Roman law and its justice is the real focus of Rom 7. It states that this law and any law, since not based on mutual solidarity, loyalty, and trust, creates chaos, not only without but also within. The Roman claim that the Caesars brought about worldwide peace, a pacification even the animals benefited from, is challenged in Rom 8. The conclusion of that chapter proves that Paul is aware of the risks and dangers of such counterclaims. And, indeed, the Romans cracked the code, and the court of the Caesar convicted Paul of blasphemy against the Caesar and thus Paul was executed. Resistance has its price.

Paul died two years before the persecution of "Christians" in Rome by Nero in 64, the date of the first appearance of *Christiani* on the stage of world history.[6] The irony of history unmasked the Caesar Nero, the judge and executor of Paul, and proved his challenger from Tarsus to be a true critic. Nero, who prided himself to be a benefactor, not only of the empire at large but also of its capital Rome in particular, had large parts of the city destroyed.[7] The lives of his subjects, their properties, and their futures meant less for him than his own fame. The city for him was less a place for people to live in than an opportunity for the powerful to make themselves immortal. The stones counted more than

---

6. Although the term was not generally used before then, not even by the members of the Christ community. The vast majority of New Testament texts do not know the term yet. It occurs three times only, and this in late texts: twice in Acts and once in 1 Peter. It seems to have been a term that was used merely locally, in Rome and perhaps some other cities. Tacitus writes his report on the persecution of the Christians half a century after the fact, that is, at a time when the early church had gained in size and expansion. This explains Tacitus's rather hostile and all too generalized remarks. They add later knowledge and judgment to the report. In the year 64, they would have been without basis, for the church was at that time all too minute for such an aggressive attitude.

7. Tacitus gives an extensive report about the conflagration of much of Rome and of its reconstruction in 64 C.E. in his *Annals* 15.38-44. As to its cause, Tacitus pretends to be objective, hinting at various possibilities, but there is no doubt that he leans to the explanation given by the historical sources surviving (Suetonius, *Nero* 38; Dio Cassius 62.17; Pliny the Elder, *Nat.* 17.1.5; Seneca, *Octavia* 831-843): the fire was the result of arson, and Nero himself the instigator. The arguments given, e.g., by Suetonius are plausible: annihilation of the outdated and ugly inner city, which in its bulk had deteriorated into a gigantic slum, and the need to make room for the new construction of a lavish urban center with the *domus aurea* that would demonstrate and celebrate the Caesar's rank as a matchless town planner. The disaster caused by the incredible blaze was bigger than the real incendiary had intended. This did not disturb him too much, since he thereby found sufficient extra space for his most prominent building, the *domus aurea*.

humans, especially more than the nonwealthy ones. This was more of a justification of his critique of the Caesar religion and the Caesar than Paul could have ever anticipated.

10

JOHN'S "HEAVENLY" JERUSALEM

1. GENERAL OBSERVATIONS

We have mentioned the author of the book of Revelation several times, hinted at his urban concerns and his similarities with the teachings of Paul. Now it is time to discuss his concluding grandiose visions of the new world as an urban world, the final chapters of the New Testament and thus the climax of the Christian Bible, a pointer lost on much of later Christian tradition. Here now the extensive presentation of the major points of his urban vision.

The Revelation of John has attracted readers again and again because of its outlandish visions of future catastrophes. The approaching year 2000 has increased this kind of curiosity. Apocalypticism is in at the end of the millennium, and the book of Revelation is usually taken to be the most prominent demonstration of such a dramatic vision of the future. Interest in the book as an authority on down-to-earth issues such as church organization would strike many as misdirected. Perhaps even more would consider it out of place if John's vision were looked at as a contribution to urbanology. Yet this essay will argue that the last book of the Bible has concrete and constructive suggestions for real churches, for the city as a central reality, and for a sane urban world.[1] The churches

---

* This essay originally appeared in *Kirche: Festschrift für Günther Bornkamm zum 75. Geburtstag* (ed. Dieter Lührmann and Georg Strecker; Tübingen: Mohr Siebeck, 1980), 351–72.

1. Scholarly interest in the book has increased in recent decades for various reasons. A good survey is given by Heinrich Kraft in his discussion of the literature on the Apocalypse in "Zur Offenbarung des Johannes," *ThR* 38 (1974): 81–98, and in the bibliography of his 1974 commentary on Revelation, *Die Offenbarung des Johannes* (HNT 16a; Tübingen: Mohr Siebeck, 1974). Günther Bornkamm made an essential contribution to the understanding of the book

that John addresses are encouraged and enabled to see themselves as concrete models of the future urban society and to act accordingly. This future society will be a global reality. It will be finalized in the new Jerusalem that is actively anticipated in the congregations of the present.

John does not advocate fleeing from the present day into the heavenly beyond. Instead, he portrays heaven as coming down to earth. For him, heaven relates to contemporary human problems. We shall observe the descent of the heavenly city.[2] The crowning conclusion of not only the entire work but also of its portrayal of the church is found in the visions of a huge city, the new Jerusalem in Rev 21:1–8 and 21:9–22:5. This visionary city takes on colors of contemporary urban reality, of its hopes and promises. Not blood, tears, and horrors are the essential points of the last book of the Bible but encouragement and constructive stimulation.

---

of Revelation, "Die Komposition der apokalyptischen Visionen in der Offenbarung Johannes," ZNW 36 (1937): 132–49 = *Gesammelte Aufsätze* (BevT 28; Munich: Kaiser, 1952–), 2:204–22. Three commentaries have lately appeared, by Eduard Lohse, J. Massingbeard-Ford, and Heinz Kraft. Elisabeth Schüssler Fiorenza has written several larger and smaller studies on the last book of the Bible. There is an overview of her work on Revelation in her article, "Composition and Structure of the Book of Revelation," *CBQ* 39 (1977): 344–66; it includes discussion of earlier proposals concerning the composition of Apocalypse, unfortunately without adequate consideration of the important studies by Bornkamm and Adela Yarbro Collins. The latter's Harvard dissertation on Rev 12 appeared under the title *The Combat Myth in the Book of Revelation* (HDR 9; Missoula, Mont.: Scholars Press, 1976). She also wrote a brief exposition of Revelation, *The Apocalypse* (New Testament Message 22; Wilmington, Del.: Glazier, 1979). Collins took up the older hypotheses of Gunkel and Bornkamm and developed them in an ingenious manner. Her study on Rev 12 makes essential methodological suggestions and brings important insights into the subject matter of the work of John of Patmos. Composition and theology of the allegedly mysterious book are clarified to a high degree. On the two last chapters of Apocalypse, see, besides the commentaries, in particular H. Kuhaupt, *Der neue Himmel und die neue Erde* (Münster: Regensbergscher Verlag, 1947); E. Bietenhard, *Die himmlische Welt im Urchristentum und Spätjudentum* (Tübingen: Mohr Siebeck, 1951); José Comblin, *La liturgie de la Nouvelle Jérusalem* (ALBO 2/37; Louvain: Publications universitaires de Louvain, 1953); idem, *Théologie de la Ville* (Paris: Éditions universiaires,1968), esp. 191–226; Mathias Rissi, *Die Zukunft der Welt* (Basel: Reinhardt, 1966); Elisabeth Schüssler Fiorenza, *Priester für Gott: Studien zum Herrschafts- und Priestermotiv in der Apokalypse* (NTAbh NS 7; Münster: Achendorff, 1972), esp. 345–416. Comblin's *Théologie de la Ville* is quite stimulating, although still too much hindered by apologetic considerations, especially in exegetical and historical respects. In the meantime, particularly through his personal engagement, Comblin has made essential contributions to the praxis and theory of liberation theology in South America, especially in Chile and Brazil. He also left a lasting impression at Harvard University through his visiting lectureship there. His *Le Christ dans l'Apocalypse* (Paris: Desclee, 1965) is important for the Christology of the book of Revelation.

2. Therefore, the new Jerusalem is not "heavenly" any longer, at least not in the common understanding of "heaven" as a quite distant religious reality, distant in time and in space.

The new creation is described as a rather playful beginning, without threat from outside or inside, without lurking fear or terror, and thus without any need of protection.³ In this the description of the new creation corresponds to the sapiential portrait of the first creation in Prov 8:30. The joy of the new world is underlined by the bride motif.⁴ Play and joy were essential elements and values of the Hellenistic urban culture.⁵

From the very beginning the book addresses ordinary congregations and their concrete experiences. The congregations and their towns are spoken of already in the first three chapters. Ordinary people are the addressees, and their churches are painted with live colors that are taken from each of their individual urban contexts. John, the prophet, has a clear organizational concept of the church, the individual one as well as all of them together, and he has a levelheaded idea of society.⁶ The church's structure, experience, and future are also kept in sight in the following chapters, and so is the urban environment. A preliminary climax is the description of the fate of the heavenly woman on earth in Rev 12; this heavenly woman symbolizes the church.

Any reader of the book of Revelation has observed that it contains sequences of seven, not just of figures but also of visions. Sometimes these series are numbered; sometimes they are not. On occasion these chains even overlap. The last sequence of seven visions begins with 19:1. It is

---

3. The walls, spoken of later on, do not exist for protection but entirely for ornamental reasons, radiating the positive character of the city.

4. Found in each introduction of both visions of Jerusalem. In 19:7, the church was described as wedded wife. Israel/Jerusalem/Zion are presented as the bride of God in Hos 2:22–25, Ezek 16:7–14, and Isa 54. Kraft gives further biblical examples for the personification of cities as women. These could easily be multiplied by pagan parallels. The biblical passages mentioned, even Hosea in 2:22–25, all contain a strong element of joy. This is also true for the motif of the pilgrimage of the peoples in Rev 21:24–26. The precious stones contribute as well to the festive flavor of the whole scene.

5. See the surveys and bibliographies in the articles on feasts, play, games, and sports in the encyclopedias *Lexikon der Alten Welt* and *Der kleine Pauly*.

6. Already the introductory messages to the seven congregations in the second and third chapters reveal the author's strong interest in a specific church concept. Akira Satake made this the subject of his Heidelberg dissertation, which appeared under the title *Die Gemeindeordnung in der Johannesapokalypse* (WMANT 21; Neukirchen-Vluyn: Neukirchener Verlag, 1966). The concrete concern of John for the churches he addresses is the main topic of Satake's essay, "Kirche und feindliche Welt: Zur dualistischen Auffassung der Menschenwelt in der Johannesapokalypse," which appeared next to mine in the Bornkamm Festschrift (*Kirche: Festschrift für Günther Bornkamm zum 75. Geburtstag* [ed. Dieter Lührmann and Georg Strecker; Tübingen: Mohr Siebeck, 1980], 329–49). In contrast to my own essay, Satake here claims that John shows little interest in the outside world. Schüssler Fiorenza emphasizes the importance of the church issue in Revelation as well.

concluded by 21:1–8 with a description of the last stage of the triumph.[7] This is, however, not the first victory scene; there were precedents to this. John had spoken of this glorious end already four times earlier.[8] These concluding visions of final glory anticipate 21:1–8. Thus, themes and tendencies of the portrait of the new Jerusalem are prepared in the preceding book.[9] The intention of each of these anticipatory "final" visions of the ultimate triumph is to clarify and to further the depiction of God's future world. These final visions of the individual sequences are condensed in the first Jerusalem vision in 21:1–8, which prepares the theme of the book's great appendix in 21:9–22:5, the second Jerusalem vision.

It will become apparent that 21:9–22:5 is not an appendix in the usual sense, even less a later supplement, but an emphatic and concluding inculcation of the critical offer of the Johannine proclamation to an oppressing civilization and to the small minority of Christ adherents whom it pressures and terrifies. This offer is that of a sane urban world. This so-called appendix finally makes it clear that the Apocalypse of John wants to present political theology, as already intimated in earlier chapters, especially 13 and 17–18.[10] In its final visions also Revelation does not intend to give a description of a day on the Greek calendars, as little as anywhere else in the book. Instead, it wants to present a concrete challenge to the present time, although done in the form of the prophetic perfect as it is best and most strongly expressed in the phrase "it has come to pass" in 21:6. This emphasis on the present by means of the prophetic perfect is already found in the many liturgical pieces, the doxologies and acclamations before. These time and again refer to the present congregation as it meets in its worship services and sings such songs. Such concern with contemporary problems is an essential intention of John's work, which is already

---

7. On 21:1–8, see Dieter Georgi and Harvey Cox, "Rev 21,1–5(8), (Jubilate)," *Göttinger Predigtmoditationen = Beihefte zur Monatsschrift für Pastoraltheologie* 26 (1971–72): 201–12.

8. In Rev 7; 11:14–19; 15:1–4; and 19:1–10. They are detailed anticipations of the themes and tendencies expressed in these concluding visions of 21:1–8. This raises the question of the composition of the Apocalypse of John. It has been thoroughly discussed in the quoted essays of Bornkamm and Schüssler Fiorenza and especially in Collins's *Combat Myth*.

9. The church as wedded wife of 19:7, the voice sounding from the throne of 19:5, God's setting up tent of 7:15, the wiping away of tears in 7:17, the eschatological service of 7:15 (see also the praise of God in 11:15–18; 15:l–4; and 19:1–8), the water of life in 7:17, and in particular the conversion of the peoples in 7:9 and 15:4.

10. Comblin and Schüssler-Fiorenza have pointed out the political and social aspect of the Revelation of John in general and of the Johannine vision of the "heavenly" Jerusalem in particular. Especially important in that respect is, besides Schüssler Fiorenza's *Priester für Gott* (here esp. 413–14), her contribution to the Schnackenburg Festschrift, "Religion und Politik in der Offenbarung Johannnis," in *Exegetische Randbemerkungen: Schülerfestschrift für Rudolf Schnackenburg zum 60. Geburtstag* (Würzburg: Echter, 1974), 261–71.

expressed in the addresses to the seven congregations in the beginning of the book. If looked at closely, the final visions are variations of the concrete preaching of Rev 2 and 3. The alleged "surplus passages" at the end, the visions of the new Jerusalem, correspond to the alleged "surplus" of Rev 2 and 3. Scholars who wanted to see the book as an apocalypse among apocalypses had no use for these alleged surpluses because nothing comparable is found in other apocalypses.[11]

The Revelation of John uses the image of the city continuously and right from the beginning.[12] It does so first in the addresses to the seven congregations, all of them in cities of Western Asia Minor, all of them of a certain importance in the urban society of the time. The Zion-temple typology, which belongs into the context of the ancient symbolism of the city, plays a great role later on in the book. We also have the image of the evil city (Rev 13 and 17–18), which is unmasked as Babylon/Rome. The

---

11. Charles assumes that the material of the last two chapters had been found by the editor of the Johannine legacy in incomplete and unorganized form, that the editor had put together this posthumous material and had integrated it into the remaining book in an incorrect manner. Charles ascribes 21:1–6a to the final vision, and of the remaining material he counts as visionary fragment only 22:3–5 to this final passage. Charles proposes 21:6b–8 as introduction to an epilogue that he lets begin with 22:7. He sees 21:1–6a ordered in the following way: 5a, 4d, 5b, 6a, 1–4c (then 22:3–5). In his eyes, 21:1–5 and 22:3–5 represent disorganized fragments of a poem of six strophes of three and four lines each. He inserts the passages 21:9–22:2 and 22:14–15, 17 between 20:3 and 4 because these pieces, in his opinion, describe the Jerusalem of the time of the millennium and do not yet describe the ultimate Jerusalem because the former does not yet exist in a sinless environment. His arguments are found esp. in R. H. Charles, *A Critical and Exegetical Commentary on the Revelation of St. John* (ICC; Edinburgh: T&T Clark, 1920), 2:144–54. Charles is, however, unable to prove that 21:9–22:4 speak of a different Jerusalem than 21:1–8. His reorganization of 21:1–8 is much too formalistic. A rhythmic structure of the text is not proven, and 22:3–5 do not really fall out of their present context. Charles also overlooks the correspondence between 21:1–4 and 5–8 as well as between 21:1–8 and 21:9–22:4. Kraft also sees redactional work in 21: 1–8 and speaks of two endings of the book, one in 21:1–5a and the other in 5b–8. He suspects a later enlargement in 21:9–22:4. On the relationships within 21:1–8, see pages 171–72 below. I am in agreement with Kraft and Collins that these verses indicate a sort of conclusion, yet they do not really constitute a closing of the book, even less the first of two. The author of 21:1–8 and 21:9–22:4 is the same as that of the preceding chapters. The Jerusalem vision of 21:9–22:4 is thematically much too closely connected with the preceding text to be able to be seen as a mere appendix. On the literary unity from 21:1 to 22:5, see also Comblin, *La liturgie de la Nouvelle Jérusalem*, 5–8.

12. On the phenomenon of the Hellenistic city, used in the following discussion for explanatory purposes, see, e.g., Ernst Walter Andrae, Ernst Fabricius, and Karl Lehmann-Hartleben, "Städtebau," *PW* 3A, 2, (1929), 1974–2124; G. Gottlieb and C. Krauss, "Stadt," *LAW* (1965), 2881–2900; Walter H. Gross, "Städtebau," *KlPauly* 5:338–40; Mason Hammond, *The City in the Ancient World* (Cambridge: Harvard University Press, 1972), especially valuable because of its extensive annotated bibliography.

urban imagery is rounded off in Rev 21 and 22 with the double portrayal of the "heavenly" Jerusalem.[13]

In 21:1–8 the image of the new heaven and the new Jerusalem is more important than the preceding judgment and the accompanying cosmic destruction; 21:5a and 8 refer back to them with a mere hint. This is surprising since much of what preceded seems to have been dominated by descriptions of catastrophes and judgment images and concepts. Earlier visions had spoken of the sea monster, the chaos dragon.[14] The evil city, too, is described in Rev 18 as a world trade port, that is, related to the sea.[15] Now, in Rev 21, John speaks of the disappearance of the ocean. Thus, the new creation is no longer presented as the island of order, barely rescued from the sea of chaos and constantly in need of protection against ferocious attacks from the ocean of primal disorder.[16]

The paralleling of the new heaven and the new earth with the "heavenly," that is, the new Jerusalem, lets these images influence each other.[17]

---

13. In 21:7 we find a direct hint of the author's interest in the connection of this presentation of the new world with the initial messages to the seven congregations.

14. See especially Rev 13. On the conscious connection of this mythologumenon with other ancient myths, see Collins, *Combat Myth*, passim.

15. On this chapter and its function, see "Who Is the True Prophet?" (25–51 above).

16. This is an essential mythical element in all ancient concepts of order. It is preserved not only in Christianity to this day but also in Western civilization at large, where the invocation of chaos always goes together with irrational fears—in each case utilized anew for a more or less authoritarian incantation of the need for order, unconsciously and irrationally presupposed as the utmost epitome of salvation.

17. Since Isa 65:17, the new heaven and the new earth belong together. They become nearly synonymous. The apocalyptic movement in Judaism (since the third century B.C.E.) further developed this combination of motifs (evidence for this in Lohmeyer on the passage). The concept of the "heavenly" Jerusalem stands in the tradition of ancient exegesis of the older biblical motif of the new Jerusalem (or Zion) as it is found in Isa 54:11–12. Here the new Jerusalem is an earthly city (see the commentaries on Rev 21:1–8). Already in Isa 54, however, there may have existed an influence from the ancient oriental motif of the heavenly city as the eternal primal image of cosmic and earthly order, i.e., of civilization, as it is found in particular in connection with Babylon. Ancient people had identified the arrangement of the stars in the sky with primal stability and order. This association was then transferred to the earthly city, which was understood as a copy of that celestial order. This connection was translated back into the realm of the stars, and their coordination was interpreted as that of a superior and eternal city. Comblin writes: "Comme *Imago mundi* la ville des païens est mythisée: elle est le paradis, l'espace sacré, le lieu de la hiérophanie, réservé, consacré" (*Théologie de la Ville*, 138); "La ville est, en soi, image du monde, un cosmos en petit" (137). See also 138 on the *Roma quadrata*. Since the world of stars had taken on the symbolic function of a celestial city and since the astral world was understood as having existed before all times, the idea of the heavenly city as preexistent was a natural consequence. This increased the aspect of unchangeability of the proclaimed stability of the urban order. The city on earth was understood as a copy of the "real" city, the model placed into the beyond of time and

The images of the new heaven and of the new earth become more concrete and real through their relationship to Jerusalem. Jerusalem comes to mean more than the physical city. It becomes a synonym for the universe and even more, for happiness, peace, and redemption. John demonstrates that for him heaven is not something far off; it does not mean the beyond in any sense of distance: heaven means the presence of God here and now. This is underlined by the descent of the new Jerusalem onto this earth. Therefore, it is not really appropriate to speak of a "heavenly" Jerusalem in the context of the intentions of John's revelation. It used to be heavenly in its preexistence. Now it is "heavenly" no longer.[18]

---

space. The earthly city mirrored the order of its celestial prefiguration, which was also identified with the sanctity of the divine. On the holy and celestial city, see Hugo Gressmann, *The Tower of Babel* (New York: Jewish Institute of Religion Press, 1928); Werner Müller, *Die heilige Stadt: Roma quadrata, himmlisches Jerusalem und die Mythe vom Weltnabel* (Stuttgart: Kohlhammer, 1966). The influence of the earlier oriental motif of the heavenly city is manifest in early Jewish passages, starting with Tob 13. Also in Shepherd of Hermas, *Vis.* 3.2.4–5 and 3.5; *Sim.* 9.3 and 9.16.1, the image of the celestial tower (older than the allegorical explanations given by the author) denotes the celestial city, with a remarkable similarity to the motif of Babylon as the heavenly city. Gal 4:25–26; Heb 11:10; 12:22; 13:14 and also other references to a celestial building (e.g., 1 Cor 3:9–17; Matt 16:17; 1 Pet 2:4–6) prove that the mythical tradition of celestial buildings was popular in the early church, sometimes with, sometimes without a reference to Jerusalem. Therefore it is not legitimate, as already pointed out by Charles (*Critical and Exegetical Commentary*, 2:161), to interpret the concept of the heavenly Jerusalem in Revelation as a reaction to the destruction of the earthly Jerusalem. John uses an ancient mythologumenon that connected the concepts of perfect cosmos with that of the perfect city, oscillating between the aspects of the primordial and of the ultimate. The growing Jewish interest in transcendence and in preexistence corresponded to the increasing dissatisfaction with the institutions of priesthood and kingship since the second century B.C.E. In these renewed and enlarged mythifications Jerusalem, as the center of the people of God, was far removed from the intrigues and corruption of earthly rulers, owners, functionaries, and their institutions; Jerusalem was returned to the transcendent God as the real builder, owner, and administrator. Charles (*Critical and Exegetical Commentary*, 2:160–61) and others show that the concept of paradise could also be connected with that of the celestial city/Jerusalem, as indeed then happens in the Jerusalem visions of the Apocalypse .

18. Kraft denies that the city passes by the seer, who is in a high place. He claims that it can be concluded from Ezek 40:2 that the city is to be visualized as placed on another high mountain. However, it can only be intentional that the text rejects the mountain location for the city, contrary to Ezek 40 and the mythical tradition of the divine mountain. The descent of the city from heaven (13:13; 16:21; 18:1; 20:1 and 9; see also 3:12 and 10:1) is an all-too-frequent image in the book, and it is always meant concretely. On the other hand, the thesis of Charles (*Critical and Exegetical Commentary*, 2:148–54 and 205) is equally untenable that in 21:1 the author speaks of the heavenly but then in 21:9 of the earthly world (of the millennium). Charles comes to this erroneous conclusion because only in 21:1 (and in 22:3–5, belonging to the same fragment according to Charles) does the text speak of a new world. Charles believes, too, that in these fragments the tree of life is absent because it has become unnecessary. Charles claims that contrary to this description of the final heavenly

2. THE NEW CITY AS WORLDWIDE DEMOCRATIC COMMUNITY

The readers were supposed to associate Jerusalem with the concept of the covenant. They were to see the new Jerusalem as the final confirmation of the ancient promise of covenantal relation between God and humans and of the trust this entails. As in the covenantal associations of Israel before, the new community is also dependent on the preceding will and action of God. In our text, the idea of the preexistence of the heavenly city expresses such confidence. The parallels, especially in Gal 4, demonstrate that the new Jerusalem stands for the miraculously (in heavenly fashion) created community of God with free people.[19]

---

reality of Jerusalem there is another portrayal of Jerusalem as a preliminary, penultimate entity in 21:9–22:2. Charles argues this way because he finds unconverted heathens mentioned here. According to Charles, 21:9–22:2 is connected with 17:1–8 because both texts are introduced with the same words: "And one of the seven angels who have the seven bowls ... came and spoke with me saying: 'Here I shall show you...'" In Charles's reading, this intimates that the present conditions are referred to, those of Babylon/Rome in Rev 17 and those of the earthly Jerusalem in 21:9–22:5. Charles refers also to the similarities between 17:3 and 21:10 and between 17:1 and 21:15. Therefore, in his eyes, 21:9–22:2 portrays the preliminary heavenly Jerusalem, which has come down onto this earth. Charles concludes from this that in 21:9–22:5. the present earth and the heavenly Jerusalem described here coexist (2:156). This preliminary heavenly Jerusalem coming down, in Charles's understanding, is identical with the millennial kingdom of Rev 20. In Charles's interpretation, the Jerusalem of 21:9–22:5, although heavenly, has descended onto a high earthly mountain and thus has become identical with the Jerusalem of Ezekiel's utopia in Ezek 40–48. However, in my opinion there is no mention in 21:9–22:2 that the celestial Jerusalem and the enclosed paradise are situated on a divine mountain on this earth, thus present but at a certain distance as well. However, neither Rev 20 nor 21:9–22:2 speak of a later removal of the city and paradise from earth into heaven after the reign of thousand years in order to be finally transformed into a new ultimate heavenly form, as Charles claims (2:157–58). The descent of Jerusalem described in 21:2 and in 21:10 is the same: from heaven to earth. It is also unimaginable in Jewish tradition that the tree of life could become unnecessary in the final Jerusalem/paradise, as Charles's hypothesis presupposes. It should not be overlooked that the glory of the city in 21:9–22:2 has even more the characteristics of the celestial city than the city in 21:1–8 possesses. The conversion of the peoples, the pilgrimage of the peoples to Jerusalem, as well as the absence of the temple belong to this. They are supposed to describe something ultimate. The angel in 21:9–10 and in 22:1 is the same as in 17:1–3. This parallel establishes the new Jerusalem as the counterimage to Babylon/Rome. What the angel shows in 21:9–27 and in 22:1–5 is not less immediate than that which is seen in 21:1–8. On the contrary, in 21:9–22:5 there is no interpretation by a celestial voice, as in 21:3–4. The second vision of the heavenly Jerusalem more immediately impresses the reading and listening audience of the book.

19. It would certainly be wrong if one would argue on the basis of the concrete polemics of Paul in Gal 4 that he had added the connotation of freedom to the heavenly Jerusalem and that Jews would not have done this. Paul clearly presupposes this synonymy of celestial city and freedom and has inherited it from the Hellenistic-Jewish synagogue.

The new city is no lifeless entity but is loved as was Israel or Zion before. However, it is also something different from the biblical people of the covenant, although clearly still related, and it is clearly more than the present Christ community/church.[20] Since the new city is presented as descending from heaven, it is clearly more than the sum of its members. It is the ultimate people of God, certainly related to the Israel of old, but the eschatological form of all of humanity.[21] It is the preceding and comprehensive live unity,[22] presented like the archetype of the tabernacle in the desert according to Exod 25:40 and 26:30, less a counterpart to the Platonic idea than to the Roma Aeterna and similar archetypes of Hellenistic cities worshiped in the local urban cults.[23] It corresponds to its original character as heavenly city that the new Jerusalem is first of all presented as God's dwelling place. However, God's tent here does not mean the tabernacle, the tent of the covenant of Israel's exodus, as was the case in 15:5, where the tabernacle, the tent of the desert, was associated with the later temple, its successor so to speak. The temple will be absent in the new Jerusalem of John.[24] Revelation 21:3 means the Shekinah, the presence of God as concrete reality. The texts quoted by Charles prove that such promise was nothing unheard of in Jewish piety, for the pious ones were certain of God's presence right now. The assurance of covenantal communal relations of God with the contemporary people of the covenant of Lev 26:11–12, repeated in our text (21:3c),[25] needed for its realization neither temple nor tent of the covenant.[26]

However, this explicit emphasis on the communal relation of God and humans means a humanizing of the notion of ideal rational order

---

20. As Schüssler-Fiorenza, *Priester für Gott*, 350–360, shows; yet her argument about the height of the wall (359–60) is not convincing (see below, 181 n. 24).

21. In the terminology of contemporary Hellenistic cities, the assembly of the free—which in the language of John means all—citizens of the city, here the city of God as the community of the free.

22. On the collective orientation of the last chapters of the Apocalypse, see Comblin, *Théologie de la Ville*, 200.

23. The novelty of this eschatological Jerusalem is rightly emphasized by Comblin, *La liturgie de la Nouvelle Jérusalem*, 9–13. It can, however, not be spoken of nondialectically, i.e., in this case not without correspondence to the biblical Jerusalem and Jewish hope. John shows with his numerous biblical and postbiblical allusions how much he is interested in such relationships. The distinction Christian/Jewish does not help at all. John considered himself nothing but a Jew. He does not know of "Christians" yet. The polemics against "Jews" in Rev 2 and 3 are those of insiders, and Rev 11 proves that the fate and catastrophe of Jerusalem and of the temple was of great concern to him.

24. Its presence is emphatically denied in 21:22.

25. Similarly Jer 38:33; Ezek 37:27; and Zech 8:8.

26. On the express denial of the temple in the second Jerusalem vision, see 182–83 below.

inherent in the oriental concept of the heavenly city. What is expressed here in the language of eschatological utopia and with the help of biblical and Jewish allusions moves in the proximity of the concrete utopia of Hellenistic cities.[27] They mean a humanization and pragmatic transformation of the abstract notions of order and perfection of the oriental ideal city as they were expressed especially in the Babylon myth.

Particularly because of the ending of Rev 20, it is surprising that Rev 21 does not refer to the selection among humans described there but speaks in an unqualified and unrestricted manner of humans and peoples as partners of God.[28] There is not even mention of an act of resurrection, let alone of the resurrection of the just ones.[29] In almost all other closing visions of Revelation, namely, in Rev 11, 15, and 19, the fulfilled community is limited to those who proved themselves in persecution. Only in 7:9–12 has John already gone further, speaking of the community of salvation as of an innumerable multitude.[30] The promise about peoples in

---

27. Already in their planning stage, contrary to the naturally grown Greek cities, the Hellenistic cities entailed a utopian element. In addition, this increased through the intended and carried out integration of the manifold ethnic and social groups and through the collective consciousness that, in encompassing the entire civilized world, transcended as well as motivated these local integrations. How much this consciousness was a general and concrete reality is demonstrated by the continuous, from time to time even explosive, multiplication of new city foundings and by the literal streaming of masses of people into the old and the new cities. (See "Socioeconomic Reasons for the 'Divine Man' as Propagandistic Pattern" and "The Urban Adventure of the Early Church," 11–23 and 53–68 above) How strongly developed this utopian consciousness was is proven by the popularity of descriptions of ideal city constitutions (not state constitutions, as often very misleadingly stated) in Hellenistic times. Only the most famous ones, those from the pens of Plato and Aristotle, have survived in full. They are already several in number, and all belong to the transitional period from the Greek to the Hellenistic age. They are not political textbooks or manuals, yet not mere theoretical playthings either. Already in the case of the political writings of Plato the reference to the city-state is slightly anachronistic, even more so in the case of Aristotle. The synonymy of city and state was in the process of breaking up, yet such anachronism is only natural because of the utopian nature of the writings. Polybius and Cicero still describe the Roman city-state, although here the synonymy had ceased to exist and the Roman territorial expansion had begun long ago. The strong use of "older" political treatises by later authors and fragmentary references to other authors indicate a wide circulation and influence of such literature. In addition, there was another genre of political science, so to speak, not less a blend of utopian and practical dimensions, yet more interested in the idea of the representative individual, namely, the Hellenistic tractates on kingship, which in turn had strong influence on the Hellenistic sapiential movement, especially in its Jewish form, and on Gnosticism.

28. The plural "peoples" is the better reading.

29. This is an interesting parallel to the latter part of Rom 11, where Paul speaks of the end time without any mention of the resurrection of the dead—and also in terms of universal salvation.

30. Which he takes back again to a high degree in the following dialogue between the "angel" and the seer in 22:6–19, a scene that has been formed in a stylistic fashion unique in

21:1-8 and 21:9-22:4 is not limited to the conditions of the limiting interpretation in 7:14,[31] but these passages again take up the radicalism of 7:9-12 and strengthen it. One may ask whether the visions of the new Jerusalem at the end of Revelation want to move toward an unlimited universalist salvation, the salvation of everyone,[32] but it would be entirely wrong to treat this immediately as a specifically "Christian" issue. Already Ezek 47:22 speaks of the fact that in the new Jerusalem strangers are treated as citizens, a thought that is contained in some versions of the prophecy of the pilgrimage of the peoples, too, although there with the clear emphasis of the distinction between the people of salvation as the people in the center and the other peoples as marginal settlers.

For the covenant community, the presence of God brings the end of the eschatological tribulation, as the seer says in allusion to Isa 25:8 and in repetition of Rev 7:17. The context of Isa 25:8 speaks of the enjoyments that accompany the eschatological meal to which the text of Revelation will soon refer. Still under the influence of Isa 25:8 but going beyond Rev 7:17, John interprets the promise in the direction of an annihilation of death, of the last enemy, as Paul calls it in 1 Cor 15:54-55. Paul also celebrates the end of this ultimate evil. It should not be overlooked that Paul introduces the quotation from Isaiah as a promise that is fulfilled in the future, yet in the following text it is taken in the sense of an eschatology that is in the process of coming true.[33] What is said in Isa 35:10 of the redeemed of Israel, namely, that they no longer have any reason to worry, is now said of all of humanity. The promise of Deutero-Isaiah, that the things of the first creation and the first exodus are over, now receives a new urgency. The end of the scene again takes up the beginning in 21:1 and generalizes it. Thereby 21:1-4 becomes a unified whole.

---

the Apocalypse but shaped according to Old Testament models, found especially in Ezekiel. The innumerable multitude is now limited to the saved believers who have proven their salvation in the eschatological tribulation. On this, see Schüssler-Fiorenza, *Priester für Gott*, 392–97, although on 389–92 she explains this Johannine passage too much on the basis of the preceding one, thus harmonizing it, and on 392–97 she speaks all too quickly of "Christians," i.e., of members of a socially distinct group. It should not be overlooked that 7:13–17 (in distinction to 7:9–12, even to 7:1–8) again speaks of the temple. Thus, 7:9–12 moves far beyond its immediately ensuing interpretation and contains an unexplained rest, which is only taken up and treated in 21:1–22:4.

31. Against Schüssler-Fiorenza, *Priester für Gott*, 397 and more often.

32. Later copyists judged that our text went too far. They could not believe this promise and therefore changed the plural "(his) peoples" in 21:3 into the singular "(his) people," more customary in the Bible.

33. 1 Cor 15:56–57. The fact that Paul and John share a certain interpretation of Isa 25:8 proves, together with much similar evidence, that both theologians shared exegetical traditions and sometimes even their tendencies.

What is hinted at by the renewed use of the motif "old" (new) at the end of 21:4 is fully confirmed in 21:5.[34] Verse 5a divides 21:1–8 into two even halves: 21:1–4 and 5–8. Whereas 21:3 (as 16:1 and 17) still speaks in a restrained way of a voice going out from the throne, the prophet now presents God directly as the speaker. So 21:5–8 is the only direct word of God in the entire book besides 1:8. The latter verse belongs only to the frame anyway, not to the main part of the book.

In its form also the divine statement in Rev 21 goes far beyond that in 1:8, for 21:5–8 is no longer addressed to the seer as the lone addressee[35] but to the entire world.[36] Thus, 21:5–8 is the climax of the entire work, its crowning speech of God. The remaining vision merely further interprets the meaning of this audition,[37] namely, as God's eschatological action, the new world and congregation with its goods, of which the unlimited presence of God and the thereby given final insight into God's essence are the most important.[38]

---

34. Referring to the immediate neighborhood of statements about old and new in the basic text Isa 43:18 and its interpretation in 2 Cor 5:17, Charles assumes that the end of Rev 21:4(d) and the divine oracle in 21:5(b) belong together, and he makes the introductory phrase of the divine oracle with its presentation of the divine speaker the introduction for both statements. Charles claims that the redactor confused the two verses and moved them together with 21:6 (only 21:6a) behind 21:1–4, which they originally preceded, namely, as "God's declaration at the close of the Final Judgment." However, it would be easier to understand that an epigone would use a biblical model and an exegetical tradition existing in the church (as 2 Cor 5:17) to guide him in reconstruction rather than to tear the text apart. Charles does not reckon with the possibility that John himself (in this similar to most apocalyptic writers) possessed and exercised radical liberty vis-à-vis the biblical text. Apocalyptic writers are not interested in copying but in imaginatively re-creating the text for the present and coming age.

35. The μοι usual elsewhere is left out.

36. If one considers the importance of 21:5–8 as a direct oracle of God, then 21:5b appears misplaced. The divine speech does not need such assurances. In addition, the presentation of the divine oracle of 21:5b appears as part of an angel's speech also in 22:6, where it is better located, namely, at the beginning of the conclusion of the entire book. Most probably this phrase appears in 21:5b merely as a copyist's or reader's admiring marginal remark that uses the terminology of 22:6. A later copyist understood this comment in the margin as an earlier correction note, only as one that was shortened and garbled. Therefore he added an introductory supplement that connected the statement, now as divine word, with the preceding.

37. See the cross-references at 168 above.

38. It is important that 21:8 is the complete opposite to what precedes, and it is not interpreted in the following passage. A similar remark occurs in 21:27, again not integrated into its own context either. In contrast, the remark in 22:3a, which excludes anything accursed from the new city, is connected with the end of the preceding verse, the description of the presence of the tree(s) of paradise, healing the peoples, thus securing the removal of anything evil. It appears that the presence of anything harmful or wicked, thing or person, in this city constitutes a contradiction to that and has the appearance of an afterthought, more

By means of the separation of the statement about the old and by means of the insertion of "everything," the statement about the new has been radicalized compared to Isa 43:18–19 and 2 Cor 5:17.[39] The creation of something absolutely new and unheard of is announced in a universal statement. As in Isa 43:19, the present tense is used, and the divine voice immediately adds in the prophetic perfect: "They have come to pass!" (i.e., all new things).[40] Miraculous eschatological fulfillment and radically new creation constitute the essence of the Johannine God. The emphasis on the new creation corresponds to a tendency of the entire work and had already been prepared by the christological references to Jesus as the vanquisher of death (1:5, 18; 3:7), by the day of the Lord as the date of the visions (1:10), by victor statements, and by doxological expressions. The statement that *everything will* become new had already been intimated by the universalist tone of the texts mentioned, and it is further expanded in 21:9–22:4 when the new city is described as the cosmos, with features of the whole earth and firmament. The prophetic perfect corresponds to the christological confidence of Rev 2, 3, and 5, to the antiapocalyptic traces,[41] and to the many challenges to the Roman power and Hellenistic urban society. In this manner of speech is expressed the prophetic confidence of the early church prophets as it was voiced every Sunday in the worship service of the congregations. Like the biblical prophets, these new prophets spoke in the name of God (and the resurrected Christ) and used without hesitation the divine "I" (or that of the Christ).

The definition of God in 21:6b also stems from the worship practice. It is a prophetic statement that was quoted in Rev 1:8 as well but has now become part of an extensive speech of God. God's rulership not only over time but also over all things is described by resorting to alphabetical letter speculations common in Judaism and paganism at the time.[42]

This all-embracing statement about God's essence is proclaimed in the worship service, more precisely during the eucharistic meal in an

---

precisely of a secondary correction, inserted by someone who could not stand the idea that in the end everyone would be saved.

39. As also compared to the many other passages from Jewish eschatology that speak of the new heaven and the new earth; see Charles, *Critical and Exegetical Commentary*, 2:203.

40. Apocalypse in general associates the neuter plural of the noun more with verbs in the plural than in the singular (ibid., 1:cxli). On the disappearance of the gloss in 21:5b, see 171–72 above.

41. For this, see 175–76 below.

42. On these religious-historical parallels, see the commentaries on 1:8 and 21:6, especially Wilhelm Bousset (*Die Offenbarung Johannis* [6th ed.; Göttingen: Vandenhoeck & Ruprecht, 1906]) and Ernst Lohmeyer (*Die Offenbarung des Johannes* [2nd ed.; HNT 16; Tübingen: Mohr Siebeck, 1953]).

immediate fashion through the prophetic voice. In this declaration, the eschatological promise of 21:6c is anticipated.[43] The concept of a covenantal reference that is peculiar to the biblical allusion in Isa 55:1 fits equally well to the meal part of the worship service of early Christ communities.[44] Some parts of the early church saw in the eucharistic meal a foreshadowing of the eschatological meal community, which in and of itself represented a renewed adoption of the paradise as a reality.[45] It is important, too, that Isa 55:1 speaks of the general accessibility of the word of God and thereby corresponds to the exegetical tradition of Isa 43:1 and 2. This is taken up in the context of 2 Cor 5:17-21, there in the direction of the reconciliation of the world. Revelation 21:4 and already 7:9-12 before hinted at similar thinking. The victor statement in 21:7 refers back to and summarizes the conclusions of the addresses to the seven congregations. The divine inheritance is promised and is interpreted as a democratization of the Nathan prediction of 2 Sam 7:14.[46] In John's Revelation, the biblical connection of new city and kingship is radicalized. The seer sees the conflicts between God and king, king and temple, and temple and city absorbed and overcome.[47] This is analogous to the self-understanding of the Hellenistic cities, especially in Roman times. Already through their outline they emphasized that they wanted to demonstrate an order that was equally open and binding for everyone.[48] However, from the victor

---

43. The parallels in Rev 2:7 and 17 speak of the wood of life and of manna.

44. So, for instance, in the Synoptic texts of the Last Supper that mirror theological and liturgical practices of groups of the early church. Paul in 1 Cor 11:26 states it differently. He explains the celebration of the Eucharist as repeated proclamation of the death of the Lord until the Parousia occurs.

45. References found in Wilhelm Bousset and Hugo Gressmann, *Die Religion des Judentums* (4th ed.; HNT 21; Tübingen: Mohr Siebeck, 1966), 284.

46. The concept of king in the Apocalypse does not appear by chance. Jerusalem was originally the royal city, and the temple was the court chapel of the king. In Ezekiel, too, this connection is still visible, although consciously reduced.

47. Ezekiel already speaks of the ultimate control of any despotic arbitrariness of kingship toward land and people (45:7-8). The cultic role of kingship is addressed below (184-86). Schüssler-Fiorenza (*Priester für Gott*, 363) points out the connection of enthronement and participation at the messianic meal in Rev 3:20-21.

48. This was underlined by the mixture of houses of different social classes in the same block, to which the Romans even added distinct rental houses and stores. The Romans later also created luxurious residential areas in some large cities. Where Greek city constitutions existed, newcomers were able to acquire the right of citizenship and to participate in the political life of the city—although this varied from place to place and from time to time as to degree and intensity. Cities with Roman citizenship tended to imitate this practice, although here the voting rights could be exercised only in Rome. Further questions of a more complicated nature, such as the issues of double and mixed citizenship and of overlap with central law, cannot be discussed here. In any event, the cynical claim, often heard today, that

statement in 21:7 and its parallels in Rev 2 and 3, one could read a reduction of the promise of inheritance, and the curse in 21:8 could confirm that. In contrast to that is the further exposition of 21:7 in 22:5, where the promise is extended to all and where there is no counterpart to 21:8.[49]

A combination of elements of the apocalyptic tradition are brought to 21:9–22:4. They are used to give the whole painting strong brushstrokes. In executing these strokes, John has not glossed over their distinctiveness but has left the individual strokes still stand out and the different colors still show markedly. Thus, a more aphoristic arrangement was quite consciously achieved. The intention of John is to set strong accents in his portrait of the new Jerusalem that are supposed to interpret the utilized and still recognizable tradition. He wants to contrast the apocalyptic background with his own praxis of visions, auditions, and interpretative reflections. With his use of older prophetic and in particular apocalyptic traditions, he does not intend a harmonization of the apocalyptic visions of the future; he wants to comment critically on these traditions. The conclusion of Revelation makes it obvious that John wants to present an antiapocalypse. This is indicated by the mention of his name as author (contrary to the pseudonymity of all apocalypses), the concreteness of the epistolary frame of the work, the seven addresses to seven identifiable contemporary communities (contrary to conscious transcendence of historical and contemporary concreteness in other apocalypses), the scheme of recapitulation (with its conscious disruption of the apocalyptic scheduling), and many other traces.

---

citizenship in the Hellenistic-Roman period was of no real value, does not do justice to the facts. Self-government and independence of certain cities, including Roman ones, from the respective central administration, even that of the Roman principate, was much more extensive than in many Western countries today. However, the cities of the Mediterranean were never able to really integrate the proletariat. This failure did not limit the ideal claim, which, indeed, the ancient social revolutionaries adopted again and again. The Apocalypse's interest in a degree of democratization that was rather radical for Hellenistic-Roman conditions is shown also by the naming and complete integration of the kings in 21:24. This, nevertheless, does not yet do away with certain traces of aristocracy in the case of God and Lamb.

49. In 21:8, unlike the universal statement in 21:4, a destruction of a part of humanity is spoken of as the other side of the new eschatological situation. This is an inexplicable paradox in these last chapters but has sufficient predecessors in the preceding chapters. It is not all too firmly embedded in its immediate context. It was mentioned already that the verse is not carried any further. Its counterpart in v.7 creates riddles as well. The composition of 21:8–8 follows the well-known blessing-curse scheme. This is however in contrast to all other victor statements, of which none has a negative counterpart. Could it not be possible that we have here a later "orthodox" correction of an all too universalistic climate as provided by the larger passage[5] ? The catalog of curses nevertheless emphasizes in a striking way the motifs of cowardice and lying. Thereby, the devilish counterpart to constancy and faithfulness could be intended, that is, to positive attitudes the entire book calls for.

In 21:9–22:4 we find various concepts and ideas of the ancient city integrated: the city of God, the heavenly city, the royal city, the Hellenistic city including its Roman modification, and especially the concrete cities Jerusalem, Babylon, and Rome. This integration has radicalized the conception of the city. Already the vision's introduction, the reference to one of the angels of vials, connects this concluding vision with Rev 16 and 17, especially with the latter, the epiphany of the devilish city Babylon/Rome. The new Jerusalem of John is the countertype of the world capital Rome, the city of cities at the time of the writer. On the other hand, the feature of the prophet's transfer onto a high mountain and many elements in the description of the city continue the heavy use of the book of Ezekiel and its critical interpretation in the earlier parts of the work, here in particular the description of Jerusalem in Ezek 40–48.[50]

Contrary to Ezekiel, John's new Jerusalem does not stand on a high mountain, the divine mountain, but comes down onto the plain, as in the first vision, in 21:1–8; more specifically, it descends into the valley through which the big river runs. The final city is situated in a river valley. In Ezekiel, the city is not described but only the temple, whereas in the new Jerusalem of Revelation the temple is absent (21:22) and with it also the temple mountain, Zion, the focus of many Jerusalem visions since Isa 2. In this and the preceding vision the motif of the preexistence of the new Jerusalem underlines the divinity, eternity, and immutability of the city. It corresponds to the oriental motif of the celestial city, which influenced Ezekiel and similar Jewish tradition as well. However, by excluding the motifs of the divine mountain and of the temple, John assimilates his portrait of the ultimate city to the consciously secularized mythical city as manifested by Hellenistic cities.[51] In the vision of Ezekiel, the divine mountain and the temple mirror heaven in its majesty (the mountain) and in its regularity and order (the geometrically regular form of the holy of holies: the cube). There is a clear division between the heavenly (mountain/temple/holy of holies) and the earthly (the not expressly mentioned city and its not specifically

---

50. But it would be wrong to assume that Rev 21:9–22:4 was simply spun out of Ezekiel (not even with the additional use of other biblical texts such as Isa 54; Zech 11; and especially Exod 28:17–21; 39:10–14). John must have had access to traditions that had already combined these texts and, using other mythical traditions, had developed them exegetically into cosmological and astrological speculations. Perhaps they had originally been priestly traditions, but they must have also found their way to Philo and Josephus.

51. See 179–80 below. On secularization, see also Comblin, *Théologie de la Ville*, 216–17. I cannot agree with Comblin's earlier argument (194) that the pagan urban utopias had been pessimistic because they originated from the separation of morality and reality. Such polarizations belong to all utopias, including the Johannine, *per definitionem*.

described population), between the cultic and the profane. Over against the picture in Ezekiel, the new Jerusalem of John is heaven in its entirety, and it is open heaven, heaven come down onto earth, in fact, heaven and earth in one. Precious stones are not mentioned in the sense of introducing elements of cultic taboo, contrary to the description of the celestial city in Tobit. Precious stones in the ancient world stand for more than beauty, purity, and clarity; they imply magic power. However, in Rev 21 this power is not apotropaic, prohibitive (except to what is unclean); it is, rather, attractive and inviting. The secular city of Hellenism has found its ideal formation.

As the temple is in Ezekiel (43:2), so in John the city is the seat of the divine *kābôd* (21:11), of divine glory and majesty. John frequently describes this presence of God as the "light reality" of the city (21:23–24 and 22:5). Cloud and veil have disappeared, brightness and clarity are ever-present: an essential intention of all Hellenistic city planning and architecture has been brought to perfection.[52]

Like the oriental city and many Hellenistic cities, the new Jerusalem has walls, too, but these walls have *permanently open* doors (21:25). This means that, contrary to the usual understanding of walls, the walls of John's city are supposed to be associated with openness, not with limitation, isolation, and protection against what is strange and unclean.[53] This is underlined by the fact that jasper is taken as material for the walls (21:18), bright and clear material, according to 21:11.

This corresponds to the contemporary Hellenistic city, in which the walls were not meant for fortification alone but also helped physically to integrate the townscape into the surrounding landscape, to reconcile civilization and nature.[54] Into this picture also fit the numerous public and private parks and gardens, paradises in the literal meaning of this originally Persian word. In the Roman version of the Hellenistic city, this integration of nature is multiplied and enlarged. So by incorporating the paradise into the new city in Rev 22, John corresponds to tendencies of Jewish eschatology as well as to the layout of the cities of

---

52. See 181–83 below. The comparison of the *kābôd* with the radiating clarity of a precious stone, of jasper, proves that the following enumeration of jewels also should be seen above all under the aspect of brightness and clarity. Compare also the description of the deity that communes through and during the meal in Exod 24:10. To understand the use and meaning of precious stones in antiquity, see the article by A. Hermann, "Edelsteine," *RAC* 4:505–52.

53. See Comblin, *Théologie de la Ville*, 138.

54. The walls were frequently built in the countryside far beyond the settled town. The original reason was probably to provide as much terrain as possible for defense. Later on, this proved advantageous for integrating agriculture and rural production.

his day.⁵⁵ This reconciliation of nature and city expresses a direct contradiction to the idyllic eschatology of the official Roman Caesar cult as it had developed since Virgil⁵⁶ and Horace,⁵⁷ especially since the erection of the *ara pacis Augusti* in Rome and since the establishment by Octavianus Augustus of the Caesar cult as the celebration of world peace. The official Roman propaganda celebrated nature outside at the expense of the city, and the leading Roman circles followed that by moving their estates to the countryside.⁵⁸ Later development is reflected in the poems of the Einsiedeln Papyrus.

Repetition of the number twelve connects the city not only with the motif of the twelve tribes⁵⁹ but, specifically due to its emphatic repetition, even more with the zodiac,⁶⁰ which is accentuated by the twelve angels of the gate.⁶¹ The new Jerusalem thereby reflects the regularity of the cyclical movements of the stars, the quietude of the eternal return in all changes. In contrast to that, order is for John no longer an astronomic-astrological counterpart; it is integrated into the living community. The rigid connection of calendar and cult is broken apart. Rationality, usually represented by the zodiac, has thereby become lively and flexible.⁶²

Not only the references to the twelve tribes and to the twelve apostles but also the New Testament and patristic parallels to the building terminology show that the eschatological building does not mean a static structure but a living community that reaches from the past and from the future into the present time.⁶³ The conception of the city as a female

---

55. The commentaries speak only of the Jewish eschatological parallels, particularly Charles, *Critical and Exegetical Commentary*, 2:160–62.

56. Esp. the fourth eclogue.

57. Esp. the *Carmen Saeculare*.

58. See "Who Is the True Prophet," 38–40 above.

59. Ten times in 21:12–22:2, in addition to variations such as the number 144 in 21:17.

60. To which the commentaries point, esp. Bousset, *Die Offenbarung Johannis,* 447 and passim; Lohmeyer, *Offenbarung des Johannes,* 170–74. They do this in following Franz Boll's important study, *Aus der Offenbarung Johannis: Hellenistische Studien zum Weltbild der Apokalypse* (Leipzig: Teubner, 1914), although they do not have the same emphasis as Boll.

61. "Originally probably symbols of the zodiac" (Lohmeyer, *Offenbarung des Johannes,* 171; my translation). At the same time, also an allusion to the angelic guardians of the wall in Isa 52:7-8 and 62:6. But the Apocalypse joins them with the gates and adds the number twelve. The twelve gates correspond to Ezek 48:30–35. Of gates also speaks *1 Enoch* in the description of heaven as a city in chapters 72, 75, and 82.

62. On the linkage of astrology and the rationality of architecture, see Vitruvius, *De Architectura* 9.

63. Gal 2:9; 4:25–31; Eph 2:20; Heb 11:10; 12:22; 13:14; Shepherd of Hermas, *Vis.* 3.2.4; 3.5; *Sim.* 9.3.3; 9.16.1; further, 1 Cor 3:9–17; Matt 16:17; 1 Pet 2:4–8; 2 Cor 6:16. Compare also the strong interest of Paul in the conception of building and constructing as a major part of church organization and communal ethics.

person, still common in the Hellenistic and Roman cities of the first century, associates easily with the biblical image of Jerusalem as bride. The image of Jerusalem is made more lively and vivid by the lack of all monumental architecture, with the exception of the description of the wall. This corresponds to the layout of the Hellenistic city, whose goal was not grandiose architecture as an end in itself but first and foremost the human community that it supported and accompanied. As is usual in Hellenistic architecture, John's city is based on enclosed space that is concerned with life and nature and based on the streets, which serve the communication among people. John does not mention houses at all. So all attention in his presentation goes to the πλατεῖα, that is, in fact to the very wide main street that is also the avenue for processions in the Babylonian and Roman city layout. Since John does not, neither in 21:21 nor in 22:2, speak of any other streets and chooses in 22:2 the syntactically imprecise formulation at the beginning of this verse,[64] he keeps open the association with a large street that widens into a plaza, that is, the association with the Greek agora. John wants to allude to meeting, assembly, and many-sided communication. The layout and architecture of the Hellenistic city exists to be filled with life and therefore can stand for the community itself.

The heavenly city has come down to earth. It is identified with the earthly Israel and is its continuation. The number twelve alludes to the tribes of Israel and to the apostles of the Christ faith. Apostles here are no longer the individual, divinely authorized missionaries, as in the letters of Paul. John still knows such migrating apostles, as Rev 2:2 proves, but in Rev 21 he wants to talk of a limited group, an institution, the Twelve, as representative for the church. Of this group of twelve Paul already speaks in 1 Cor 15:5 and takes them to be witnesses of the resurrected Christ.[65] Since the 60s of the first century C.E., this group of twelve was brought together with the term *apostle*, as the later stage of the Synoptic tradition and the Acts of the Apostles prove.[66] Through the relationship

---

64. μέσῳ τῆς πλατείας αὐτῆς. John fails to clarify whether this phrase belongs to what precedes or to what follows. "Either these trees are arranged in two rows, one on either bank of the river (one row thus coming between the street and the river), or they are placed on either side of the space that lies between the street and the river" (Charles, *Critical and Exegetical Commentary*, 2:176).

65. He neither says nor excludes that they were disciples of Jesus. He does not say that they had already been singled out during the time of Jesus, even less that they had been extraordinary followers. The possibility that the circle of the twelve was constituted by a chance experience of a shared vision of the resurrected Christ cannot be excluded either.

66. The relationship between the twelve (disciples) and the twelve tribes is found in Matt 19:28 as well, clearly a post-Easter text. The twelve then were associated with a or the leading circle of Jesus' disciples, which then (around the turn of the century) slowly absorbed the apostle title completely.

to the twelve tribes and the twelve "apostles," the celestial city is connected with history. It is remarkable that the gates represent the relationship to the older history and reality of Israel. This relationship to Israel is identified with the openness of the city, whereas the relationship to the history of Jesus is seen in the foundation and the walls, an application of the most recent history. The use of the motif of the disciples of Jesus on the one hand and the apostles on the other as foundations of a heavenly building is known from other texts, from Matt 16:17 and Eph 2:20,[67] but the anachronism of the "architectonic" preordination of the "twelve" in relationship to the Israel motif is surprising. One would expect the reverse order. However, the new world turns everything upside down, not only what is customary but also what is expected. The mention of the twelve tribes and the twelve apostles in their interrelationship helps to bring the heavenly Jerusalem completely down to earth, and with it the celestial world. The new earth has absorbed heaven. The secularization of the Hellenistic city has found its fulfillment.

By way of the peculiar enumeration of the directional points in the description of the wall (east, north, south, west in 21:13), the author again intimates a reversal of the customary. Even in the itemization of the precious stones, customs and expectations are shaken. The complete identification of the presented stones is impossible for the modern reader.[68] There are nevertheless sufficient hints. In addition, there are relationships to the description of precious stones on the breastplate of the high priest in Exod 28:15–20 (according to 28:21, to be related to the twelve tribes of Israel as well).[69] This makes it clear that John had this biblical listing in mind but did want to identify his own enumeration with the biblical one. There is also a relationship between precious stones and the zodiac. Philo (*Mos.* 2.133) and Josephus (*Ant.* 3.7.7) have associated the stones on the priestly breastplate with the zodiac, and there is further evidence for this correspondence of zodiac and jewels.[70] However, the individual identification, the relationship, is so far secured that the normal sequence can be compared with that in Revelation. This permits one to conclude with Charles: "The signs or constellations are given in a certain order, and this (is) exactly the reverse order of the actual path of

---

67. The description of the lead figures of the Jerusalem church as στύλοι according to Gal 2:9 is a related image as well.

68. See the commentaries.

69. Compare further the LXX text of Exod 36:17–21 (39:10–14) and also the description of the king of Tyre in Ezek 28:13 LXX.

70. Charles, *Critical and Exegetical Commentary*, 2:167–68; Lohmeyer, *Offenbarung des Johannes*, 171.

the sun through the signs."⁷¹ By means of this "confusion" of the sequence of the walls and the stones, John seeks to show his readers that the new heaven, the one that had come down to earth, has a different order, is truly new. The new city's measurements, given by the angel, result in a regular cube, a copy of the Babylonian temple tower.⁷² But the Greeks also saw perfection in the square. This is even more the case with the Hellenistic city. It is famous for its grid pattern, the layout of the streets in rectangular pattern, sometimes in square format. This is supposed to embody a just, reasonable, and from all angles clear order that serves everyone equally well.⁷³ Whereas in the concluding vision of Ezekiel the angel gives normal measurements, the dimensions of the new city are overwhelming in John's image (21:16–17). The territory of the new Jerusalem of 12,000 στάδια in all directions had the extension of the civilized world west of Parthia or, rather peculiarly, the extension of the entire area that Alexander the Great had covered in his campaigns. The only difference is that this eschatological cosmopolis is as high as it is wide and long.⁷⁴ The geographical correspondences are certainly not matters of chance but are linked with the cosmopolitan claim of this ultimate image and challenge the contemporary urban culture with its ideological claim and promise. The new Jerusalem is the perfect Hellenistic city.⁷⁵

If the gates each consist of one giant pearl and, according to 21:25, are nevertheless always open, their immeasurable value and beauty are meant to be accessible to everyone. The twice-stated, consciously paradoxical expression "pure gold, like pure (or transparent) glass"⁷⁶ seems to be an allusion to the celestial world, namely, to the firmament flooded with sunlight in the heat of noon.⁷⁷ Contrary to depictions of the new

---

71. Charles, *Critical and Exegetical Commentary*, 2:167.
72. Bruno Meissner, *Babylonien und Assyrien* (Heidelberg: Winter, 1920–25), 1:313.
73. Lohmeyer, *Offenbarung des Johannes*, 173.
74. Here a difficulty arises. Merely 144 πῆχα = 70 meters is indicated for the walls. If this meant the height of the wall, it would result in a ridiculous proportion compared with the incredible extension in length and breadth. The explanation sometimes offered that John wanted to describe a ramp that would carry the dome of the sky does not satisfy because this would compete with the cubic form. In addition, the passage on the measurements of the city also contains the statement (21:16) that the city was as high as it was wide and long. Since there is no mention here or later of any other measurable structure than the wall, the height can only refer to the wall. Then, the indicated measure of 144 cubits must refer to the thickness of the wall.
75. Rev 21:17 expressly says that the large numbers are realistically meant, for they are related to human measurements. Thus, the city corresponds in certain ways with extensions within the range of experience of humanity.
76. Rev 21:18 and 21, once for the mural structure, the other time for the street.
77. See further what was said above (176–77, esp. n. 52) about jasper.

Jerusalem in Ezek 40–48, Isa 65, Zech 2, and Tob 13, the covenantal relations in the new Jerusalem of John are not oriented on the cultic presence of God in the temple.[78] God and the Lamb stand for the temple.[79]

In this, the vision of John corresponds to the ideal Hellenistic city. While in the oriental and the Greek city the sanctuary or sanctuaries were situated in the center of town and the city oriented toward them, the Hellenistic city was a secular town. It was defined by its population and characterized by its streets and plazas as an area in which one came together in order to communicate.[80] The new Jerusalem is such an open, democratic city.[81] God and the Lamb are mayors and citizens at the same time, *primi inter pares*, free among free, *principes* as the first citizen of the Roman Empire, the Caesar. So Rev 21–22 is not only a counterpart to Rev 17 but also to Rev 13. God and lamb make the idea of the principate come true, whereas the Roman *princeps* is perverted to a monster that destroys the earth.

In 21:21, Revelation presupposes Isa 60:19 and Zech 14:7, which describe the eschatological break-in of God's glory in Jerusalem as an invasion of an inexhaustible flood of light[82] that surpasses the creation of light at the first creation. Sun and moon are no longer necessary.[83] As in Trito-Isaiah, light, *kābōd* (= glory), and Yahweh are identified, to which the Lamb is added in Revelation. John then also takes up the widely known feature of the pilgrimage of the peoples that Paul and other circles

---

78. This is no "Christian" invention. Tendencies to distance oneself from the temple and its priesthood grew in Judaism since the second century B.C.E. at the latest. The priestly sect of the Essenes and the lay sect of the Pharisees prove that this could be done with high self-confidence, even cultically oriented. The Essenes broke with the privilege, too, which Ezek 44:23–24 reserved for officiating priests, namely, to teach the differences between pure and impure. The Pharisaic scribes of the so-called synod of Jamnia took over this task officially and under neglect of the temple, which did not exist any longer. There was no concern for the role of priests in this adjudication any longer either.

79. Perhaps Charles is right in his assumption that 21:22 originally read: καὶ ναός κτλ ... ὁ γὰρ κύριος κτλ ... ναὸς αὐτῆς ἐστιν, καὶ τὸ ἀρνίον ἡ κιβωτὸς τῆς διαθήκης αὐτῆς.

80. On the communicative purpose of the city and of the urban community, see Comblin, *Théologie de la Ville*, 203–4, although not with sufficient consideration of the particular character of Hellenistic cities, which had radicalized this aspect of the urban.

81. On the democratization of function, of office, and in particular of authority and power in the Johannine conception of the New Jerusalem, see Comblin, *Théologie de la Ville*, 221–22. Comblin also points out correctly (224) that John envisions the end of the state with his depiction of the new Jerusalem.

82. The width of the streets, the multiplicity of plazas and parks, and the great number of public buildings with a great deal of free space around them demonstrate the interest of the planners of Hellenistic cities in airy arrangements and free incidence of light.

83. Against Charles, *Critical and Exegetical Commentary*, 2:171.

of the early church had used as well.[84] The particular variant of the Isaiah text, the addition of the kings, is adopted, too. The aspect of the open city is developed far beyond Trito-Isaiah,[85] and John lets peoples and kings even contribute to the splendor and honor of the city. The original wealth of the city and the influx of new treasures are meant as counterparts to the depiction of Babylon/Rome in Rev 17 and 18. John leaves out the depiction of the return of Israel immediately following in the basic Isaiah text. This means that he first gives the impression that the population of the new Jerusalem consisted merely of the (pagan) peoples and of the archrogues of apocalyptic ideology, the kings. Only in 21:27 does he add the reference to those inscribed in the Lamb's book of life. This reference provides a bridge to the remaining work. However, by considering kings and pagan peoples in their entirety as being enrolled in the book of life, the connection is established not only with the universalism of 21:3 but also especially with that of 7:9–10. The negation of 21:27a cannot amount to a real limitation, even less a contradiction. It reads rather as an assurance of the purity of the new world, an assurance that emphasizes God's miraculous will of grace already intimated before.

With these points John can claim that the eschatological city realizes ideals that the pluralistically oriented Hellenistic city intended: the reconciliation and integration of all nations and the equalization of all classes,[86] all under the banner of education, here alluded to with the motif of light, a common metaphor for education. At the same time, it is an image that generalizes in a democratizing fashion the symbol of light used in Deutero-Isaiah (42:6; 49:6) for the mission of the servant of the Lord, later applied to all of Israel and then to the propagandistic and educational task of the missionary activity of Judaism.[87] The intention of the biblical Babylon (Gen 11) to unite humanity is now successfully observed. The new Jerusalem fulfills another ideal that the Hellenistic cities strove for but never accomplished: the reconciliation of town and countryside. In the city of John's utopia, there is no longer any differentiation between inside and outside. All are full citizens. The new city is paradise as well. It integrates nature. It gives the water of life and holds the tree of life, not

---

84. About the motif of the pilgrimage of nations, see Comblin, *La liturgie de la Nouvelle Jérusalem*, 23–27, and Dieter Georgi, *Remembering the Poor: The History of Paul's Collection for Jerusalem* (Nashville: Abingdon, 1992), passim.

85. The doubling of peoples in 21:24 and 26.

86. The idea of universal reconciliation is already presented in 2 Cor 5:17–21, going beyond Isa 43:18–19, and has gained new dimensions in Rev 21 and 22.

87. As Paul proves in Rom 2:19. He has transferred this motif to the mission of the church in 2 Cor 4:4, 6 and Phil 2:15.

merely once but in infinite variety in the form of the avenue alongside the river and the main street.[88] There is no prohibition or curse any longer that would shield anything from God's human partners, nothing that would resemble the negative sides of Gen 2 and 3.

The emphasis is on the river. This image is taken from the vision of Ezekiel.[89] However, in contrast to that prophet's description, the miraculous water now no longer flows out of the temple but now comes out from under the throne of God and the Lamb. Parallel to Jewish language usage, Revelation takes the throne to be the symbol of God's power and presence.[90] Taking this into account, it is all the more striking and must be conscious intention that in 22:1–4 both thrones remain empty. Prior to that, the text had already spoken of the lightlike omnipresence of God and the Lamb. John is not interested in following Ezekiel in making the river that now comes out from under the throne (in Ezekiel it comes from the temple) into a growing influx into the Dead Sea. John emphasizes rather that the river flows through the entire city. The connection with the great avenue and the rows of trees makes it obvious that a comparison with Babylon is intended.[91] The image of the wide boulevard stems from the Roman version of the Hellenistic city.[92] The new Jerusalem is "Babylon *rediviva*," the epitome of the evil city revived. This means the reconciliation of the primeval rebellion of civilization against God. It means the end of the dispersion of the people of Israel, and all peoples,

---

88. Most commentators agree that the neuter singular ξύλον here is supposed to mean a plurality and not just one tree because of the reference to the river's two sides and to the street. The grammatical construction makes it difficult to decide whether the second row of trees is supposed to be visualized between river and street or whether river and street run side by side and the row of trees is then beyond the street. It is not impossible either that a third row of trees is meant, running in the middle of the street along both lanes, so to speak. It is clear that there is a row of trees on the other side of street and river, that is, beyond the river.

89. But see also Joel 3:18 and Zech 14:8–11 (yet there, two streams flowing in opposite directions).

90. See Ezek 43:7 (the throne is here identical with the presence of God).

91. See already the motif of the cube and that of the celestial city, both of which are related to Babylon.

92. While the Hellenistic city knew only regular rectangular or squarelike layouts of streets with little emphasis on the extension of the individual road, the Roman pattern emphasized more and more the axial ordering of roads. This included singling out one or more main streets and included a certain tendency to the grand street, the avenue or boulevard, a return to the old oriental procession street. In the new Jerusalem of John, there are no longer any processions. Their necessity has disappeared (i.e., the maintenance and increase of fertility and of protection against human and nonhuman enemies). This is correctly stated by Comblin, *Théologie de la Ville*, 206: "La grande avenue de la cité mythique est exorcisée. Dans la cité de Dieu, il n'y a plus de processions."

and their eschatological reunion and reconciliation. Abundance of water and the accompanying monthly harvest offered by the trees of life put an end to the constant threat experienced by Babylon and other oriental and Hellenistic cities due to the desert, lack of water, thirst, and famine. The city of the last days shares with its Hellenistic and Roman predecessor an irresistible force of attraction. It is truly able to give space, life, and even healing to all without distinction, thus fulfilling the utopian hope of the masses that streamed into the Mediterranean cities and lived there.

The vision ends with renewed emphasis on the present, now adding the visibility of God and the Lamb in the city.[93] That God can be visible and concretely present, thus constituting and maintaining covenantal communion, is an old covenant motif, and therefore John immediately supplements it with the service motif.[94] The visibility of God and the Lamb is further interpreted as radiating brightness, as omnipresent illumined essence of God, as *lux invicta*. The correspondence to this majesty that distributes and communicates itself everywhere is the kingship of everyone.[95] The community of those who adhere to Jesus looks ahead

---

93. About the close linkage of God's visibility and presence with openness, communication, and community in the city, see ibid., 204 (and 225). Page 214 also has important things to say about the critical questions that the understanding of God in Rev 21 and 22 puts to contemporary conceptions of God and their social aspects.

94. On the vision of God and the worship service, see Schüssler Fiorenza, *Priester für Gott*, 379–82 and 382–84.

95. Schüssler-Fiorenza (ibid., 384–89) already sees in the names on the forehead more than merely eschatological sealing, namely, the bearing of headdress of rulership (something like that of a vice-king). In her opinion (168–73, 198–203, 237–62, 283–90, 334–38, and several more places), the Johannine idea of the promise of kingship (and priesthood) stems from the early Christian baptismal confession, which is based on Exod 19:6. She shows that John emphasizes the christological reference and thereby underlines especially strongly the motif of rulership. On the omission of the concept of priesthood in Rev 22:1–5, she gives her opinion on 401–4. Comblin (*La liturgie de la Nouvelle Jérusalem*, 18–19) is correct in arguing that, insofar as priesthood, mediation, and cult belong together, there can no longer be mention of priesthood in the new Jerusalem. Schüssler Fiorenza agrees with Comblin on this. One must agree with her, though, in that the Johannine understanding of priesthood is not exhausted by this aspect but that the motifs of service and of rulership belong to it as well, both of them now democratized. She shows as well (370–72), in referring to 2 Tim 2:11–12 and Rom 5:17, that the motif of eschatological mediation is a very old tradition in the early church, and she also sees it behind the antignostic criticism in 1 Cor 4:8 (see also ibid., 373). In the emphasis of John on the future character of co-rulership (on the Aion formula, ibid., 368–74) she wants to see an anti-enthusiast. i.e., antignostic tendency. It is no doubt important that in the antiheretical messages in Rev 2 and 3 the victor statements are particularly pointed. But the interest of the author goes not so much in the direction of anti-enthusiasm, rather more toward the formation of a theologically founded critical political consciousness, as he continues doing later on too, especially in Rev 13, 17, and 18, and then finally, summarizing and crowning everything, in Rev 21 and 22.

toward the real city, the city of the "new age," to the ultimate unification of Jerusalem, Babylon, Alexandria, Antioch, Athens, and Rome as the completion of these and all cities but also as the reconciliation and promise of and for all the people of the entire world.[96] Heaven as world, the world as city, and the city as a democratized world[97]—with such an image ends the Revelation of John and proves itself thus to be an authentic child of the Hellenistic-Roman world, a truly urban world, in which there is a countryside too.

---

96. Comblin, *Théologie de la Ville*, 197: "La venue de la nouvelle Jérusalem est l'achèvement de l'histoire de la ville. Elle est la conclusion de l'effort gigantesque de l'humanité que nous appelons urbanisation." See also 203.

97. Although not a democracy in the sense of modern Western constitutions but rather in the sense in which Aristides 26.60 describes the Roman Empire in an idealizing fashion: κοινὴ τῆς γῆς δημοκρατία ὑφ' ἑνί τῷ ἀρίστῳ ἄρχοντι καὶ κοσμητῇ. This conception is radicalized by John, since this ἄριστος is totally transparent, as Comblin emphasizes again and again.

11

THE WRATH OF THE DRAGON: PATRIARCHY'S LAST STAND

In antiquity as well as in modern times, the village and the countryside were and still are full of wit and humor; yet already in ancient times urbanization meant also an intensive accumulation and refinement of the aspects of laughter. The Hellenistic and Roman cities in particular became roaming places for jesters, jugglers, and jokers. It is high time that we drop the unfortunate assumption that the Bible had at best a merely marginal interest in jocundity. The Bible shows more humor than the reader usually gives it credit for. There is not only a good deal of irony, sarcasm, and satire but also outright humor and comedy. Most people would expect it the least in the last book of the Bible, which usually is associated with blood and gore. The book pokes fun at the power play of the Caesar, describes it as comedy. This is an efficient attack of the centralizing tendencies of imperial politics and Caesar religion, so foreign to the nature of the urban society of the Greco-Roman world, however picked up again and radicalized in the monstrosity of modern

---

* This paper was presented in March 1985 to the Theological Opportunities Program of Harvard Divinity School. TOP is a very successful continuing education program, mostly for women interested in theological issues, and it is self-governed. The Faculty of Divinity is used as resource for the lectures, and it assigns an advisor, which I was in the 1970s and 1980s until I left for Frankfurt. The essay deals with a major accompaniment of the bourgeoisie, the nation-state and nationalism, that has functioned as a continuous detriment to the well-being of the municipalities and urban society, not only despite the occasional beneficence to the cities but often enough because of it. Munificence of the nation-state has a tendency of being a golden persuasion that suffocates the autonomy of the urban communities so necessary for them, and the bounteous plenty can all too quickly be replaced by austerity where the municipalities are used as milking cows for the greater glory of the state.

nationalism, a sick offspring of the bourgeoisie, allegedly supportive of civic life but in fact a sinister parody of it, indeed patriarchy's last stand, an anachronistic burlesque.

As I wrote this paper on Rev 12, one of the most complex and debated texts in the New Testament, I decided against an academic approach and for a more meditative style. I used the reflections and results of historical-critical exegesis for the purpose of penetrating the drama of this chapter. I presuppose most of all the thorough analysis given to that text by Professor Adela Yarbro Collins in her book *The Combat Myth in the Book of Revelation*.[1] Professor Collins has pursued her studies on Revelation further in later publications, particularly in her brief commentary on the Apocalypse and her book *Crisis and Catharsis*.

With Professor Collins I date the book in the 90s of the first century, toward the end of the reign of Domitian. With her I presume that the author combines two stories in Rev 12. His editorial additions are also clearly visible. The two stories are (1) the story of the woman giving birth, fleeing, and being pursued by the dragon (12:1–5, 14–16) and (2) the battle in heaven between Michael and Satan (12:7–9). The justification for my procedure lies in the fact that the author was able to create a new unit out of the different parts, the similarities as well as the contrasts, partly through playing on the associations of the readers.

The Bible reader trying to understand the rich imagery of Rev 12 will attempt to read it against the foil of the story of another encounter between a woman and a reptile, the snake's temptation of Eve in Gen 3, the narrative that for millennia has been understood as the seal on the fate of humankind, most of all of womanhood. However, if one tries this story of Gen 3 as a foil for Rev 12 one will notice surprising differences. The woman of Rev 12 is not a mate to anyone, neither man nor God. She is queen of heaven, clothed with the sun, the moon under her feet, the zodiac as her crown. This woman is divine and does not need salvation. Thus she is meant to represent something more than Eve, even more than Zion, Jerusalem, or Israel, female figures of larger than human size in the Hebrew Bible. She brings divinities to mind, most of all wisdom and Isis.

Whereas Eve is tempted, the queen of heaven of Rev 12 is threatened—by the dragon, the snake. Why? Because this woman is to become mother, first of one child, then of many. Nothing is said of a father in our story. The children mentioned are truly hers and hers alone. What causes the wrath of the dragon? Not her being the queen of heaven but her becom-

---

1. HDR 9; Missoula, Mont.: Scholars Press, 1976.

ing mother; the new race she is about to bring forth is a threat to the dragon—and she is coming down to earth.

Thus, this threat by the woman is of a twofold kind. First, it is expressed in an old-fashioned manner. The child born first is described as crown prince, a boy who is to become ruler over all nations. As we learn later in Rev 13, the dragon is interested in world dominance. Therefore the baby boy is his rival, a rebel, in fact. In terms of ancient myth, the dragon that claims the reign represents chaos, the young rival manifests the new order.

Later on in Rev 12 we learn that this baby boy will not remain alone. The woman will be a mother to many more. The baby boy will have to share his role with many sisters and brothers. Thus the threat is secondly and most of all not that of a new monarchy but that of democracy. This democracy is one defined not by power but by the keeping of the ordinances of God, which is identified as keeping the witness of Jesus. The witness of Jesus is understood by John as the active expectation that the world of tomorrow will be created, structured, and maintained not by power and power-brokers but by forgiveness, understanding, and sharing, and this expectation goes together with the knowledge that this is subversively true already now.

The heavenly queenship of the woman in Rev 12 is not that of superior heavenly knowledge, wisdom, and power, as her counterparts wisdom and Isis would have it, but it is her ability and willingness to motherly exposure, deliverance, and nurture in time of human crisis. This motherhood providing a rebelling race is not forced upon her but is of her own free will, not withstanding the suffering of threat and flight. It is all for the sake of a fundamental change. The bringing about of a new race means the bringing about of a new creation, this time not by male killing but by female life-giving. As her first child is raptured and put into safety, the woman protects her further offspring by leaving her heavenly power base and fleeing into the desert, from an ancient perspective a suicidal move, heaven being the area of divine power whereas the desert is the place of demons and chaos, certain physical and spiritual death; thus the flight into the desert is a certain descent into hell.

Biblical and Jewish tradition, of course, know that this place of mortal and spiritual dangers can be turned into a place of refuge, as the story of Israel's exodus and many more examples prove. Likewise in the case of the queen of heaven the descent into hell turns into a protective flight, with nourishment of miraculous providence as well.

It is most interesting that God does not appear as a main actor in the scenes of Rev 12. Events seem to occur without the deity as stage-director. God appears more like the stagehand who in an awkward situation helps the prima donna with a few signs of endearment. Even as the author shifts the attention of the drama from the woman's flight once more to heaven and starts a new act, God does not take center stage, nor does the child. The atmosphere of threat and danger of the first phase now turns into outright battle, but neither woman, crown prince, nor God join in this fight, as one might expect. Only the dragon does. However, whereas in the first phase one might have suspected the dragon as a figure of the underworld, the second scene clearly puts him into heaven, into the role of a major angel. John makes him the state attorney of the heavenly order, God's prosecutor. But the state attorney apparently goes for a higher office, and only an emergency measure, the countercoup of Michael and his fellow angels, can stop the coup of Satan and his angels.

What first smells of fist fighting and power play among the big boys turns out to be a question about true order. The many versions of the myth of divine combat parallel to the scenes of Rev 12, in the ancient Near East, in Egypt, and in Greece, justify always the governing patriarchal order and claim that it has won out over chaos in primordial times. What is order and what is chaos is not questioned even when chaos is considered to be lingering on, as existential disorder under the surface of society or as evil thought in one's own heart.

John, however, though speaking in the language of myth, does not talk about something primordial but about something only a little while ago. John concedes that Satan had a claim on heaven until recently. Satan had this claim not on heaven alone but even on order. Now, what if the child was not a threat to Satan's order but of order as such? What if the rapture was an illegitimate intrusion into the divine order? What if Michael covered up for an illegal entry and the hiding of a usurper, the boy? Did Michael not interfere with proper law-enforcement?

Later we learn that Satan's main charges were leveled against the allegedly faithful. What if they were indeed a conspiring gang? What if the faithful were the real sinners, rebels against the all-pervasive order, questioning not only reality but challenging the order that protects us all? Would not the takeover of the woman's seed mean that the stronger no longer controls, that the above is no longer above but below? Does the customary pyramid of power not represent a saving order instead? Is Satan not the real protector of the world of order, whereas the woman and her seed represent true chaos, upsetting the world, causing catastrophe?

Michael's coup is portrayed as a close call, and it resolved matters in heaven alone. Satan and his angels are thrown out. The access to the baby boy of the queen of heaven is denied to them, and so is further pursuit of their claims in heavenly quarters. But not so on earth, not so with respect to the woman and her further children. They are pursued by the dragon.

It appears frivolous to us that the author interrupts the story, nevertheless, in order to let us hear a song celebrating victory. Is that not premature? We shall see when we return to the hymn. Presently we shall follow the story.

We have already spoken about the fact that the desert, originally a place of danger, has turned into one of protection for the woman. More explicitly, the desert as a place where chaos dwells would be expected to be Satan's domain, turning against the woman. However, the dragon's tools turn against him. The desert shields the woman. Now the dragon uses another instrument of his against the woman: abundance of water, the deadly flash flood striking the unbewaring desert traveler, tearing away everything and either drowning the woman or carrying her to the dragon defenselessly.

The dragon does not succeed, however. Another instrument of his, the underworld, does not cooperate with the dragon either but helps the woman. The earth opens, and the underworld takes in the flood. Then with a masterful stroke of his pen the author all of a sudden adds the sea, and thus a combination of two weapons of the devil, the abyss as well as the ocean, appears, and the ocean now separates the dragon from the woman and her children, not threatening her as one would expect but protecting her. Thus the story ends on a curious note: "And he stood at the sand of the sea." The reader is moved to say, "Poor dragon!" His dominion has turned against him. His powers have revolted, making his purpose and efforts futile—the utmost of irony.

This irony is reflected in the triumphant song in the middle of the chapter. The revolt of the dragon's media is meant to prove that the conviction expressed in the hymn is not mistaken but justified. Patriarchal order is in disarray. Its last stand is that of the dragon like a kid standing at the shore of the sea with all his marbles washed away. The boy turned a spigot, and a flood came, the nightmare of the sorcerer's apprentice putting even the sorcerer out of his wits.

It is quite interesting that in the central hymn of our chapter the victorious warriors, Michael and his angels, are not celebrated. On the contrary, those who did nothing are celebrated, first of all God and Christ, and then, in a surprise move, the faithful. They are celebrated as the victors. The active battle in heaven is not the real fight, but the dragon is overcome by the quiet rebellion of the fellow-travelers of the Lamb on earth. Thus the scene in heaven is only a cinemascope reflection of the real thing on earth. But does this not mean that Rev 12 speaks of earthly rebellion in a condoning, indeed encouraging fashion? Whom do John and his friends challenge? Whose world dominance do the woman and her offspring threaten?

This comes out in Rev 13. This chapter provides us not with a continuation of the story of Rev 12, but it gives us a rerun, a variation of the story of the dragon, now represented by the two beasts, the representatives of the dragon who rescues some of his marbles from the sea, as it were. In Rev 13 a ruler and his prophet represent the threat of the dragon to the woman and her offspring. Here the author of Revelation lifts the veil of his imagery, intimating that more than an individual dream journal is intended. John, victim of Roman banishment on the island of Patmos, writes to his fellow-believers on the mainland of Asia Minor, and in this document, which is to be smuggled out, he denounces and attacks the very system that keeps him hostage, and he denounces its religion. He challenges the Roman state and the Caesar religion.

The Roman system reformed by Augustus and celebrated in the Caesar religion appeared to the ancient world as an enlightened system of law and order, justice and peace, humane and not despotic, clearly the most humane system the world had seen thus far. John, however, denounces this system as the epitome of despotism, the utmost of repression. The Caesar religion is seen as an all-penetrating manipulation of consent, a civil religion of allegedly mutual loyalty and solidarity, but all the more stifling and exploitative. In Rev 13 and later in 17 John portrays this system in mythological terms, in patriarchal colors. It is trinitarian; there is the dragon as the transcendent father, the first beast as the son, the alleged savior and redeemer; and the second beast functioning as the spiritual agent, the organizer of the church of the beast and its worship.

What is described as a rather transcendental encounter in Rev 12 is revealed in Rev 13, 17, and 18 as systematic, political, social, and economic threat and repression. John's dreams are not just insights into individual psychological conditions but are insights into social and political predicaments of which the individual condition is but a part. But is not this assessment of the Roman system defamation? Its achievements, peace and a stable world, were obvious in light of the previous one hundred years of civil war and over against the barbaric systems of other potentates. John's denunciation and resistance could be correctly interpreted as advocacy of anarchy and chaos, as undermining of the commonwealth, of the common good not just of the rich and powerful but also of the common people. The Jesus believers, a gang of anarchists? The book of Revelation, a handbook of terrorism? Is it not too much terror that the book describes, terror against the establishment as well as against the commoners?

John is aware of the precarious dimension of his message, which is an attack on an order more humane than any other before. Thus he concedes the heavenly position of Satan, his role as attorney of the heavenly order. Moreover, he acknowledges the power not just of the Caesars' establishment but also of the Caesar religion, the ability of the Caesar to create and maintain consent, to have the polls come out in his favor—and without any rigging of the results.

The great mother and her children, the noncollaborators, stand there squarely in the middle of the book of Revelation, however, ridiculing the governing power, taunting its claim of eternity, proclaiming its self-destruction and collapse.

Domitian, the Caesar of John's time, is no longer; the Roman Empire is gone. Before it went to pieces, however, it was able to co-opt a major part of the church of Jesus Christ, turning the Christ faith into the official Caesar religion. In the name of Jesus the officers of the Caesar now invoked and enforced loyalty to the Caesar, the consent of what was supposed to be the commonwealth.

The appearance of the modern age came with the nation-states slowly dissolving the Roman Empire, now called the Holy Roman Empire. We understand the appearance of nation-states as a breakthrough of civilization. They even brought democracy. All these nation-states developed nationalism. Seen through the critical eyes of the author of Revelation, this nationalism everywhere has the marks of a religion, the dominant religion, the religion that provides the excitement and protection of national consent. In almost all cases, particularly in that of Western democracies, the churches support this national religion, and, in fact, modern nationalism can claim biblical roots. The Caesar religion of today is nationalism. Nationalism is the perfection of patriarchy.

So what about the triumphant song of Rev 12? What about the biting story of the dragon standing at the shore of the ocean, wrath turned impotent? Is not the talk about patriarchy's last stand mocked by the experience of the dragon's power for two thousand more years? Has not John been proven wrong? Where is the queen of heaven? Co-opted too? Is not motherhood together with flag and apple pie one of the three pillars of our national consent?

The final breakdown of the dragon's dominance will happen when the mothers, real and potential, take the apple pies and throw them at the flag and teach their children to do likewise. There he stands, the dragon of patriarchy, draped in the flag, covered with apple pie.

12

SHOULD AUGUSTINE HAVE THE LAST WORD ON URBAN THEOLOGY?

1. INTRODUCTION

We have observed several times already that although the early church in its majority demonstrated an urban concentration some opposite tendencies developed slowly. They started in the second generation and gained momentum in the second century. The person who gave these deurbanizing tendencies full justification and final swing was a double convert first from paganism and then from Manicheanism and later became bishop of the Northwest African diocese of Hippo: Augustine (354–430). He made the church finally turn its back to the big cities of the Mediterranean that had turned into colossal slums. He made the turn decidedly toward the small towns and the countryside, the *pagus*. The inhabitants of the villages in Latin were called *pagani, pagus*-dwellers, a term that in earlier days urbanized Jews and members of the early church had identified with idolatrous and ungodly polytheism, *paganism*, that is, primarily a sociological concept that then was changed into a negative religious qualification. Augustine was the theologian and politician who finally stood for a complete turnaround of these initial connotations. Due to his efforts a "paganization" of the church, its message, and its theology came about. Augustine made a tremendous and successful effort to reinterpret Paul as the mastermind of that change, thus supporting the claim that this change was no turn at all but the original and divine intention.

---

* Based on a paper given on 1 November 1991 at a symposium of the School of Protestant Theology of the Johann Wolfgang Goethe University in Frankfurt on Main on "Religion in Multicultural Context."

The change that was not supposed to be one meant also to a high degree a de-Judaizing and Latinizing of Paul, in the sense of the Latin culture of the fourth century, no longer that of the first centuries B.C.E. and C.E., with its pluralistic urban outlook. The Latin theology Augustine represented emulated a good deal of the ideological changes the Caesar religion had made to the Latin heritage. The city of old was replaced by the church as salvation machine, something the Caesars would have liked their empire to be. Augustine's Paul, although a complete contrast to the authentic one, became the Paul of the church, slowly even seeping into the churches of the East and their theologies.

2. GOODBYE TO AUGUSTINE

2.1. Augustine as Interpreter of Paul

This essay takes up the question as to why theology at large and Protestantism in particular as an institutionalized entity never made themselves at home in large cities. All the essays in this collection deal to varying degrees with the curious absence of urban concerns in institutional theology before and after the Reformation.[1]

This blindness of academic theology toward the city, particularly in its larger forms, is not limited to Protestantism but reaches deep into the Middle Ages. It is, in fact, an inability to grasp the urban social situation as a challenge and a call to undertake a different kind of theology than that of typical small towns. Since the Middle Ages, large cities have never been seen as a theologically relevant phenomenon or as a proper subject of theological inquiry. This disinterest is not inherited from the early church but has a later origin. It caused an essential break in the social concern of theological inquiry and caused a major change in the character of theological discourse. In fact, the early church was essentially urbanly oriented. The transformation of Christianity into the Roman state religion went hand in hand with a strong preoccupation of the church with the countryside and small town. The Germanic invasion of the Mediterranean increased this tendency, and the resulting orientation characterizes all Christian churches around the globe to this day. Later on, when factual coexistence between urban developments and certain theological changes occurred—such as in the case of the contemporaneity between the beginnings of scholastic theology, in particular that of Thomistic theology, and

---

1. In particular, pages 218–20; see further 255–82, 283–307, 343–66.

the strengthening of the medieval city—these relationships were never discussed let alone integrated into theological conception. Instead, they were pushed to and beyond the margin of theological reflection.

In his book, *The Conscience of the Eye: The Design and Social Life of Cities*, sociologist Richard Sennett has pointed to the fatal influence of Augustine's *De civitate Dei* on the development of ecclesial consciousness and in particular of urban consciousness in the world of Christianity.[2] He establishes the plausible thesis that Augustine's influence affects city consciousness even today in concrete and practical ways, not only in Europe but also in the United States.[3] Thanks to the arguments of Augustine's *De civitate Dei*, cities with a Christian background have not consciously furthered multicultural developments and structures but merely let them happen or actively tried to prevent them.

Sennett takes his departure from Augustine's statement in chapter 1 of book 15 of the work quoted. Here, in following the conclusion of the story of Cain and Abel in Gen 4, Augustine makes the following observation: "Of Cain is written that he founded a city, yet Abel being a sojourner built none. For the city of the saints is above although it creates citizens here as well, where they do their pilgrimage until the time of their reign approaches." In many translations of Augustine, the Latin term *civitas* used by Augustine is all too quickly identified with the state, which modern readers easily and erroneously equate with the modern territorial state. This would be incorrect, for Augustine first and foremost thinks of the ancient city as the representative or epitome, at least the capital, of the political community—a phenomenon still existing in Roman times.[4] The external occasion for the writing of *De civitate* is not the

---

2. Richard Sennett, *The Conscience of the Eye: The Design and Social Life of Cities* (New York: Knopf, 1990). On Augustine, see further Peter Brown, *Augustine of Hippo: A Biography* (New York: Dorset, 1967); and Alfred Schindler, "Augustine/Augustinismus" TRE 4: 644–98. The following articles on Augustineanism in the Middle Ages, Reformation, and modern times can also be read as accompaniment and supplement to the ideas presented above, although this was not necessarily the intention of the authors.

3. One should add that this is the same elsewhere in the world as the megalopolises in "Christian" Latin America or the capital of the Philippines, the only "Christian" country in the Far East, demonstrate. They have the same basic problems as the large cities and metropolitan areas in non-Christian countries.

4. According to Schindler, the *civitas dei* in Augustine is to be understood as "Summe all jener vernuftbegabten Wesen, die Gott über alles und alles andere um seinetwillen lieben" Augustine's *civitas diaboli* is determined by the "Selbst-liebe bzw. 'superbia' (d.h., wie Gott sein wollen')" (Schindler, "Augustine/Augustinismus," 680). A positive evaluation of the Augustinean *civitas* concept as much as of the so-called two-regiments doctrine is found also in Ulrich Duchrow, *Christenheit und Weltverantwortung: Traditionsgeschichte und systematische Struktur der Zweireichelehre* (Forschungen und Berichte der Evangelischen

decline of the Roman Empire as a territorial state but the conquest and plundering of the city of Rome by the Vandals in 410 C.E.

Before the passage quoted from book 15 about the fratricide Cain founding cities, Augustine had said that Cain belonged to the *civitas*, the urban community of humans, that he was a *civis* of this *saeculum*. Abel, instead, was a citizen of the heavenly city. People who know their Bible also know that Augustine, in this emphasis on the transcendence of the only true city, is referring to the Epistle to the Hebrews in the New Testament, where we find the claim: "We do not have here a lasting city, but we search for the future one" (Heb 13:14). The whole eleventh chapter of this epistle had this heavenly city in mind as the goal of hope. In these texts, Hebrews picks up prophetic and apocalyptic traditions that are seemingly confirmed by the last book of the Bible, the Revelation of John. I have spoken of its visions of the new Jerusalem above. Augustine is of the opinion that another New Testament text is in his favor: 1 Peter, where the believers are described as "strangers and refugees." This is actually a legal definition of the relationship of the believers to the urban society, a definition that also calls on Ps 39:13 (Gen 23:4; 47:9).

Later, Augustine writes in chapter 5 of the same book 15:

> Therefore the first founder of an earthly civic community [*civitas*] was a fratricide. Overcome by envy, he killed namely his brother, the citizen of the eternal civic community [*civitas*], who was (merely) sojourning on this earth. Thus (the following) is not astonishing: long after that at the founding of that *civitas* that was to become the head of the *civitas* about which we are talking and which was to rule over many peoples, this (*civitas*) corresponded to this first example and archetype as the Greeks call it, which is an image of (its) particular kind.[5]

Then Augustine presents Romulus, the founder of Rome, as murderer of his brother. The earthly and visible city is thus the product and sanctuary of murder and manslaughter. In the case of the foundation of Rome, the search for glory was the reason for the murder; in the case of Cain and Abel, it was envy, for Augustine, the more evil, a truly devilish reason.

Studiengemeinschaft 25; Stuttgart: Klett, 1969]). Duchrow's statement that *civitas* in Augustine means "Staat, Herrschaftsverband, Stadt, Bürgerschaft, Bürgerrecht" completely misses the social-historical problematic of the term spoken about above. The oft-repeated claim, also found in Schindler and Duchrow, that the opposite of the *civitas dei* in Augustine, the *civitas diaboli*, did not include the concrete city and the state is plainly palliative.

5. The Latin construction of the sentence is rather complex. It is obvious, however, that the "which is an image of (its) particular kind" (*quaedam sui generis imago*) implies the murderous nature of the earthly city as innate and continuous since the very beginning.

Augustine here suspects the spatial contrast of *here* and *there* as much as the temporal antithesis of *now* and *then*. In using this polarization, he believes he has Paul's letter to the Galatians on his side, where in chapter 4 Hagar and Sarah are confronted. Of Hagar, Paul says in that context: "She is Mount Sinai in Arabia." This mountain Sinai is then equated by Paul in a hazardous exegesis with the earthly Jerusalem and associated with slavery. Of Sarah, Gal 4:26 says that she is the "upper Jerusalem," that is, the heavenly Jerusalem. It is the "free (city) that is our mother (that is, of the adherents of Christ)."

Since Paul in this passage parallels the contrasts of *here* and *there* and of *now* and *then* with that of *flesh* and *spirit,* Augustine feels himself entitled—using his internalizing exegesis of Paul—to internalize the contrast of these two cities, the *civitas terrena* and the *civitas dei,* as well. Augustine also introduces the contrasts of *inside* and *outside* and of (sexual) *sensuousness* and (asexual and ascetic) *virtuousness.*

Augustine develops the idea of the new Jerusalem as the heavenly world in conscious debate with pagan Roman theology. In this context, the term "urban theology," *theologia urbana,* shows up, but it is used by Augustine in an ironical sense. It occurs in Augustine's critical discussion of the theology of the Roman statesman and scholar Varro, who lived from 116–27 B.C.E. His main work, the forty-one books of the *Antiquitates rerum humanarum et divinarum,* made him the primary theologian of the Caesar religion.

Varro's gigantic work is preserved for us merely in fragments and this through the quotes in Augustine's *De civitate Dei.* Augustine distinguishes three kinds, three genera, of theology: the *genus mythicum,* the *genus physicum,* and the *genus civile.* Augustine's differentiation thus is between a mythical, a natural, and a civil theology. The civil theology, that of and for the citizens, can be seen as popular theology too, or, as Varro denotes it, as a theology of and for the people, a folk theology.

This third kind, the *theologia civilis,* Augustine ironically calls *theologia urbana,* that is, urban theology. Augustine means that in a belittling sense: a *merely* urban (i.e., particular) theology. Instead, Augustine promises a universal theology, valid for the entire world once and for all.

In Varro's classification, urban theology, folk theology, deals with the reasonable treatment of the question of which cults need to be publicly recognized and furthered in the city, that is, which cults are supposed to widely influence and determine the urban culture. This includes the erection and maintenance of public cultic buildings and thus relates to land and property distribution and to road construction, since access to these buildings and their rites needs to be guaranteed by the municipality. The monuments of the city and especially the theater are, as in all Hellenistic-Roman townships, religious entities too. The theater is also the seat of the people's assembly. Augustine identifies the *theologia civilis,* or, as he sarcastically says, the *theologia urbana,* with the mythical theology and in a biting fashion calls them both "theatric theology."

The question of whether and how certain cults were to determine the urban culture was for Varro a matter of the *populus,* of the people and its organs of government, not only a matter of the priests, poets, and philosophers, but especially of the democratic organs of the city, that is, of the people's assembly, senate, and magistrate. For Augustine, this relationship of urban theology to the public and the people was anything but commending; it was too little heaven-related and far too particularistic.

The differentiations within the individual cities and between the cities, the incredible plurality of the Mediterranean culture that also kept the borders to the east, south, and north open, these needed to be overcome by a unified and generalized Christian religion, according to Augustine. He could explain the need for such simplification by this pluralistic culture's religious, in fact, polytheistic, dimension. The monotheist Augustine understood and recommended generalization and uniformity within and outside of the church as liberation. For him, particularization and multifariousness were inappropriate fetterings, not only in religious and theological respects but also in that of civilization. The voice of the people, the *vox populi,* was for Augustine not something to which church and theology should be exposed and be answerable. The people of the church could and must listen attentively, pray, and sing hymns. For Augustine, the Christian freedom he praised no longer had any room for a legal voice of the church people, not to even mention the liberty of the general city population.

Augustine turns the freedom of the citizen into a completely internal matter. It is the freedom "that frees us from the tyranny of sin, death, and devil." The very realistic conception of peace present in the Hellenistic-Roman world and also the extremely concrete, materially meant hope for peace in the biblical message is turned by Augustine into an inner peace that continues in heaven as an eternal enjoyment of sentimental peacefulness and happiness.

In his discussion of Roman religion and theology, Augustine distinguishes between *civitas terrena* (the earthly *civitas*) and the *civitas caelestis* (the heavenly *civitas*) and sets them against each other. Rome vicariously stands for the *civitas terrena,* the earthly *civitas.* Augustine, in following the Apocalypse of John, identifies Rome with Babylon, but these are more than mere cities for him. They are the inhabited earth in its entirety. Augustine can also call it *civitas diaboli,* "city of the devil." On the other side, that of the *civitas caelestis* (the heavenly *civitas*) or of the eternal city (the *civitas sempiterna*), he sees the "heavenly Jerusalem," identical with the *civitas dei*, the *civitas* of God.⁶ As Augustine is speaking of the *res publica terrena* (the earthly republic) and contrasting it with the *res publica caelestis* (the heavenly republic), he still uses the classical terminology of Rome as city, but in both cases he subversively shifts beyond the concept of the single city to the idea of the territorial state.⁷

As already said, the sack of the city of Rome was the point of departure for writing *De civitate Dei*. However, one of the essential theses of the book is that it does not really depend on a concrete city such as Rome in any decisive sense, not even as far as the existing Roman Empire is concerned. Augustine closes his eyes in particular to the manifest economic and social decay of the cities of the Mediterranean. He thereby only reconfirms the decision the allegedly "orthodox" church had made long ago: to devote its interest more or less completely to small towns and even more so to rural areas and villages.

According to *Civ.* 2.28, those who are destined to real (heavenly) life are saved from this prison, this place of demonic impurity and fettering, already during their (temporal) life time "have been moved by the name of Christ ... and out of the night of most pernicious godlessness into the light of the most beneficial fear of God." Those who are saved in this fashion assemble "for chaste celebration, in reputable separation of the sexes..., where they learn that one has to live here piously, limited in time in order to gain after this life the blessed permanent life."⁸ The church of Augustine is quite concretely an institution of salvation, "where Holy Scripture and the teaching of righteousness are proclaimed in front of the entire congregation from an exalted place, to the listeners who act accordingly for salvation, to those who do not act accordingly for judgement."

It is characteristic for Augustine's theological ideas and equally important and fateful for the history of their consequences that Augustine fails to consider the concrete fact that the organized church in which he himself holds office and exercises power in an autocratic fashion has in fact become the state religion. It is constitutive for Augustine's ecclesiological

---

6. In the latter, he finds a *curia* as in the city of Rome, namely, the *curia caelestis*, for him the assembly of the (good) angels who have to be distinguished from the fallen ones.

7. Thus the term *civitas* actually means the city community. It has not lost this meaning in Augustine yet. We shall see that the meaning "territorial state" is already to be found, but it has not yet taken over. The connotation of "city" is still strong.

8. In this puritan description, the parallel to Manichean thought is again obvious. When for Augustine's symbolic counterpart of the heavenly city, namely, the *civitas terrena*, the origin and growth of the city and procreation belong together as negative aspects, this is even radicalized Manicheanism, for the latter had a certain tendency to the urban despite its negative attitude to sexuality.

ideology that the church remains essentially threatened, even fought against, constantly embattled. This threat and fight are not of a real but of a mythical nature. The alleged evidence for this threatening of the church is artificial, an imagined facade. The "hatred of the world" is a cipher that is constitutive for Augustine's theology, in modern lingo a "virtual reality," but it is an unrenouncable basis for the theology of the church's self-understanding and power that Augustine relentlessly advocates.[9] The "reward of the saints," the heavenly life of the believers in the enjoyment of heavenly leisure, would not be serious enough for Augustine if life here on this earth would forgo the pressure of an eschatologically interpreted life situation, including constant hostility from human enemies with demonic or satanic wire-pullers in the background.[10] For this alleged suffering has a causative function and importance for receiving citizenship in the eternal and imperishable community of the heavenly city, the *civitas sempiterna*.

The bishop Julian of Aeclanum, a younger contemporary of Augustine, accused him of having merely superficially converted from Manicheanism to the Christianity of the "catholic" church. This thesis has been taken up again by Alfred Adam, who has brought new evidence from newly found original Manichean sources that support his allegations.[11] The constitutive dualism of good and bad and the mixture of both

---

9. This is why Augustine, his predecessors, and his successors are obsessed with discovering heresies and denouncing heretics. The existence of heresies and heretics is fundamentally, indeed ontologically, necessary for this theology of struggle where anything positive has to have something fearful as foundational counterpart.

10. The claim is common that this is an adoption and continuation of the eschatological thinking of the early church. This is, however, simply wrong, for an essential element of the eschatology of the early church is the realization that their own organization is a minority and that it has to take threats seriously from other groups and from the establishment. The specific apocalyptic form of eschatology that had been used in the New Testament as well possessed this realism of a threatened minority, too.

11 In his essay, "Die manichäische Herkunft der Lehre von den zwei Reichen bei Augustine," *ThLZ* 77 (1952): 385–90, Adam's portrayal of the Manichean origin and dimension of Augustine's doctrine of the two *civitates* has unfortunately remained only a sketch. In the context of the restoration of the German Federal Republic that occurred under "Christian" signs, such a claim as that of Adam was anything but welcome. For reasons that were politically understandable, it was never taken up, let alone worked out and continued. Peter Brown at the end of his Augustine biography distances Augustine from Mani and Manicheanism. He shows at various places, however, how much the "catholic" bishop Augustine was still in agreement with Mani and Manicheans; this agreement still plays an important part in Brown's concluding discussion (Brown, *Augustine of Hippo*, 381–97). Therefore, it is impossible to understand why in the following chapter Brown's treatment of Augustine's doctrine of predestination fails to undertake the necessary comparison with the Manichean teaching of predetermination. Schindler treats the theme Augustine/

in the present world, the identification of sin and desire, the doctrine of sin as an inheritable matter mediated sexually and literally by means of the genitals, all these are basic Manichean ideas, merely superficially camouflaged. In addition, we find the concept of a basically mythical evolution of salvation, merely superficially historicized. In Augustine's theology, the many demons and agents of salvation of the Manichean myth receive seemingly historical faces that are in reality just thinly covered abstract figures.

Augustine's concept of the church as a magically operative institution of salvation corresponds to Mani's thinking. Just as in Mani's theology, this church concept also claims to entail manifest revelation of salvation, means of salvation, and organs of salvation. Augustine's engagement for Holy Scripture as a firm canon is most easily understood in the light of Manicheism's mythified but nevertheless real interest in writings and in a bookishly fixed form of written tradition. Neither in Judaism nor in the majority of Christian groups prior to Augustine is his extremely high estimation of scriptures as canon to be found. The only real parallel in Hellenistic-Roman times exists in Mani and in Manicheanism. There we have an extreme interest in what is written by holy forces and hands.

Particularly important for this comparison is the concept of soul, the understanding of self as developed by Augustine. It presupposes the refined psychology of Manicheanism. Mani had inherited the gnostic interest in the self and its advanced psychological embellishment. Mani developed this further and conducted studies that can be called psychoanalytical, creating a corresponding peculiar therapy, which he made part of his work and its myth. Without Mani and Manicheanism, Augustine's *Confessiones* cannot be understood, neither in their origin nor in their composition. Authentic Manicheanism was, however, more conscious of the reality of the city and of urban existence than Augustine was.[12]

Augustine's Manicheanism became more virulent than Manicheanism proper, because in its Augustinean version it received a concealed

---

Manicheanism all too superficially. Duchrow gives it more extensive attention. Especially in his book *Sprachverständnis und biblisches Hören bei Augustine* (Hermeneutische Untersuchungen zur Theologie 6; Tübingen: Mohr Siebeck, 1965) he pursues this subject in a more thorough manner. He nevertheless veils the obviously mythical and dualistic orientation of Augustine in an apologetic fashion and overlooks the telling fact that Augustine's extreme preoccupation with questions of discipline has its best parallels in Manicheanism.

12. It certainly would be interesting to study the question as to how much Augustine's conversion to "catholic" Christianity was a reaction to fundamental urban elements in Manicheanism.

existence that was distorted due to the concealment. The distortion of Augustine's Manichean tendency, and at the same time its success in world history, were due to the Christian-Manichean mythical elements saddled with essential features of the Roman state ideology. This was synonymous with social provincializing, contrary to the originally urban tendencies of the early church and of Manicheanism. What defenders of Augustine praise as the biblical and historical elements in Augustine in fact stems for the most part from the state-sustaining Roman political ideology and the legends that supported it. For Augustine, as for the Romans, especially those that were conditioned by the Caesar religion, history was essentially heroic history, that of heroic men who proved themselves in their battle against the evil powers of this world. It is true that Augustine brings many biblical examples as well, but he treats them like the Roman ones. He denies their historical continuation in the Jewish experience, whereas he considers Roman history to be continuous and of essential importance for the present. Indeed, he sees in Roman nature a greater natural relationship to Christianity than in Judaism. The climax of that argument is found in the following sequence of thought, ghastly as well as disastrous in its consequences. According to Augustine, the Roman Empire expanded "thanks to the competence of its great men." About the Jews, Augustine says the following:

> the Jews were especially correctly [the Latin text says *rectissime*] given for the glory of the Romans [*istorum gloriae donati sunt*]. For we see that those who aspired and achieved earthly fame by means of their magnificent virtues [*qualibuscumque virtutibus*; i.e., the Romans] conquered the others [the Jews] who by means of [their] great vices [*magnis vitiis*] killed and cast out the one who had brought true fame and the eternal *civitas*. (*Civ.* 5.18)[13]

It is certain that Augustine believed to be following Paul, for instance the pseudo-Pauline insertion in 1 Thess 1:14–16. In reality, however, he lets himself be directed more by the image of Paul in the Acts of the Apostles than by the Paul of the letters. In Acts, Luke has Paul state that the Jews merited their condemnation by God and that this damnation is lasting, despite Paul's elsewhere emphatically stated opinion of the lasting election of Israel (Rom 9–11). For Augustine and his countless epigones, the history of the world is the judgment of the world. For this idea of God's governance of times (*gubernatio temporum*) Augustine sees

---

13. This anti-Jewish attitude shows in other passages too, for instance in 18.46, where the adversities the Jews have experienced are turned into counterfoils and testimonies for the truth of Christianity.

the Jews as the prime paradigm—indeed the only true paradigm, because in the case of the Romans and their many successors in imperial power, corruption, and lawlessness the judgment of God was and is never seen as consistent and fatal, as it is claimed for the Jews.

Augustine directly and indirectly uses the Roman *virtus* and with it also the Roman *mos* as leading concepts. It is mere pretense that Augustine replaces the *mos maiorium* with the biblical ethos. Augustine's ethos, more closely looked at, retains the character and structure of the *mos maiorum*. Within this context—not within a New Testament one—is Augustine's emphasis on forgiveness of sins to be found. Contrary to the historical Paul, Augustine sees the forgiveness of sins as an essential heritage of the apostle. The internalizing of Roman categories in Augustine is not Pauline at all; it is Manichean.

A further sign of the continuation of the Roman state myth in Augustine is that for him the goal of salvation—no longer mediated by the state but by the church—is "the true and perfect luck," *felicitas,* a circumlocution for the Roman Fortuna. Although for Augustine this is no longer a city goddess, as she had been throughout Hellenistic-Roman civilization, the connotations of Fortuna in *felicitas* remain "deposit of faith," that is, of *fides.* Thus Fortuna remains the basis of motivation for the members of the church, the citizens of the true, the heavenly *civitas,* that is, for the new and authentic Romans, unto whom Augustine projects the essential constitutional ideas and goals of the Roman state religion.

Interpretations of Augustine again and again overlook that the Cicero text *De republica,* which Augustine has been shown to have used for his conception of *De civitate Dei,* has in its center Scipio's dream, in which the life of the essential, the real and true citizens, namely, the statesmen, is also described as a pilgrimage into the heavenly home and into heavenly happiness. These statesmen in Scipio's dream have to endure the hardship of life in their service for the *res publica Romana*. They have to prove themselves in the service of the state in order to receive the heavenly reward (i.e., *per aspera ad astra*).

The difference in Augustine is only that the number of heroes and martyrs is increased and the promise of the heavenly reward is carried over to the saints and to those believers who truly endure all hardship sent to them by the providence of God in the battle against Satan's forces. Only for the superficial eye is the pilgrimage motif in Augustine taken from the New Testament, in particular from the Epistle to the Hebrews. In reality, Augustine has interpreted the relevant New Testament motifs on the basis of the *Somnium Scipionis.* According to *Civ.* 5.16, the examples of outstanding Romans are incentives for the believers. The patriotism of these Roman heroes serves as a paragon for the spiritual path of the believers to the heavenly fatherland.

In 5.5, 12, 15, 17, and 18 Augustine treats the achievements of the Romans who are supposed to be models for the Christians.[14] Forgiveness comes in addition and finally secures citizenship in the eternal homeland.[15] God makes the believers happy in the beyond, just as happened to the meritorious Romans before. Cicero, too, would have understood that Augustine seeks the true "riches of the souls" in the future and equates them with the final, the *vera libertas,* but also with the *amor laudis*. The entirely selfless, service-oriented understanding of the transcendental reward for the engagement for freedom Varro would have grasped as well—"not out of the desire to be praised by humans but out of love for humans (namely) to liberate them"—although the pagan Romans would have had problems with the sin and devil concepts that Augustine also elaborates here. Augustine can speak of the success of such state-supporting morality with the pride of one who himself belongs to such an enterprise, as was the expansion of the Roman Empire thanks to its great men. That these Roman men served the country well that Augustine himself still feels part of is self-evident to him; only heaven he will not grant them. He has taken over their image of heaven and of heavenly rewards but has transferred it to the Christian heroes and their train.

2.2. Paul Himself

Shaped by Augustine and the Reformers who were strongly influenced by the bishop of Hippo, we read Paul to this very day as an apostle of *Entweltlichung* (desecularization). Rudolf Bultmann has presented Paul in such a fashion, among others in his *Theology of the New Testament*. A Pauline text such as Phil 3:20 seems to confirm Augustine and all of his epigones: "Our πολίτευμα is in heaven, whence we expect the Lord Christ as savior." Exegetes have, however, continuously overlooked that Paul, on the one hand, comes very close here to the concept of the service for the state as it was in his days certainly as manifest as it was expressed in the *Somnium Scipionis* a century earlier, but then, on the other hand,

---

14. Here and elsewhere Augustine, of course, blends anti-Roman polemics with his praise; the Romans, however, are still always at the pinnacle of non-Christians.

15. At the end of 5.17. Augustine's dependence on Roman political theology and morality creates peculiar, oftentimes forced parallelisms: obedience, courage, renunciation, contempt of earthly goods, poverty, faithfulness, sacrifice (in the face of the challenge of heretics, then also sacrifice of bodily life, of one's own blood), discipleship (*askēsis*, self-denial). Augustine permits the use of the term *virtue* for those Roman attitudes, which he considers exemplary.

departs from it all the more evidently. Since Augustine takes as his point of departure the understanding of the essence and task of earthly existence as expressed in *Somnium Scipionis,* his distance from the intention of the text quoted from Paul can be made all the more obvious. According to the *Somnium Scipionis,* the true politicians who really can shape the world have their essence not from this world, but they are "stars" in the literal sense, namely, stars of heaven. They have their vocation from above and toward the above as well, that is from the heavenly world and toward the heavenly world. This distinguishes them clearly from the *plebs* of this world, sets them apart from the masses, which look merely to the this-worldly in pleasure and despair. *Entweltlichung* in the sense of astral mysticism belongs to the political ethics of a Cicero, a Seneca, or a Nero.

Looked at more closely, the deliberations of Paul in Phil 2 and 3 do not show anything of such *Entweltlichung,* which according to the *Somnium Scipionis* is a privilege of the elite. Augustine later again took up this elitist tendency, the emphasis on the extraordinary, and it has remained predominant in Christian exegesis and ethics ever since because of their dependence on Augustine. Paul, on the contrary, accepts the frailty and perishability of human existence, even if it means shame in his own biography, manifest in particular in his persecution of the adherents of Christ. He is not at all interested in the elitist elevation of the "stars." Instead, he emphasizes the democratic multiplication of the exemplar. He dismisses all secrecy and mystery mongering of the great man and his claims of special gifts and insights, distinguishing him from the common people. Paul insists instead on understanding, comprehending, and integrating everyone, in full respect even of the "lowest."

The text quoted from Philippians refers in its context to the resurrection of the dead and sees it as a transformation of the body of lowliness into a body of glory. Paul, however, puts the resurrection of the dead under the "power with which he (the Christ) can subdue even the universe under himself." Behind the transformation hoped for stands the same power that has humbled itself for the sake of all humans—not only for the sake of the believers. It is the power that in Jesus has made God equal to all humans, according to Paul and to the tradition of the early church that he quotes in Phil 2:6–11. It is the power that means the obedience of the human Jesus, his saying yes to the conditions of human existence—death included. According to the hymn quoted in Phil 2:6–11, this power, however, forces the powers that claim to rule the world to recognize Jesus, making them confess his lordship.

For Paul and the tradition he quotes in Phil 2, it makes no difference whether the superterrestrial, terrestrial, and subterrestrial demonic powers fully see all that or not. The song Paul quotes speaks of recognition of the lordship of the humiliated Jesus over the world and their powers *de jure* and *de facto*. In that hymn and in the Pauline context, a denial is expressed of the claimed superiority of the allegedly higher over the seemingly lower, of the allegedly better over the seemingly worse. According to the pre-Pauline tradition and also according to Paul, this fundamental criticism of the seemingly normal concept of power and rulership is the secret of the superiority of Jesus over the superhuman as well as the human powers.

Jesus' obedience to the conditions of createdness is in Paul's eyes the secret of Jesus' glory. In this, the crucified Jesus is distinguished from all the alleged "stars" of this world, not in the least the political ones. The rulership over the world that Jesus the Christ exerts means the removal of all claims of rulership that alienates and murders people through power and violence. It implies liberation from the idea of an almighty God who allegedly rules the world in such an inhuman fashion. Paul's Christology and already the Christ hymn of Phil 2 entail the liberation from "big brother" in whatever form.

The third chapter of Paul's letter to the Philippians has been read by many as a description of spiritual distancing from the world. In reality, this text has a democratizing egalitarian tendency and point. This democratizing perspective is found in all the surviving epistles of Paul that he himself wrote, from 1 Thessalonians to Romans. Paul's God does not sit on a throne as almighty king above the clouds but moves within and through his Christ to and among humans. In the Christ of Paul, God is humanized, and this humanization of God is continued in Christ's incorporation in the community of Christ adherents.

The entire body of Pauline letters is a conscious discussion not only with the urban culture of the Mediterranean but also with its top, the Caesar and the political ideology and eschatology of the Caesar religion. Paul contrasts the fascinating utopia of the Caesars with another utopia that adopts and radicalizes essential ideals of the libertarian-egalitarian pluralism of Hellenistic city culture and its urban constitution.

Augustine actually should have been made aware by his choice of the term *civitas*, with its predominant urban connotation continuing during his time, that the addresses of Paul's epistles were not directed to the church as a whole but to congregations, ἐκκλησίαι, in individual towns and cities. Augustine pretends against the Pauline texts before him that Paul means the whole worldwide church as an institution when he uses the term ἐκκλησία. For Paul, however, the ἐκκλησία is institutionally tangible only in the concrete assembly, ἐκκλησία, that meets in the name of Jesus the Christ at a certain geographical place, for Paul mostly in towns and cities. Augustine completely overlooks the fact that the local variation in the different epistolary addresses of Paul is reflected in the contents of the different letters as well. They really go into the particular situations of the congregations addressed. These are not limited to particular personal problems of the group spoken about and to. Behind them shows also the special profile of the surrounding town or—in the case of the Epistle to the Galatians—the entire region.

Paul did not invent the term ἐκκλησία as a definition of the Christ congregation. He inherited it in this function from the first churches. Greek-speaking Jews from the Diaspora who had joined the Christ community had applied the term to their own assemblies. They had adopted it from the city culture of the Mediterranean, where it was used as an administrative term of urban self-government. The term ἐκκλησία here meant the people's assembly, as they were customary in the free cities of the Mediterranean. These assemblies would meet in the local theater and debate and decide the local problems. A lively picture of such an ἐκκλησία is found in Luke's description of a meeting of the people's assembly of Ephesus in Acts 19. In adopting this name, the Christ community, although knowing themselves under the rule of the God of Israel, entered into competition with the local assembly of the free citizens in the theater of the town.

If the Christ community in the respective city presented itself as God's ἐκκλησία in Corinth, Thessalonica, Philippi, or Antioch, they took up this local identity and particularity as a double claim. They asserted that the problems and fate of the particular town were best represented and pursued by their assembly and also that in their assembly the unity of all assemblies of Israel's God in the entire ecumene was present as they met in a specific location. There was no other representation of this unity than the local one. This approach and understanding mirrored the societal and political principle of organization that kept the entire Hellenistic world, even in its Roman form, more closely together than army or central administration.

The organizational character of the Hellenistic kingdoms and the Roman Empire has been often correctly called a "confederation of cities." The pluralistic urban culture of the Mediterranean was apparent first and foremost in the individual cities and towns, with the local ἐκκλησία being the primary manifestation of the whole. The synagogues of the Jewish Diaspora had imitated that principle. They did not feel subordinate to the Jerusalem temple and its priesthood but equal to them. Thus, the praxis and terminology of the Greek-speaking Christ communities had a long and widespread history behind them, even if the term ἐκκλησία was not commonly used in the Jewish Diaspora. However, if we were not lucky enough to have the writings of Paul and the book of Acts, we would not speak today of a common terminology in the early church either.

As I already stated earlier, Paul and his Hellenistic-Jewish colleagues in the Christ mission concentrated their activity on the cities of the Hellenistic-Roman world. There is only one exception in Paul's known career, his mission in the province Galatia, most probably mainly on the Anatolian high plains close to the modern Ankara. His mission seems to have been work in the rural areas and small towns, yet, as we shall see, even here urbanization was under way. The third and fourth chapters of Galatians demonstrate clearly that even in addressing the problems of these communities Paul did not want to do without essential terms, motifs, and arguments of urban culture.

Already the choice of the letter genre aims at a typically urban means of communication, and Paul sticks to that in relating to the Galatians. In the argumentation of Gal 1 and 2, the relationship of the Christ communities in two large ancient cities, each a metropolis, played a major role: Antioch and Jerusalem. The Antiochene Christ community at the time of writing had grown into the largest ἐκκλησία of the early church.

In Gal 2 Paul describes a synod in Jerusalem that had been demanded by the Christ community in Antioch. This assembly was something like a constitutional synod of the early church at large. Here the decision was made to recognize the dialectic of diversity within the oneness of the gospel as the basic constitutional principle. The multicultural character of life as experienced in the urban environment of the Hellenistic-Roman world was acknowledged as the basic pattern for the church as a whole too. This multicultural dimension of the environment was of a religious nature as well, for the various lifestyles—whose mutual recognition was the basic concern of the constitutional assembly in Jerusalem—were formed by religious traditions and experiences, not only of various forms of paganism but also of various forms of Judaism.

Paul's report of the synod makes it clear as well that the gospel was not a unified dogmatic entity but a process of proclamation and preaching as shared praxis, with all the variety the different local situations brought with them. The two main provisions of the constitutional arrangement were the establishment of the congregations of Jerusalem and Antioch as two different metropolitan centers (mother cities in the Greek and Hellenistic cultural sense) that would support a Torah-related community style (Jerusalem) and non–Torah-related community style (Antioch), the latter more alongside the pagan experiences. The later dogmatic assumption that the early church conceived and pushed through something like a third, the Christian, way as something completely new, fallen from heaven as it were, is without evidence. Paul, certainly the most independent critical mind we know of in the early church, nowhere presents us with such a third ideology or ethics. All his arguments, reflections, and suggestions work with given elements of his environments, never dogmatizing and petrifying any of his results of deliberation but continuously remaining open for new insights and suggestions as they came out of the ongoing communal and environmental dialogue.

Apparently Paul and his dialogue partners at that constitutional assembly in Jerusalem adopted for their plans to build and structure the Christ communities and their interrelationships the solutions that the Mediterranean urban society had found for the interrelationship between and within cities. After the clash with Peter and the Antiochene church, reported in Gal 2, Paul and his congregations founded later further developed such structures of horizontal mutual relationship as means of governance and unity. In contradistinction to modern urban culture, the Hellenistic-Roman urban culture had not undertaken social and societal integration from above, through central national institutions and political authorities, and not via the individual at the bottom. There was nothing like the artificial "melting pot" procedure à la Dewey and company.

Integration in the urban environment of ancient Judaism and the early church happened by recognizing the differences and particularities of the divisions of live groupings on the one side and the propagation of the community of education on the other. The latter was not supposed to destroy or even absorb the former. Education was nothing "national,"[16] not even under Roman dominance.[17] Education transcended the particularities of certain territories and their historical and social particularities. Education had a multicultural community in view. The cities became the main locations of the integration via education. The multicultural dimension showed rather drastically in the suborganization of the cities into πολιτεύματα. They were far more than our modern city districts. They were rather semiautonomous parts of the city shaped by regional or ethnic or religious associations or by all of them together. In their exchange among one another and between the cities, they contributed to the intracultural networking texture and cultural identity of the whole—within

---

16. It is still all too common to use the term *nation* in its modern understanding for the description of ancient phenomena. Nowhere in the ancient world existed anything like a modern nation. The Latin term *natio* means something completely different from the modern term *nation*. The Latin meaning was still maintained in the official definition of the "German" Empire from Charlemagne in the eighth century to the Habsburg monarchy in 1806, when the Habsburg emperor was forced to abdicate his claim to the German Empire and the latter was dissolved. The title was "Holy Roman Empire of the German Nation." That German Nation was completely different from, indeed the opposite of, Bismarck's German nation of 1871 and following. Even less must one speak of ancient nationalism. It never existed anywhere. It slowly originated in sixteenth-century France and England.

17. How little nationalism was present in Roman education already showed in the dominance of the Greek language, Greek religion, Greek rhetoric, and many more Greek and Hellenistic cultural features in the education of Romans.

the single city such as Antioch, Corinth, Rome, and so forth as well as within the Hellenistic-Roman culture as an urban world culture at large.

As in the Hellenistic culture at large, each unit—whether state or region or municipality—developed a prideful confidence of best representing the whole in its particular part, as did also the districts and subcommunities in the individual cities. Cohesion was produced first of all by the attempts of the different units and subunits to best represent the whole, its ideals, and its mission. This was the basis and stimulant for horizontal exchange as well but also the red thread of a unified corporate consciousness.

The constitutional synod of the early church mentioned organized the distribution of the missionary activity among Jews and Gentiles. As prerequisite for this distribution, the constitutional treaty settled the relationship of both major groups: the (more conservative) Jews and (more liberal) Hellenistic Jews together with the Gentiles, each defined by a certain lifestyle, of which there were subdivisions, too, but still some overall commonness. Each of the two major groups was associated with one of the two mother cities, Antioch or Jerusalem, both understood as metropolis, mother city, in the sense of the center of (sub)cultural identity and support, a terminology and custom that reached back into the early Greek period but never ceased completely. This division permitted the living together of different groups with different lifestyles, subcultures as it were, in a common larger community, here the church at large.

This contractual solution at the Jerusalem synod demonstrates a pragmatic use of given models of the Hellenistic-Roman urban and intraurban structures by the early Christ movement. It is significant that the constitutional dimension of this Jerusalem conference and its character as a synod among equals fell into oblivion.[18]

---

18. Already in the Acts of the Apostles it is a one-sided affair, in which the Antiochenes merely beg whereas the Jerusalem authorities decide and decree. Later generations no longer wanted to know of this Jerusalem conference as a constitutional meeting because one had given up on the prime agreement of Jerusalem, its multicultural consent with its polychrome religious coloring. Augustine as well as his "Christian" theological predecessors, contemporaries, and successors interpreted this conference of the glorious past as the documentation of the subordination of the Gentile church under a central church government. The major reasons for the conference were pushed aside, and so were its results. The location Jerusalem and the Torah-orientation of the Jerusalem representatives of this synod were reduced to trivialities, in fact to something that history had already done away with. Jerusalem was in ruins, and Torah-obedient Christians were turned into neglected persons, still in existence but without status and recognition in the allegedly "catholic" church. The conference in Jerusalem was even seen as the beginning of the self-marginalization, indeed self-removal, of Jewish Christianity, now seen as completed. Augustine's *De civitate Dei* is a real exemplar of this development of the early church and of a praxis in which the belief in

Closer attention to the social situation in the province Galatia during Paul's time makes it seem less extraordinary that Paul uses so many urban elements in this letter as well. The congregations addressed in the epistle must have come from many different social groups and from different religious environments. The three most distant influences we need to count on are Celtic, Jewish, and, of course, Roman backgrounds. The Roman province Galatia was particularly rich in immigrants, foreigners indeed. In this region the Roman administration worked hard to establish larger townships through the accumulation, fusion, and incorporation of villages and small towns.

In the Epistle to the Galatians, there are several universalistic aspects, the most famous one in 3:28: "There is neither Jew nor Greek, neither slave nor freeborn, neither man nor woman, for you are all one in Christ Jesus." This thesis of the unity in Christ despite all diversity of social conditions has its parallel in the universalism of Hellenistic-Roman urban culture. This universalism was shaped by the utopian hope that the city would be able to respect all ethnic, racial, social, sexual, and other differences and could overcome, that is, integrate them into a larger whole, though not at the expense of their particularity.

It is not without reason that Paul introduces into this universalist context, at the end of Gal 3 and the beginning of Gal 4, the issue of education, παιδεία, the great equalizer and unifier of the Hellenistic-Roman world. However, Paul does not trust this claim of unification in liberty that contemporary culture associates with παιδεία. He identifies παιδεία with the law, which he interprets negatively, law as universal, as cosmic law. Paul describes the law as a prison guard and a beating pedagogue. What παιδεία, the education of the Hellenistic-Roman world, promises to Gentiles and Jews, this, so Paul, only the Christ creates by means of the gospel, because thereby the divine loyalty to humans is documented. This implies that the appearance of the Christ has moved trust in God and solidarity among humans into the center; it is no longer a merely marginal appearance at the heavenly rim or at the threshold of the imperial palace—with God and the human governor themselves still clearly above and removed into a beyond (of palace or heaven).

The Pauline congregations, as stated previously, incorporated the Hellenistic-Roman idea of society as a confederation of cities especially

---

Christ included mere lip service to differences in thought and lifestyle. In reality and even *de jure* one tended to monopolize one's own dogmatic conviction—if one had the power—and one pushed—although in a camouflaged fashion—for one's own lifestyle. One tried to portray this in the most generalist fashion, hoping that it might win out if the power relations permitted.

well. This federative principle had produced a sense of equality within and between the cities. This eased the possibility of a worldwide balance. Corresponding to that Paul argues in 2 Corinthians in the context of the organization of the collection for Jerusalem for the necessity of equality between the Christ congregations. He does it with the use of the appropriate Greek term for equality, ἰσότης. This term in classical and Hellenistic Greek is synonymous with the term Paul prefers, δικαιοσύνη, "righteousness," or in Paul's understanding even more "solidarity." Righteousness not merely as equity but as equality was an urban phenomenon, fundamentally democratic.

In the parallel discussion in 2 Cor 9, written shortly after the fragment in 2 Cor 8, Paul can use terms and ideas of proverbial wisdom and popular philosophy. Thereby he is able to bring the idea of God's righteousness and solidarity and their human equivalents into the horizon of reason, especially urban reason. Righteousness was, since Plato, the recognition of the function that had been parceled out to each individual and of the particular function that came with it, appropriate for that person. It enabled its realization. In all of that the city dweller was in view. Not only the internal but also most of all societal equity and balance was seen as the consequence of concrete righteousness. Thus, righteousness was essentially a social, indeed, a political term in its most literal sense, a social term that was related to the urban community, the community of the πόλις. Only within this context can it be understood that the term δικαιοσύνη became a legal and juridical term as well.

In the Hellenistic period this term was associated with the concept of the (theatrical) role. Now righteousness became even more concretely than under Plato the ability to recognize the role and task posed by the deity and/or fate to the individual. One had to gain and exercise the confidence to play one's role. Part of δικαιοσύνη was to understand the relationship of the individual role to the roles and tasks of others and to the concept of the whole community, of society and of the cosmos at large, and to exercise one's personal role within that context appropriately. This meant that one did one's best to ensure that others were enabled to play their own roles as well. The slogan *suum cuique*[19] expresses this understanding of one's role as the fulfillment of one's personal obligation. It was originally formulated by Stoic philosophy and meant the *suum cuique distribuere,* namely, distributing each and everyone his or her appropriate role. This way of understanding life as role-playing had

---

19. Which the Prussian kings later adopted as their mode of conduct—interpreted in the Presbyterian understanding of responsibility and work ethics.

far-reaching consequences for the understanding of essential societal phenomena, not the least for the term *righteousness*.

It is Paul's opinion that this *suum cuique distribuere* that the Hellenistic-Roman society expected for everyone happens in the body of Christ. This Pauline motif of the body of Christ stands in critical competition with the contemporary understanding of the *Imperium Romanum* as a cosmic body with the Caesar as its head. With this motif of the body of Christ, Paul does not want to describe an elevated and distanced select society, as Augustine and many others later understood. When Paul uses this motif in 1 Cor 12 and in Rom 12, he wants to outline a model for society and calls on the congregation addressed to be a model society for their environment. In the community of the body of Christ, all persons possess different gifts, but all gifts are equal. Everyone is of equal value compared with everyone else. Variety of gifts does not constitute different qualities or values. Each and every one is important and valuable for all. The differences of the gifts guarantee the unity within the single congregation and even the unity among all Christ communities together. For contemporary readers, pagan or Jewish, this was indeed the draft of a model society of urban constitution. They would have seen the point and would have taken it as a critical challenge, though they might not have agreed with the enactment. They would have taken it as a challenge on their own level. This also means that the Pauline description of communal life can be seen as a conscious development of the Stoic and popular philosophical development of the concept of δικαιοσύνη already alluded to, although this term does not occur in 1 Cor 12 or Rom 12. Paul sees the local Christ community and the totality of all of them around the Mediterranean as a manifestation of "righteousness/solidarity."

In 2 Cor 9 Paul personifies δικαιοσύνη after the example of middle-Stoic and popular philosophy, which would also transform abstract philosophical terms into persons. The δικαιοσύνη Paul discusses here in such a personified fashion is first of all the relationship within the individual Christ community but also all the relationships between the various Christ communities throughout the world. As δικαιοσύνη as relationship turns into a person, the community is changed into a person as well. Just as the Hellenistic city, that is, the civic corporation as person, consisted of smaller πολιτεύματα, individual smaller communities that communicated among one another, so it was also on the level of the ecumene, or, in Stoic formulation, on the level of the κοσμόπολις.[20]

---

20. Later on Paul's conception of ecclesial organization and political power was hierarchically and spiritually interpreted. This already happened before Augustine but even more so by the bishop of Hippo, and this has remained so with most interpreters until today.

Paul is, of course, of a utopian inclination, but so were all of his contemporaries. Lewis Mumford has correctly pointed out that the city of antiquity was a utopia in stone. This was especially so with the Hellenistic and the Roman city. For instance, Paul's utopian hints at the universal nature of the Christ community do not constitute a dream world. Paul's conception corresponds to the idea of complete freedom as it expressed itself in the Greek and Hellenistic city. However, the liberty that Paul has in mind is more radical than the Greeks or the Romans had ever intended: it entails the complete surrender of all segregation by gender, race, status, ethnicity, education, culture, and so forth. Particularly with respect to education, strong differences remained in the Greek cities and in Hellenistic-Roman society, even where emancipation with respect to other social divisions was contemplated. Upward mobility never broke the barrier between the educated and the noneducated. Only the former were truly free.

In 2 Cor 3:12 Paul sees the adherents of the Christ community entitled "to use much παρρησία" because of their hope that the life-giving glory and freedom of the spirit spoken of before is with all of them—a utopian phenomenon indeed. This παρρησία of all members of the Christ community, women, children, slaves, and foreigners included, is in parallel as well as in critical competition with the freedom of speech of the free citizens of the Greek and Hellenistic city. Here παρρησία meant the right to say anything one wants, to thereby prove one's courage to be open, and to contribute to the truth through this exercise of freedom—and this for the benefit of the whole community and everyone in it. In his interpretation of Paul, Augustine expunges this gift of civic freedom. He does not appreciate it within the political community and has even less room for such concrete liberty in the spiritual community of the believers in Christ. Augustine's exegesis of Paul, in fact, means the final death stroke to Paul's revolutionary position. Augustine's exegesis of 2 Cor 3 in his writing *De spiritu et littera* changes this world-shaking chapter into a moralistic discussion about the relationship of the individual to sin, sin being understood morally. This robs Paul's teaching on justification of its heart and of its nerve. The church as a hierarchical institution was given free play. The power option had finally won out over the freedom option. Justification again became the righting of might.

Whenever in the history of interpretation exegetes have tried to point to even mere traces of political concreteness, especially of democratization, in Paul, these findings were immediately refuted as unrealistic and utopian and were confronted with an alleged Pauline realism that was and is anything but realistic; instead, it is completely internalized, individualized, spiritualized, and transcendentalized.

3. PROPOSALS FOR TOMORROW

This essay presupposes the Protestant thesis that Paul's teaching of the justification of the godless is the basic Protestant principle. At the same time, it argues that it will take some effort to bring back some of the original color and flavor of Paul's own understanding of the concept. We must regain, in particular, Paul's interest in making this concept basic for a corporate consciousness. People such as Augustine have changed this orientation into a cliquish one, which has turned churches into sects, as which United States law sees all churches, no matter what size. The Roman Catholic Church is simply a little bigger sect than the Amish.

Augustine's individualizing and deurbanizing interpretation of 2 Cor 3 and other essential Pauline texts has followed and strengthened a compromise the post-Pauline generation already felt compelled to make. The end of the world had not come, although all theologians of the first generation of the early church, including Paul, had predicted it. Instead, time continued and this without major changes; the Caesars kept ruling. The best way out for the theologians of the post-Pauline generation seemed to be to free the basic ideas of end and beginning from any corporate, social, or political aspect and to transfer them into the internal experience of the individual. The idea of the end of the world was interpreted as a merely cosmic act, was severed from the internalized dimensions of eschatology and transferred into an indefinite future.

The falsifying mutation of the Pauline message of universal justification and reconciliation of the godless by and with God, its perversion into an individualistic, ghettoized teaching of sin and forgiveness, completely covered the corporate dimension that had been critically addressed to the concrete urban community. The real points of Paul's teaching were disfigured, veiled, and finally removed. Patriarchy, hierarchy, centralism, conformism—all unmasked as antiurban in Paul's constructive criticism of the concept and praxis of corporateness—again had their way, even in the church. The tendency in ecclesial bodies is still to lead from above, to misunderstand ethics as morals that can be used by those in power to discipline and control attempts at self-government. Democratic ventures in the churches still succeed less than in nonchurch contexts. There are even still Protestant theologians who claim, without receiving basic contradiction, that democracy is a worldly thing and therefore does not really have a place in the church. A theology based on Paul's critical views should know differently.

The history of exegesis of the Bible proves that centuries and even millennia of exegesis can cover and deform the texts. The Bible on one side is overinterpreted. This, however, is true merely with respect to the interpretation by the major established churches. This kind of interpretation tends to yield to power plays. As soon as one moves a little away from this direction the Bible turns again into an undiscovered continent. We should open new inroads and then hand over this *terra incognita* to the next generations for their own discoveries and surprises.

We have already spoken of the grand vision that ends the last book of the Bible. We have noticed that the Jerusalem coming down is not what the church's misinterpretation in following Augustine wanted it to look like, namely, something like an island of the blessed, eternal happiness, something like a never-ending session in the ice parlor, heaven as an immortal "Baskin Robbins," with never-ending nice weather. No, John's the new Jerusalem is a true city, alive, moved, and moving. Its topography as city in the valley and along the big stream has betrayed its secret to us, that it is the revived, the reconciled Babylon, the justified great witch. Thus the Bible ends with an urban vision of the concrete communal justification of all of us godless people.

In Augustine, expanding time, Christ's return failing to appear, lead to an internalization of the concept of justification but also to a separation of the doctrine of justification from the idea of and need for corporate organization. The latter could now start forming a centrally, hierarchically led institution of salvation, a cultic machine that had its own life, isolated from the challenges of the proclamation of justification and reconciliation, from the needs and promises of ordinary urban life. The Roman Catholic pontiff is truly the successor of the Caesar as *pontifex maximus*. The Roman curia is indeed the successor to the Roman curia of old, with the increment of the Caesars' bureaucracy. Eschatology was reduced to the doctrine of the last things, including confirmation of the elect just ones and eternal torture of the unbelievers, an eternal Gestapo dungeon.

Paul's proclamation of the justification of the godless does not allow such isolation of eschatology. This proclamation is itself eschatological, a teaching of judgment, reconciliation, and new beginning, of reconciliation within judgment. In an urban theology, the intent of the idea of justification, that God's solidarity creates reconciliation and solidarity, should be taken up and furthered. Such dimensions transcend the borders of faiths and churches. The Roman Catholic Church is an excellent and promising example. The increasingly authoritarian centralism and control from the top have been answered worldwide with stunning neglect of Rome's ordinances and increased ecumene at the basis of the church. Roman Catholic priests and lay people even in an allegedly Roman Catholic country such as the Philippines take more heed of their fellow Christians of other denominations and even of their non-Christian neighbors than of their hierarchy, even less of pope and curia. There is a growing trust at the basis and cooperation in facing and overcoming the fatal consequences of more than three hundred years of Catholic and more than one hundred years of Protestant imperialism on the Philippine islands. The present pope with all probability will be the last centralist pontiff. His successors need to be advocates of increased decentralization and democratization if the Roman Catholic Church wants to be of help for the world of tomorrow. The Church has great potential for this task, given its worldwide experiences and many officially unrecognized and unbeatified saints among the poor throughout the world .

An urban theology for tomorrow needs to regain the curious blend of Utopia and pragmatism that is found in the Pauline adaptation of urban consciousness or that of the Apocalypse of John. The mobility found in the new church and presupposed by Paul and John was not limited to a few spiritual stars but was common in the congregations. This mobility belonged to urban culture and was—already because of the job situation—not rare in the lower classes. The metaphor of the sojourning people of God, extremely sentimentalized and internalized by Augustine, belongs in the New Testament text into the urban reality. Augustine and his spiritual relatives have removed it from that concrete context with disastrous consequences.

In the letters of Paul as much as in the Epistle to the Hebrews, this mobility, this sojourning, is oriented alongside the mobility of God, God's move toward the human race as it became reality in the Son of God turned human.

An urban theology for tomorrow must put an end to the theological nonsense of limiting the figure of God's incarnation and humanization to the history of Jesus of Nazareth. The biblical evidence for that does not exist. Theologians usually refer for that extremely consequential syllogism to two occurrences of ἐφ-ἅπαξ and interpret it as "once and for all," but this interpretation of the relevant passages in Paul, Hebrews, and 1 Peter is false.[21] Paul himself has understood the body of Christ as the continuation of the incarnation of Christ, in the sense of the incorporation of the Christ in the community who is identified with the Christ (1 Cor 12:12). The Epistle to the Hebrews also interprets the Christ story as a

---

21. Rom 6:10 is a baptismal text and does not even speak of Jesus himself but gives a general rule, that the death (of every human) ends sin for him or for her, while 1 Pet 3:18 states in confessional fashion that Jesus Christ died once for our sins, and that also clearly means for all. The same tradition is used in Heb 9, the text that most often uses the adverb "once" in the New Testament. It speaks of the death of Jesus Christ as a sacrifice for sins, as a sacrifice once and for all, in contradistinction to the sin offerings in the temple. There is no reference in any of these texts to the incarnation of God or Christ. Only a church such as the Protestant one that could make the Christ event synonymous with sacrifice for sins (prepared in part by Anselm of Canterbury) could use such texts as an argument that the incarnation was only a once-and-for-all event.

continuum. This realizes the biblical motif of the sojourning people of God. Properly looked at, this motif already possesses incarnational dimensions in the Old Testament. The sojourning of the Christ community under the Christ is the main concern of 1 Peter as well.

The solidarity Paul speaks about does not exhaust itself in the Christ communities; it does not end at the community's borders. It moves to the weak, impoverished, powerless, disenfranchised, victimized, and marginalized at large. It respects and supports their creative integrity. This is primarily the continuation of the incarnation, the humanization of God. An urbanized church and an urban theology should consciously approach our cities and speak of the Christ communities as *communes,* as places where the meaning that is embodied in the Latin term is taken more seriously than is customary in modern municipalities.

The true dispensers of power and creators of sense and meaning for the world of tomorrow will not be the nations, not even their federation(s). The true federation will be the one that is situated at the base, between the communes and communities that imaginatively and creatively discover their commonality of existence and work, beyond all borders and in mutual exchange and support. Thus may develop an authentic corporate communal consciousness for our time.

We have seen that in the new Jerusalem of Rev 21 and 22 God and his Christ blend with their people, becoming citizens among citizens. This is entirely in agreement with the urban theology of Paul. Despite the devil and other enemies of humanity, the commune is the goal of all of God's ways.

13

THE INTEREST IN LIFE-OF-JESUS THEOLOGY AS A PARADIGM FOR THE SOCIAL HISTORY OF BIBLICAL CRITICISM

1. INTRODUCTION

Augustine had given further credence to one instrument of the Hellenistic and the Roman city, the concept of the "divine man." The cult of the extraordinary individual was continued in the celebration of the biblical and the Roman past, particularly in Augustine's Christology. Augustine completely neglected the massive criticism that Paul in his Christology and in his teaching of justification had leveled against such veneration of the portentous individual and of any achievement orientation. Paul had accused such praxis and thinking as being not only disastrous for the person and for the church but also for the human community at large, and that meant especially for urban life. In the Middle Ages, the church followed Augustine's guidance instead. It picked up further the trend that was found already in the life-of-Jesus theology of the gospel tradition: Jesus, the spiritual hero as the great achiever, a seemingly urban concept that in form of the Caesar religion and of the church's adoption of it had contributed heavily to the demise of the ancient city. The medieval society adopted this concept and made it multipliable, a seeming "democratization," to be imitated by the burghers in the old and new cities and towns. Their walled-in communities were anything but healthy. Were their successors in the subsequent ages really healed from

---

*This article is an enlarged form of a paper I gave at the Annual Meeting of the Society of Biblical Literature in Kansas City, Missouri, in November 1991.

the mass-suicidal spirit of self-justification, self-aggrandizement, and competitiveness that had developed with the hero worship and the achievement orientation? Not really. The problems of such pursuits have remained with us until today and are embedded in much of our biblical scholarship and theology at large.

Historians, including biblical critics, are not known for exposing themselves to the same kind of historical criticism that they apply to everything and everyone else. The historical situation of contemporary exegetes and their social conditions usually remain uninvestigated and thus, from a historical-critical and sociohistorical perspective, unquestioned. The various hermeneutical inquiries that different forms of liberation theology have recently developed provide a beginning for such a necessary self-study. They need, however, to be expanded.

The following observations take their departure from the social situation of the author as a person belonging to the white male European and American bourgeoisie. They explore the historical dimensions of this context. The long-standing interest of European and American scholarship in the historical Jesus serves as a paradigm for this inquiry. An abbreviated form of this study can be found in my article "Leben Jesu Theologie/ Leben Jesu Forschung" in *Theologische Realenzyklopaedie*.[1]

In that article I had intended to start with Hermann Samuel Reimarus (1694–1768) as I had in the earlier article on the subject. In the meantime, however, my experiences in Germany and the United States had thoroughly changed my perspectives. Previously I had been open to a sociohistorical point of view, yet the years from 1960 to 1990 had given this perspective further flesh and blood. Lecturing on the Jesus question from the first century to the present day at Harvard Divinity School in the 1970s contributed to this awareness. Albert Schweitzer's *The Quest of the*

---

1. Dieter Georgi, "Leben Jesu Theologie/Leben Jesu Forschung," *TRE* 20:566–76. Further discussion and bibliographies can be found in Gustav Pfannmüller, *Jesus im Urteil der Jahrhunderte* (6th ed.; Leipzig: Teubner, 1951); Dieter Georgi, "Leben Jesus Theologie," *RGG* 4:429; Dennis Duling, *Jesus Christ through History* (New York: Harcourt Brace Jovanovich, 1979); Eduard Schweizer, "Jesus Christus I, Neues Testament," *TRE* 16:671–726; Rowan Williams, "Jesus Christus II. Alte Kirche," *TRE* 16:726–45; idem, "Jesus Christus III. Mittelalter," *TRE* 16: 745–59; Karl-Heinz zur Mühlen, "Jesus Christus IV. Reformationszeit," *TRE* 16:759–72; Walter Span, "Jesus Christus V. Vom Tridentinum bis zur Aufklärung," *TRE* 17:1–16; John Macquarrie, "Jesus Christus VI. Neuzeit (1789 bis zur Gegenwart)," *TRE* 17:16–42; idem, "Jesus Christus VII. Dogmatisch," *TRE* 17:42–64. In my article in *TRE* I had to refrain from enlarging the aesthetic and artistic dimension of the Jesus theme I had touched upon in my article in *RGG*. More on this can be found in Pfannmüller, *Jesus im Urteil der Jahrhunderte*; Karl-Josef Kuschel, *Jesus in der deutschsprachigen Gegenwartsliteratur* (Zurich: Benziger; Gütersloh: Mohn, 1978); and Otto von Simpson, "Das Christusbild in der Kunst," *TRE* 17:76–84.

Historical Jesus had hinted that the scholarly interest in the historical Jesus always had been more than a part of the history of ideas.[2] These hints now gained stronger meaning for me. I became more interested in the social environment of the inquirer, my own as well as that of others, present and past. In addition, the analysis of the social and political context of the so-called New Quest had become a scholarly concern of mine in the 1970s.[3]

In trying to understand Reimarus I had to confront four facts. First, comparing Reimarus's efforts with later ones, including those of the New Quest, I found that the common distinction between an allegedly improper interest in the life of Jesus and a seemingly proper interest in the public career of Jesus was an apologetic excuse. It was of little value because most people interested in the historical Jesus had been aware of the fact that the major part of Jesus' biographical life was unrecoverable and that, therefore, the interest had to focus on Jesus' public career as the essence of Jesus' life. This selective concentration of the Gospels was not that different from what the Hellenistic world understood as interest in the *bios of* someone, that is, not life in the sense of an extended series of events but rather the essence of someone's life.[4] Second, neither Reimarus's quest nor that of his followers was neutral but had a clear theological purpose: to gain a verifiable reconstruction of the public career of Jesus of Nazareth and to put this reconstruction into the middle of the reflection of theology and faith, turning this "true" Jesus into the center of theological discourse. Third, Reimarus's efforts and interests and those of his successors were and are not just theological or philosophical findings of individuals driven by their personal idiosyncrasies, and particularly their emotional urges. They were and are embedded in wider drives that extend far beyond the persons involved.

Fourth, in pursuing Reimarus's quest for the historical Jesus I found traces and connections not only in the Hamburg of the author of the

---

2. Albert Schweitzer, *The Quest of the Historical Jesus: A Critical Study of Its Progress from Reimarus to Wrede* (New York: Macmillan, 1968).

3. James Robinson, *A New Quest of the Historical Jesus* (SBT 25; London: SCM, 1959). In preparing the article in *TRE*, modern social history struck me in a peculiar way, too. My computer together with ca. 140 disks, that is four years of work, including backups, was stolen from my office at Frankfurt University, with all the material on the article in question, and this just a quarter of a year before the extension of the deadline ran out. What is found now in the *TRE* article mentioned is an emergency recovery measure.

4. I have dealt with this topic in "The Records of Jesus in the Light of Ancient Accounts of Revered Men," in *SBL 1972 Seminar Papers* (ed. Lane C. McGaughy; SBLSemPap 6; Missoula, Mont.: Scholars Press, 1972), 527–42.

Apologie, that is, not only in his academic and personal background.[5] The far-ranging curiosity and learnedness of Reimarus provided many more leads into places and people far beyond his own time and location. Following these leads carried me into the Reformation, the Counter-Reformation, and the Middle Ages. Then I suddenly found myself again in my own professional field, the history of New Testament times and the New Testament itself, but I now looked at it from a much wider sociohistorical perspective.

My book *The Opponents of Paul in Second Corinthians* had acquired a much wider scope in its development from the original German to the later English version.[6] The increased sociohistorical perspective proved helpful also in this new venture. The connections between the ancient discussions about the divine man and their religious, social, and economic contexts and interests reappeared, albeit in varied forms, in the medieval and modern quest for Jesus.

Brevity demands that I give only sketches. For illustrative reasons these will concentrate heavily on persons. The price for this will be a great deal of shorthand with respect to the description of social situations and developments. The sketches are in this perspective but so brief that I must risk the charge of falling back into a mere history of ideas. In my view this outline is not that. Contrary to the opinion of some modern sociologists, ideas are quite often social benchmarks.

In doing so I clearly move far beyond my own professional field. My presentation is literally an extended act of trespassing in my neighbor's garden. Social history is meaningless without such interdisciplinary transgressions with all the risks and dangers of dilettantism.

Readers of my book on the opponents of Paul, particularly of the English version, may remember that I argued that in the early church there were already tendencies to portray Jesus of Nazareth as a verifiable demonstration of the extraordinary. In this approach the extraordinary was identified with the divine as well as with the spiritual but was concretely available in the here and now. With all due concern for the distance in time and respective developments of thought and terminology, I would claim that the terms *objectivity* and *verifiability* can be used to describe the concern of these people in the early church.

---

5. Hermann Samuel Reimarus, *Apologie oder Schutzschrift fur die vernünftigen Verehrer Gottes* (ed. Gerhard Alexander; 2 vols; Frankfurt am Main: Insel, 1972); a collection of an older edition of fragments by D. F. Strauss is found in Hermann Samuel Reimarus, *Fragments* (ed. Charles H. Talbert; trans. Ralph S. Fraser; Chico, Calif.: Scholars Press, 1985).

6. Dieter Georgi, *The Opponents of Paul in Second Corinthians* (Philadelphia: Fortress, 1986).

In the English version of my book on Paul's opponents in 2 Corinthians I indicated the place of this kind of christological interest within the cultural and socioeconomic context of the Hellenistic-Roman world.[7] Our modern market economy with its orientation toward performance has much in common with the cult of the extraordinary in Hellenistic-Roman society and its market economy. Even the multicultural dimension was already part of that competitive socioeconomic structure. Those missionaries of Jesus who propagated the extraordinary qualities and performances of the man from Nazareth and claimed similar strengths for themselves competed and collaborated within the conditions of the Hellenistic-Roman market, of which the religious market was an essential part, as any excavated agora or forum proves.

This missionary competition was basically an urban effort despite rural and small-town references in the Jesus tradition, which it used. These rural references do not necessarily imply true concern for the plight of the peasantry but could easily function as merely idyllic features. I have shown this in my essay "Who Is the True Prophet?"[8] The Gospel of Luke and to a greater extent Acts furnish many examples for this idyllic interest of urban writers as well.

In my book *Theocracy in Paul's Praxis and Theology*[9] I have developed my arguments further in order to show that Paul presents a very different option from the opponents in 2 Corinthians, different also from a sociopolitical perspective.[10] Paul's option was not dependent on an objective and verifiable reconstruction of the public career of Jesus of Nazareth but actually rejected such an approach. Paul was by no means alone in this. The book of Revelation, for instance, presents another example of the fact that within the early church other forms of dealing with the Jesus figure were consciously developed besides the one that dominates much of our Gospel tradition and Acts.

---

7. Ibid., esp. 358–450; see also my essay, "Socioeconomic Reasons for the 'Divine Man' as Propagandistic Pattern," 11–23 above.

8. See 25–51 above.

9. Dieter Georgi, *Theocracy in Paul's Praxis and Theology* (trans. David E. Green; Minneapolis: Fortress, 1991), 61–71.

10. In my book *Remembering the Poor: The History of Paul's Collection for Jerusalem* (Nashville: Abingdon, 1992), I discuss further the economic dimensions of Paul's stance. In "Should Augustine Have the Last Word on Urban Theology?" (195–220 above) I argue that Augustine quite consciously moved away from the urban orientation of Pauline praxis and theology.

2. FROM AUGUSTINE TO CUSANUS

In late antiquity and in the early Middle Ages the social and economic conditions and possibilities of the Mediterranean society changed drastically. In *De civitate Dei* Augustine demonstrates that the forces of the church that had gained the upper hand had given up on the ancient city and now consciously concentrated on small towns and rural areas.[11] Whereas the church of the first and second centuries had represented basically an urban religion, the church after the third century increasingly followed the leads of the governing economic and social forces of the empire away from the cities. Christianity became a small-town and rural religion. The growing slums of the cities lost interest for the church. The impoverished masses of the cities provided cheap labor for the rural domains and the industrial plants in the countryside. They were used by the church as easily available pressure groups to smoke out the remaining nests of the pagan intellectual and religious elite in the cities and to attack Jewish citizens in the former urban centers. The interest in Jesus of Nazareth as a divine man dwindled and was replaced by that in Christ as king and pantocrator—a merely superficial turn toward the Christology of Paul and the book of Revelation, in light of which the Gospels and Acts now were read. This was a misreading not only of the Gospels but also of Paul and Revelation.

This approach changed drastically in the southern and western Europe of the eleventh and twelfth centuries. Most of the cities of western and southern Europe we now know originated in that period either as reawakened ancient cities or as new settlements. Sizable markets again developed in these urban centers. These markets were created by the ever-increasing number of craftsmen and merchants in the cities—the essential "burghers," freemen in these "burghs" or "boroughs," that were not just fortified places but locations, legally singled out and set apart.[12] These burghers, craftsmen and merchants alike, received special duties and privileges. They were active and protected in industry and commerce and thus established an intermediate social group, wedged between landlords and peasantry. Industry and commerce now became major sources of wealth, which no longer came from real estate, war, and

---

11. Augustine, *The City of God* (FC 8; 3 vols.; trans. Demetrius B. Zema et al.; Washington, D.C.: Catholic University of America Press, 1977).
12. On the nature and development of the bourgeoisie, see the articles by Adolf Armbruster, Werner Conze, Hans Freyer, Gerhard Köbler, Bernhard Moeller, and Oskar Köhler on "Bürger/Bürgertum" quoted in Georgi, "Leben Jesu Theologie," 573–75. These articles also give sufficient literature in English.

farming alone. This new class of burghers was a new economic and social force. Universities sprang up in the growing cities. They provided education not only for the nobility and clergy but also in an ever-increasing way for the offspring of the class of burghers, giving them chances for upward mobility. Universities thus provided an effective base for gaining economic, social, and political influence upon society.

In this environment interest in Jesus as a superhuman individual became prominent again. This Jesus was touchable as a human but at the same time much larger than ordinary life, ready again to influence and determine human beings, and now in particular those of the new, bourgeois class. Life-of-Jesus theology developed further in close interplay with the socioeconomic and ideological evolution of the European bourgeoisie, as one of its motors as well as its conscience. The formation of conscientious and responsible burghers called for an ideal that was able to inspire and direct individuals who would represent and shape the new societal vision. The evolving life-of-Jesus theology would provide that germinal stimulation.[13]

The new theological era was introduced by Anselm (1033–1109), the Italian nobleman turned English theologian and archbishop of Canterbury.[14] His work and contribution are often presented in too isolated a form, concentrating on his theology and ecclesiastical politics against the Norman king, that is, chiefly as a predecessor to Thomas Becket (1118–70). In such a view Anselm's interest and contribution to education as a forming and training of the will is unjustifiably marginalized if not forgotten, even though it was a major concern of Anselm's since his days as a monk at the monastery in Bec. This interest in the shaping of the individual will was not limited to monastic formation. It extended to the moral and religious education of young people at large and the creation of personal responsibility and freedom among pupils. It was certainly not limited to the feudal elite alone but extended to others as well, thus reconciling the Britons and the Normans and providing for a new

---

13. In selecting and organizing the material for my article, "Leben Jesu Theologie" with its limited space I used pragmatically the 50s of the different centuries as focal points. This captured most of the changes. This seemed to be justified to a degree also by the curious observation that in most cases the major pushes in the sociohistorical development of the life-of-Jesus theology happened in these decades. Echoes of this pragmatic and selective approach can still be heard in this essay, although it is much enlarged; a thousand years do not easily fit into an essay, and heavy selection thus remains necessary.

14. See Franciscus Salesius Schmitt, ed., *Anselmi Cantuariensis Archiepiscopi Opera Omnia* (2 vols.; Stuttgart: Frommann-Holzboog, 1984). For an English edition, see Jasper Hopkins and Herbert Richardson, eds. and trans., *Anselm of Canterbury* (3 vols.; Toronto: Mellen, 1975–76). "Cur deus homo" is found in vol. 3.

intermingling. Anselm's thoughts were prototypical and influential for the growing bourgeois consciousness, first in Britain and then very soon on the continent. His interest in the dialectic was an expression of his concern for the *ratiocinari*, the process of thought that argued openly and conclusively. His phrases, *ratio necessaria* (necessary reason), *sola ratione* (by reason alone), and *Christo remoto* (with Christ in suspension) speak of a new trust in rational thinking and respective inquiry that is accompanied by the interest in consciousness, self, free will, and *rectitudo*, being right and doing right, not just on the divine side but also on the human side. He considered these features as they belonged to humans before the fall and as they were restored through Jesus Christ's own conscious will demonstrated by his incarnate life and sacrificial death. They were then communicated through the church's institutions and their influence upon social life, through the sacraments and education.

The dogma of the incarnation thus received a psychologically realistic and personal flavor again, one that was even stronger than the earlier concept of the divine man. The life of Jesus gained a reasonable and therefore clear dimension, was placed into a legal frame of reference, and was thus related to the social order as well. Harold Berman in his fascinating study *Law and Revolution* has shown that this was part of a revolutionary change, represented chiefly by the monk Hildebrand, who became Pope Gregory VII (1020/25–85, pope from 1073–85). [15] A societal will was formed in order to respond to the new socioeconomic conditions and developments with a marked educational effort, an effort that was able to focus on the ideal of the outstanding and leading individual and to multiply the ideal into a great number of conscious and responsible selves. As a human individual who transcended the normal, the extraordinarily gifted person became a model relevant and formative for society. In such an ideal individual, societal intention and conscious development ran together to a degree that the Hellenistic-Roman world had not known.

Gregory VII, of nonaristocratic origin himself, was one of these giants. Besides him there were any number of great personalities of regal and aristocratic stature, but also other popes, bishops, and clerics. An increasing multitude of artists, poets, and scholars joined the ranks of the extraordinary individuals in the eleventh to thirteenth centuries, among whom were an increasing number of the bourgeoisie. This interest and these developments, however, were not limited to the Latin world but

---

15. Harold Berman, *Law and Revolution: The Formation of the Western Legal Tradition* (Cambridge: Harvard University Press, 1983).

found expression in the Greek East as well.[16] In the Byzantine world were people such as the encyclopedic genius and philosopher Constantine Psellos, often mentioned under his monastic name Michael (1018–96/98).[17] He opened the way for the realization of the ideal of a renewed ancient educational formation, a paideia in neoplatonic understanding. He advertised it as a bridge between antiquity and Christianity. It is not unimportant, moreover, that the ancient Alexander romance blossomed anew in the East as well as in the West.

Although certain trends in theology since John Scotus Eriugena (ca. 810–77) seemed to tend toward mere speculation, a combination of philosophical cosmology and theological metaphysics, the adaptation of Eriugena by Hugh of St. Victor (ca. 1096–1141) continued the central interest of Anselm in the individual Jesus of Nazareth.[18] Hugh's work is the first of many subsequent examples of the fact that mysticism could support the rationalist concern for objective verifiability that concentrated on the man from Nazareth as the center of everything. Augustine's influence helped Hugh even more than Anselm before him to put the figure of Jesus into the process and developmental scheme of the salvation machine that Augustine had conceived the church to be. The sacramental as well as hierarchical structure did not contradict this renewed interest in mysticism and asceticism but accompanied it.

Thus the issues of power and control were not contrasts to this new program but rather related to it naturally, as was prominently demonstrated by the great mystic Bernard of Clairvaux (1090–1153).[19] He proved that the miraculous as well as the suffering Jesus, together with the imitation of this Jesus, could become elements of schooling in and exercising of

---

16. Hans-Georg Beck, *Kirche und theologische Literatur im byzantinischen Reich* (Munich: Becksche Verlagsbuchhandlung, 1959).

17. Christian Zervos, *Un philosophe néoplatonicien du XIe siècle. Michail Psellos, sa vie, son oeuvre, ses luttes philosophiques, son influence* (1920; repr., Burt Franklin Research and Source Works, Byzantine Series 41; New York: Franklin, 1973).

18. Esp. Hugh of St. Victor, *De Sacramentis* 2.1 (PL 176:371–416); for an English edition, see Hugh of Saint Victor, *On the Sacraments of the Christian Faith (De Sacramentis)* (trans. Roy J. Deferrari; Cambridge: Medieval Academy of America, 1951).

19. See Jean Leclerq, C. H. Talbott, and H. Rochais, eds., *Bernardi Opera* (8 vols.; Rome: Editiones Cisterciensis, 1957–76). For a German translation, see Agnes Wolter and Eberhard Friedrich, trans., *Die Schriften des honigfließenden Lehrers* (6 vols.; Wittlich: Fischer, 1934–35). The first one and a half volumes contain Bernard's sermons for the time between Advent and Easter, i.e., the christological section of the church year, and thus deal heavily with christological issues. For English editions, see *Saint Bernard's Sermons on the Nativity* (trans. by a priest of Mount Melleray; 1921; repr., Devon: Augustine, 1985); and Bernard of Clairvaux, *On the Song of Songs* (trans. Kilian Walsh; 4 vols.; Spencer, Mass.: Cistercian Publications, 1971–80).

ecclesiastical and political power. The secular world was called to watch and to reflect, and so they did, and not only the princes. I have shown elsewhere that the concept of sovereignty has evolved out of the medieval ideal of the aseity of God.[20] The earthly Jesus of the Middle Ages was not far removed from that concept but rather a necessary expression of it.

The particular individual Jesus of Nazareth was the prominent exemplar of divine power. The Council of Chalcedon of 451, in accordance with Pauline Christology, had neglected the claim of Pope Leo I (died 461) in his letter of 449 to Bishop Flavian (died 449/450) that Jesus' miracles were essential elements and proofs of his divinity.[21] In contrast, Thomas of Aquinas (1225–74) took the letter of Leo as the decisive interpretation of the council's declaration in every respect.[22] In this light Thomas, in the third part of the *Summa Theologica*, reinterpreted Chalcedon by emphasizing the miraculous power of Jesus as most distinct.[23] The divine, that is to say, the higher power in Jesus, did the miracles. This power was also the force in Jesus' resurrection and ascension, supported by the transfigured soul of Jesus, which was the prefiguration of the potential that humans could gain in following Jesus. Not only Thomas argued thus, but also the Franciscan monk Giovanni di Fidanza Bonaventure (1221–74).[24] He had strengthened the idea of the potential of Jesus by emphasizing Jesus' identity with divine wisdom and therefore associating the individual Jesus with the possession of superior knowledge, its disbursement, and its enactment. This ideal was one that the new universities were about to put into practice through the schooling of brains and

---

20. See the preface to Georgi, *Theocracy in Paul's Praxis and Theology*, vii-xi.

21. Leo's letter is found in H. William Pereival, ed., *The Seven Ecumenical Councils* (NPNF 2/14, New York: Scribners; Edinburgh: T&T Clark, 1916), 255–56.

22. On Aquinas's use of Leo's letter to Flavian, see Ignaz Baker, "Die christologische Problematik der Hochscholastik und ihre Beziehung zu Chalkedon," in *Das Konzil von Chalkedon: Geschichte und Gegenwart* (ed. Aloys Grillmeier and Heinrich Bracht; 3 vols.; Würzburg: Echter, 1952), 2:923–34, esp. 937–39.

23. See Petrus Caramello, ed., *Thomae Aquinatis Summa Theologica* (2 vols.; Rome: Marietti, 1950). For an English edition, see Thomas Aquinas, *Summa Theologica* (5 vols.; trans. Fathers of the English Dominican Province; Westminster, Md.: Christian Classics, 1981).

24. *Doctoris Seraphici S. Bonaventurae S. R. E. Episcopi Cardinalis Opera Omnia* (10 vols.; ed. Collegium A. S. Bonaventurae; Ad Claras Aquas: Collegium S. Bonaventurae, 1882–1902). For an English editon, see Bonaventure, *The Mind's Journey to God* (trans. Lawrence S. Cunningham; Chicago: Franciscan Herald, 1979). For a German edition of Bonaventure's *Hexaemeron*, see Bonaventure, *Das Sechstagewerk* (trans. Wilhelm Nyssen; 2nd ed.; Munich: Kösel, 1979). See also Zachary Hayes, *The Hidden Center: Spiritual and Speculative Christology in St. Bonaventure* (New York: Paulist, 1981). Aquinas's teacher, Albert the Great (ca. 1193–1280), had already stressed the sapiential dimensions of Jesus Christ.

wills of the young elite. It is amazing to note how through Augustine's and Leo's Latin, that is, Roman, triumphalism the images of the great ones of the pagan Roman past became hermeneutical images for reading and interpreting Jesus and the Gospels, and so indirectly the ideology and anthropology of the imperial cult also crept in.

For Thomas as for Bonaventure, the particular and the extraordinary coalesced in Jesus. It followed that the preference for the divine in Jesus turned out to be an enlargement of the human potential. The discussion of Christology in the third part of the *Summa* is preceded by an elaborate presentation of the anthropological issue in the second part. Thus Thomas's final portrayal of Christology reads as the *specialissimum* (most special case) of anthropology, which is the *generalissimum* (most general case). This is supported by Thomas's claim that the incarnation and life of Jesus prepared the way for human deification and that, contrary to Paul, justification was most of all associated with the resurrection, not the death of Jesus. For the future development of the societal impact of theology, especially Christology, it should be decisive that Thomas interpreted the purpose of revelation and justification as the influencing of the human will.

Bernard of Clairvaux had been the first to use the figure of Jesus as a model for reflecting on the nature and impact of experience.[25] Jesus' experience and the experience of the believer encountering him coincided. Subsequent thinkers would reconcile this concept of experience with that of Aristotle. In this form meditation on Jesus added another essential element to the bourgeois consciousness as it went about exploring not only its growing environment but also itself. In Thomas's christological discussions in the third part of the *Summa* the considerations of the experience of Jesus played an important part. Thomas called Jesus' experience *scientia experimentalis*, a highly presentient term, and associated it significantly not only with the imagination but also with active reason.[26] Increasingly since the twelfth century the Franciscans, particularly in

---

25. On "experience" here and in the following discussion see Eilert Herms, "Erfahrung II. Philosophisch," *TRE* 10:89–109; Ulrich Köpf, "Erfahrung III. Theologiegeschichtlich/ 1. Mittelalter und Reformationszeit," *TRE* 10:109–16; and Joachim Track, "Erfahrung III/2. Neuzeit," *TRE* 10:116–28.

26. In his discussion of experience in the Middle Ages (see previous note), Ulrich Köpf unfortunately and unjustifiably separates religious experience and experience directed toward the world. Even within the religious experience the discussions on the experience of Jesus are set apart too much. Eilert Herms, in discussing the systematic theological aspect of experience, presents no reflection on the theological dimension of experience in general but limits himself to the experience of the status of salvation/grace ("Erfahrung IV. Systematisch-theologisch," *TRE* 10:128–36).

England and Scotland, stressed the concept and practice of experience. In their opinion the exterior form of the experience related to the world at large, but it grew out of the inner experience and gained status and life beside it, not the least in the academic and scientific environment. The Franciscans had been formed by a style of piety and teaching that concentrated on Jesus. This theology presented to the burghers of the cities an ever-increasing consideration for the individual. Praxis, experiment, and experience were integrated into this growing interest in the individual. Roger Bacon (ca. 1214–92) was a representative of that interest, a clear indication of an increase of the blending of spirituality and worldliness, not at all unrelated to Franciscan piety, theology, science, and education.[27] Roger Bacon said that the individual did have priority, not only according to its intention and operation but also because of its dignity. Such a view prepared the way for John Duns Scotus and to a greater degree William of Ockham.[28]

The Scottish Franciscan John Duns Scotus (ca. 1265/66–1308),[29] the son of wealthy landowners, developed further the individualistic and dynamic interest of the Franciscans in the intellect and the will of the self, divine as well as human. He saw the humanity of Jesus as the decisive interface between the divine and the human experiences of intellect and will. He defined the divine, Jesus, and the human self all in distinction from other selves. Duns Scotus's discussion of the absolute will and sovereignty of God must be seen in the light of the growing importance of the national state and its royal sovereign at that time, particularly in Britain, not in antithesis to and at the expense of the bourgeoisie but in growing collaboration with it.

---

27. See Roger Bacon, *Opus major* (ed. John Henry Bridges; 3 vols.; 1897–1900; repr., Frankfurt am Main: Minerva, 1964), 1:xxxix–xliii and the subsequent statements of Bacon in *Opera hactenus inedita* (ed. Robert Steele and Ferdinand M. Delorme; 12 vols.; Oxford: Frowde, 1905–40), 2:96. On Bacon, see Herbert Grundmann, "Bacon, Roger," *RGG* 1:832–33. Bacon also edited and annotated a secretive scientific text, "Secretum Secretorum," falsely attributed to Aristotle and allegedly dedicated by him to Alexander the Great (see Bacon, *Opera hactenus inedita*, vol. 5).

28. On the themes discussed here see Heinz Heimsoeth, *Die sechs großen Themen der Abendländischen Metaphysik und der Ausgang des Mittelalters* (5th ed.; Darmstadt: Wissenschaftliche Buchgemeinschaft, 1965); Theo Kobusch, Ludger Oeng-Hanhoff, and Tilman Borsche, "Individuum/Individualität," *Historisches Wörterbuch der Philosophie* 4 (1976): 300–23; Wolfgang Janke, "Individuum/Individualismus I. Philosophisch," *TRE* 16:117–24.

29. *Joannis Duns Scoti Doctoris Subtilis Ordinis Minorum Opera Omnia* (26 vols.; based on the edition of Lucas Wadding; Paris: Vives, 1891–95), here esp. vols. 8–21 on the sentences, the so-called "Scriptum Oxoniense." The new critical edition of the Vatican is not yet complete. On Duns Scotus, see Reinhold Seeberg, *Die Theologie des Johannes Duns Scotus* (Studien zur Geschichte der Theologie und der Kirche 5; Leipzig: Dieterich, 1900), esp. 234–336.

Since the twelfth century there had been a tendency to interrelate the motif of the kingdom of God and/or of Christ with these concepts. Jesus Christ was the natural link. There were various ecclesial and royal expressions of that connection, both imperial in tendency, with pertinent interests in realization. Revolutionary alternatives also existed, along with tendencies toward complete internalization of the concept of the heavenly kingdom. In none of these cases was there a separation of the interest in Jesus and the interest in the kingdom of God and/or Christ but rather an intimate connection.

In the fourteenth century the bourgeoisie had to recover from the previous bad experiences, namely, that the hopeful attempts at a comprehensive emancipation of the cities and of their markets from feudal grasp had been successful merely in part. The attempts were perhaps most successful in Britain where the Hundred Years' War actually helped the bourgeoisie. Here also the monetary evolution advanced the most. The bourgeois succeeded least in central Europe. The bourgeoisie in general still lacked mass, and with it power. Therefore, a general interest in concentrating on the growth of societal consciousness could be observed both in the development of efficient forms of expression and in the evolution of strategies of alliance.

Francesco Petrarch (1304–74) made the ancient world of Greece and particularly Rome a model for his times and the great men of the ancient world the formative ideals.[30] A little later the Byzantine philosopher Georgios Gemisthos Plethon (1355–1452) in Mistra on the Peloponnesos renewed the Hellenistic-neoplatonic image of the ideal human person with an emphasis on the heroic.[31] Several hundred years later Reimarus would delve into Plethon's thinking first by way of the work of one of Plethon's critics and then through the work of Plethon himself.[32] The nature mysticism of Plethon possessed some analogies to the natural theology of Reimarus.

Meanwhile the Franciscan order had developed nominalism. Within this frame of reference, William of Ockham (ca. 1285–ca. 1350) started to

---

30. In Francesco Petrarch, *De viris illustribus* (ed. Guido Martellotti; Florence: Sansoni, 1964); on Petrarch, see Ernest Hatch Wilkins, *Studies in the Life and the Works of Petrarch* (Cambridge: Medieval Academy of America, 1955); Ralph Roeder, *The Man of Renaissance: Four Lawgivers: Savonarola, Machiavelli, Castiglione, Aretino* (New York: Viking, 1977); Paul Oskar Kristeller, *Eight Philosophers of the Italian Renaissance* (Stanford, Calif.: Stanford University Press, 1964), 1–18.

31. Eusebius Stephanou, "Plethon,"' *DThC* 12 (1933): 2393–404; F. Masai, *Pletho et le platonisme de Mistra* (Paris: Les Belles Lettres, 1956).

32. Hermann Samuel Reimarus, *Matthaei Camariotae Orationes duo in Plethonem de Fato* (Leiden: Wishoff, 1721).

emphasize the *res individualis* as the only reality. This concept was clearly not limited to the area of logic and language but was intended to portray the individual as the entity that formed, supported, and maintained the divine, the world, and society. It was a breakthrough in the concept of the individual as a phenomenon that was to form and support society in the future.[33]

Since Bacon this discussion about the individual and individuation makes use of the terms *proprium* and *proprietas* for the purpose of differentiation. The double meaning of the Latin terms appears in this usage. The Latin words were not merely employed to imply "proper" in the sense of "peculiar" but "property" in the sense of material property owned by the individual. Ockham's emphasis on the will and on the property of the individual was ontologically grounded and had ethical pointers; it was thus originally intended to further the Franciscan ideal of surrendering property.[34] The outcome of this train of thought, however, was the opposite, namely, the founding of the ideal of individual property, which was formative for British and European societies to come and eventually for Western society as a whole.

In this terminological and sociohistorical context of the strengthening of British bourgeoisie, certain features of the English language developed. At that time the French term *proprieté* was split in English into "propriety" and "property." In the same vein the Latin *personalitas* was broken up into "personalty," that is, personal property, and "personality"; *realitas* became divided into "realty" and "reality."

The decline of the papacy and imperial power and the growth of nation-states in the West encouraged the increase of administrative approaches. At the same time the bourgeoisie gained inroads into the

---

33. William of Ockham, *Opera philosophica et theologica* (10 vols.; St. Bonaventure, N.Y.: Editiones Instituti Franciscani Universitatis S. Bonaventurae, 1967–68). Ockham treated the concept of *individuum* especially in the first book of his "Super Quattuor Libros Sententiarum" (vol. 3 of *Opera Plurima*) and in the "Expositio Aurea" (vol. 4 of *Opera Plurima*); see William of Ockham, *Opera Plurima Lyon* (London: Gregg, 1962). Already a brief look at Leon Baudry's index (*Lexique philosophique de Guillaume d'Ockham: Étude des notions fondamentales* [Paris: Lethielleux, 1958], s.v. *individuum*) indicates that the term means much more than logical problems. See also the selection of texts by Stephen Tornay, *Ockham: Studies and Selections* (La Salle: Open Court, 1938). On Ockham, see Joseph Klein, "Ockham, Wilhelm," *RGG* 4:1556–62. See also Alister E. McGrath, "Homo Assumptus? A Study in the Christology of the Via Moderna with Particular Reference to William of Ockham," *EThL* 60 (1984:) 283–97.

34. On the understanding of the concept of will in Duns Scotus, see Walther Köhler, *Dogmengeschichte von den Anfängen bis zur Reformation* (3rd ed.; Zurich. Niehans, 1951), 338–45. On Ockham, see Tornay, *Ockham*, 62–76; and Baudry, *Lexique*, s.v. *intentio* and *voluntas*. On Ockham's understanding of property, see Kurt Flasch, *Das philosophische Denken im Mittelalter* (Stuttgart: Reclam, 1987), 456–59.

central power machineries, not in opposition to the growing idea of the state's sovereignty but in support of it. The development of *devotio moderna,* only insufficiently translated as "modern piety," was not an antithesis but an accompaniment to this. This new form of piety and lifestyle met the need of the newly formed individual to feel empowered from within.

Ockham already had spoken of the particular individual, Jesus, as a human person who had developed under God's self-limiting power and will. Ockham had presented this individual, Jesus, as the model for the human individual for the fulfillment of its tasks. Around 1450 this individualism had found stronger and multiple expressions. Gabriel Biel (before 1410–95), one of the main representatives of *devotio moderna,* preached about the earthly Jesus as a paradigm for the spiritual life and recommended following Jesus.[35] Nicholas of Cusa (1401–64), also an adherent of *devotio moderna,* shared an interest in the individual with the philosophy and theology of nominalism.[36] Nicholas saw in Jesus something historically particular or accidental. Exactly in that which appeared to be peculiar, however, he envisaged the unification of everything that tends to split apart. Jesus for him was the active original image and paradigm for humanness, humanity, and every individual. Here, in the human particularity of Jesus, he saw the divine likeness as well as the human likeness, so that the particularity of the human individual was shaped in a paradigmatic fashion. The ego of Jesus brought into final form what was singular and personal in every individual, not in contradiction to the whole but as its expression, namely, as the manifestation of the meaningfulness of creation and creature.

3. THE FIFTEENTH AND SIXTEENTH CENTURIES

The fifteenth and sixteenth centuries showed a strong movement in the direction of democratization. Chivalry as a military and social order began to lose its political and economic influence. This shift had begun with the troubadours who had idealized chivalry and so had made it transferable. With the growth of their economic influence and democratic power, the commons slowly adopted the ways and means of chivalry. Knighthood for centuries had been saturated with motifs of following

---

35. Gabriel Biel, *Sermones,* (4 vols.; ed. Wendelin Steinbach; Tübingen: Leynburger, 1499–1500); Heiko Oberman, *The Harvest of Medieval Theology: Gabriel Biel and Late Medieval Nominalism* (Cambridge: Harvard University Press, 1963), esp. 217–80 and 340–60.

36. Richard Haubst, *Die Christologie des Nikolaus* (Freiburg: Herder, 1956); Pauline Moffit Watts, *Nicolaus Cusanus A Fifteenth-Century Vision of Man* (Studies in the History of Christian Thought 30; Leiden: Brill, 1982).

Jesus and of the Holy Land, so the adoption of chivalric ideals by the commoners frequently also entailed the transfer of such religious motifs.

The kingdom of God, love for Jesus, and the Holy Land on the one side and society, its constitution, its institutions, and its forces on the other moved toward one another. The *cavaliere, caballero,* or *cavalier* became circumlocutions for the new societal ideal of the *uomo universale* or *honnête homme* as it spread from the aristocracy into the bourgeoisie.[37] The title "gentleman" could be bought; the "yeoman" could purchase the "esquire." Academies that had been founded by dukes to train knights now made chivalry the ideal, the model for young people mainly recruited from the bourgeoisie. These academies on the Continent and the public schools in England also trained young burghers for clerical and administrative offices of the state. Novels about knights became folk literature.

A major paradigm and force in this encounter and transfer was Ignatius of Loyola (1491–1556). In his thinking and praxis the ideal and the social sides of chivalry are strongly linked. In his *Spiritual Exercises* (completed in 1540) the history of Jesus was portrayed as a superhuman but formative model under inclusion of the Easter stories.[38] This model was skillfully used to form the individual will and to school individuals for the dialectic interplay of individual and collective planning. Although the overall direction of Ignatius's thought and praxis was still clerically and centralistically inclined, even institutionalized, with the religious order and the papal church as the points of orientation, the Protestant caricature of Jesuit morality was and is wrong. This caricature misinterprets Ignatius's concept of obedience and overlooks the Protestant sides of the Jesuit order and its direct connection with the Enlightenment exemplified in Jesuit missionary activity outside of Europe and in the later attack by Friedrich Spee of Langefeld (1591–1635) on the persecution of witches (see below).[39]

---

37. Pietro Toldo, "Le courtisane dans la littérature francaîse et ses rapports avec l'oeuvre de Castiglione," *Archiv für die Studien neuerer Sprachen und Literaturen* (Braunschweig: Westermann) 104 (1900): 75–121, 313–30; 105 (1900): 60–85; see also Roeder, *Man of the Renaissance;* Walter Schrinner, *Castiglione und die englische Renaissance* (Neue deutsche Forschungen 234; Berlin: Junker & Dünnhaupt, 1939).

38. On Ignatius, see Karl Rahner, *Ignatius of Loyola* (trans. Rosaleen Ockenden; London: Collins, 1979); idem, *Betrachtungen zum ignatianischen Exerzitienbuch* (Munich: Kösel, 1965); Ignatius of Loyola, *Exercitia Spiritualia S. Ignatii de Loyola et eorum Directoria* (1919; repr., Rome: Monumenta Historia Societas Jesu, 1955); idem, *The Spiritual Exercises of St. Ignatius* (trans. Anthony Mottola; Garden City, N.Y.: Image, 1964); Heinrich Boehmer, *Ignatius v. Loyola* (ed. Hans Laube; Stuttgart: Koehler, 1941).

39. An example of unfair presentation is Heinrich Boehmer, *Die Jesuiten* (ed. Kurt Dietrich Schmidt; Stuttgart: Koehler, 1957).

The contribution of Spain toward the later Enlightenment was even stronger in Juan Huarte de San Juan (ca. 1529–ca. 1591). He was a physician, philosopher, and pedagogue. His *Examen de ingenios para las ciencias* (1575) is essential for the history of the bourgeois concept of genius.[40] Huarte identified the "talent" of Matt 25:14–30 with the "charisma" of Paul's discussions in 1 Cor 12 and Rom 12. Huarte interpreted this phenomenon as *ingenio,* the connection of extraordinary gift and natural talent. Huarte presented a manual for discovering and pedagogically improving such an extraordinary, ingenious predisposition.[41] In his description of the highest talent, the royal one, Huarte put the figure of Jesus in the center. He understood his portrait of Jesus as paradigmatic. The drawing bore all the traces of the ancient divine man, interestingly enough, as a blond-haired man.[42] Huarte's book closed with technical suggestions for the biological reproduction of boys. This was not without reason, for in this kind of bourgeois thinking reproduction, production, education, and formation in the sense of manipulative selection and breeding were closely related, along with technique and pedagogy. Huarte's depiction of the correct reproduction of what appeared socially valuable and preferable ended with another portrayal of Jesus in which Jesus was drawn as truly human. True humanity included divinity, and in divinity's merger with humanity the miraculous appeared already in the natural. Here was a prototype for the ingenious personality, the exemplary genius. This genius, however, was not high and above but rather a model and thus multipliable in the objects of pedagogical inventiveness and formative manipulation.[43] Here major interests of the

---

40. Juan Huarte de San Juan, *Examen de ingenios para las ciencias* (ed. Esteban Torre; Biblioteca de la literatura y el pensamiento hispanicos 14; Madrid: Editora Nacional, 1976); Malcolm Kevin Read, *Juan Huarte de San Juan* (Boston: Twayne, 1981).

41. Huarte's argument was that if variations already exist in supernatural gifts then they exist all the more in natural gifts. Huarte wanted to argue for *ingenio* as a differentiable given but also as formable and improvable. But as Huarte's argument moved along, the Spanish term *ingenio* (Latin *ingenium*) became less and less pluralistic and more and more hierarchically differentiated. In the end he aimed at the exceptionally, specially equipped genius. In the reception of Huarte this tendency became even stronger.

42. Here Huarte went beyond the royal office in its constitutional sense and presented a paradigm for the great personality, the highest genius, which the pedagogical scrutiny and effort had to find and form. This is proven by the fact that Huarte followed this discussion of Jesus with that of Adam as royal person.

43. Huarte wanted to show that Jesus, already through his nature, even without using supernatural wisdom could drive out evil and choose the good. Jesus was for Huarte the true human, divine and miraculous already in his natural appearance and action and therefore the exemplar for the ingenious personality. This was stated without the cynicism of Machiavelli found in *The Prince*. This ingenious personality, moreover, was to function as subject and instrument of educational sensitivity and skill.

bourgeoisie in reproducing and strengthening itself had found a more radical expression that urged educational implementation.

The secular model for this planned superhuman personality, as a socially and politically efficient power figure, was *The Prince* of Nicolo Machiavelli (1512/13).[44] Machiavelli had understood this figure as a negative model. Later, however, *The Prince* became almost proverbially associated with the name of Machiavelli (1469–1527). *The Prince* influenced modern thinking about the proper actions of statesmen but also about the allegedly realistic individual political and societal existence, indeed the existence of the realistic individual altogether. An ironic, even satirical understanding of *The Prince* initially prevailed, made world-famous through Cervantes' (1547–1616) *Don Quixote*.[45] This sad figure of a knight was a foolish counterimage to that of the *caballero* but also to *The Prince*. Whether the image of Christ as fool had influenced Cervantes is an interesting theme in the study of his work. The majority of the prophets of the Enlightenment shared with Cervantes the ironical, that is, satirical, interpretation of the Prince.

Martin Luther (1483–1546) took a rather critical stance toward the historical Jesus, as his attitude toward the Synoptic Gospels proves. This attitude is vividly expressed in his prefaces, especially that to the Gospel of John, which he vastly preferred over the first three Gospels. Luther used the stories and sayings of Jesus as mere illustrations for the message of the cross.[46] By 1550 the Synoptic Gospels, especially the Gospel of Matthew, nevertheless had gained center stage in Lutheranism, particularly through the efforts of Melanchthon.[47] Melanchthon was interested in educating the populace, in particular the bourgeoisie, according to the ethical image of the figure of Jesus. With this attitude went an interest in translating the concept of the kingdom of God into ecclesial and even societal realization.

---

44. Nicolo Machiavelli, *The Prince* (trans. and intro. Harvey C. Mansfield; Chicago: University of Chicago Press, 1985); August Buck, *Machiavelli* (Darmstadt: Wissenschaftliche Buchgesellschaft, 1985).

45. Miguel de Cervantes Saavedra, *Don Quixote* (1615); ET: John Ormsby, *Don Quixote* (Great Books of the Western World 29; Chicago: Benton, 1952).

46. See Luther's preface to the New Testament and his reflections on the question of the noblest writings of the New Testament in the so-called September Bible of 1522. See Martin Luther, "Vorreden auf das NT," *WA* 6 (1929): 1.

47. Philipp Melanchthon's "Unterricht der Visitatoren" (1528) (see *Werke in Auswahl* [7 vols.; ed. Robert Stupperich, Gütersloh: Mohn, 1951–75] 1:265–71) already contained an explicit warning against a premature reading of John's Gospel in the elementary education in the so-called Latin schools. Melanchthon recommended the use of Matthew's Gospel instead.

This was even more strongly the case with Martin Bucer (1491-1551), who in 1550 composed one of his most influential works, *De regno Christi*, written in Cambridge, England, and dedicated to the English king Edward VI.[48] This study was concerned not only with religious matters but also with political ones, such as *administratio populi aut civitatis* (the administration of the people or the state). For Bucer this implied reforms of the church as well as reforms of state, society, and economy. He was interested in the well-being of all burghers, which would presuppose a godly as well as a reasonable and rational life. This concept anticipated the ideals of the Enlightenment and the American Revolution. For Bucer such a life was possible only within the context of the kingdom of Christ. This kingdom expanded into the world as society; it achieved this expansion in the process of sanctification and in the missionary witness of its citizens, the elect ones. Thus it would penetrate all realms of the world with the spirit of Christ. The medium of this penetration should be the example of the elect ones, their activities within and through public offices, including secular ones. Bucer believed that another major means of this penetration of the world and the realization of the kingdom of Christ was the education of children.

For Bucer the incarnation, life, suffering, and death of Jesus were demonstrations of his love that conquered sin and restored the rights of God's children. Bucer understood the crucifixion as an exaltation that made Jesus' earthly life a prototype to be imitated for the purpose of sanctification. This imitation took place in obedience to God and love toward the neighbor along one's own way toward one's own glorification. Faith, sanctification, church, and also the kingdom of Christ were terms of process for Bucer. Their aim was perfection, the glorification that had already begun in the resurrection of Christ. In the combination of all these ideas the foundation for the bourgeois concept of progress was laid. For Bucer neither bourgeois freedom nor happiness nor progress were imaginable without controlled education and discipline. The church was the place of purification, the exemplary frame of reference for the ethical action of believers. From there school and university were supposed to receive the formative guidelines they were then to communicate in their educational efforts for the well-being of the society and every individual.

---

48. Martin Bucer, *De regno Christi* (vol. 15 of *Opera Latina*; ed. Francois Wendel; Pans: Presses Universitaires de France; Gütersloh: Bertelsmann, 1955), 15; Wilhelm Pauck, trans. and ed., *De Regno Christi Melanchthon and Bucer* (LCC 19; Philadelphia: Westminster, 1969); Wilhelm Pauck, *Das Reich Gottes auf Erden Utopie und Wirklichkeit: Eine Untersuchung zu Butzers "De Regno Christi" und zur englischen Staatskirche des 16. Jahrhunderts* (Berlin: de Gruyter, 1928); Gottfried Hammann, *Martin Bucer 1491–1551 zwischen Volkskirche und Bekenntnisgemeinschaft* (Stuttgart: Steiner, 1989).

4. FROM MILTON TO REIMARUS

It speaks for Bucer's political and socioeconomic farsightedness that he saw in the England of Edward VI the best-prepared soil for the final realization of his plans for ecclesial and societal reforms. His radical as well as concrete eschatologizing of Christology, ecclesiology, and ethics anticipated the Puritan program and its enactment in the first bourgeois revolution, the English Civil War, and found its new expression in the writings, poetry, and actions of that revolution's prophet, John Milton (1608–47).[49] Its nationalism, even imperialism, understood itself as a coming to terms with the concreteness of Christ's rule, not to the detriment of bourgeois liberty but as its accompaniment. Jesus represented for Milton the triumph of reason over temptation and passion; Jesus rendered freedom to the individual and, in conjunction with freedom, gave the inner paradise. In reliving this freedom Christ's example was realized again. The Puritans would bring this program to the shores of North America, and Jonathan Edwards (1703–58) would finally give it a distinctly American character.[50]

During the first half of the seventeenth century Protestant orthodoxy was at its height. Within all the overly abstract and refined language, their great concern was the degree of reality in the work of Jesus, particularly his death. This realism increasingly also included the dimension of experience. There was growing experiential awareness. It was not only reflected dogmatically but also disbursed through hymns and

---

49. John Milton, *The Works* (ed. Frank Allen Patterson; 20 vols.; New York: Columbia University Press, 1931–40); Arthur E. Barker, *Milton and the Puritan Dilemma (1641–1660)* (Toronto: University of Toronto Press, 1942); Herbert C. G. Grierson, "Milton, John," *ERE* 8 (1980): 641–48. The importance of Milton's "De Doctrina Christiana," and in particular his concept of the "kingdom of Christ," for his entire thought and work needs to be stressed (see Barker, *Milton and the Puritan Dilemma*, 193–214, 260–90, and 293–330).

50. Jonathan Edwards, "An Humble Attempt to Promote Explicit Agreement and Visible Union of God's People in Extraordinary Prayer for the Revival of Religion and the Advancement of Christ's Kingdom on Earth Pursuant to Scripture Promises and Prophecies concerning the Last Time," *Apocalyptic Writings* (vol. 5 of *The Works of Jonathan Edwards*; ed. S. J. Stein; New Haven: Yale University Press 1977), 307–436; see also idem, "Covenant of Redemption: Excellency of Christ," in Jonathan Edwards, *Representative Selections* (ed. C. H. Faust and T. H. Johnson, New York : Hill & Wang, 1962); idem, "A History of Redemption," in *Works of President Edwards* (ed. Sereno E. Dwight; 10 vols.; New York: Converse, 1829–30), vol. 3 On Edwards, see H. Richard Niebuhr, *The Kingdom of God in America* (2nd ed.; Hamden, Conn.: ShoeString Press, 1956); Ernst Wolf, "Edwards, Jonathan," *RGG* 2:309–10; Conrad Cherry, *The Theology of Jonathan : A Reappraisal* (Bloomington: Indiana University Press, 1990); Mark Valeri and John F.Wilson, "Scripture and Society from Reform in the Old World to Revival in the New," in *The Bible in American Law Politics and Political Rhetoric* (ed. James Turner Johnson; Philadelphia: Fortress; Chico, Calif.: Scholars Press, 1985), 13–38.

prayerbooks, not the least by stalwarts of Lutheran orthodox Christology such as the two friends Johann Arnd (1555–1621) and Johann Gerhard (1582–1637), both of whom were heavily influenced by earlier mystics. In their edifying literature as well as in many contemporary hymns, the presentation of the experience of Jesus, often in a rather dramatized fashion, was made to coincide with the depiction of the experience of the believer, that is, the soul, frequently with an equally dramatic tone. Friedrich Spee, mentioned above, was a forceful representative of this approach, with a strong emphasis on Jesus and the experience of Jesus, but he stressed the global dimensions of such an encounter more strongly than did his Protestant peers.[51] The new musical form of the aria emphasized that even more strongly. This literature, in language as well as in experiential expression, helped to strengthen the tendency of the bourgeois to express themselves in their indigenous language in a refined fashion that would at least equal the aristocratic formation of former times. In Germany this tendency received additional urgency not despite of but because of the devastation of the Thirty Years' War.

I have pointed already to the fact that a strong connection between Spain and the Enlightenment existed and that the Jesuits provided a major bridge to that period. A particularly important mediator, much respected in the period of Enlightenment, was the Spanish Jesuit theologian, philosopher, and pedagogical artist Baltasar Gracián y Morales (1601–58). His main literary work was, among others, an example of a positive reception of *The Prince*. Gracián was not really a conformist.[52] Out of caution, he allowed part of his writings to appear only under the name of his brother. He never moved away from the Jesuit order, however. Even in his last major tract, *El Comulgatorio (The Table of the Lord)*,[53] he gave an introduction to the communion entirely in the method of Ignatius's exercises: a meditative study of biblical texts relevant for communion aiming at the emotional, intellectual, and volitional finding of the

---

51. Friedrich Spee von Langenfeld, *Cautio Criminalis seu de processibus contra sagas liber* (Rinteln: Petrus Lucius, 1631; 2nd ed., Frankfurt am Main: Johannes Gronaeus, 1632); idem, *Trutz Nachtigall Oder Geistlichs poetisch Lust Waldlein* (Cologne: Godefridus Otterstedt, 1649; new ed. Gustav Balke; Leipzig: Brockhaus, 1879); idem, *Guldines Tugent Buch das is Werck und Übung der dreyen Göttlichen Tugenden Glauben Hoffnung und Liebe* (Cologne: Friesen, 1649; new ed. Franz Hattler; Freiburg: Herder, 1887). A survey of Spee's works is found in Carlos Sommervogel, *Bibliothéque de la Compagnie de Jésus* (new ed.; 12 vols.; Brussels: Schepens; Paris: Picard, 1890–1960), 7:1424–31.

52. As is often claimed.

53. Baltasar Gracián y Morales, *Obras Completas* (ed. A. del Hoyo; 2nd ed.; Madrid: Aguilar, 1960); Thomas G. Corvan, *The Best of Gracián: A New Translation* (New York: Philosophical Library, 1964); Virginia Ramos Foster, *Baltasar Gracián* (Boston: Twayne, 1975). Corvan's book has been especially helpful in preparing this synopsis.

self and decision-making. The essential bridge for achieving this was the effective encounter with the earthly Jesus.

It is possible to draw a synopsis of the ideas from the major works of Gracián, chiefly from *Oraculo Manual y Arte de Prudentia* (1647), but also from *El Heroe* (1637), *El Politico* (1640; ed. 1646), and *El Discreto* (1646). Such a synopsis provides a stunning resemblance to the features that make up the image of Jesus as presented through the next three hundred years up to the present day. All these books show Gracián's pedagogical concern, that is, an interest in educational policy. It is important to note that Gracián was also attractive to Arthur Schopenhauer and Friedrich Nietzsche. With his concept of the ideal personality, Gracián gave a mode to *The Prince* of Machiavelli that made this figure a typos usable as pedagogical paradigm for the education of the bourgeois individual. This alteration, however, was not thinkable without the heroizing meditation on Jesus of the Jesuits.

Gracián's hero possesses genius, ingenuity, intellectual presence, insight, foresight, oversight, passion, but also trust in God. He is active in word and deed. Gracián's hero devotes himself to God and true religion in piety and obedience. Gracián shared a strong skepticism with Machiavelli. His hero must not only withstand conflict but must also camouflage his heroic intention. This intention needs to appear as mysteriously waiting for the right moment of the final demonstration. This hero knows humankind. In his care for his fellow humans and in his love for nature he proves that his heart, often in a romantic and sentimental fashion, is full of hunger for ideal beauty. He renders himself to the examination of his individual talents and power, and he passes this examination. Thereby he confirms his consciousness about himself as much as the symbolic values for which he stands. In these conflicts the hero proves his abilities to stand suffering and humiliation. He demonstrates constancy, consistency, patience, and power of will. He is even ready to die when it is time. In his speech and actions he is full of contrasts and contradictions—in short, a fascinating personality.

During the seventeenth and eighteenth centuries the market finally became the decisive force in western Europe. Mercantile considerations now were dominant, and the bourgeoisie pushed more and more for control. Two movements linked in a dialectical relationship, one sentimental and one rationalist, dominated: Pietism and the Enlightenment.[54] Both

---

54. On the Enlightenment, see Emanuel Hirsch, *Geschichte der neueren evangelischen Theologie im Zusammenhang mit den allgemeinen Bewegungen des europäischen Denkens* (2nd ed.; 5 vols.; Gütersloh: Mohn, 1960); Rainer Piepmeier, "Aufklärung I. Philosophisch," *TRE* 4:575–94; Martin Schmidt, "Aufklärung II. Theologisch," *TRE* 4:594–608; Hermann Greive,

grew out of the bourgeoisie and shaped it; both were interested in the self, its illumination, and its liberation. Both saw the self as threatened, indeed enslaved by impersonal dogmas and institutions.

Both were interested in experience and method. Through the efforts of both movements, history became the magic wand of bourgeois consciousness and developed a critical stance toward such enslaving forces of inauthentic history by which the individual was kept the object of history. These movements worked on a critical reconstruction of authentic history in which the individual was to be the acting subject. Authentic history was understood as a progressive evolution that enabled seeing established privileges not as supernaturally or biologically given but as gained, inherited and, therefore, temporary, to be replaced by the authentic, earned recognition of contemporaries. History was used as a critical instrument, as the vehicle of emancipatory reconstruction for the freedom of the self, the bourgeois, the *citizen*. The church history of Gottfried Arnold, for instance, although a hallmark of Pietism, has much in common with the historical criticism of scholars of the Enlightenment.

The difference of both movements from much of older Protestant mysticism appeared in a concern for change, not just of the individual or group but also of social conditions and the world. The formula of changing the world by changing individuals was not only that of Pietism, and this change of will was not limited to the inner life but included social change as well. Rationalists and Pietists wanted to be "practical" in every respect, even religiously. Doctrinaire theology was despised as much as petty legalism. The goal was a practical piety, an internalizing as well as an ethicizing of religion that would, however, concretely radiate and bring about change for the better. The concept of progress was not limited to the Enlightenment alone. Education was a passion of both movements. Both trends also supported European imperialism.

This concept of concrete freedom needed models for what Max Weber later—in a completely false interpretation of 1 Cor 12 and Rom 12, but rather like Huarte—would call the charismatic personality. Jesus was portrayed as such a leader. Jesus and his God were seen by the Enlightenment and Pietism as agents who activated the pious as well as the reasonable, responsible, and humane individual, providing room for

---

"Aufklärung III. Jüdische Aufklärung," TRE 4:608–15. On Pietism, see Martin Schmidt, "Pietismus," *RGG* 5:370–81; idem, *Wiedergeburt und neuer Mensch* (vol. 1 of *Gesammelte Studien zur Geschichte des Pietismus;* Witten: Luther, 1969); idem, *Pietismus* (Stuttgart: Kohlhammer, 1972); idem, *Der Pietismus als theologische Erscheinung* (vol. 2 of *Gesammelte Studien zur Geschichte des Pietismus;* Göttingen: Vandenhoeck & Ruprecht, 1982).

freedom of choice and self-determination, liberty to move and to create. Both Pietism and the Enlightenment portrayed Jesus as the person who transformed the cultic and metaphysical elements of religion into the personal and private, essential for the liberated bourgeois individual in its stewardship efforts in a born-again, that is, enlightened life.

Jesus stood for the concept of mature individual consciousness in which others could find themselves and were enabled to risk and to regain themselves, thus discovering their soul and true life, authenticity and identity, propriety, and with that, it was to be hoped, also property. Talents, prefigured by Jesus, and imitated in the educated, pious, and reasonable life, were understood as God-given rights in critical opposition to everything that owed its existence merely to tradition, status, or class. *Egalité* and *fraternité* followed easily, but it was a disciplined freedom, the freedom to act responsibly.

Much of the criticism of Pietism and the Enlightenment was directed against Roman Catholicism and Catholicizing tendencies, but there had been much influence from Catholicism, and there was still quite a bit of cross-traffic and common interest. The Pietists, for instance, were influenced not only by Continental and English Protestant mysticism but also by Spanish and French (i.e., Roman Catholic) Jesus mysticism. Such relationships made it easier to continue the common Christian anti-Semitism and to make Judaism the incarnation of everything antibourgeois: cult and legalism, dead tradition, clericalism, and hierarchy. Thus Judaism again became the main counterfoil, only now to bourgeois culture and individualism.[55]

Pietism in Germany had been a major force for the survival of the lower aristocracy and the bourgeoisie through and after the devastation of the Thirty Years' War. It had been shaped during that period but had much earlier interdenominational and international roots that slowly grew together into a multifaceted movement. It nevertheless had a definite profile that in this form lasted into the late eighteenth century. In Pietism Jesus was experienced and felt quite literally in the readings and narrations of groups and individuals concerning Jesus as an efficacious power.

---

55. This happened despite such philosophers as Baruch Spinoza (1632–77), Moses Mendelsohn (1729–86), Charles de Montesquieu (1689–1755), and Gotthold Ephraim Lessing (1729–81), and such theologians as Paul Felgenhauer (1593–1677) and Friedrich Christoph Oetinger (1702–82). As Philipp Jakob Spener (1635–1705) proved, the tolerance of Pietism against the Jews on the whole did not go beyond an acknowledgement of pre-Christian *Heilsgeschichte* and the advancement of mission to the Jews together with the integration of converted Jews into the circles of the born-again. For details, see Gerhard Müller, "Antisemitismus VI. 16. und 17. Jahrhundert," *TRE* 3:143–55; and Erika Weinziess, "Antisemitismus VII. 18.–20. Jahrhundert," *TRE* 3:155–65.

In these pietistic exercises, a subjectifying of the objective text happened, an indwelling of Jesus in the born-again, inspired persons. This intimate experience was frequently expressed in terms of erotic mysticism. Intensive scrutiny of the self and its conscience prepared and accompanied these encounters with Jesus, who called for free decisions, first the conversion and then the daily acts of will and practice of the sanctified life.

The influence of the Spaniards Ignatius, Huarte, and Gracián upon the Enlightenment, especially in Germany, was tremendous. Ignatius's influence was obvious. Huarte and Gracián were partially translated: Gotthold Ephraim Lessing translated Huarte's *Examen de ingenios para las ciencias*. Lessing knew also of Gracián, as did Christian Thomasius, who was impressed by him. One of the most influential teachers of Reimarus, the polyhistor Johann Franz Buddeus (1667–1729), was an expert in European philosophical and theological discussion, particularly that of Spain, and not the least in the works of the Jesuit Francisco Suarez (1548–1619), who had renewed Ockham's individualism.[56]

The work of Reimarus (1694–1768) marks the beginning of the outright scientific approach to the life-of-Jesus theology and a definite increase in the already-existing interest in objectifying verifiability. Reimarus possessed a broad education and a far-ranging knowledge not only of classical but also of contemporary and international literature. His interests were not limited to British deism alone. Reimarus's father-in-law was Johann Albert Fabricius (1668–1736), the most influential classical philologist of his time. The fourteen volumes of his *Bibliotheca Graeca* meant a new cultural and educational program, since the Enlightenment thus far had concentrated almost exclusively on Latin texts.

Fabricius's intention and effect went beyond the small circles of the learned. He clearly had in mind the lecture halls and classrooms of public schools at large. Fabricius made Reimarus his fellow worker, a schoolman as well. Reimarus's move from central Germany to the north, to the harbor city of Hamburg, brought him into one of the most important and oldest shipping and trade centers of Europe, a city proud of its old burgher traditions. The pupils whom Reimarus was to teach were future merchants, industrial producers, and owners of wharves who would live in a world formed even more by the bourgeoisie than before.

It is of note that in the early eighteenth century interest in Alexander the Great awakened again, particularly in France and Germany. It was visible in Fabricius's works. Fabricius's interest did not limit itself to

---

56. On the influence of Jesuit theology, especially that of Suarez, on the German discussion, see Ernst Lewalter, *Spanisch-jesuitische und Deutsch-lutherische Metaphysik des 17. Jahrhunderts* (Darmstadt: Wissenschaftliche Buchgesellschaft, 1967).

Alexander the general and politician but extended to the Alexander romance and the Alexander legend, in other words, to the mythical afterlife of this ancient hero. The figure of Alexander began again to appear in works of pictorial art in the late seventeenth century. This person who had been considered an exemplary divine man in Hellenistic-Roman culture began to fascinate the bourgeoisie in its final ascendancy.

Reimarus's dissertation of 1719 was about Machiavellism.[57] Thus Reimarus participated in the continuous debate about *The Prince* and its subsequent effect. In Reimarus's later portrayal of Jesus one finds certain traces of *The Prince*, but in an ironic coloring that corresponded to the ironic-satirical understanding of Machiavelli's famous figure in the Enlightenment at large. Reimarus described the ambivalent efforts of Jesus to gain the kingship of the Jews. According to Reimarus, Jesus wished to obtain the royal rule. At the same time, however, Jesus had to seek this secretly because he feared the threats of the establishment. Therefore, this political mission had to fail, Reimarus said. Jesus' career ended in catastrophe and godforsakenness. Reimarus, however, saw an ethic in Jesus' moral testament that survived the disaster of his political mission and the conversion of his own figure by the disciples, Paul, and the church after his death. This ethic was in fact a republican morality. It did not need a lasting superman. It was closer to Machiavelli's *Discourses* than to *The Prince*.[58] The Jesus of Reimarus built on trust and a rather relaxed attitude, and from that he projected the concept of the will of his heavenly Father, who presupposed the good intentions of the heart and a reasonable sentiment and, therefore, expected the observation of the so-called double commandment of love. This ethic contained a practical piety in the perfection of an emotive heart and healthy reason.

5. THE NINETEENTH CENTURY

The two hundred years since this description of Jesus' ethic have changed astonishingly little the outline that Reimarus gave to it. With respect to Jesus' personality, however, the majority of the life-of-Jesus theologians after Reimarus made many changes. The ironic side of his portrait of Jesus disappeared entirely, and with it his distancing from *The Prince*. Instead, an increasingly less disguised adoration of genius, the

---

57. Hermann Samuel Reimarus, *Dissertatio Schediasmati de Machiavellismo ante Machiavellum praemissa qua sibi locum ... benevole concessum vindicat* (Wittenberg: Gerdes, 1719).
58. *The Discourses of Nicolo Machiavelli* (trans. Leslie J. Walker; London: Routledge & Paul, 1975).

divine man of old, which had lost out in Chalcedon, was now in final bloom in theology at large as the ecumenically recognized and authorized Christology. The view that Jesus had been a genius of sorts became dominant in the late eighteenth, nineteenth, and twentieth centuries, not only in Germany but also in western Europe and North America, among both Protestants and Catholics. Differences between conservative and liberal Christology in this respect were of minor importance.

The accompanying concept of the kingdom of God was not deeschatologized, as it has been often unjustly claimed since Johannes Weiss and Albert Schweitzer. Rather, the idea of the kingdom of God of the Gospel tradition became integrated into the reigning bourgeois *regnum:* eschatology with its dialectic of finality and historicity, utopia and realism, individual and society, election and fate, giftedness and educational manipulation, risk and planning, reason and sentiment, introvertedness and responsibility, production and enjoyment, capital and charity. In this context it developed further.

It was symptomatic that in the revolutionary decades at the end of the eighteenth century G. W. F. Hegel, transplanted into a centuries-old urban society, moved away from the historical Jesus of his formative years in the small-town environment of Suebia.[59] He turned now to a Johannine and even more Pauline Christology of a more complex and corporate dimension. In this transition his theology and philosophy came into their own. As the revolutionary development abated, however, the interest in the historical Jesus gained momentum again. The attempt of David Friedrich Strauss (1808–74) to reverse this and to give the life-of-Jesus question a critical and revolutionary turn again—following the revolutionary trends of the early 1830s—did not succeed, although initially it appeared as if it could. Following Reimarus's distinction between pre- and post-Easter and picking up Hegel's theologically based notions of collective consciousness, Strauss had claimed that the theological relevance did not lie with Jesus' earthly career but with his afterlife in the Christ community in which Jesus had become the object of the collective consciousness of the disciples.

The middle of the nineteenth century was characterized mainly by rather conservative reactions to Strauss's *Life of Jesus* (1835).[60] Even the

---

59. This major change happened in Frankfurt am Main, the old free imperial city. On this see Dieter Georgi, "Georg Wilhelm Friedrich Hegels Frankfurter Jahre (1797–1800)," in *Gott in Frankfurt: Theologische Spuren in einer Metropole* (ed. Matthias Benad; Frankfurt am Main: Athenäum, 1987), 79–95.

60. David Friedrich Strauss, *Das Leben Jesu kritisch bearbeitet* (Tübingen: Osiander, 1835); idem, *The Life of Jesus Critically Examined* (ed. Peter C. Hodgson; trans. George Eliot;

revolution of 1848 did not make any major difference to this. Critical scholars such as Strauss's teacher Ferdinand Christian Baur (1792–1860) interfered and prevented the end of the life-of-Jesus theology.[61] They played down the quantitative and even more the qualitative impact of the post-Easter elements in the material on Jesus and insisted on the importance of the historical Jesus, of his claim in words and deeds for piety and theology today. Even a representative of the working class, Wilhelm Weitling (1808–71), did not stray far from the established bourgeois road. Whereas he actively helped prepare the revolution of 1848, Weitling also wrote meditations on Jesus under the titles "Humanity as It Is, and as It Should Be" (1838) and "The Gospel of the Poor Sinner" (1843).[62] Here Jesus' teaching and actions were presented as a communism of and for all humanity; for Weitling, Jesus was the great and far-sighted individual of a rather intimate, indeed a bourgeois, privacy and a great personality still.

The bourgeois restoration after 1848 thus could easily maintain interest in life-of-Jesus theology. Evidence of this is the very successful *La Vie de Jesus* (1863) of Ernest Renan (1823–92).[63] This work was something like a historical novel with romantic sentiment and idyllic character. Here Jesus was depicted as a unique personality, full of unspoiled naïveté but at the same time full of dignity and wisdom, the ideal image of bourgeois nostalgia. The fact that Renan's Jesus was an idealized rural figure who was destroyed by the terrifying and deadly metropolis did not contradict the bourgeois flavor; instead, it reflected the many bourgeois portrayals of country life. The description of Jesus' end fitted the views of liberal bourgeoisie as well: Renan's representative of an uncorrupted biblical Judaism was destroyed by a hardened Jewish establishment.

There it was again: the great individual Jesus, sufficiently human to allow identification with him but also sufficiently lifted above the masses that he could be seen as a beacon. This was not a phenomenon of leisure, however. The times were hard and demanding. In this respect also Jesus was exemplary, a man of risk and challenge, calling others to take risks. This fit the bourgeoisie, which was often self-critical to the point of

---

Philadelphia: Fortress, 1972). This translation unfortunately is based on the fourth edition, not on the first or second.

61. Ferdinand Christian Baur, *Vorlesungen über neutestamentliche Theologie* (1864; rev. ed. Werner Georg Kümmel; Darmstadt: Wissenschaftliche Buchgesellschaft, 1973); idem, *Kirchengeschichte des 19. Jahrhunderts* (1862/63; ed. Heinz Liebing; Stuttgart: Frommann, 1970).

62. Wilhelm Weitling, *Das Evangelium des armen Sünders: Die Menschheit wie sie ist und wie sie sein sollte* (ed. Wolf Schäfer; Hamburg: Rowohlt, 1971).

63. See vol. 1 of Ernest Renan, *Histoire des origines du Christianisme* (7 vols.; Paris: Lévy, 1863–83).

masochism and which prided itself on its readiness to face competition and conflict, even under warlike conditions, whether in the market or in the hardships of what amounted to institutionalized civil wars in the exercises of bourgeois democracy. The frequent shooting wars in which Jesus went in the knapsack too—for all parties involved—were another aspect of the same phenomenon.

How much the bourgeois consciousness of today formed the Jesus debate is proved by the term *messianic consciousness*. This concept pretended objective verifiability in the face of the history of religion, yet no historian of religion could provide evidence for such a consciousness. A circular logic was at work: the answer set the question. No other historical individual from New Testament times had possessed this consciousness; therefore, the analogy of such a messianic consciousness did not exist, and it must not be. The uniqueness of Jesus' consciousness was the concern; it was the goal as much as the point of departure. The interest was not in historical parallels at all but in the idealization and historicization of a central contemporary concept, of the consciousness of the (great) individual.

The messianic or eschatological consciousness of the bourgeois Jesus, liberal or conservative, was his freedom of the heart, his courage to face the demands of the situation at hand as any responsible manager would have to, or at least as a charismatic leader would. Given the seriousness of life, retrospection about details did not count as much as the great lines, the individual events not as much as the personality. The gestalt was what counted. Uncovering the secret of the personality, the unity of work and deed, was the task.

6. IS THERE A DIFFERENCE BETWEEN THE "OLD" AND THE "NEW" QUEST?

Around the turn of the twentieth century there were signs of a "Burgher-Dämmerung," not limited by any means to Germany. The history of religion school in Germany was part of an international educational movement that challenged the structures and goals of established education on all levels. The founding of the University of Chicago and the immediate involvement of that institution in the city's plighted life was one of the major signs of this movement on the North American side of the Atlantic Ocean.[64]

---

64. The interest in adult education and in university extension was also strong in Great Britain.

The criticism of life-of-Jesus theology by such scholars as Johannes Weiss (1863–1914), William Wrede (1859–1900), and Albert Schweitzer (1875–1965) must be seen within this context.[65] The successful mythicizing of the origins of dialectic theology proclaimed its uniqueness by asserting that World War I and its immediate aftermath had set into motion an unprepared and unparalleled cultural and theological revolution. However, the so-called theology of crisis must also be seen as part of the strong criticism already active in the wider context of the scholars mentioned.[66] The concrete and critical engagement of the history of religion school, not the least that of Ernst Troeltsch (1865–1923), at this distance appears closer to Karl Barth (1886–1968) and Rudolf Bultmann (1884–1976) than the common myth permits. Troeltsch engaged himself in politics more than they did, and therefore he was unjustly denounced as the last and failing prophet of cultural Protestantism. In fact, Barth's and Bultmann's criticisms, along with their challenge of life-of-Jesus theology, belonged belatedly to this "Burgher-Dämmerung" of pre–World War I as well.

The common argument that the pro and con of Schweitzer's *Quest of the Historical Jesus* applied merely to the Continental, and most of all to the German, scene has been corrected sufficiently by Daniel L. Pals.[67] Here it is possible to observe how well British life-of-Jesus research and theology fit the bourgeoisie. In Britain, even before World War I, a skeptical critique and countermovement that was not merely dependent on developments on the continent also occurred.

The origin of the so-called New Quest in the early 1950s, its rather explosive spread, not only in Germany but also worldwide, and its continuing life were and still are a complete surprise for the historian— at least on the surface.[68] There were no new methods or truly new

---

65. William Wrede, *Das Messiasgeheimnis in den Evangelien* (Göttingen: Vandenhoeck & Ruprecht, 1901); Johannes Weiss, *Die Predigt Jesu vom Reich Gottes* (Göttingen: Vandenhoeck & Ruprecht, 1901); ET: *Jesus' Proclamation of the Kingdom of God* (trans. and ed. Richard Hyde Hiers and David Larrimore Holland; Philadelphia: Fortress, 1971); Schweitzer, *Quest of the Historical Jesus*.

66. Not only in the heritage of Christoph Blumhardt (1842–1919), Hermann Kutter (1863–1931), and Leonhard Ragaz (1868–1945), as is often claimed.

67. Daniel L. Pals, *The Victorian "Lives" of Jesus* (Trinity University Monograph Series in Religion 7; San Antonio, Tex.: Trinity University Press, 1982).

68. Given the fact that the literature of and on the New Quest in the meantime is legion, and also because of the existence of such a thorough journal of it as Werner Georg Kümmel, *Dreißig Jahre Jesusforschung (1950–1980)* (BBB 60; Königstein: Hanstein, 1985), a comprehensive compilation of Kümmel's reviews on the question in *ThR*, I have refrained from a detailed report and have drawn the larger picture instead. I should, however, mention a sample of contributions to the New Quest (besides Robinson, *New Quest of the Historical*

methodological insights, no new texts or any other new historical evidence that had direct bearing on the problems of historical authenticity of the Jesus tradition.[69]

There was a clear reversal of the principle of burden of proof. All those advocating something like a life-of-Jesus theology argued increasingly that that principle was favoring those who started with the

---

Jesus), including not only strictly historical-critical studies but also those of a more systematic-theological nature: Ernst Käsemann, "Das Problem des historischen Jesus," *ZTK* 51 (1954): 125–53; repr. in idem, *Exegetische Versuche und Besinnungen* (2 vols.; Göttingen: Vandenhoeck & Ruprecht, 1960–64), 1:187–214; idem, "Sackgassen im Streit um den historischen Jesus," in *Exegetische Versuche und Besinnungen*, 1:31–68; Günther Bornkamm, *Jesus von Nazareth* (Stuttgart: Kohlhammer, 1956) ET: *Jesus of Nazareth* (New York: Harper, 1975); Gerhard Ebeling, "Die Frage nach dem historischen Jesus und das Problem der Christologie," *ZTK*, Beiheft 1 (1959): 14–30; repr. in idem, *Wort und Glaube* (3rd ed.; 3 vols.; Tübingen: Mohr Siebeck, 1960), 1:19–82; idem, "Kerygma und historischer Jesus," in idem, *Theologie und Verkündigung* (HUT 1; Tübingen: Mohr Siebeck, 1962), 19–82; Ernst Fuchs, *Zur Frage nach dem historischen Jesus* (Gesammelte Aufsätze 2; Tübingen: Mohr Siebeck, 1960); Eberhard Jüngel, *Paulus und Jesus* (HUT 2; Tübingen: Mohr Siebeck, 1962); Willi Marxsen, "Zur Frage nach dem historischen Jesus," *TLZ* 87 (1962): 575–80; Wolfhart Pannenberg, *Grundzüge der Christologie* (Gütersloh: Mohn, 1964) ET: *Jesus, God and Man* (Philadelphia: Westminster, 1977); Hans Küng, *Die Kirche* (Ökumenische Forschungen 1/1; Freiburg: Herder, 1967), esp. 57–99, ET: *The Church* (New York: Sheed & Ward, 1967); Hans Küng and Pinchas Lapide, *Jesus im Widerstreit: Ein jüdisch-christlicher Dialog* (Stuttgart: Calwer Verlag, 1976); Hans Küng, *Christ-Sein* (Munich: Piper, 1974), esp. 111–401; ET: *On Being a Christian* (Garden City, N.Y.: Doubleday, 1976); Herbert Braun, *Jesus: Der Mann aus Nazareth und seine Zeit* (Themen der Theologie 1; Stuttgart: Kreuz, 1969); ET: *Jesus of Nazareth: The Man and His Time* (Philadelphia: Fortress, 1979); Edward Schillebeeckx, *Jezus het verhaal van een levende* (Bloemendaal: Nelissen, 1974); ET: *Jesus: An Experiment in Christology* (New York: Seabury, 1979); Jürgen Moltmann, *Der Weg Jesu Christi: Christologie in messianischen Dimensionen* (Munich: Kaiser, 1989); Howard C. Kee, *Jesus in History: An Approach to the Study of the Gospels* (New York: Harcourt, Brace & World, 1970); idem, *What Can We Know about Jesus? Understanding Jesus Today* (Cambridge: Cambridge University Press, 1990); Joachim Gnilka, *Jesus von Nazareth: Botschaft und Geschichte* (HTKNT suppl. 3; Freiburg: Herder, 1990); ET: *Jesus of Nazareth: Message and History* (trans. Siegfried S. Schatzmann; Peabody, Mass.: Hendrickson, 1997); Friedrich-Wilhelm Marquardt, *Das christliche Bekenntnis zu Jesus, dem Juden: Eine Christologie* (2 vols.; Munich: Kaiser, 1990–91); Marinus de Jonge, *Jesus, the Servant-Messiah* (New Haven: Yale University Press, 1991).

69. The attempts of the "New Quest" did not remain without criticism: e.g., Rudolf Bultmann, *Das Verhältnis der urchristlichen Christusbotschaft zum historischen Jesus* (SHAW Philosophisch-Historische Klasse 1960/3; Heidelberg: Winter 1960), 5–27; Karl Barth, "How My Mind Has Changed," *EvTh* 20 (1960): 97–106; Dieter Georgi, "Bleibende Aufgaben, die uns Rudolf Bultmann stellt," *Evangelische Zeitstimmen* 59/60 (1971): 66–76; Walter Schmithals, *Jesus Christus in der Verkündigung der Kirche* (Neukirchen: Neukirchener Verlag, 1972); Siegfried Schuiz, "Die neue Frage nach dem historischen Jesus," in *Neues Testament und Geschichte: Historische Geschehen und Deutung im Neuen Testament: Oscar Cultmann zum 70. Geburtstag* (ed. Heinrich Baltensweiler and Bo Reicke; Zurich: Theologischer Verlag; Tübingen: Mohr Siebeck, 1972), 33–42

assumption of the authenticity of the biblical texts concerning the historical Jesus—with the exception of the most outlandish features, such as certain miracles. Inauthenticity needed to be proven, not authenticity. This was argued despite the obvious nature of the texts as being thoroughly shaped by faith in the continued presence of Jesus after his death. This reversal of the burden-of-proof principle did not happen by way of methodological argument but by way of decree. The arguments that the supporters of the New Quest make against the few remaining critics are in fact of a theological nature. The governing argument is that faith since its inception was connected intimately with the historical reality of Jesus, as a historical person but also as a historical agent in word and deed. The kerygma of the church essentially was anchored in the teaching and actions of Jesus, so the claim goes. If that connection were cut, the faith of the early church would not have existed, and our faith would turn into illusion. Only the historical Jesus would prevent theology from sliding into myth, docetism, and mystery religion.

Again the old interest in a life-of-Jesus theology forced its way into New Testament scholarship. The interest in a reconstruction of the historical Jesus' public career makes it an allegedly verified and objectifiable center of theology and faith. It is remarkable and often taken as a proof of correctness that despite a great number of differences in detail the images of Jesus in the New Quest possess a common profile. It has, therefore, proved possible for me to establish something like a synopsis of the major views presented within the purview of life-of-Jesus theology on both sides of the Atlantic. It was amazing to me to what extent the synopsis of Gracián and that of the New Quest concurred.

The question of the last thirty years of life-of-Jesus research is about Jesus not so much as a passive object of history but as an active subject of history. The focus is chiefly on his individual consciousness, his will, his activity, his way, all of which point toward the question of his claim and success. Since the latter obviously appeared more as a failure, the reflection of the New Quest centers on Jesus' intention that climaxed in his urge for a decision and on his consequent death as an intended risk. The work of Jesus is discussed in the double fashion characteristic of bourgeois thinking: (1) the work of an individual is both the sum of conscious activity in a history of conscious will and the responsibility of the self; (2) the individual's heritage, known and shaped by the individual in advance of the *exitus*, works beyond the death of the individual and guarantees continuity both within the conscious remembrance of the individual's original and surviving environment and beyond. For the New Quest, this work of Jesus outlasted his death, so his death was no catastrophe.

The theological thesis of God's identification with the crucified one on Easter turns for the New Quest into the thesis of God's identification with the historical, critically verifiable claim of the historical Jesus, and this identification is understood as Jesus' continuation as a person. This continuation is seen in the resurrection appearances. These are interpreted as the continued effect of Jesus' personal claim that in his activity the eschatological salvation of the kingdom of God had already been realized. This heritage, namely, the disciples' memories of their concrete experiences with Jesus, according to the New Quest shaped the lasting image of Jesus, his gestalt, and comprised the outlines and trends of Jesus' kerygma, attitude, intention, and fate. It is understandable, therefore, that this reconstructed knowledge of the historical Jesus becomes a major criterion for the examination of the post-Easter kerygma.

Jesus' allegedly unique claim also presupposes an equally unique experience of God in the view of the New Quest. Whether Jesus used for himself popular Jewish titles of dignity remains debated. It appears unquestioned, however, that Jesus possessed an extraordinary consciousness about himself and his mission and that he consciously stood and acted in the place of God, although he enclosed this claim in mystery. Therefore, Bultmann's expression of Jesus' implicit Christology is eagerly accepted as a proven fact; it is simply overlooked that Bultmann spoke merely of a possibility. For the New Quest, Jesus' unique consciousness, this implicit Christology, is sufficient reason for the explicit post-Easter Christology in which Jesus turned from the subject of faith to the object of faith. Many scholars, moreover, see this faith in Jesus already prefigured and prepared in the relationship of the disciples and others to Jesus before Easter. For the scholars of the New Quest, Jesus' claim before Easter does not fit any stereotype of traditional eschatological expectation; it is precisely in this uniqueness that it can be observed by scholarly means.

For the New Quest the kingdom of God remains central—the theme that since the Middle Ages had remained so fertile for the development of bourgeois consciousness. In Jesus' announcement of the coming of the kingdom of God, the new representatives of the life-of-Jesus theology see the essential eschatological claim of Jesus expressing itself. They find this eschatological claim not only in individual sayings but also in Jesus' entire work, in the radical nature of his proclamation and in his actions. His expectation of the kingdom of God in his coming and in his demand of discipleship is seen in a dialectical relationship.

For the bourgeois individual and especially for the modular great personality, delineation, demarcation, and differentiation are the necessary dialectical counterpoints to continuity. The claim of the uniqueness of Jesus belongs here and is strengthened by a continuous religiohistorical singling out of the man from Nazareth. Fortunately, an increasing number of life-of-Jesus scholars in the meantime have slowed down or even given up on distancing Jesus from Judaism. The majority, however, maintain this approach, while the crudest forms of anti-Semitism slowly pass away from this form of argument for Jesus' uniqueness.

The New Quest associates a radical exposition of the will of God, whose essence is seen in his creative and gracious will, with Jesus' proclamation of the kingdom of God. Most often this concept of God's will in Jesus' proclamation, particularly as full of grace, is still set in antithesis to the letter of the law and even more to the rules created by humans. The majority of life-of-Jesus scholars still consider Jesus' coupling of love for God and love for neighbor, especially love for the enemy, and his emphasis on forgiveness of sins, demonstrated actively in Jesus' joining with sinners and outcasts, as a challenge to the foundations of established Jewish religion and as a momentous move toward something different and new.

In his miracles, understood as eschatological signs, Jesus' emphasis on God's radical sovereignty with its eschatological challenge and criticism allegedly demonstrated liberation from that which was customary and established as well. Therefore, the violent end of Jesus' career would have to be seen as having been within the foreseeable, even as the intentional consequences of Jesus' preaching and actions. Jesus would have gone to Jerusalem in full awareness of the mortal risks his challenge implied. His death would have been within the consequences of his life. The conflict with the Romans would have been marginal, only a further consequence of Jesus' basic conflict with the Jewish establishment.

Returning to the questions concerning the sudden and explosive origin and spread of the New Quest, I observe the main cause in the continuous social and historical situation of the whole quest for the historical Jesus, that is, its location within the evolution of bourgeois consciousness, not just as an ideal but as an expression of a socioeconomic and political momentum. The contemporaneity of the New Quest with the end of the New Deal and the restoration of the bourgeoisie in the United States and Germany after World War II and within the confines of a burgeoning market-oriented Atlantic community is not accidental.

14

THE RELIGIOUS DIMENSIONS OF THE WORLD MARKET: A FAREWELL TO THE MIDDLE AGES

1. INTRODUCTION

The social nature of the pursuit of life-of-Jesus theology to the present day has also an economic side that is intimately related to the development of the world market and world trade. That world markets and trade have their major locations in the cities of the globe is a matter of course. In their modern form the churches are increasingly outdone as being inefficient activators of trade and market by the new religion, that of neoliberalism, which advertises globalization. It takes the global market as a factual reality and celebrates it at the same as a cult, a utopia of sorts that no one has really seen despite the billions of dollars shot around the globe day by day. In this cult the world as city is turned into "the global village." A historical-critical assessment of these allegedly "modern" or "postmodern" battle cries unmasks them as still medieval. The farewell to the Middle Ages is a task yet before us.

---

* The following paper was delievered at the Bonhoeffer Symposium at the University of Greifswald, Germany, on 10 May 1997. This symposium is a regular affair organized by the German Bonhoeffer Society and Union Theological Seminary in New York, the symposia occurring alternately in the United States and in Germany. See note 5 for further details. The following form of the paper is modified and enlarged. I want to dedicate it to the memory of my fellow "doctorandus" Heinz Eduard Tödt. It belongs in the context of the discussion about Dietrich Bonhoeffer's understanding of religion and "religionlessness." Tödt added essential points to this discussion. Bonhoeffer's conception of religion and of "religionlessness," in my opinion, again and again integrates the topic of reality and, in an implicit fashion, that of consciousness—not as abstract phenomena but as related to concrete realities. Among them we must also count the economy.

In the following essay I shall show that our economical thinking and its practice are not modern but a product of the Middle Ages. They were produced by medieval theology, especially that of mendicant monks. Their theology formed our "modern" economic consciousness, even our understanding of society, its character, and its function. These are therefore still under the influence of a certain scholastic, especially mendicant, conception of religion, world, and society. The Reformation has done little to change that. This is contrary to common contemporary assumption as informed by Max Weber. His main thesis of capitalism being a product of Calvinism cannot be further maintained. Modern capitalism originated in late medieval Britain and evolved out of mendicant theology, coming to fruition in the late fourteenth and fifteenth centuries. It helped to turn around an economic catastrophe. Thus, our economy and economics are at their very base and in their structure heavily religious, even theologically conditioned.

Our economic consciousness is not the reflection of an invariable reality and its inalterable laws; it was formed as much as our economic reality within a certain historical period. The same was true of the corporate consciousness preceding it, which arose in the Hellenistic-Roman period and deteriorated in the fifth through ninth centuries. In the tenth century, something began that has been convincingly called a revolution by Harold Berman in his fascinating book *Law and Revolution*.[1]

All this gives us theologians a basic right to involve ourselves in the discussion on economy and economics. Religion and religious consciousness are our fields of scholarly expertise. This consciousness is anything but isolated; a theologian who understood this and pursued this inclusiveness at the expense of his own life was Dietrich Bonhoeffer. His three major works need to be looked at simultaneously: his *Christology*, his *Ethics*, and his last visionary reflections in the *Letters from Prison*.[2] I will try to interrelate and integrate the challenges that I see in these works and transfer them to the relationship between religion, justice,

---

1. Harold J. Berman, *Law and Revolution: The Formation of the Western Legal Tradition* (Cambridge: Harvard University Press, 1983).

2. There exists a "trajectory" between the Christology lecture of 1933 and the fragments from his last years. The metaphor of the trajectory means a ballistic curve and entails the idea of necessity, indeed computability, of the relations between individual points on the curve and to the curve as a whole. There is indeed a consistency in Bonhoeffer's development from 1933 to 1945. Between 1933 and 1945, Bonhoeffer's concept of the presence and dominion of the Christ clearly determines his understanding of reality and world more and more (see, for instance, the introduction of his *Ethics*). The countertrajectory of dualism, discussed in this essay, which had been predominant in Christian theology since Augustine, increasingly tended toward zero.

and economy.³ I will take up and convey some of the intellectual stimulation for a just economy within a just society of tomorrow that arises from such a comprehensive view of these three works by Bonhoeffer.⁴

The theme of the conference at which this essay was first delivered, "Economic justice and the consequences of the globalization of the labor market," addresses a relatively new point of economics, new at least as far as public consciousness of it is concerned: the internationalization, indeed globalization of the labor market.⁵ There is a certain circumlocution of

---

3. The importance of Bonhoeffer's Christology for a new consideration of the economic situation is also treated in Peter Selby's book *Grace and Mortgage* (London: Darton, 1997). He takes a somewhat different approach, but his and my studies complement each other to a certain degree.

4. The subtitle of this essay intimates that I differ from Bonhoeffer in an essential point. I do this specifically because I agree with Bonhoeffer's own tendency in the mentioned works. Bonhoeffer was far ahead of his time, especially that of the political, societal, economical, ecclesial, and theological restoration after 1945. The restoration in the German churches after 1945 proves that Bonhoeffer's hypothesis of our time as having come of age has not come true. Bonhoeffer had claimed that secularity and the disappearance of religion prove such maturity. German churches and theology instead revived the concept of *Volkskirche*, the people's church, a term that had been used since 1848 in a decidedly antirevolutionary and reactionary sense and was fully discredited by its enthusiastic employment in the majority of German Christianity of Nazi Germany. A bourgeois life-of-Jesus theology, already thought dead, was reanimated in the 1950s and found acceptance in the church and to some degree also in society. The established churches again found new power in the legal situation of the Federal Republic that was and is disproportionate to the actual importance of the churches. All this and much more prove that full age and secularity, claimed by Bonhoeffer for the present time, have again moved into the distance. I shall go even further back in this essay. I shall show that even the modernity of our age is in question because it can be argued that what we consider to be most modern, namely, our economic theory and practice, are outdated. It is especially they that demonstrate the erroneousness of the common assumption of the end of the Middle Ages; the Middle Ages are, in fact, still continuing. The world's coming of age that Bonhoeffer talks about is not yet at hand. The religionless society does not exist, and true secularity is absent. Christian conservatism and, indeed, fundamentalism have entered many boardrooms of corporations in the United States and are doing so elsewhere too—with little attention paid to this by the academic disciplines of economics, business administration, and theology, neither in the United States nor in Europe. This does not include the coming of age; on the contrary, it changes from the status of a phenomenological reality, implied by Bonhoeffer, to that of a critical challenge and a task of proclamation. It must be stated again and again against the continuation of a medieval collective consciousness today. Bonhoeffer's emphasis on the character of the coming of age as a critical process needs to be taken even more seriously than Bonhoeffer himself does. The predominance of an ideologized theory over praxis needs to be finally unmasked and overcome. The coming of age is indeed noticeable in the praxis of world society, occurring in the streets everywhere, but it needs to be understood and interpreted in a critical economic as well as theological theory.

5. The fascinating papers of the Simpson couple at this conference have given excellent examples for using Bonhoeffer's thoughts and actions as challenges to ours for a different

this new development. One speaks now of "human capital." It is still a very loose concept and implies many different things. It will potentially radically modify previous assumptions and practices. It certainly sees the labor force as an element of capital, available worldwide, globally usable, and transferable.

This idea of human capital participates in the assumptions, actions, and problems of capital at large, not just in terms of capital but also in terms of international production, international trade, and the world market. In the light of globalization, human capital is presently still seen as something essentially passive, with respect to its availability, and thus seen more in its exploitative sense. Yet capital is not something passive—as working capital it is active. The idea of working is usually applied to the monetary side of capital alone and to aspects associated with that. If this meaning is carried over to humans as humans, then this human capital has to be seen as working in a human way, as not being passive but active, original, and creative. Looked at this way, capital in the form of active human capital could produce a major, indeed, a revolutionary change. The final vision of my essay aims in this direction.

In approaching the issue of globalization in an ecumenical perspective, I limit myself for reasons of time to the dimension of the so-called world market.[6] In many different ways it is linked up, even widely synonymous, with world trade; so as I talk about world market, world trade is most often implied, too.[7]

---

tomorrow. They have demonstrated that systemic unemployment as a necessary accompaniment of a globalized capitalist economy can be overcome by a subversion of the governing rules of the game. This can be achieved through a blend of communal and personal involvement, imagination, clever stubbornness, conscious interdependence, mutual help, and interactive protection. They have demonstrated what black experience and black leadership can mean, not only for the black community but also for the community at large. What they have shown to be the case on the local and regional level can be extended into larger areas, if the communities and churches on these levels accept the challenge. They do not yet do this to a sufficient degree, least of all the organized provincial and national churches, even less the World Council of Churches or the Roman Catholic Church.

6. Since this essay addresses the *ecumenical* perspective, I have taken the liberty to use that term in its original sense as it was familiar to the authors of the New Testament, namely, in the meaning "worldwide," truly universal, not in its present sense, which is much narrower, limited to an ecclesial perspective, namely, churches worldwide.

7. It is significant that the *International Encyclopedia of Social Sciences* introduces its article on the theory of international trade with the following sentence: "The theory of international trade is that branch of economic theory concerned with trade between nations and, more broadly, with all aspects of the economic relations between nations" (Harry G. Johnson, "International Trade," *IESS* 8:83). This sentence completely overlooks the fact that much of world trade today is defined and controlled by multinational corporations that have moved far beyond the reach and even more beyond the control of individual nations. These

As we use the term *market* and try to visualize what I have said before, we encounter major problems of definition, problems that are more than semantic. They increase if we enlarge the perspective and speak of the world market. There is general agreement that the market is the place of meeting and exchange of economic agents, the buyers and sellers. In the market, prices, wages, and profits are set and gained in the process of exchange. Here the allocation of economic resources and the distribution of income are brought about, too. Products and labor are part of the market as well.

As soon as we try to spell this out, the market turns into an abstraction. It is no longer identifiable with a certain place on the map. Instead, it becomes an ambiguous concept, a universal name more than a concrete reality that can be grasped. Market today is indeed a complex as well as enormously abstract entity. It entails all phenomena and structures of the process of economic exchange. Not only what comes into the market and what comes out of it is important but also all sorts of interests, not merely economic ones but also political and social concerns. Many different legal aspects appear, not merely of law relating to the economy directly but also of constitutional, international, and other forms of law. Even cultural perspectives are important.

The market is an object as much as a subject. It is treated as a thing as well as a person. People and society affect it, and it affects them. It is determined by behavior as well as determining behavior. Therefore, the market is also a political and sociopsychological, even a cultural and anthropological, phenomenon.

As soon as one wants to become concrete about the market, one must suffer many questions with respect to what kind of market one has in mind. Although the questioners themselves use the term *market* without differentiation, their questions immediately split up the concept into many different aspects and entities. These in turn are established and maintained by definitions, by differentiation in naming that produces and utilizes terms like name tags. Talking about the world market as the sum of it all merely camouflages the problems of identification and definition of the market.

There is the stock market as well as the automobile market, the book market as well as the oil market, and so on. When people speak of the market, they may have the conditions in mind, such as free trade, that determine the exchange, or they may be talking of the market in the sense

---

multinational corporations have larger budgets than most nations present in the assembly of the United Nations, certainly also much more influence. In fact, some multinational corporations compete with major industrial nations in terms of economic power and influence.

of its defined boundaries, often not the economic ones, but those of a geographical, sociological, or political nature.

The complexity of the concept market increases as soon as a certain major contributor to the market enters the picture: industry. Its appearance also enlarges the degree of abstraction of the concept market in an astonishing way, no matter what kind of industry is involved, whether productive industry or service industry. To what kind of market does a firm such as Siemens belong, a worldwide firm with highly diversified production lines and multinational subindustries and sales organizations? What about the consequences of the fusion of Daimler-Benz and Chrysler? This, in turn, leads us to another market, the stock market, for the larger an industrial enterprise is the more active it is on the stock market.

What I am trying to say with all this is that the unifying reality of the market consists to a large degree in its abstracted name and the latter's cumulative potency, more precisely, in the constant process of definition and redefinition of the market. The market is not defined and redefined merely by advertisement. Active factors in this continuous process of naming and renaming are all the people and agencies that involve themselves in this entity that is considered to be the market or that one wants to consider as such. In addition, many people and agencies are passively usurped and integrated into the "market" by forces of various kinds, most of them beyond the control and even knowledge of these passively engaged persons and groups. Both this active and passive integration are essential elements of the alleged "self-determination" of the market and of the factual determination of all of those who are involved. Economic agents, enterprises, and market segments take part in this continuously changing process of definition. Self-assessment of the participants plays a role, but so does assessment by others. Essential influence is also exercised by the academic disciplines of economics and business administration and, in addition and very significantly, by national and international institutions, especially by those that are politically and legally responsible for such classifications. This leads us to the political powers on many levels as major players in the establishment and change of the market, not the least the game of definition and redefinition.

In anticipation of later reasoning, I want to hypothesize that much of what is going on locally, regionally, nationally, and worldwide in the modern market reality is reminiscent of Ockham's "realistic conceptualism."[8] According to this philosophy, reality is not something "out there,"

---

8. This term was coined by Philotheus Boehner, "The Realistic Conceptualism of William Ockham," in idem, *Collected Articles on Ockham* (ed. E. M. Buytaert; New York: St. Bonaventure, 1958), 156–74.

something physically existing. Real is only the individual "thing"[9] that has been "de-fined," that has found its "limit"-ation by a naming process, that has become a concept.[10] The market as such and its universality do not have their reality "out there" either, do not "really" exist; they exist primarily as abstract concepts.

We are accustomed to assume that the economy, at least in the common contemporary perception, follows general laws, more or less ironclad. For many today, economy and reality are identical. Therefore, we turn to economics as the scholarly discipline that demonstrates and explains to us these laws, the causes, reasons, and goals of the economic occurrences. We believe that here we learn about the determinants of our present reality. Economists show us, we trust, that these economic occurrences are essential as well as general necessities that follow rules, that are rational, reasonable, clear, and intelligible. Economy and order are more and more considered to be identical. The economy is looked at and used as the real factor of organizing everything. It is more and more put above political responsibility and power. The economy and its main players and agencies do feel and are made to feel less responsible to society and its political organization and to the political representatives of the will of the people. On the contrary, politics and politicians increasingly answer more to the economy, industrialists, bankers, and economists and less to their constituents. Our understanding of the world of economics, our economical planning and decision making, as well as our reactions are conditioned by such beliefs. It has created a certain image in the public mind that is constantly determining reactions and decisions on the public level and also in personal life and relations.[11]

The density and influence of this common understanding of economy and market was revealed in recent times in the reactions that one could hear and read in the West when Soviet socialism and its vassals broke down. These reactions were rather quickly adopted in the East and also taken to be self-evident, thereby demonstrating that the Western market economy functions not only as a common Western but, in fact, global religion. It is a form of belief, an ideology that does not even need to justify itself any longer. It is camouflaged as rational and realistic—indeed, it is reality itself, as much the Roman Catholic belief system and practice was the reality in the Middle Ages. I refer, for instance, to the

---

9. The *res*.

10. This "nominalism" claimed to be empirical and scientific and became the basis for Anglo-Saxon Empiricism.

11. Whether also in the mind of the economist and in the scholarly discipline, it is not my business to discuss. I am speaking of the public perception of economy and economics.

many editorials in serious newspapers and magazines in the year 1989. I am thinking also of the speeches of the candidates in the last two U.S. presidential elections, particularly the speeches of the main contenders.

I take here the term *religion* as it is used in sociology of religion. I quote, for instance, Clifford Geertz: "[Religion] relates a view of the ultimate nature of reality to a set of ideas of how man is well advised, even obligated to live. Religion tunes human actions to a view of the cosmic order and projects images of cosmic order onto the plane of human existence."[12] In a similar fashion, Robert Bellah sees religion "as the most general mechanism for integrating meaning and motivation in systems of action."[13] Our economy and economic thinking are embedded in our corporate consciousness and heavily conditioned by it. This corporate consciousness of ours is of historical origin, a product of certain massive changes, conscious as well as unconscious. It is thus open to more or less drastic modifications as well.[14]

2. SOME SELF-REFLECTION

Religion does not provide a secret access to the complexities of economics. Theologians do not know more about economics than economists

---

12. Clifford Geertz, "Religion as a Cultural System," in *Anthropological Approaches to the Study of Religion*, (ed. Michael Banton; A.S.A. Monographs 3; London: Tavistock, 1963), 4.

13. Robert Bellah, "Sociology of Religion," *IESS* 13:411. One could also mention Luther's definition of God in his explanation of the first commandment in the Larger Catechism.

14. My essay asks the question whether being religionless can be a phenomenological option for theology at all. Religion(s) as observed and described by the disciplines of the academic field of comparative religion cannot be wiped aside. They are phenomenological facts. The option of Karl Barth of denouncing all religions as improper is a dated expression of Christian imperialism. Bonhoeffer still uses the term *religion* as a critical concept in the context of a critical-theological analysis—a limited application of Barth's criticism. However, he limits it mostly to Christian phenomena that he defines as pseudoreligious or pseudoreligion. The prefix *pseudo-* implies the critical dimension, certainly not shared by those criticized. They either understand their approach or interpretation as religion and/or theology proper or do not concede that their approach or interpretation is religious at all. In this essay I work with the assumption that many of the religious phenomena described, conscious as well as unconscious, are indeed pseudoreligious because they are either "religious" cover-ups for self-justification and individual as well as institutional security, power acquisition, and powerpreservation or are camouflaged as realistic phenomena and processes, behind whose "worldly" facade are rather fixed products of religious ideology and expressions of blindness to the real world. People responsible for this blindness defend it with certain ontologies, which are what Bonhoeffer called metaphysics. In fact, greed for profit and lust for power have driven such processes of pseudoreligious camouflaging, with church and world combining forces in cozy alliance.

do. They do not have patents for the future either. However, we theologians can consult and contribute to matters of economy because the economic reality has always been and still is heavily infused with irrational, religious, and theological elements, matters we as theologians are knowledgeable about. Thus we can contribute to the critical assessment of the present economic consciousness and to the necessary building of a new economic consciousness.

I am a biblical scholar who has always refused to be reduced to the New Testament part of the Bible alone.[15] My area of particular expertise is Judaism, paganism, and the early church in the six-hundred-year period from Alexander to Constantine. Relating this period to the New Testament and vice versa is my daily professional bread. I have always felt responsible for the history of interpretation as well, for the history of interpretation of the so-called Old Testament in the New and in its contemporary environment and for the history of interpretation of the New Testament in our present time. I learned to understand history of interpretation as being much more than a mere history of the conceptual reception of New Testament texts and ideas. The historical milieus of these receptions are important, not the least the socioeconomic ones. This has brought me to the assignment of this essay. It is the outgrowth of the course that I taught at Union Theological Seminary in 1969 and 1970. Its title was "Glaube und Geld: Cash and Creed." This lecture course and my present reflections took their departure from my studies on the collection of Paul for Jerusalem and its relevance for the present, but also from other research of mine in the history of New Testament times in general, and further from many years of reading on the history of biblical interpretation and its effects. For me, this history of interpretation and effect

---

15. My theological formation and my professional activity in biblical studies grew under the influence of Rudolf Bultmann, Günther Bornkamm, and Ernst Käsemann but also of Joachim Jeremias, Karl Georg Kuhn, William Manson, and Eduard Schweizer, as well as of Peter Brunner, Hans-Joachim Iwand, Edmund Schlink, Tom Torrance, and especially Ernst Wolf, in a wider sense also of Karl Barth and Dietrich Bonhoeffer. In order to interpret the whole of the biblical tradition fairly, it has proved not only to be necessary to extend the research of the New Testament texts to their religious-historical and socioeconomic environments in Bible, Judaism, paganism, and the early church. In addition, a full understanding of the texts necessitated a theologically as well as sociohistorically oriented investigation of the history of interpretation and of the history of the effect of the biblical texts, and this examination has to keep in mind church, politics, economy, and culture in later periods and to the present day. My essay illustrates what, in my opinion, must be considered a demythologizing and "religion"-less interpretation not only of biblical terms but also of biblical subject matters. I believe that this does justice to Bonhoeffer's observation that the biblical reality to be interpreted comprises much more than that what Bultmann had implied with his claim of an existential interpretation of the Bible.

of the Bible always included the relevant socioeconomic contexts of these interpretations.[16]

3. THE ANCIENT ORIGIN OF THE WORLD MARKET

Biblical scholars and Bible readers should be familiar with the formation of corporate, even societal consciousness and their transformation. Biblical scholarship (i.e., exegesis and history of interpretation) cannot overlook that their object, the Bible, entails major changes of corporate consciousness. Let me name as examples the origin of the faith of Israel, the evolution of the period of Israelite monarchy, the exile and its fruits in the postexilic period, and the major changes that took place around the turn from the third to the second century B.C.E., with the New Testament as one of its conclusions. Let me also mention the evolution of rabbinical Judaism and of the various forms of so-called Christianity between the First Jewish War and the end of the second century and then especially point out the occurrences around Constantine.[17] They all relate to major reinterpretations of the biblical heritage.

To this day the Bible, and in particular the New Testament, are nevertheless read by many, even by a good number of biblical scholars, as documents that came from a niche, not only as to geography but also as to subject matter. In much of New Testament exegesis it is overlooked that Palestine possessed worldwide connections in New Testament times. Since the beginning of the second century B.C.E., Palestine, especially the Jewish part of its population, had been an active partner in the Hellenistic world.

The Jewish Diaspora extended from Spain to Persia at least. This is especially important for the understanding of Paul, who grew up in the

---

16. Much of my thinking on economy has evolved around reflections on the collection of Paul for Jerusalem. See Dieter Georgi, *Remembering the Poor: The History of Paul's Collection for Jerusalem* (Nashville: Abingdon, 1991). However, already my dissertation, *Die Gegner des Paulus im 2. Korintherbrief* (WMANT 11; Neukirchen-Vluyn: Neukirchener Verlag, 1964), and even more its English translation, *The Opponents of Paul in Second Corinthians* (Philadelphia: Fortress, 1986), dealt with socioeconomic and political dimensions of religious-historical phenomena in New Testament times.

17. "Christianity" did not exist yet in the first century. Using the term *Christian* for the first generation of the early church is anachronistic. Paul and his contemporaries did not know this term. It originated at the earliest in the second generation. The early church was a form of Judaism. "Christianity" became an entity separate from Judaism only on the threshold from the first to the second century C.E., and even then a not insignificant Torah-oriented branch of the church did not concur with that move. It contradicts the historical knowledge and theological insight of today to marginalize and denounce the latter group as heretics.

Diaspora. We must read his letters as being written by a person who had daily acquaintance with the phenomenon of world trade, and this is true for his audiences as well. The Hellenistic-Roman markets were no abstractions; they were physically real. They were visible in the centers of the towns and cities spread all over the Mediterranean and beyond, into Africa and into Germany, into Britain and into the areas of modern Afghanistan and Pakistan. The Parthians, heavily controlling the Eastern markets since the first century B.C.E., had, despite their opposition to the Romans, become thoroughly connected with the Hellenistic-Roman market society. The markets Paul and his readers knew were connecting links with the world at large. This market's trade included Ireland as well as Vietnam and increasingly also China, first by sea, later by land. The steppes and savannas south of the Sahara as well as Ethiopia were connected with that "world market," as were Russia and Scandinavia. The land route to China, the so-called silk route, was increasingly used, and the connection between China and Rome was fully and officially established via that route around 100 C.E.

As Paul speaks of the world, he has this vast area in mind, its people in their manifold variety and in their intensive relations and communications. Trade and market were the major strings and nodes of his world. The market for the society of Paul's time was also the place of demonstration of the worldwide interest in performance and achievement. Not only material goods were presented on Hellenistic-Roman markets but also spiritual ones, among them religions. These markets became the major centers of propaganda and missionary activity. Thus, competition did not happen among merchants and traders alone, nor was it limited to the stadium, but there was also competition among nonmerchants on the markets, people who presented their intellectual or spiritual wares, doing their best to stand up to the expectations of a performance- and achievement-oriented market society, a society interested in athletic competition in all fields of societal experience, religion included.

As he writes his letters, Paul has in mind this market-oriented world, the corporate consciousness of this society that already transcended the Mediterranean by far, a worldwide society, of which Judaism is merely a part—although a rather large and, for that matter, very active one. The Pauline fragments collected in 2 Corinthians deal in particular with the competitive and also the monetary dimensions of this worldwide society. Paul's polemics against his opponents in these fragments of 2 Corinthians demonstrate that Paul takes issue with the achievement orientation of a competitive society. They also show that Paul is thinking about money quite intensively, not as barter but as a universal communicator of personal and communal relation, of interest as participation and sharing. Contrary to Aristotle, he looks at money as a heavily symbolic and thus communicative phenomenon, relating to legal and cultic conditions and situations as well.[18]

Paul's reflections on money in 2 Corinthians and elsewhere are the most intensive deliberations on the subject that have come down to us from the ancient world. Paul develops the final stage of his theological thinking on grace, Christology, justification, church, and freedom in these reflections on money, in the contexts of his discussions of remuneration and of the collection for Jerusalem.

In the history of exegesis of Paul, these passages have nevertheless been almost forgotten, even more in the church in general. They are hinted at only when a moralizing pressure is intended for the improvement of a Sunday collection. Paul's reflections on money are completely unknown to circles outside the church. Economists to this day still quote Xenophon and even more Aristotle on money but never Paul. He had taken on the corporate consciousness of the world of his day, governed by the Caesar as well as by the market. But the concreteness and directness of his communications have been individualized, spiritualized, and moralized by the church because the church did not want to further pursue the political, social, and economic dimensions of Paul's teaching on justice as solidarity nor his Christology, in which power is turned into weakness and weakness into power. Such thinking would have too much troubled a church that had decided to share power with the governing forces of state and economy.

In his missionary preaching Paul had refused to use Jesus as a great personality, as a divine man.[19] He did this in emphatic contrast to such attempts of other "apostles," that is, other missionaries of the church who had consciously entered into the competition of an environment that was obsessed with performance. Paul's refusal proves his denial to yield to the rules and conditions of the contemporary market and achievement-oriented society. His debate with the congregation in Corinth, and thereby with the preachers and missionaries who had contradicted Paul and gained support among Corinthians, demonstrates that certain circles in the early church had eyes set on collaboration with the rules of a society that was conditioned by demonstrable and verifiable power—religious, political, social, and economic. These circles,

---

18. This is much more in tune with the origin and character of money in the ancient world than Aristotle is. On the origin of money and money-based economy, see Gunnar Heinsohn, "Privates Grundeigentum, patriarchalische Monogamie und geldwirtschaftliche Produktion: Eine sozialtheoretische Rekonstruktion zur Antike" (Ph.D. diss., Bremen, 1983).

19. θεῖος ἀνήρ in Greek.

although unknown to us, won out over Paul and co-opted him by means of misrepresentation. This happened through pseudonymous writings, especially the so-called Pastoral Epistles, and through a falsified portrait of Paul in the Acts of the Apostles, where Luke paints Paul as a successful hero, a "super-apostle" exactly like the opponents Paul fought against in the fragments of 2 Corinthians. So Luke—clearly a fan of Paul—made him a posthumous turncoat, an emphatic mouthpiece for what used to be Paul's opposition during his lifetime. Ever since that "conversion," Paul was the great achiever, champion or villain, for the branch of the church that won out. The foe of any personality cult became its major advocate. In order to make this radical change of perspective certain, the victorious church—contrary to Paul's pleading in 2 Corinthians—put the earthly Jesus and with him the Gospels into prominence, and indeed pointed preference,[20] reading them as having established the earthly Jesus as the great personality, the glorified martyr who made it straight into heaven because of his extraordinary performance and achievement.[21]

This was no challenge to a culture that cherished martyrs such as Heracles, Socrates, Caesar, and many others. Constantine finally gave his blessings to that approach by making this a-Pauline and anti-Pauline church into the state religion. Augustine finalized the moralizing and individualizing misreading of the letters of Paul, most prominently in his tractate De Litera et Spiritu (On letter and spirit)—a complete disfiguration of one of the basic texts used, namely, 2 Cor 3.

---

20. The liturgical practice in Orthodox and Catholic churches puts the reading of the Gospels ahead of and above other biblical reading, and this has remained the case, even in the high-church forms of Protestantism. One stands up for the Gospel reading and remains seated as other texts of the Bible are read.

21. Which certainly was in decisive contrast to the original intent of most of the surviving Gospels, with the lone exception of the Gospel of Luke. Mark, Matthew, John, and the newly discovered *Gospel of Thomas*, too, all deal critically with the temptation of forming a personality cult around Jesus. More or less extensive fragments of so-called "apocryphal" Gospels make evident that the so-called canonical Gospels were not the only ones written and preserved in those days. Yet the "canonical" ones were those that corresponded the most to the sociopolitical interests of the part of the church that aimed to increase the church's public influence by conforming to the norms of the governing circles of society. The preserved Gospel tradition demonstrates an incredible variety of possibilities in the shaping of the Jesus phenomenon, certainly not limited to the concentration on a verifiable power-laden earthly figure.

4. THE MEDIEVAL REFORMATION OF A WORLD MARKET AND THE CONCEPTIONALIZATION OF A WORLD ECONOMY

Our often-quoted laws of economics were conceived, born, and developed in medieval history.[22] The social and economic development of that time certainly played a role in this, but a far more important one was that of scholastic thought, in particular its adaptation by mendicant friars. These created a new consciousness that included a new understanding of society and economy, of trade, market, and money. People such as the monk Hildebrand, the later Gregory VII, brought about a revolution. A change of corporate consciousness occurred in southern, central, and western Europe in the eleventh century. The letters of Paul remained pinned down to their established apoliticized, spiritualized, and moralized reading. The canonical Gospels became the lead documents for this revolution of society. A world arose that was governed by pope and emperor, by bishops and feudal rulers, a world of lords and vassals on the surface. Yet the veins and nerves of medieval society became the monks and the burghers. A major vessel of this new consciousness became the nascent bourgeoisie.

A sociopsychological structure was developed in which theory and practice were bonded, with theory coming first and practice derived from that, contrary to everything we can learn from the Bible in general, and Paul in particular, where praxis created and informed the theory.[23] Pastoral counseling, as institutionalized and professionalized attention, reflection, disciplinary and consultative practice in the confessional, offered the heartbeat for this new culture, its economy, and the consciousness that bore it. Augustine's thoughts became an essential factor in this new conception. It carried his stamp in the form of its marked dual structure, its polarized understanding of heaven and earth, God and devil, believers and unbelievers, high and low, inner and outer, soul and body, church and state/society, and so on. A heightened spirituality formed the basis. It was made to relate to a wide circle of professions and lifestyles in a greater variety than ever before, and did so with respect to extensity and intensity. It greatly affected people's conscience, volition, decision, and activity. It formed the individual and the public will.

---

22. See Odd Langholm, *Economics in the Middle Ages: Wealth, Exchange, Value, Money, and Usury According to the Paris Theological Tradition 1200–1350* (Studien zur Geistesgeschichte des Mittelalters 29; Leiden: Brill, 1992).

23. On this new structure of urban life, see Lester K. Little, *Religious Poverty and the Profit Economy in Medieval Europe* (Ithaca, N.Y.: Cornell University Press, 1978), here 197–217 under the title "Urban Religious Life" (see also the subsequent two-page conclusion).

Indeed, it shaped the individual itself. Although the individual was made to believe in his or her independence, the individual was nevertheless turned into a willing instrument of church and society. Media for this formative process were primarily pulpit and confessional as supportive literature, but also a far richer liturgical life, richer in matters of form and of space. A modernized canon law did its work effectively, too.

There was also the duality of clergy and monks on the allegedly "spiritual" side and the majority of people in church and society, "the world," on the other side. Among those who lived an "evangelical life" were those who worked out the theory that was to be applied to the two ways, the "evangelical" and the "worldly."[24] Practice became application, application of theory, the worldly practice even more than the evangelical practice. The theory was comprehensive, indeed all-embracing. The so-called spiritual life was the extended leash that connected people to theory, not only as basis but also as control and discipline. This discipline was presented and understood as an essential element of spiritual life.

In two essays I have shown the importance of then newly developed life-of-Jesus theology for these theoretical ideas and socioeconomic developments.[25] The theological concept of the "divine man"[26] that Paul had so emphatically fought against in 2 Corinthians was picked up from the Gospels again: "The particular individual Jesus of Nazareth was the prominent example of divine power." Thomas interpreted Jesus' alleged miraculous faculties as decisive in the God incarnate. He called Jesus' experience *scientia experimentalis*. Such a concept of experience became quite relevant for the Scottish Franciscans from Roger Bacon on. The theology and piety of the Franciscans had been shaped on the concept of the life of Jesus. "This theology presented to the burghers of the cities an ever-increasing consideration for the individual. Praxis, experiment, and experience were integrated into this growing interest in the individual."[27] Theological theory, especially of these mendicants, put heavy emphasis on the individual's intention, volition, and decision. Theology since Anselm had bound together reason, the law of nature, faith, theology, ecclesial, societal, and personal life. All this together formed an order of

---

24. It was significant that one chose the term *evangelical* as the signifier for the monastic life that was distinguished from normal life and followed the rules of the canonical Gospels, especially the Sermon on the Mount.

25. Dieter Georgi, "Leben-Jesu-Theologie/Leben-Jesu-Forschung," *TRE* 20:566–76; idem, "The Interest in Life-of-Jesus Theology as a Paradigm for the Social History of Biblical Criticism," *HTR* 85 (1992): 51–83, repr. on 221–54 in this volume. Subsequent references are to the version appearing in this collection.

26. The miraculous person, the θεῖος ἀνήρ.

27. Georgi, "Interest in Life-of-Jesus Theology," 229, 231.

reason. Monastic cell, pulpit, confessional, teaching chair, and podium were the instruments of the monks, even more so when the mendicant friars entered the scene. Shop, desk, parlor, and market became the instruments of the burghers.[28]

The individual and individual will became main concerns of societal formation, the human as actor and agent of heavenly and earthly transactions. This increased when a Seneca renaissance had brought the individual even more into the center, not the least among the Franciscans. The individual for Seneca was the smallest societal entity that could own property.[29]

The friars did not change that as they assumed a major role in theological teaching. On the contrary, they demonstrated an increased concern for the economy. They had observed the growth and spread of trade and of the profession of merchants in much of southern and western Europe. They had seen that these growing forces of southern and western society did not even mind trading with infidels. One would imagine that the mendicants would have observed these developments with contempt, would have denounced this bursting of greed and warned against its spread. For such negative judgment the monks could have invoked the biblical distaste for money grabbing and the injunctions against usury.

---

28. The correlation of money, economy, and religion that was common since the origin of money in ancient Greece was further strengthened in the Middle Ages. There are already many proofs of this in the field of languages. One could mention first the terms *credit* (*credo*!) and *debit*. Then there is the semantic field of the Latin *fides*, already used in its Latin variations with concepts of monetary and economic transaction. This is enlarged by one of the English translations of *fides* as "trust," a very creative semantic field in the world of Anglo-Saxon business. The Middle Ages and early modern times saw a real bloating of the fundamental connection of faith and money. At the same time, this intimate connection was covered up, as shown in the tendency to separate the terms *faith* and *belief* as such from all material relationships, to *entweltlichen* (desecularize) and spiritualize them and their religious synonyms, contrary to the usage in Greek and Latin languages before, and also contrary to biblical language. The Reformation with its hypertrophic understanding of "faith" contributed further to the seeming separation, in fact, coverup, of the factual network of relations between religion and money. This increased the dual disguise, so fatal in the Middle Ages already. Newer research on Pauline usage has challenged the translation of the terms πίστις and πιστεύειν with "faith" and "belief," a matter of course for traditional Protestant theology and exegesis. "Loyalty" and "trust" make more sense for the divine and the human side of the matter as well, embedded in the context of "solidarity," the more proper translation for the Pauline δικαιοσύνη. I have dealt with this in my *Theocracy in Paul's Praxis and Theology* (trans. David E. Green; Minneapolis: Fortress, 1991).

29. A concept by which our contemporary social, cultural, and economic consciousness is still conditioned.

At first sight such an interpretation appears supported by an intensive and continuous interest of medieval theology, even more that of the friars, in the biblical prohibition of usury and its contemporary meaning and application. However, closer analysis of these many reflections on usury and its application betray continued attempts to minimize the definition of usury, to allow the merchants more maneuverability and to widen as well as deepen the perception of economy. These theologians produced theological reflections that could be taken as handbooks in economics. It seems to be a contradiction in terms, but the followers of Saint Francis reflected about economics the most and furthered economic thinking. Some of the more radical advocates of poverty were even in the forefront of such reflection, which furthered economic thinking among "secular" people as well, and intentionally so. The mendicant theologians, in particular some of the radicals, provided space, direction, moral discipline, as well as encouragement—even motivation—for the economy and the merchants of their days.

The medieval theologians, including the friars, agreed with Aristotle that private property was a most essential means for societal order. They believed that it was not original with the human race, yet under the conditions of the present age—after the fall—it was an essential tool against chaos and so of redeeming value. The mendicants saw property as well as economy as important parts of the Christian life. In these deliberations, the concept of capital grew. Radical friars such as Peter Olivi, although advocating radical poverty for the mendicants, thought up dramatic theoretical visions of economic situations and problems, as scarcity and desire, utility, objective and subjective values, incentive and acquisition, wares, skills, and wages, need and just price, banking, conscience, and wisdom. Olivi and other friars stressed the importance and freedom of labor, but they distinguished labor increasingly from *industria* and allowed the latter to be assigned to enterprising merchants. Most of these ideas evolved in tractates that dealt with the biblical injunction against usury. These treatises tried to give the theory its proper application in the confessional. It was supposed to help enterprising people in public life. Peter Olivi was the first to speak of a *ratio seminalis* of capital.[30] Herewith the concept of capital as a working entity was born, and this in the context of God's providence and plan of salvation and an emphasis on the spiritual importance of poverty.

The theory of money held by the scholastics was also more or less identical to that of Aristotle. They understood money as the replacement

---

30. It is found in the sixth *dubium* of Olivi's tractate *De Usuris et Restitionibus*.

of barter. This idea of exchange also determined their conception of economy. Free exchange of wares, labor, and money was the demand of scholastic economics. This freedom related to fairness and justice. It included the idea of fair and just pricing. Scholastic, and particularly mendicant, economy looked favorably to the market as the place where that exchange and fair balancing would happen and mirror its "righteousness" in a fair price.

In Scottish Franciscan teaching and preaching on private property, an important change happened. Private property was now moved from the area of natural law into that of the positive law of state and society. This change freed the upcoming bourgeoisie and its industry and commerce even more from the holds of ecclesial teaching and control.

William Ockham was the Franciscan theologian who put subjectivity into the center. He did it not merely in a theoretical, academic but also in a historical, biographical sense. As regards private property, he claimed that the powers of possession and jurisdiction were natural powers, given by God to all human beings, infidels included, even after the fall. In every human, Christian or not, the will is seen as the power that translates God's own will into action. "By their natural powers, men can still act virtuously and legitimately."[31]

These ethical views of Ockham stem from the last period of his life, after he had been forced to appear at the papal court in Avignon to answer the accusation of heresy, related most of all to his advocacy of radical poverty. To this day scholars wonder whether there had been two Ockhams, as it were: one more theoretically interested, prior to Avignon; the other more politically minded, after Avignon.

I am convinced that there were not two Ockhams. Rather, it is again the distinction between theory and practice spoken of above. There is a continuous line in which the earlier Ockham by means of his theoretical thoughts prepared the path for the application, namely, the expansion of the worldly side and its power. As Ockham defended radical mendicant poverty, he increased the Augustinean polarity of the two worlds I spoke of before. At the same time, Ockham insisted on the rights of both sides of that polarity. He upheld that the connection between both was maintained by God, by the sacraments, and by the power of persuasion as executed in preaching and the pastoral care of the church, especially the mendicants. Ockham's theoretical thoughts are much less elevated into complete abstraction than is usually assumed. His dealing with *res* and

---

31. Gordon Leff, *William of Ockham: The Metamorphosis of Scholastic Discourse* (Manchester: Manchester University Press, 1975), 629.

realitas with *proprietas* as property, his insistence on the power of naming things, his concept of contingency, on will and volition, all provided a basis for his later thoughts and their encouragement of the worldly side. As I wrote earlier, "Ockham ... started to emphasize the *res individualis* as the only reality. This concept was clearly not limited to the area of logic and language but was intended to portray the individual as the entity that formed, supported, and maintained the divine, the world, and society. It was a breakthrough in the concept of the individual as a phenomenon that was to form and support society in the future.[32] The believing and reasoning individual already belonged to the earlier Ockham; so did the concept of the unity of believers as being truly a universal one. It must not be overlooked either that the idea of the liberty of the individual, developed by the mendicant theologians and advanced by Ockham, was held in golden fetters—and remains so to this day: this individual was and is an element of a system, a wheel in a well-constructed machine, furthered by instrumentalized spirituality and the togetherness of richness and poverty.

This advanced mendicant thinking helped decisively in turning around a major socioeconomic crisis Britain experienced in the second half of the fourteenth century. Various blows of the Black Death, the Hundred Years' War, and social and religious rebellions had led to depopulation, famine, and other forms of devastation.[33] A great number of serfs had been freed by their impoverished masters and had turned into agricultural laborers without land. The landlords had land but insufficient money to buy or maintain labor. So the laborers could dictate the price because they had become too few, and the landlord had to compete for them and did so with excessive wages.[34]

In this socioeconomic crisis the Franciscan thinking became a major motivational force for the lower nobility and the social group called the gentry to react creatively, especially in the more distant countryside. Since the established social structure was extremely weakened, lower nobility and gentry united in these areas,[35] and they formed, first around noble estates and then also without them, differentiated but tightly knit,

---

32. Georgi, "Interest in Life-of-Jesus Theology," 233.
33. William Langland gives a drastic description of the situation in his *Piers Plowman* from the second half of the fourteenth century.
34. On this and the following, see Gunnar Heinsohn and Otto Steiger, "Geld, Produktivität und Unsicherheit in Kapitalismus und Sozialismus oder: Von den Lollarden Wat Tylors zur Solidarität Lech Walesas," *Leviathan* 9 (1981): 164–94.
35. Priests and even more so monks always mingled with them and performed their pastoral counseling.

interdependent as well as interactive, structures. This was a new, less feudal form of the client system with extensive division of labor, including commercial, legal, and spiritual service. We could call these enterprises production companies. It was the origin of the basic units of the capitalist economy. The most important products were cloths of various kinds.

The extreme depopulation had caused a complete deterioration of the legal structure of the land base of agriculture. This led to intensive reassessment, aggressive repossession, and ingenious rearrangement of real estate. Land, naturally the most immobile entity imaginable, became most mobile, an important good of trading. This radical shift in the understanding of the "immovable" was another major building block of capitalism. The term *realty* was coined in those days, an imaginatively British way of concretizing *realitas*. The implication was, of course, that only those who had realty had reality.[36] The rearrangement happened in particular with respect to land use. Wool was the most profitable resource. Therefore, sheep grazing was increased tremendously, with a growing appetite for more and more land. That helped to depopulate the countryside further and drove many more farmers into the city after they had sold their land cheaply.[37]

The third pillar of the origin of British capitalism was the turning of debts and credits into capital assets. It happened on the production side and on the distribution side. On the production side, the relationship

---

36. This splitting of one original French term, brought over by the Normans, into two different English ones happened frequently at that time. I have already spoken about this in Georgi, "Interest in Life-of-Jesus Theology," 234. There are many more examples than those I list there. It is important for our inquiry to note that the division of these originally French terms into two English ones each time created a distinction between a more fundamental or even ontological term and another, more pragmatic one, the latter with a more socioeconomic or moral aspect. It is quite interesting, indeed significant, that this division of original French terms into two English ones happened between the fourteenth and sixteenth centuries, the period I have described above in which British capitalism emerged. The establishment of a distinction by means of such English splitting of a French concept is demonstrated as a significant social differentiation in the case of the French term *villain*. It is maintained in English, but another one, *villein*, is added. Both terms should actually mean the same. The division might even have utilized two different spellings already in French, yet there not associated with a difference in meaning. The socioeconomic differentiation of the time caused the linguistic differentiation in English, after which only the first term, *villain*, signifies the villager proper. The second term, *villein*, comes to mean the vagabond and troublemaker who does not accept the social changes and the new conditions. In French, on the contrary, both meanings still are covered by the same word.

37. A good illustration of the vicissitudes of capitalism: the original deficiencies it promises to diminish if not cure—in this early case, that of depopulation—are in the end increased even more.

between landlords without money and agricultural laborers without land was resolved through the issuance of debt certificates by the landlords to the workers, who bought their necessities with these certificates, which were then also traded. On the distribution side, merchants began to order wool or cloth from the British producers in advance against a down payment and credit for the remainder. They also sold the options against credit to interested parties, mostly across the Channel in Europe. Much of the currency used in this foreign exchange was in papers drawn upon monetary institutions in London or Calais.

These socioeconomic changes in Britain quickly imparted themselves upon western, central, and southern Europe in the fifteenth century. The Reformation did not bring drastic changes to this system. Luther's *To the Christian Nobility of the German Nation* was a brief attempt to interfere, yet the German reformer did not continue it.[38] Bucer and Calvin tried to challenge and reform a little longer and a little more intensely the duality of the system I talked about, also trying to discipline the already observable excesses of commerce and production. Both invoked the kingship of Christ over the entire world, including king and burgher,[39] but the duality quickly returned in the form of the organized community of the believers over against the rest of society and world.

Two hundred years later a compatriot of the Scottish Franciscans tried to employ enlightened Scottish Presbyterianism against the abounding wild growth of capitalism in Scotland and England. Adam Smith's concept of market is an application of an enlightened understanding of the Presbyterian concept of universal theodicy to the economy run wild. His idea of enlightened self-interest has more to do with Bucer's and Calvin's understanding of divine illumination of the creature than with the unbridled greed of the robber barons of his days. His vision of the market is supposed to provide the necessary bridling.

V. THE PRESENT CHALLENGE

Today it appears that in our secularized society capitalism as such is without any religion. Indeed, major established churches have little direct

---

38. And this despite the remarkable fact that the document that really started the protest of the Reformation, Luther's famous ninety-five theses of 31 October 1517, attacked the Middle Ages right in their core, the connection of economy with decommunalized, professionalized, and institutionalized pastoral care.

39. Curiously enough, this resembles some of the arguments and actions of John XXII, the opponent of Ockham, although without the triumphalist dimensions and without the papal and episcopal aspects.

contact with commerce and industry; even less do they have a real hold on them. This is even truer with respect to the influence of academic theology on economics and economy. However, the close association of Pietists and fundamentalists with economy, even in its most blatant capitalist version in the United States and in Germany, speaks against the assumption of a complete secularization of capitalism.[40] Recently a study by Norbert Bolz and David Bosshart has shown that capitalist economy has taken over the religious vacuum left by the decreasing ability of church and theology to relate to contemporary society and its economy.[41] "Today, not the churches but the temples of consumption are the places of modern religiosity."[42] "Capitalism in the stage of saturated markets of consumption is turning into the ultimate 'last' religion of this world."[43] "Capitalism has become the strongest of all religions.... Capitalism succeeded in making wares into our gods."[44]

This is a challenge to church and theology. Bolz and Bosshart, in my opinion, merely describe what has been a fact in capitalism all along. Capitalism's influence has increased merely because economy alone had

---

40. It needs to be emphatically stated that the present union between Pietism and political and economic conservatism in Germany and in Anglo-Saxon countries contradicts the actions and thoughts of Pietists in the eighteenth and even the nineteenth century. These awakened ones distinguished themselves frequently from their socially and politically conservative, establishment-oriented religious environment by their intensive, occasionally even radical social engagement, often demonstrating ingenious as well as practical imagination and corresponding social criticism. In his book, *The American Religion: The Emergence of the Post-Christian Nation* (New York: Simon & Schuster, 1992), Harold Bloom unfortunately has not dealt with North American Pietism of earlier times, which was characterized by similar activities of social criticism and engagement such as those mentioned above. Bloom concentrates on modern forms and sees them as manifestations of what he describes as the obsessions of U.S.-Americans with religion. According to Bloom, radical individualism and fundamentalism do not exclude but include each other. In his analysis, which declares Mormons and Southern Baptists as particularly characteristic for the United States of tomorrow, Bloom states: "Authority, in the context of the American religion, is another form of gnosis, another knowing, and what it knows is that it must replace the purely secular authority brought about by the American Revolution" (271). One could debate the use of the term *gnosis* by Bloom. It is very unfortunate, yet significant for his limited approach, that Bloom does not consider the rather obvious question of the close connection of faith and money and of religion and market in the phenomena he describes. He does so despite his intensive occupation with U.S.-American religious conservatism and therefore also more or less directly with the politically conservative forces of past and present, including the so-called conservative revolution of the Republicans.

41. *Kult-Marketing: Die neuen Götter des Marktes* (2nd ed.; Düsseldorf: Econ Verlag, 1995). The translations are my own.

42. Ibid., 11.

43. Ibid., 22.

44. Ibid., 248.

to fill the void that, in the dual structure of society described above, was created because the church and theology no longer had the importance of the past more than half a millennium. Should both now return to their old roles and compete with the gods of consumption? No. What Bolz and Bosshart prove is most of all the decline of the duality we have seen as being basic for capitalist economy and society. Church and theology after 1945 have failed to provide the same religious-cultural support for the capitalist revival after the war that cultural Protestantism and cultural Catholicism had given to capitalism into the first third of this century.[45]

There is no reason for theology or church to continue any variation of the idea of the two kingdoms.[46] On the contrary, there is need for a renewed meditation on the meaning and impact of Paul's theology. Those who want to make us believe that the conception of two regiments as developed in the history of interpretation of Paul is a proper exposition of Paul's intention have no good arguments in Paul's authentic writings themselves.[47] A new occupation with Paul's work beyond the fatal trajectory from Luke over Ignatius, Tertullian, the scholastics, and on to Luther could contribute to the evolution of a new corporate consciousness. We have a chance to rediscover Paul's conception of the rule of Christ over the entire world. It is not meant as the rule of a more or less despotic

---

45. The attempts since 1953 to revive and continue the life-of-Jesus- theology had considerable success in church and theology but almost no resonance in the economic world. The basically conservative tendency of this Jesus renaissance found its correspondence in the renewed decommunalizing and professionalizing of pastoral care and counseling even in Protestant theology, training, and practice. This led in many places to an almost complete identification of ministry and pastoral care. Bonhoeffer's warning against an overestimation of professionalized pastoral care remained unheeded. This allegedly new emphasis on spirituality and the pastoral approach nevertheless remained without much effect toward the outside because it lacked the theological foundation and weight of preceding efforts.

46. This would contradict the tendency in the development of Bonhoeffer's theology from the lectures on Christology and from his ethics to the last reflections in prison, a tendency that in reality was a growing polemical move away from the traditional theology of the two empires, although Bonhoeffer tried to separate Luther's own version of that doctrine from that which he considered a distortion. The synchronic strengthening of the christocratic line in Bonhoeffer and its relationship to creation and world as a whole unambiguously prove that Bonhoeffer also moved away from Luther's understanding of power.

47. The described conception of duality reaching from Ignatius to Luther with the Middle Ages in the center still stands behind the modern idea of the legal and institutional separation of state and church. This duality is maintained even in form of the alleged secularization. The latter has led, in fact, to a strengthening of the phenomenon of "civil religion" as well as to an analphabetism concerning religion and theology among the majority of the intellectuals. These *illiterati* are, therefore, robbed of all critical and constructive faculties that would be necessary to overcome the continuing dualism and achieve a constructive vision for the future.

individual together with his worldly vassals. It is rather a rule under the dialectic of power and powerlessness, strength and weakness, solidarity and justice, person and community, giving and sharing. The Christ in this rule is a corporate personality, communing, dialoguing, sharing, and exchanging through us and with us. This Christ of Paul is not above the world but within the world and for the world.

Through such rethinking, theology can be liberated from its present apologetic, indeed defeatist, attitude. Theology does not need other academic disciplines in order to establish its scholarly value and status. Theology is as much science as other fields and should cooperate with them in the process of bringing about a new worldly consciousness, not of the Western world plus a few nations in the Far East exploiting the remaining world and even the poor and unemployed in their own countries, but a consciousness that heeds the entirety of the human family.[48]

We stand at the eve of the experience of capitalist economy. It has taken an ultimate, clearly eschatological flavor. Capitalist economy is all of a sudden left without competitors, particularly the one it had to deal with during the last one hundred years: socialism or rather communism organized by totalitarian states. During that time, capitalism did not find the time to really line up with the society it was basically allied with, the democratic society. Contrary to an often-heard claim, capitalism with its inherent social Darwinism is heavily anarchic with suicidal tendencies. It is not and never will be inherently democratic.[49] If capitalism were to become democratized, it would become something essentially different.

Capitalism, contrary to common assumption, is not a constructive system either. We have seen that a basic element of evolving capitalism in the Middle Ages was its or the market economy's claim that it was an essential factor of order in society. In reality, however, capitalism and the market it dominates are on the road of self-destruction. That the market is about to destroy itself, even more in the age of multinational corporations who constantly diminish their number by fusing into megacorporations, is a realistic possibility. A true democratization of corporations, the industry, the economy, and the market could prevent that. I want to give some quotes from a basically procapitalist but nevertheless highly critical

---

48. The worldliness and the majority age that Bonhoeffer has in view is, closely looked at, a new corporate consciousness. It is a world reconciled with God and with itself, which is conscious of its weakness and does not use this weakness any longer as an excuse and a basis for the exercise of power but as point of departure for common constructive action.

49. The Nazi period has proven how fast and easily capitalism can collaborate with fascism, and the same game, the collaboration with totalitarianism, is being played again in present China.

book by Lester C. Thurow, *The Future of Capitalism; How Today's Economic Forces Shape Tomorrow's World.*[50] This book by the former Dean of MIT's Sloan School of Management presents the Castle Lectures in Ethics, Politics, and Economics at Yale University in 1995/96.

His discussion of the relationship between capitalism and democracy is conducted under the critical title: "Democracy versus the Market." He begins with the following sentence:

> Democracy and capitalism have very different beliefs about the proper distribution of power. One believes in a completely equal distribution of political power, "one man, one vote," while the other believes that it is the duty of the economically fit to drive the unfit out of business and into economic extinction. "Survival of the fittest" and inequality in purchasing power are what capitalistic efficiency is all about.[51]

After extensive debate of these contradictions—in which Thurow presents the self-destructive dangers of capitalism and warns against false assessments with regard to one's own indestructibility in the face of the disappearance of the communist competition—he comes to a rather drastic statement: "Values or preferences are the black hole of capitalism. They are what the system exists to serve, but there are no capitalistic theories of how values arise, and no capitalistic theories of how values should be altered or controlled."[52] The assumed self-evidence concerning capitalism's ability to survive as it can be found in leading circles of the West, and more recently even in countries of the East, is not shared by Thurow. Although he does not speak expressly of the possibility of the suicide of the so-called free market that threatens to lose its own liberty by means of its own design, Thurow does not exclude it either.

Thurow calls for sailing anew into a new world in a way comparable to Columbus's journey to the New World. He calls the ship that bears the discoverers "capitalism." This image clearly contains utopian elements, which is laudable. My observations and suggestions are meant as a critical contribution to the utopia of this and many other contemporary economists, not the least also the Nobel-prize winner of 1996, professor of economics at Columbia University in New York, William Vickrey, who unfortunately died two weeks after the Nobel-Prize committee had chosen him. His 1993 presidential address to the American Economic Association, titled "Today's Task for Economists," charts out a new road

---

50. New York: Penguin, 1996.
51. Ibid., 242.
52. Ibid., 277.

as well.[53] The subject of the Bonhoeffer symposium, namely, unemployment, Vickrey considers a matter of importance. He argues for the necessity of removing it completely, and he considers it possible within a few years—if the insight and political and economic will are present.

Vickrey and others like him demonstrate that an old goal and measuring stick of conservative market economy finally might take hold. I am thinking of the principle of the greatest possible degree of welfare for the greatest number of people. Today, in a time of increased ecological consciousness, we would have to replace the term *people* by the term *creatures*. Ecology and economy belong indispensably together in a world that wants to survive.

---

53. This address is found in William Vickrey, *Public Economics: Selected Papers by William Vickrey* (ed. by Richard Arnott et al.; Cambridge: Cambridge University Press, 1994), 432–53. Vickrey's last work, which he had written shortly before the announcement of his winning of the Nobel Prize by the committee, bore the title, "Fifteen Fatal Fallacies of Financial Fundamentalism: A Disquisition on Demand Side Economics." It is on the website of the economics department of the Columbia University in New York: http://www.columbia.edu/dlc/wp/econ/vickrey.html. In this rather compact study Vickrey has, among other things, presented a devastating critique of the senseless, even ludicrous demand for a balanced state budget. This demand has become the magic word in the Western world, and the institutions of international finance control have spread it worldwide as gospel. Looked at economically, so Vickrey, this demand as an exclusive one makes no sense, is even economically and politically fatal. The political ideas and intentions behind such an absolute demand are clear. Conservative, indeed reactionary, forces have activated in a very clever fashion the fear of the lower middle class concerning debts, the fear of taking loans and of running into debt in the context of the normal family budget, and have manipulated it for the purpose of covering up their real intention, minimizing the social responsibility of the rich—in particular the big corporations, especially the multinationals—and for the purpose of justifying the reduction of their "tax burdens." This assists the constant threat and outright bribery of many corporations to leave the state or the country for some other "cheaper" place that proves more open to their bribery—much to the detriment of that new place, usually in the south of the globe. The devastating consequences of such manipulation strike home more and more in the countries of the north, too. Their social nets get smaller and smaller, and the holes within the nets keep growing. The transnational institutions, the European Union and the United Nations, are possessed with questions of money and currency that have replaced political reason and foresight, which should attack the international bribery mentioned and reduce it with a very much improved international law and a forceful judicature, both feared like hell by the international business world. Given the development of economy and education during last century and their increasing tendency to separate themselves from the democratic process, it appears appropriate that the predemocratic concept of separation of powers be enhanced and the three powers be enlarged, that is, that economy and education become the fourth and fifth powers. This would recognize that these two powers are major forces in present society as well. Their transformation into constitutional institutions would make them transparent factors in the process of mutual control and enhancement of the essential powers of society and thus diminish the destructive proclivity of economy and education with respect to the democratic fiber of society.

This would be an occasion of again adopting thoughts of the old Presbyterian federal theology that had come to fruition in the development of Anglo-Saxon democracy and had found an even stronger realization on the western side of the Atlantic among the Covenanters and their epigones. We can again take up these attempts and use them for a radical rethinking of the possibilities and problems of a truly social market economy. The direction of this enterprise needs to be what the English revolution of the seventeenth century and the beginning years of U.S.-American democracy had concentrated in the term *commonwealth,* this ingenious English translation of the Latin term *res publica.* Common weal and general welfare were meant by this, yet not only these but also common wealth, that is, wealth shared more or less equally by all citizens, and this centuries before the *Communist Manifesto.*[54]

In this our common task, we must avoid a basic flaw that Thurow's image of the journey of discovery into the future holds. He compares this journey, in which society and economy are united in a democratic venture, with that of Columbus. However, Columbus's journey into the Americas can be called a discovery only from a European perspective, not from the perspective of the American Indians. Our corporate journey into a new future must not repeat the conquering and exploitative flaws of the confusion of perspectives of the "discoverers" of the sixteenth century. The Europeans took away from the natives of the Americas what these peoples owned. In fact, the economic miracle of the Europe of the sixteenth and seventeenth centuries was due to a much greater crime than the grand larceny reluctantly being admitted into the history books; it was the destruction of the Native American society and of the ecology of its continent.

The future we are setting sail for is not ours; it belongs to the future generations, not only to those of our own children and grandchildren but also of to those of the peoples in the poorer countries. Both our thinking and our future actions should not interfere with the freedom of these new

---

54. The term *commonwealth* first appears in the fifteenth century. Puritan theological and political thinking had adopted and integrated it into their concept of covenant. Coming from this soil, this term then became a concept of state law in the Puritan Revolution of 1648/49 and found its weighty expression in the ruling of the state-council of 1649: "that the People of England and of all the dominions and territories thereunto belonging are, and shall be, and are hereby constituted, made, and confirmed to be a Commonwealth and Free State, and shall henceforward be governed as a commonwealth and Free State." Four U.S. states carry the title *Commonwealth:* Kentucky, Massachusetts, Pennsylvania, and Virginia. How much of the revolutionary emphasis of the years 1648 and 1649 still exists in these titles or in that of the "British Commonwealth" may be asked with good reason, but it is obvious that this tradition is not yet dead.

generations but should enhance their chances truly to make their future their own. The ship that bears us is not reserved for a select few. It holds all creatures and all creation.

15

IS THERE JUSTIFICATION IN MONEY?
A HISTORICAL AND THEOLOGICAL MEDITATION ON THE FINANCIAL ASPECTS OF JUSTIFICATION BY CHRIST

A fool may make money, but it takes a wise person to spend it. (English proverb)

1. INTRODUCTION

We have noticed already the realistic social, legal, and economic dimensions of New Testament spirituality. It deserves further discussion, though, that Paul is very much aware of the urban fact that cash and creed are intimately interrelated. This shows in his treatment of the issue of the collection for Jerusalem. Their financial aspect is not only integrated into Paul's biography but also interrelated with the major themes of his theology, especially with Christology and the concepts of trust, grace, and justification. They have to be rediscovered as being extremely concrete and in their concreteness relevant for urban theology.

Biblical studies, theology, and the church at large are unaware that the authentic writings of Paul contain some of the most elaborate literary reflections on the flow of money surviving from the ancient world. The important texts in this regard are, principally, 2 Cor 8 and 9, the other passages on the collection for Jerusalem, the reflection on financial support from the Philippians, and, finally, the discussions on remuneration in 1 and 2 Corinthians.

Paul's reflections on money are intimately related to central theological issues and interwoven with his life and the lives of his congregations.

However, the usual scholarly presentations of Paul's theology and his biography to this day discuss these financial and organizational issues only in the most abstract terms, giving them marginal status at best. This is even more the case with the use of the Pauline correspondence and its message in the contemporary church. Stewardship Sundays are the place in church life for Paul's collection texts, and there they are utilized, but only as snippets.

Despite the fact that ancient reflections on economy, and particularly on the flow of money, are rare, social and economic historians have never dealt with the Pauline texts on money. As far as literary evidence is concerned, the three ancient authors presented briefly below dominate the discussion. This is particularly true of Aristotle, whose hypothesis that money developed out of the exchange of goods prevailed until recently, with major consequences for the history of economics and also for our contemporary understanding of money.

Reworking my thesis on the collection for this volume has given me the opportunity to reconsider the relevance of these Pauline texts and to relate them to my own social-historical inquiries into the interplay of Judaism and the early church with their pagan environment. The economic crises and changes at the end of our millennium, those in my own country and in the United States not least among them, have furthered my insights and opened for me new perspectives. This essay took shape when East Germany was simply usurped by the economic strength of West Germany under the leadership of a party that claims to be Christian. This experience has sharpened my views. The economic crises around us make it more urgent for theology and the church to remember that the frame of reference of one of their most commonly used authors, Paul, has been unnecessarily curtailed.

A renewed acknowledgment of the interrelatedness of life and theology in Paul will engender fascinating suggestions. Life here means not only Paul's personal life, but also his communal and social life as well as that of others. It includes economic issues directly. This suggests that the church needs to begin to reflect on justification by Christ in its financial offices as well as in its pulpits. It further implies that lay Christians will no longer view Christology as a mere matter of personal opinion but as something that has relevance for their workplaces in the various branches of the economy. It follows as well that Pauline theology cannot be left to professional theologians alone but belongs to the praxis of the church at large, a church that is not removed from the world but rather acts as a challenging and stimulating part of the world. The letters of Paul as a textbook for schools of economics and of business administration? Why not? So long as they do not replace the other textbooks, it could only enrich the curriculum.

The recent crises of economic structures have led to intensive debates about the nature of the economy and of economics. The theory of money, its character and its function, is at present under vivid discussion. The origin and history of money are still a matter of controversy. All this makes a reflection on Paul's contribution to these discussions opportune.

Paul's ideas and suggestions appear even more relevant today because the many and various studies on money that have appeared in recent decades have gone far beyond the economic value and function of currencies. The political and social sides of money have been argued about for quite some time, as have its ethical dimensions.[1] In addition, the relationship of economy and money to the law and legal order have found increasing attention.[2] Moreover, the recent deliberations on the sociology of money have also uncovered its communicative importance,[3] and the psychological aspects of money have also received much recognition.[4] Compared with this, the theology of money has been relatively ignored.[5] However, within this concert of theories the ideas and suggestions of Paul do not look strange at all. As does the contemporary discussion, Paul's ideas on praxis and theory of money go far beyond the metallic value of coins.

---

1. Aristotle treated these categories in his discussion of economy and money, as will be shown further below. In their focus on the ethical dimensions of money, Christian theologians of the Middle Ages and the Reformation strongly emphasized certain issues, such as interest, but very much limited themselves to a moralizing approach. Since Marx's critical contributions to the socioeconomic debate, the three categories mentioned have found considerable treatment. Georg Friedrich Knapp has stimulated many debates concerning the state's role in the issue. Concerning the social side of economy and money, Talcott Parsons has furthered the discussion, building on George Herbert Mead, Max Weber, and Emile Durkheim. See also note 3.

2. This relationship of economy/money and the legal order has been seen by Aristotle. In modern times Georg Friedrich Knapp has stressed also the legal element in his monetary theory. Naturally, the negative sides of the relationship between the monetary and the legal were permanent targets of biblical prophets, but also of ancient Greek and Roman satirists. Today the growing complexities and intricacies of the financial and economic systems, and the white-collar crimes exploiting this fact, have led to ever-increasing financial and economic legislation. The creation of related branches of the judiciary corresponds to this situation. The intimate interplay of economy, money, and legal order since the beginnings of the economy of the West, which based itself on private property, will be shown below.

3. Since Talcott Parsons's elaborate discussion of this, scholars such as Klaus Heinemann have furthered this insight. Jürgen Habermas has devoted the last two chapters of the second volume of his *Theory of Communicative Action* (Boston: Beacon, 1984) to this issue; for his critical reflection on Parsons's position on money, see 199-300.

4. See, for example, Ernest Bornemann, *Psychoanalyse des Geldes* (Frankfurt: Suhrkamp Verlag, 1973).

5. Wolfgang Lienemann's collection of essays by various authors (*Die Finanzen der Kirche* [Munich: Kaiser, 1989]) on this subject indicates that this may be changing.

As we have seen (and shall see more), the historical dimensions of economy and economics, money included, have gained renewed attention. New suggestions have been made about the origin of money, its understanding, and its function in the ancient world.[6] My study of these matters in the context of the history of New Testament times threw new light on the Pauline correspondence. I have integrated my research on 2 Corinthians and on the collection into the general picture of the ancient environment, not only with respect to the history of religion and social history but also with regard to the ancient economy. The Pauline correspondence increasingly became a primary source for my understanding of the ancient world. The following essay is intended to make these ancient thoughts relevant for today through a meditation on the theological texts of Paul within their historical context. I hope to communicate not only my thoughts but also my fascination with this subject, so that my actual suggestions can stimulate further thinking on the part of my readers.

2. SOME GENERAL REMARKS ON THE ECONOMIC SITUATION OF PAUL'S THEOLOGICAL DISCOURSE

2.1. The State of the Ancient Economic Discourse

Paul's writings presuppose a monetary economy of worldwide proportions with a common (Roman) currency and an easy exchange of other currencies. This means that he was familiar with an urban society with a universal market structure. He must have taken for granted industry, division of labor, trade, and a labor market that included slave labor. Financial institutions were present. There existed during this time

---

6. I shall use in particular the ideas of Gunnar Heinsohn and Otto Steiger, who themselves built heavily on the work of John Maynard Keynes and Frank H. Hahn. Heinsohn's observations are not limited to the historical origin and evolution of the economy of the first millennium B.C.E. but portray its continuing character and structure down into the first century C.E. as well. Moses Isaac Finley's minimalist hesitation against reading modern economic perspectives and criteria into ancient economic structures (*The Ancient Economy* [Berkeley and Los Angeles: University of California Press, 1973]) too quickly and too strongly calls for some caution in the use of Heinsohn's terminology. A world market in its modern sense did not yet exist, nor had independently productive capital and coinage defined what money was. However, Finley has overemphasized these points. An expansive network of markets flourished, as did the equivalents of checks, and written obligations were traded. See in this regard F. M. Heichelheim's less minimalist view on these issues in *An Ancient Economic History* (3 vols.; Leyden: Sijthoff, 1958–70).

a strong wisdom tradition that discussed these economic issues.[7] Since Paul invokes wisdom, it can be taken as a matter of course that he was well attuned to this tradition. While he distances himself from the apocalyptic and gnostic denunciations of any kind of temporal economy,[8] he does not share the positive attitude that Jewish missionary wisdom held toward a performance- and market-oriented society.[9] It is clear that while Paul presupposes an effective economy, he consciously neglects certain economic principles and elements important to his day and to ours as well.

Outside of Paul's writings, Aristotle touches upon monetary issues in his discussion of economics in *Pol.* 1.2–5 (especially chapters 3–4)and also in his treatment of revolutions in 5.3–5.[10] Money plays an important role in other literary and nonliterary remains as well (for instance, in the studies of the Elder Cato), but never in the form of a continuous reflection. Economic deliberations are presented in the dialogue *Oeconomicus* by Xenophon, and in the treatise *Oeconomica*, which comes to us under the name of Aristotle and reflects a good deal of his ideas but had most probably found its final form only during the third century B.C.E. In none of these sources does one find anything similar to modern textbooks or manuals on economics or business administration, or (certainly) anything like an introduction to social work. The texts offer economic reflections and provide technical advice, to be sure, but these considerations are embedded in general ethical, social, and political discussions. Some passages even take a storytelling approach, and piety features rather

---

7. See, for example, Prov 6:1–5; 11:1; 16:11; 20:10; Sir 8:12–13; 10:26–27; 11:10–11, 18–19; 13:21–23; 14:3–6; 20:12; 22:26–27; 24:30–32; 26:29; 27:2; 29:10; 34:1–11; 37:11; 38:24–39:11; and 40:13–14.

8. In apocalypticism this hostile stance showed in the tendency to associate, indeed identify, state power and wealth—that is, economic and political strength—with corruption and sinfulness (see *1 En.* 62–63; 94:6–104:13). Jewish gnostic wisdom adopted and radicalized this sweeping criticism of temporal power relations and their institutions, as did, for instance, the *Letter of Eugnostus* and the *Apocalypse of Adam*.

9. For instance, the individual and collective prosperity that Philo promises in *De Praemiis et Poenis* (*On Rewards and Punishments*) to the faithful is not projecting a distant eschatological future, isolated from the present experience by something like a supernatural parousia, nor is it a fully realized eschatology, but rather something in between. Modern theological terminology calls it "realizing eschatology."

10. The numbering of Aristotle's *Politics* is that of the Loeb edition. The discussion of the origin and use of money takes up a relatively small portion of Aristotle's treatment of household management (*oikonomia*), whereas wealth getting and trade, as larger economic issues, occupy much of chapters 3 and 4. Here the close relationship between economy, money, and trade with politics, law, constitution, and ethics can be seen. Aristotle's reflections on the origin of money and the character of the flow of money carry a strong moralizing tone.

prominently. Only Aristotle in his *Politics* deliberates to a larger degree on the monetary side of the economy.

In Xenophon's dialogue on economics, property and profit are phenomena of social relations. Their main value is not of a financial but of an unquantified, social kind. Profit means primarily usefulness in and for human relations. It is of interest to note that Paul's strong emphasis on righteousness in his arguments for the collection finds its parallel in Xenophon's use of the terms *righteous, just, righteousness,* and *justice* in the context of economics, by which he means the management of a house, particularly an estate.

Pseudo-Aristotle claims in his treatise that the economics of a private household, a city, a province, or a kingdom are basically comparable; economics is for him literally *oiko-nomia:* the regulation of a house, despite the many variations in detail.[11] What render these economic contexts different are such things as the procurement of funds and other economic means and their use. Risks and catastrophes are taken for granted in these economies, but the need for imagination and resourcefulness is equally taken as a matter of course.

2.2. Juridical Elements of the Ancient Economy, Particularly Its Monetary Structure

In my book *Remembering the Poor* I have shown that Paul makes an easy association between righteousness and justification on the one hand and the collection on the other. The automatic response of a Protestant theologian to this discovery of the proximity of a discussion of the flow of money to the central doctrine of the Reformation is to find it shocking, if not blasphemous. This is particularly so when one remembers that Paul did not draw this connection on the grounds of the doctrines of election and sanctification, as Max Weber claimed for Calvinist economics. Paul's association is much more direct.

My studies subsequent to the writing of the German version of my book on the collection have demonstrated to me that from its inception ancient Mediterranean urban society interrelated economic issues naturally with political, social, juridical, and religious ideas as well as with ethical concerns. I present the major arguments for this claim in the following paragraphs. I shall describe the primary working principles of the

---

11. Michael Rostovtzeff has discussed this in *The Social and Economic History of the Hellenistic World* (Oxford: Clarendon, 1941), 1:440–46.

Mediterranean economy during this period and the role of money, market, and religion within it. Then I shall demonstrate and interpret the selective use Paul makes of these issues.

How one understands the origin of the Greco-Roman economy of the first millennium B.C.E., particularly its monetary and market structure, has a direct bearing on how one understands our own today. The old Aristotelian idea that money arose out of the barter system because guaranteed metallic value facilitated and objectified exchange has lost ground recently. It appears more convincing that the concept of private property stood at the beginning of what we now call Western civilization, that is, Greco-Roman society, and that the social and legal orders were intimately associated with it. From its start the monetary system presupposed a high degree of abstraction and numerical quantification, and this in turn rested on a basic societal shift away from an orientation that was highly mythical in character to one that was less so.

It is most plausible that abstract notions of right, measurable, and divisible performance and production and the market as a place for the exchange of surplus production originated together with private property. It seems reasonable to suppose that a sense for quantifiable signs evolved with this objectification of business. The minted coin became the expression of this process.

Recent research has demonstrated that, after an intermediate state of Mycenean-type cultures and economies, the Mediterranean economies of the first millennium B.C.E. were born out of catastrophes and governed by the fear of future disasters, which later were still remembered as the chaos that threatened both the legal and economic order of society.[12] Individuals who had fled natural catastrophes congregated together and formed communities, not from a feeling of solidarity but out of common

---

12. Gunnar Heinsohn ("Privates Grundeigentum, patriachalische Monogamie und Geldwirtschaftliche Produktion: Eine sozialtheoretische Rekonstruktion zur Antike" [Ph.D. diss., Bremen, 1983], 45–57, speaks of major natural disasters in the early centuries of the first millennium B.C.E. and their immediate social consequences for matrilineal tribes. In the words of the English abstract attached to his book (278–79): "Among archaeologists the consensus is growing that the Mycenean tribute economy collapsed in huge natural catastrophes whose causes are disputed. At the same time they agree that the origin in the 8th century B.C.E. of civilization in the polis with individual male ownership cannot so far be explained satisfactorily. In proving that Mycenae was not destroyed in the 13th/12th centuries but in the 8th century B.C.E. we can show that serfs (of the Romulus type) successfully rebelled against their masters who had become destabilized through catastrophes and that—probably aided by tribesmen who had also become uprooted by the catastrophes, but also by noble deserters of the Theseus type—they divided up the feudal estates amongst themselves in order to prevent people from their own ranks rising and becoming new overlords."

interest. These communities began as democracies of shared penury. The persons gathered agreed upon equal shares of land as their private property, forming the basis of the new form of patriarchal economy, that of the city-state.[13] Fear of overindebtedness and a return to poverty remained inherent threats. Gaining and maintaining stock and liquidity through labor beyond sustenance-work were the means of protecting oneself against unforeseeable risks. One began with one's own labor, then that of family members, debtors, and slaves. It was beneficial and created additional security to lend one's own assets to other citizens who had had bad luck. This lending against security and credit promised better liquidity in times of future adversity. It lowered the costs of maintaining stock in the form of natural goods and provided additional protection. Thus the risk of holding stock and maintaining liquidity decreased, and one gained assets through the interest one placed on debtors' returns.[14]

Catastrophe and credit, protection and promise, and many more terms to be used here intimate that for ancient culture and society the divine was consistently in the picture. Debts and contracts called for witnesses and sanctions, all divine prerogatives. Temples became involved rather early as trusted institutions. Their trust became quite real in terms of testifying, depositing, crediting, and collecting interest. The priests witnessed and certified the contracting and trading of debts; they wrote and executed obligations against fees and interest. These obligations were traded beyond the original parties and provided profit to the temple and further traders involved. Thus the temple became a bank, and money became an abstraction, depersonalized and dematerialized.[15]

---

13. See ibid., 53–100. In the words of his abstract: "This [the dividing up of the feudal estates] is the origin of private ownership, with the individual free peasant who initially can at best feed one wife and therefore has to forego polygamy, which had been the due of the chiefs and feudal lords, in favor of monogamy."

14. See ibid., 113–56. He summarizes on 278: "The abolition of the collective security provided by tribe and estate forces the private owner who now suffers from an individualized existential risk—in a way he is his own debtor—to increase his output in order to obtain a security stock as liquidity to cover himself against unforeseeably large risks. This stock is at the same time a potential lendable asset against a premium whose size is measured according to the assessment of the existential risk when it is lent to others—or oneself, if a private owner is not successful in obtaining a liquidity stock he has to ask for credit in an emergency. This the successful stockholder is happy to grant as it relieves him from the expense incurred in caring for his reserves of animals or grain. But he does not want to lose the security for which he has after all laid in this stock." For Heinsohn, this sequence of developments accounts for the origin of debt bondage, which he describes as "the preliminary stage of interest." The latter is coming about as a replacement of debt bondage after its revolutionary abolition (e.g., in Athens under Solon).

15. The idea of the cultic origin of money has been particularly emphasized and developed by Bernhard Laum. He claims that money originated as a substitute for produce and

Temples usually were not private property but were jointly owned by the gods themselves and the respective cities. For these stored and traded debts and the interest growing out of them, people needed legalized and nominalized tender. Minted coinage was born, guaranteed by the gods and the cities, symbols of their power and protection and of the value they guaranteed. This value, symbolized by the coins but represented also by the written obligations behind them, was not economic alone but was social, political, and religious as well.

The accumulated interest called for the production and exchange of goods—that is, for commodities—and for a market in which to trade and redeem them. Performance, achievement-oriented surplus, production, division of labor, and trade that transcended local boundaries came into being, stimulated, guided, and guarded by deity and state alike.[16]

It is highly significant that the political theology and the reforms of Augustus and his successors (as well as such eastern Mediterranean philosophers and theologians as Plutarch) reemphasized Theseus, Romulus, Aeneas, and other founding figures of Greek and Roman urban societies. Virgil, who was so influential in the evolution of Roman political theology of the first centuries B.C.E., paid increasing attention to Hesiod, an author on whom Gunnar Heinsohn has drawn heavily in his reconstruction of the origin and development of an economy based on

---

animals as sacrificial gifts. He does not see the interplay between private property, debt, security/interest/obligation and money, nor the role of temples. He leaves out entirely the advanced Mediterranean economy of classical and Hellenistic times.

16. See Heinsohn, "Privates Grundeigentum," 157–95. His summary of this reads as follows: "If now [after the abolition of debt bondage] the creditor unexpectedly requires liquidity before the expiration of the credit, he can avoid a loss of substance by passing on his claim to the liquidity premium to the new provider of liquidity. Now this contract is active money.... The interest claim arising from the illiquidity of the creditor stands for goods that are not yet available, which now have to be produced—via surplus production—as commodities which constitute the market when they are redeemed. For the purpose of witnessing and executing the debtors' obligations as embodied in the bills of exchange, the temples generate banks, which receive considerable shares of the interest as a basis for their granting security on behalf of the creditors who become depositors. As this income in kind in turn demands high expenditure for its maintenance the banks eventually proceed to lending their property claims against interest in the form of depersonalized and denaturalized money" (279). Temples as the first banks and as ongoing banking enterprises remain in the picture even after the origin and growth of secular money institutions. The characteristics of the Mediterranean and Near Eastern economy, together with its evolution in the first millennium B.C.E. and beyond into the first four centuries C.E., are summarized by Heinsohn under the two chapter headings "Private Property and State, Individual Existential Risk and Storage of Liquidity, Credit and Debt Bondage, Interest and the Production of a Monetary Economy, Slavery and Coinage," and "Division of Classes, Division of Labor, Population Explosion and Depopulation" (my translation).

private property. The propagandistic intention was to make the social and economic traits personified in such figures a matter of public consciousness in Paul's own world.

2.3. Critical Omissions of Common Economic Motifs in Paul

Paul's failure to employ certain of these elements and characteristics of the Mediterranean economy in his discussion of the collection, given their wide currency, proves to be very striking. As I have pointed out, Paul makes every effort to avoid speaking of the collection as if it were a tax. However, for readers who knew of the tax Jews paid regularly to the temple in Jerusalem, this association would have been natural. Therefore, it would have been clear to them that Paul's skirting of this issue was an intentional oversight. Paul never allowed the Jerusalem temple to enter onto the stage, although he did play with the motif of a voluntary gift for the temple (2 Cor 9:15). If for no other reason than it was the central edifice in the Judean capital, one would have expected Paul to refer to the temple in speaking of the Jerusalem collection, yet he made no mention of it.

The same reticence holds true in his use of the concept of the pilgrimage of the peoples. He merely alludes to it, never quotes it in full. The biblical and Jewish expressions of this motif focus, if not on the temple itself, at least on Mount Zion, that is, the center of Israelite and Jewish sacrificial worship. Paul's silence on this idea of a cultic center, therefore, becomes telling. Paul almost appears to tease when he constantly plays with different variations on the theme of sacrifice. But it is always *spiritual* sacrifice; he keeps out the idea of real sacrifice at the temple completely.

Given the ancient financial and economic structures described, references to debts and obligations as well as to their redemption would only be natural. The customary understanding of Paul's doctrine of justification even inserts metaphors to that effect into the Pauline language and interpretation—against the evidence of the texts.[17] In keeping with this pattern Paul does not mention how the money he wants collected is to be produced. Labor and production would normally be associated with a structure that was built on debit and credit. Contrary to its claims to bank on trust, this system was not built on confidence and faith but rather on distrust, diffidence, disbelief, debt, and obligation, behind all of which

---

17. The only exception is in the context of Paul's discussion of the collection in Rom 15:27, where the Gentiles are described as debtors to the Jerusalem church. But here the usual creditor-debtor relationship is turned on its head; the rich are debtors to the poor.

lurked anxiety and fear. Paul's message offers freedom from all of these fetters. Why, then, should he allow such language to enter into the argument again and to corrupt his encouraging reflections on the collection? Paul's meditations on justification, which are predominantly of a positive nature, speak more of freedom for than freedom from.

As we have seen, in speaking of the collection Paul espoused a negative attitude toward the concept of self and toward the adoration of the private, privatization, and private property. In 1 Cor 16:2, personal gain is mentioned only as something to be set aside to facilitate the collection for others. There is no mention of either calculations (as to proceeds, investment, or possible quantifiable yields) or of order or law in Paul's discussion, even though all these terms belonged to the ancient market economy, especially in its contemporary Roman form.[18]

The many participants in Paul's collection, most of them urban people accustomed to the market economy and its terminology, must have noticed these omissions. Two texts that deal with the issue of collection, one for Jerusalem (Gal 2:1–10) and one for Paul (Phil 4:10–16), show that Paul knew the vocabulary of business language. The end of 2 Cor 8 proves that Paul did not shy away from down-to-earth matters of organization if he were so inclined. Thus Paul's reticence to employ the language of the market economy must have had a purpose.

2.4. The "Trust" Structure of Ancient Economic Mobility and Monetary Circulation

2.4.1. In the Mediterranean World

There is more to the interplay of religion and economics in Paul's times than the phenomena described above. It is certain that members of the Hellenistic-Jewish Diaspora, like Paul, knew such documents as 1 and 2 Maccabees. The story of Heliodorus in 2 Macc 3 and 4 certainly supports the argument made earlier that temples were banks of deposit and served as a sort of savings and loan association. The legend of the angel's intervention during the attempted temple robbery gives credence to the belief held worldwide that the gods would safeguard not only the temples but also the deposits held there. Not only the priests but also creditors, debtors, and traders depended on this protection.

---

18. Concerning the origin and character of the social and economic concept of order, Heinsohn has made very intriguing observations and suggestions.

This credibility of the temples' financial role and economic importance reached far beyond the deposits and the financial business transacted in the local temples. The temples as "credit" institutions protected commerce beyond the city precincts, and they supported and guarded the mobility of merchants, creditors, and debtors in international trade. These people did not confine themselves to the places and persons with whom they had credit. They did not stop at the boundaries of the Mediterranean or even at the outermost reaches of the Hellenistic culture. Commerce and trade had become worldwide, with black, brown, and yellow faces appearing on Mediterranean markets, and with Mediterranean tongues being heard on sea and land routes extending deep into Asia, the northern countries, and Africa.

Who protected these people when they traveled that far? Who else but their gods, who not only sailed with them but also sailed in front of them. Mutual recognition of cults and the discovery of one's own god or goddess in a foreign deity enabled a major worldwide credit structure. Money as a mobile, circulatory agent followed this development. One soon learned that the value of the currency and circulation in the markets were mutually dependent, although occasional inflations, often state manipulated, from time to time added to that flow.

The divine protecting presence with these attempts to transcend human boundaries was possible for the ancient mind because of the vertical connection between the gods and humans. The horizontal economic circulation would remain stable only if this connection with the heavenly forces held. One of the most important forms of this interplay is described in the contractual, as well as religious, formula *do ut des,* "I give in order that you give."[19] This formula did not function in only one direction; it did not simply flow from humans to gods (as the common Christian caricature of pagan religion wants it), or merely from god to humanity (as Christians claimed of their own religion). Rather, it worked both ways for Christian, pagan, and Jewish religions alike.

This interchange could be described as a circle or, better yet, a cycle. It could be expressed by two Greek puns: the divine gift and grace as χάρις correlate with εὐχαριστία (gratitude), and the divine glory as δόξα with δοξολογία (glorification). The character and range of this correlation have been demonstrated in my book on the collection.[20]

This cycle was one of mutual benefit and growth. The stronger ones, the gods, gave of their strength to the weaker ones, the humans. These

---

19. The idiom is often attributed to Cicero, but it is much older.
20. Dieter Georgi, *Remembering the Poor: The History of Paul's Collection for Jerusalem* (Nashville: Abingdon, 1992), 102–4, 107–9, and 138–40.

returned the divine gifts through worship in the form of thanksgiving and glorification. The continuation of the strength and richness of the gods, their ability to give more and more, depended on this multiplied feedback from the human, the poorer side in this exchange.

The Hellenistic mind would associate especially the goddess Tyche with this cycle, the deity distinguished by her bountiful gifts. Tyche was more than mere chance or happenstance; she was not simply capricious. Her concerns went beyond individual luck and advantage. Tyche featured prominently as constructive ability, empowerment, promise, and guidance in an increasingly urbanized world. She was associated with the city goddesses, each of whom was seen as her manifestation, the divine essence of the community of each city. The goddess Tyche was the positive potential of the community; the city goddess was the embodiment of the Tyche's interest in constructive welfare and chance.

2.4.2. Paul's Critical Adaptation of This "Trust" Structure in His Concept of Spiritual Worship

I have argued that Paul's concept of grace and gift in 2 Cor 8–9 is not far removed from these associations and includes even the concept of divine growth through increased human thanksgiving and glorification. It should be remembered in this context that for the Hellenistic social mind the guidance and protection of the gods were not confined to individuals but extended to the community at large. This would certainly entail the economy of the πόλις, to the extent that Tyche would relate to the economic well-being of the city and its citizens. I have shown elsewhere that the ancient reader would associate the concept of τύχη with Paul's concept of χάρις.[21] This is all the more the case with the collection because here financial motifs enter the picture from the outset. Successful trade and God-given gain were ascribed to Tyche and Hermes, especially in their Roman forms of Fortuna and Mercury. The latter for Hellenistic-Roman culture was the journeying god who guided and protected merchants and other travelers, among them pilgrims and missionaries.

In 2 Cor 8 and 9 the original contractual purpose of the collection for Jerusalem has receded into the background. The collection has now been transformed into a paradigm for ecumenical communal exchange in the form of a financial communication. This is all the more important because it evidences a dialogue Paul had engaged in with the society of his day

---

21. Dieter Georgi, "Reflections of a New Testament Scholar on Plutarch's Tractates 'De Alexandri Magni Fortuna aut Virtute,'" in *The Future of Early Christianity: Essays in Honor of Helmut Koester* (ed. Birger A. Pearson; Minneapolis: Fortress, 1991), 20–34.

and its economic structures. In these critical socioreligious reflections, continuously furthered in debates with friends and opponents, the issues of performance and power made their way even more to the fore than in Paul's earlier texts. These were issues that pertained to the competitive market economy and to the religious forces that sustained it. In the discussion that the fragments of 2 Corinthians represents, the Pauline understanding of christology and justification by Christ gains its final form. It is then laid out in the Epistle to the Romans, to which the information on the collection forms the conclusion. This letter was intended as a new start but in the end became the final farewell and testament of the propagator of justification by Christ, by grace, and thus by trust alone.

In the collection, a cycle of grace occurs in which money is the expression and means of a process that moves human hearts and draws people together. Thus the mobility and ready exchange of money become a manifestation of the power and essence of the Christ movement as a missionary phenomenon. The collection turns into a demonstration of the interplay of divine gift and human gratitude. This is not, however, abstract. Both the gift and gratitude are from and to real people, for the benefit of both. Money becomes a concrete expression of χάρις in that the personal gifts, the χαρίσματα of the givers move toward the χαρίσματα, the gifts, of the recipients. Χάρις and χαρίσματα are not on the side of the givers alone but on that of the recipients as well, with divine grace providing a bridge back and forth. In this spirit 1 Cor 16:2 uses the concept of a graduated voluntary contribution related to one's prosperity, which assumes equity not of quantity but of quality.

Paul presupposes a material cycle that understands δόξα (glory and splendor) and χάρις (grace and gift) as substances of light. Paul uses the religious dimension of the Hellenistic economy, the vertical circulation described above, to interpret the concept of money flow in a more religious way. In this interpretation he redirects and adds the vertical cycle (god-human-god-human, etc.) to the horizontal one, into which he integrates the incarnate deity, as the quote from the traditional formula in 2 Cor 8:9 proves.[22]

---

22. Here I differ greatly with my friend Karl-Josef Kuschel, who on 379–82 of *Geboren vor aller Zeit: Der Streit um Christi Ursprung* (Munich: Piper, 1990) thoroughly demythologizes 2 Cor 8:9. He explains the richness of God's agent here as the spiritual riches of the historical person Jesus of Nazareth. This is in line with Kuschel's general attempt to downplay the importance, often even the existence, of mythological language in the New Testament. The very realistic context in which 2 Cor 8:9 speaks of actual money flow contradicts Kuschel's attempt at spiritualization. In his interpretation of 2 Cor 8:9 the cross of Christ must come necessarily into a moralizing light, which contradicts all references to the cross in Paul. I have demonstrated the fact that Paul's understanding of the spiritual has to be seen according to

The collection of funds for Jerusalem in Paul's interpretation transforms the idea of an economy geared toward growth of production and profit, as the Hellenistic economy already was. The Hellenistic market economy obviously used interest as a major instrument of growth. Paul instead presupposes the biblical prohibition of interest (Exod 22:24; Lev 25:36–27), now extended to everyone. Increase of wealth for him needs to be common wealth. The money collected for Jerusalem grows also, but into a universal divine worship. The money involved becomes a social force, a gift from community to community. It is intended to forge the vitality of the community to which it is given as well as the health of the community donating. Here obedience and simple kindness are blended. In this process the subjugation of the universe under the Rich One who had become poor has begun, and the unification of humanity has been initiated.

This sharing becomes a manifestation of the body of Christ, the community of the justified godless and poor ones who have become rich and who are living under the leadership of the one who has become impoverished and weak. A spiritual movement takes place from God to the churches, back and forth among them, and then back to God. In so doing, the cultic and sacred are replaced by an active ecumenical partnership, which includes also economic sharing.

Spiritual worship means for Paul the multipersonal, multifaceted, and multidimensional life of a community that understands itself as a model society contrasting and redeeming the society around it. The ideas of the circulation of money and of economic growth have been exchanged for the circulation and growth of the grace of God among people, even the growth of Godself for the benefit of all humans. This greatly enlarged picture has absorbed concepts of personal potential and action, of interest and of profit and of a worldwide net of markets.

Paul's presupposition is that creation and created life originate in and are maintained by grace, so thanksgiving, the returning of grace, is called for. The collection in 2 Cor 9:1 is termed a blessing, which is understood as a bountiful yield, as working capital. Its interest and profit consist most of all in the responses, the blessings of the beneficiary party and the enrichment of the communal relationship of givers and recipients. The gift of blessing creates, maintains, and enlarges the community.

This process is associated with love, the atmosphere of Christ's body, the global realm of Christ. In this atmosphere the persons giving are

---

the ancient perspective, which does not exclude mythical ideas of substance but rather incorporates them.

taken over by grace, which makes them realize that in giving they are in fact being given to. Rather than depleting their own stocks, their treasure boxes are filled as a result of their giving to others. In this vision, magnanimity proves to be more economical than miserliness.

2.5. Social Aspects of Ancient Economic and Monetary Relations

2.5.1. Righteousness and Its Equivalents as Accompaniment of Economic and Monetary Relations

Quite in accord with this, although not without precedent in the ancient world, Paul introduces in 2 Cor 8:14–15 the term ἰσότης ("equity/equality"), a concept highly esteemed in Hellenistic culture. For many Hellenistic readers this would be entirely appropriate in a discussion pertaining to finances. The adage "Money is the great equalizer" was not unknown either, although not in the same wording.[23] The tendency of Paul is to exploit the dimensions of the synonymity of equity, equality, righteousness, and justice and to explore critically the alleged equalizing power of money. He wants to move beyond the legal and economic equality that Hellenistic culture and its market-oriented society represented. Theoretically, for Hellenistic culture equity and equality as synonyms of righteousness and justice were the basis and moving force of society. For Paul righteousness precedes equity and equality. However, in keeping with his wisdom background, Paul understands righteousness as efficacious divine power. It brings about equity and equality. For Paul ἰσότης is a divine force among humans, making them equal "from equity (as divine potency of efficaciousness) to equality (as human experience, legal, social, and economic reality)," as the statement in 2 Cor 8:13–14 could be abbreviated in a pointed way.

In this context money does not rob debtors of their integrity and identity. On the contrary, both haves and have-nots possess and owe something in this interaction to the other party. In this positive and constructive capacity money does not move external things alone but also the inner life of persons, and it is fed back from the beneficiary to the

---

23. It is most often stated cynically, as for instance in the proverbial expression in Ovid's *Amores* 3.8.55: "Dat census honores" ("Income assessed by the census doles out honors"; compare *Fasti* 1.217). The whole poem complains that wealth establishes esteem and power across the board, without regard for differences of class, status, talent, or merit. Petronius's *Satyricon* pokes fun at the freedman Trimalchio, who, because of his wealth, believes in his equality with the freeborn, especially the senatorial and equestrian class.

benefactor, not as an expression of self-humiliation but as a demonstration and experience of equality. In this process money truly becomes an equalizing agent, a democratizing instrument.

For Paul this kind of monetary momentum is not wishful thinking; he sees it happen in space and time—"at the present time"—in the actual collection activities of people he knows and to whom he relates. The collection is being undertaken for certain partners he knows well. He wants the delegates to meet them, so that personal intimacy as an integral part of a universal community can increase.

The discussion of equity and equality in Paul is much less abstract than its counterpart in Aristotle, as Paul's communities are more concrete than the philosopher's from Stagira, who was never allowed to become a citizen of Athens, the city he lived in and admired so much. Paul's arguments, activities, and suggestions stem from communal praxis and move therein. According to Paul's concept of communal equity and equality, money no longer serves as a differentiating, distinguishing, isolating, and expropriating agent. It does not segregate people from one another or separate them from their economic means, as if the latter were capable of operating independently, abstracted from human brains and hearts.

The exchange, to which money is intimately related and by means of which it has its life, is an exchange among persons as equals and peers. Redemption does not belong at the end of a creditor-debtor relationship. It is the basis of all human solidarity, where people are related in their shared poverty, that is, their common godlessness. Redemption is the engagement of the Rich One who became poor (2 Cor 8:9) in order to make all humans rich—namely, all those who share in the common poverty—not the believers alone but all of humanity. Paul presupposes universal poverty and universal redemption. Global equalization is in view, a sweeping exchange and settlement with transpartisan, transemotional, rational, as it were objective, features—elements normally associated with coined money and its proper use.

As I wrote my study on the collection of Paul, I did not deal with the biblical passages on the Sabbatical and the Jubilee Years as possible backgrounds to Paul's thinking while he composed 2 Cor 8 and 9.[24] Today's global discussions about large-scale settlements of debts have brought actuality and relevance to these biblical ideas. They may have been at the back of Paul's mind. An analogy to these biblical motifs of restitution,

---

24. The Sabbatical Year appears in Exod 21:1–11; 23:10–11; Lev 25:1–7, 18–22; Deut 15:1–18; see further Ben Zion Wacholder, "Sabbatical Year," *IDBSup*, 762–63. The Jubilee Year appears in Lev 25:8–17, 23–28, 47–55; see further Adrianus van Selms, "Jubilee, Year of," *IDBSup*, 496–98.

minus their financial aspects, is found in the rather concrete Roman notion of the secular cycles of 110 years or so. Paul must have experienced once under Claudius's principate the secular games that celebrated the official revolutionary restitution and renewal of the Roman Empire and its institutions. In a contemporary theological and ethical reflection on Paul's collection, these analogies have to be brought into play. They demonstrate how much general institutional renewal was thinkable in Paul's time, and they correspond well to ideas and phenomena described in this study and these essays.

Shared penury is not only at the origin of private property. Common experience and wisdom say that each individual starts and ends life penniless. We know that relentless accumulation of money and investments merely into property and goods is deadly, suicidal, at the very least from a social point of view, but most probably also from an economic one. Staggering inequity that moves fatalistically toward the insolvency of one party, blocking countermoves from that party or any outsider, is humanly and politically bankrupt. This is particularly true in a democratic society. It appears also economically unwise; the end of buyers and competitors would be the end of the market.

Equalization of debts is in line with Paul's notions of divine *grace*, the spiritual worship he sees set in motion and the universal equality he presupposes and finds brought about by grace. The regularity of the intervals of seven (Sabbatical Year), forty-nine (Jubilee Year), or 110 years (Roman secular cycle) is more rational than infrequently and erratically arranged monetary shake-ups, currency reforms, or international debt settlements of recent vintage.

2.5.2. Utopian Dimensions of Economic and Monetary Relations

It is obvious that money in the Pauline texts on the collection possesses utopian dimensions. "Remembering the poor" refers first of all to the eschatological title and privilege the early church in Jerusalem prided itself on and for which it was respected. Also in the context of economy and money, the projection into the future, and the anticipation of it, are customary; in John Maynard Keynes's words, "Money connects with the future."[25] Money always has been associated with hopes for better times, individually and collectively. Without hopes there would be no stock market, and these hopes are very often literally speculative. To reflect upon the utopian aspects of the stock market would be as appropriate as a discussion about the eschatological dimensions of capitalism. There is

---

25. *A Treatise on Money* (London: Royal Economic Society, 1930), 3.

always a "not yet" directly beneath the stock market's surface. An "it will definitely improve in the future" is immediately invoked as soon as structural difficulties of the market show. The messianism of the free market blows its horn the most in times of economic crisis, such as recessions or worse, more easily of course if it is someone else's crisis.

In the Pauline texts and activities, the money to be collected for Jerusalem was viewed first as a means of "remembering the poor," that is, the church in Jerusalem as the avant-garde of God's new age. That meant one stood not for oneself alone but anticipated the people of the new age, who would consist of the people of God restored and all pagan peoples gathered around. The money was to be used to give the Jerusalem Jesus community financial backing in its attempt to achieve a reasonable degree of economic security for its strenuous witness, needed most of all for those members who were not yet settled and/or were unemployed.

As the collection evolved independently on Paul's own mission field, it was transformed into a more general paradigm. Expressed in the traditional vocabulary of biblical scholarship and contemporary theology, as used also in my original study on the collection, Paul's concepts and terminology concerning the collection remain "eschatological" But over against the traditional and prevailing contemporary scholarly use of the term *eschatological*, it has to be stated that eschatology and eschatological issues included tangible utopian dimensions and aspects. Eschatology did not relate solely to the individual; on the contrary, biblical and Jewish eschatology developed collective social visions. This collective perception could be found also in pagan eschatology, which was very much alive in Hellenistic culture, even more in its Roman form. Eschatological awareness had increased since the time of Augustus and was particularly active in the latter part of Claudius's and during Nero's principates.

Alexander's empire had been a creation and vivid manifestation of intensive utopian thought and activity.[26] This remained the case with new variations under Alexander's successors: under Hannibal as well as his Roman enemies; the various Mithradates; and among the many revolutionaries of the third to first centuries B.C.E. and C.E. Each of these persons stepped easily into that visionary pattern and attempted to bring to life a social utopia. Jewish utopias, literary and political, have to be seen within that concert as well, both in the Diaspora and in Palestine, which was part of the Hellenistic world culture.

---

26. Alexander's pursuits and achievement were still seen in this way long after his death. Plutarch's various reflections on Alexander give evidence of this in the latter part of the first century C.E.

2.5.3. Justification of the Poor Ones as Concrete Utopian Praxis

It has been a fatal side of much of Protestant exegesis that the rational as well as utopian elements of Paul's understanding of justification have been weakened or even covered up. As Paul transforms his understanding of justification into a praxis and theory of the collection, the climate of a pragmatic utopia becomes apparent. In the terminology of established Reformation theology, Paul's reflections on the collection and on money, if brought out in their full historical meaning, qualify for the verdict of "enthusiasm" as it was leveled against revolting peasants, anabaptists, and spiritualists.

In fact, any attempt to cast views and perspectives of faith directly into the vision of a real communal way of life, not governed and controlled directly or indirectly by state authorities or state-established church bodies, was counted by the Reformers among the heresy of enthusiasm. However, this fear of religious enthusiasm made much of Protestantism blind to all kinds of enthusiastic ventures that quickly arose in secular disguise, capitalism among them. The churches of the Reformation failed to develop practical and theoretical instruments with which to approach critically the apparent messianism of the capitalist idea and practice, as they grew further in the post-Reformation period. The church's denunciation of interest as usury did not help and was given up rather quickly.

The justification of all humans as thoroughly impoverished ones is a reasonable proposition for Paul, a basis for understanding and changing the world and humanity. In 2 Cor 9 Paul stresses the proximity of justification and reason. As justification is his point of departure for structuring true community as a model society, he perceives of this new society as a more reasonable one. This rationality does not establish distance of viewers and operators from people and things. The concept of the rational for Paul coincides with the concern and engagement of God as well as the members of the community for others.

Paul argues emphatically for a God engaged in the human demise and impoverishment; Paul fights against a distant and unengaged deity. The deficiency of the pagan deities in his eyes would not be that they were too human but that they were too little involved in the human dilemma. Justification is not important merely between God and the individual but comes about and manifests itself in the interrelatedness of God, the world, and all humanity.

God's righteousness is the origin of human righteousness, but the latter is allowed to reflect and represent the former in full. This righteousness mirroring God's own is not a pious possession of the individual. It is the liberty of integrated human beings, incorporated into a body of justifying grace and love. This is a free space where rights, personhood, and communal relations are given, and mutual assistance exists in accordance with God and God's self-impoverishing agent. The intent is to embrace the entire human family by this concord. The intermediate realization of this is supposed to happen in the church, the model society that is charged with a realistic anticipation of that nonvoracious/mutually supportive humanity.

This justifying grace creates wise and reasonable, in a word good, praxis, in which personhood and the identity of persons is formed through relatedness and concern for others. This praxis is not to be confused with the treadmill tug and drudgery or with money hunting either. It is giving instead of gaining, thanks instead of interest, confidence instead of credit, trust instead of security, community instead of market, spiritual worship instead of temple cult, charisma instead of property. This praxis avoids the power that grows out of fear and that leads to exploitation and violence. Instead, this praxis affirms the power of weakness and poverty because such power allows for authentic engagement, reliable yield, and true growth. A multiplication of thanksgivings follows from this and will engage people further in this expression of gratitude. This will create radiating strength. This praxis will instigate and invigorate truly humane—relational, ethical, and consciously political—elements in the economy and will make them transparent.

The self is no longer the entity that is capable of giving and securing freedom through self-liberating activity. Personal freedom is even less enhanced through acquisition, holding, and accumulation of property with the false hope of the ultimate security of the self—not only suicide but also the death of the economy. Rather, freedom is the experience of liberation from the self. The isolated individual and his or her private property are governed by the fear of indebtedness and thus of spiraling poverty, with no security left. For Paul freedom is liberty from necessity and hurt. It is the diametrical opposite of the Stoic ideal of *autarky*, self-sufficiency. Autarky means, for Paul, the simplicity of an open, trusting, and faithful heart. Only this liberation enables reasonable deliberation, free will, and free decision. Only this freedom releases the person from the necessity of being obsessed with self-concern. In this way God bestows power and freedom for an active life in a free community.

The concepts of private property and private ownership find no place at all in Paul, nor do the accompanying notions of credit, debt, obligation, interest, dividend, profit, market, temple, or bank. Why? Because they presuppose and foster fear of catastrophes, and through fear they lead to estrangement, expropriation, and exploitation—false security indeed.

From Paul's viewpoint money does not create, but it stimulates, facilitates, and sets in motion the process of thanksgiving. It has been shown that Paul has a concept of growth, too, and that he sees money as an expression of such growth. However, he views it always in the context of the return of divine grace, mediated through χαρίσματα and accumulated thanksgiving. Thus Paul locates growth in the context of shared righteousness, the mutual respect for equality and integrity.

2.5.4. Can Any Money Be Just?

Is there anything like money that is just?[27] The dream that there could be just money if there could be neutral money—that is, indifferent money—has been around for a long time. But every effort to bring this about has failed. Cash is never cold or indifferent; it is always involved in the heat of human exchange and gains temperature in that exchange. Attempts on the part of governments to tame and control tightly what they mint, print, and issue have not succeeded either. Money, indeed, is an intimate friend of the market. Money has regulated the market, has always even been part of the market. Money is a trading object, the market's most prominent expression. Does the solution lie in leaving money and the market to their own devices?

Does the market possess its own independent laws? There is sufficient evidence that money and market bend given laws of society if left unchecked. They become a law unto themselves. However, money and the market are not only means of the economy but are also means of communication within a community and between communities that all need to be fair and just. Money and market are creations of the community and have to remain the community's children if they want to survive and flourish. Behind all financial credit there must be communal trust, and this must come from a broader base than the local community. Already the Hellenistic-Roman economy had learned that such communal trust had to occur on an international scale. The economy is bound to fail if it is dictated from any side (private, group, or state), because it will have lost its communal authenticity and force. The community and the market are not identical; the community has to remain above the market, all the more the international community above the international market.

---

27. This question is dealt with by Wilhelm Gerloff, *Geld und Gesellschaft* (Frankfurter Wissenschaftliche Beiträge; Kulturwissenschaftliche Reihe 9; Frankfurt am Main: Klostermann, 1952), 214–75, esp. 214–36. Gerloff reminds us that Aristotle also dealt with this issue, though not with the same terminology.

Accordingly, money and market have to remain expressions of the community's basic right and its manifestation in communal laws. This right will dissever its righting power if it fails to remain communal. Then it is no longer everyone's right but that which belongs to some people, to some groups, or to some institutions in particular. If the creditor has a prerogative over the debtor, or vice versa, the rights of each suffer. The laborer must not be cheated of his or her wages, nor the saver or investor of his or her savings or investments, provided that these entitlements are fair and just according to the basic right that joins all members of the community equally, and in a world market that must include the farthest and lowliest as integral peers. These persons must have equal standing. Their identity and integrity must be respected by the world economy fairly and justly.

It has often been said that money is a means of social communication. But is it as yet in the authentic sense of social? Does it not reward the rich and powerful more, while continuously disappointing the poor and weak? There is doubtless more to the value of money than its nominal or market value, more to it than its buying power. The presence or absence of money increases or decreases the social value and standing of persons; it increases or decreases their social acceptability and importance. This relates also to the subjective feeling of value that people have of themselves. Thus their identity and integrity are affected. Can it be in the true interest of a community that pauperization occurs in its midst? that any one of its members loses in reality her or his personal rights and standing through loss or lack of monetary means? Can the community suffer that because of financial or economic insufficiency certain members fall short of rights and potentials others maintain? Is that just "too bad" for those persons or groups? Is it not rather "too bad" for a community that permits this to happen without immediate intervention?

There is no indifferent or cold money, but what is its true warmth? Is it that of greed or that of caring? For Paul the answer is clear: investment in the hope of and for the deficient ones is the truly warm money. Paul returns to the poor as the target of the collection in Rom 15. This proves that in the interim the poor ones have remained the foil of Paul's reflections on the money flow. This raises the question of whether the ability to discover and respect the dignity and integrity of the poor, their gift and witness to the society, is not for him the crucial economic issue.

2.5.5. The Poor Ones as the Heart of the Wisdom of a Just and Humane Economy

In Rom 15:26 Paul returns once again to the issue of poverty. It has been demonstrated that there the economic side of poverty is more directly emphasized than in Gal 2:10. The collection is now meant "for the poor ones among the saints in Jerusalem." In all probability, heavy investment in the creation and maintenance of the economic stability of the Christ community in Jerusalem remains the direct financial objective of the collection, certainly with the distribution and use of the funds left to the discretion of the recipients. Some real estate and building projects for the meeting purposes of the Christ community in Jerusalem and their guests may be in the picture as well, but they are certainly not the primary goal. The main focus is on the economically impoverished ones.

It would be wrong to presume that the poor are now regarded by Paul as merely deficient—social and economic debris, as it were—thus at best objects of the condescending charitable activity of those better off. On the contrary, whereas the powerful monetary contribution of the Diaspora churches in Rom 15:27 is reckoned among "the fleshly things," and as such represents the weak and ephemeral matters of a passing world, the poor ones among the Jesus believers in Jerusalem are taken as representative of "the spiritual things" Jerusalem has to offer. It is primarily the poor ones who stand for these spiritual things. Paul's argument about the exchange of the fleshly against the spiritual is taken from the rules of religious competition, more precisely from the rules of the religious market, a rather important sector in the wider Hellenistic market economy. The outcome of this critical interpretation and application of competitive market language is that Paul gives the poor ones higher market value.

On the basis of the generalizing reflections since the Epistle to the Galatians, this emphasis on the poor ones as embodying a more direct blend of an economic and theological issue makes sense. The poor in the Christ community of Jerusalem above all stand in place for the main gift of that church to the rest of the churches. They preserve the focus of the Easter witness on the word of the cross: the Rich One who had engaged himself for and among impoverished humanity (2 Cor 8:9). This is the dignity of the poor ones of Jerusalem. Since Paul has transformed the collection and the Jerusalem church into a general paradigm, this is true for the poor elsewhere, too. There is a gift, a witnessing quality in their lives, ideally but also practically, even economically. They point to poverty as the basis for human and societal existence; they remind the society of its constant fringe. They are a continuous reminder and a challenge to all who believe themselves to be removed from poverty, who might even have barricaded themselves into golden fortresses while boasting of their security. The witness of the poor testifies to the non-poor who want to flee their human condition with the help of money that they are no longer justified by Christ but by money and the power therein. Poor people, the disenfranchised, and all those at the margins of society give evidence against society's false pride placed in wealth and strength at the expense of others. The poor and disenfranchised, the marginal people, invoke the community's unfinished business. The poor and disenfranchised point to society's deficiencies and failures, identifying them not as mere oversights or individual failures but as systemic weaknesses and collective sins.

But the poor testify also more than any well-stocked bank to the potential, the gift, that is in the human not having, not possessing. There is first of all the sapiential insight that, contrary to the boast of the powerful, the ones who "can make do" with little prove more than the ones who "can do" with much. However, the poor point further to the redemptive engagement of Christ to whom humanity owes its survival. They herald the chances opened by that redemption. The poor call up the not-yet of society, the new vistas awaiting a community prepared to yield more power in order to gain more future. The poor ones challenge the sterility of a rich society, give it incentives to be imaginative and innovative with respect to new material investments and with regard to new spiritual engagements.

A community that turns first and foremost to its allegedly hopeless cases, to those who appear at the end of their rope materially, physically, socially, legally, psychologically, and spiritually, is clearly the more risk-conscious, the more courageous, imaginative, and inventive. It is the economically more stable and promising entity, setting up a model for the wider society to do likewise.

To discover the dignity and the charisma of the poor, the inflicted, and the disenfranchised, hearing and understanding their witness as that of individual persons and of groups, is about as difficult as understanding the scandal of the cross, which the poor resemble. Because the poor also share more intimately than others the power that is manifest in the cross of Christ, investing in the poor, empowering them, has as its consequence the true empowerment of those who seem more fortunate. The poor ones in biblical terms are not the rear guard of the past but the *avant-* of the future. Therefore, the call to invest in the poor ones represents the central, not the peripheral, concern for a market society that wants to be truly economical, a society that really desires to invest in the future.

16

BULTMANN WAS NOT FIRST:
JOSIAH ROYCE AS INTERPRETER OF PAUL

1. INTRODUCTION

Urban theology is not the business of an ivory tower, even less of professional specialization. It is first of all a matter of praxis, the praxis of everyone concerned. There is no doubt, though, that professional theologians can be conscious parts of that praxis, whether students or professors. The following two essays present two professors, one of philosophy and one of philosophy and theology, who were very conscious trespassers. They crossed not only lines between academic disciplines but also lines between academe and laity. Both were quite conscious of their own praxis and developed their philosophical and theological thought on the basis of their praxis consciously relating to their social situations.

The first, Josiah Royce, came from the countryside, out of the backwoods of the Rocky Mountains, but he very determinedly became a city person, first as a student in the area of Berkeley, California, later as a professor in the area of Boston, Massachusetts. One of his later and most influential students, George Mead, became as professor in Chicago a stimulating force not only in the new university there but also in the process of rebuilding Chicago after the great fire. Critically reflecting on

---

* This paper was initially given at a meeting of the Society of Biblical Literature in Chicago. Richard Hocking, retired professor at Emory University, an eminent authority on Royce and the son of the Royce student William Hocking, gave it the honor of a paper of response. This and the discussion at the meeting, which Charles Hartshorne joined also, contributed to a major improvement of this paper, which was again given at a faculty luncheon of Harvard Divinity School in the spring of 1982.

the California situation during and after the gold rush and the rather unlawful stealth of that state out of Mexican hands and debating such historical matters with eyewitnesses, Royce showed how community evolved out of chaos. Out of these observations and findings he developed concepts of proper association and of communal loyalty that he refined later on as professor of philosophy at Harvard University. He then tested them against the teachings of Paul and of John of the New Testament and presented his finds in lectures on "The Problem of Christianity," first of all not to an academic audience but to a lay audience in Boston, Massachusetts, later on to an audience of nonspecialists in Oxford, England. All this was not the common professorial attitude in those days.

In this essay I want to address issues that are at the heart of urban health in all cities of the globe that house universities, and most of them do. I wish to deal with several problems that endanger academic sanity today. There is first of all the result of the claimed need to specialize for the sake of saving and improving scholarship, namely, research that ends up with knowing more and more about less and less.

Second, we experience an increasingly apolitical turn of academic pursuits, a neutrality that is but the coverup of the university's turning more than ever into the handmaiden of oppression and imperialism. Nuclear insanity is the same blatant expression of a pervasive corrupt understanding of academic freedom that claims that what it can do it must do—and does, in fact, for whoever pays best.

Third, we face a worldwide defeatism of theologians with respect to the importance of their work for university and society at large. The ancient arrogance of the queen of the sciences is in danger of turning into the cowardice of a bumpkin who rushes for the protective back of whoever proves his lordship by showing the brightest colors of faddism.

Fourth, I try to prove that it can happen that amateurs may see better than specialists, in fact do anticipate major insights of the research of professional scholarship. This should not be news to scholars, because what is true research other than the ability to see anew, to become amateurs again or, in biblical terms, to become children again, thus overcoming the brainwashing and petrifaction of established academic pride. Irreverence, particularly against oneself, is an essential dimension of scholarship, but it is not cynical, instead adventurous, curious, and enjoying itself—despite all the encountered frustration.

2. SOME GENERAL REMARKS ON JOSIAH ROYCE

Let me now turn to a great companion of my American voyage, Josiah Royce. I got to know him by accident. My wife and I went through the catalogue and shelves of the San Rafael Public Library in Frank Lloyd Wright's marvelous civic building looking for books on California, the state we had chosen as our residence for the next years. I found among others a book simply titled *California* by an unknown author, J. Royce. We took it home. Looking through it back in San Anselmo, I discovered that I might not get from it too much contemporary information on the greatest state of this great union, but I found a fellow Hegelian who told me quite a bit about the beginning of the state of California. He did so in uncovering the manipulative myth of the Bear Flag state, a myth still surviving in 1966 and soon to be further implemented by a man called Ronald Reagan, a true successor of John Charles Fremont, whom Josiah Royce opposed so much. In reading about the California of the 1840s I also learned about the real America and about the fight of the real community against the corruption thereof. The theme of this paradigmatic book is still pursued in the last great work of this now-forgotten Harvard professor, *The Problem of Christianity*.[1]

His first strike is against an old sacred cow of bourgeois Christianity. The religion and theology of white people in the West have centered since the end of the seventeenth century, indeed since the Middle Ages, on the historical Jesus. This Jesus promised immediacy. He corresponded to the reigning individualism, especially to its Cartesian form among academically trained or influenced people. The historical Jesus seemed to give verifiable objectivity, and emphasis on Jesus of Nazareth also satisfied the strong antidoctrinal trend since the Enlightenment. The historical Jesus could please even the half-brother of rationalism, anti-intellectualism.[2]

It is usually held that the rediscovery of Jesus' eschatology by Johannes Weiss and Albert Schweitzer, the critical review of the life-of-Jesus research, and the analysis of the bias of the Gospel of Mark by William Wrede first shattered the confidence of the life-of-Jesus movement and its theology. Then, so it is believed, dialectical theology,

---

1. The community Royce is talking about is especially the urban community. Its nature, its growth, and potential decay, its deficiencies and strengths are elaborated upon. This makes Royce's work one on urban philosophy, more specifically one of urban philosophy of religion. The book *California* I speak of above is mostly about the growth, problems, and promises of the urban community in California. Modern communitarians fall far short of the depth and range of the communitarian philosophers Peirce and Royce.

2. The interest of white people in the historical Jesus is different from the concentration on Jesus by black people in the United States or by people in the Third World. In these contexts, the "I" vis-à-vis Jesus is absent. Instead, they make the community and Jesus merge and unite them with the people of the old covenant. The bourgeois interest in "historical objectivity" is lacking.

especially Bultmann, launched the fatal blow. The opposition that Bultmann's *History of the Synoptic Tradition* and his introductory statements in his *Theology of the New Testament* found in this country seemed to indicate that one saw in him the first theologian who wanted to remove the historical Jesus from the center of attention.

The first announcement of the death of the historical Jesus, however, came in 1913 from an American, Josiah Royce (1855–1916), when he delivered his Hibbert Lectures at the Manchester College in Oxford, England, his lectures on the problem of Christianity.[3] The first part of the lectures he had already delivered a few months earlier at the Lowell Institute in Boston.[4]

Royce reflects the frustration over the confusion and inconclusiveness of life-of-Jesus research as one could have gotten it also from Albert Schweitzer's *Quest of the Historical Jesus*. Royce betrays acquaintance with Hegelian (especially David Friedrich Strauß's) emphasis on the productivity of early Christian collective consciousness,[5] but Royce rightfully denies that this had a decisive influence on him.[6]

Royce can simply point to the textual fact that the majority of New Testament writings, not just Paul, show little or no interest in the earthly life and career of Jesus of Nazareth. He recognizes, moreover, that the Gospels, especially the Gospel of John, have a rather free attitude toward historical accuracy.

Royce uses Paul's writings as the basis for his discussion of the character of early Christianity. He is not deceived by the quantity of Paul's writings. He does not portray this apostle as an outstanding and thus isolated person but as representative for early Christianity, that is, in a role Paul presented himself in through style, content, and declared intent of his correspondence. Royce does allow for major initiatives by leading individuals (e.g., 1:184–85) but sees them embedded in communities. Their activities stem from, are conditioned by , and relate to the larger whole. Thus he breaks with the Protestant preoccupation with great personalities as the main objectives in the study of religion, culture, and society.

---

3. The lectures were published in the same year by Macmillan (New York). On Josiah Royce, see the comprehensive article by James Collins, "James Joyce: Analyst of Religion as Community," in *American Philosophy and the Future* (ed. Michael Novak; New York: Scribner, 1968), 193–218. Collins gives an extensive bibliography. See also Frank Oppenheim, *Royce's Voyage Down Under: A Journey of the Mind* (Lexington: University Press of Kentucky, 1980). The edition of *The Problem of Christianity* used below is the two-volume reprint (Chicago: Regnery, 1968).

4. For a lay audience of elderly women.

5. Which is in the background of Bultmann and Dibelius as well.

6. About the relationship of Jesus and Christ, read *Problem of Christianity*, 1:198–99.

Royce sees the Gospel of John in its reflection on the impact and influence of Jesus as rather close to the theology of Paul. Here Royce anticipates Bultmann's approach in the *Theology of the New Testament*, where Paul and John function as the two pillars of early Christian theology. Royce even claims that the Fourth Gospel supports the Pauline notion of the close interrelationship and interaction between the Christ and the community—basing this argument heavily on the farewell speeches in John's Gospel, especially on John 17 (1:206–13). It appears to me that Royce here has the edge over Ernst Käsemann.

Royce's explicit interest in christological problems, especially in the Trinitarian aspect and the two natures, is rather rare among his contemporaries, especially in theology. The contributions of theologians of the late nineteenth and early twentieth centuries to the christological discourse are at best weak—Karl Barth being the exception—mostly nonexistent. Royce, instead, stands in the tradition of Hegel, the greatest contributor to Trinitarian theology and Christology in the last 200 years, outdoing Karl Barth as well. But both issues, Trinitarian and christological, intimately relate to ecclesiology. For Royce, the community is the embodiment and expression, not only of the Christ, but also of the Trinitarian deity.

The traditional Christian doctrine of the two natures finds a very original translation, that of the two levels, the human nature actually meaning the level of the individual, the divine nature suggesting the collective level (1:164–79, 201–5). Both stay in an unmixed as well as undivided relationship. Although these doctrinal deliberations are no direct discussion of Pauline theology, they help to clarify the revelatory character of the future of Jesus Christ and the relationship between Christ and spirit, both as presented in Paul. The intimate connection between Christ's divinity and humanity and the Christian community is also of importance for Pauline theology. One could even argue with Royce that Paul contemplates the incorporating power of the divinity of Christ as spirit. In any case, Christology for Paul not only speaks about the impetus and divine cause of the new life and of the community but also renders the creative pattern for the community and the life of the individual within it. Thus, we have an interplay of Christology, ecclesiology, and anthropology (1:164–96).

Just like Paul in his concept of the body of Christ, Royce sees anthropological issues subordinated to the community (quite similarly to Paul in 1 Cor 6:12–17). The individual does not constitute the community, but the community reconstitutes the individual. In and through the community, the individual finds his or her true identity.

3. HERMENEUTICAL SUGGESTIONS

The problems of interpretation and understanding are for Royce not mere conditions for reflection but are intimately intertwined with the subject matter. I see in this an indirect theologizing of Paul's method and style of communication. Royce pays close attention to the way Paul expresses himself. Royce does not merely list and expound Pauline topics. In Royce's translation, interpretation takes the place of Paul's proclamation. One can even say that Royce's interpretation of the saving and reconciling process, relating memory and hope, building and maintaining community, also stands for justification in Paul. The Pauline notion of justification also shows in Royce's association of faith and loyalty.

Compared with more recent hermeneutical ventures, Royce's hermeneutics remains closer to Paul but also appears as superior to that of Martin Heidegger, Rudolf Bultmann, and their students because the process of understanding is seen as something corporate.[7] Contrary to all post-Heideggerian theological hermeneutics, Royce deals in with essential questions that we also find in Troeltsch (1:200–205), and Royce treats them with greater critical and constructive force than Jürgen Habermas presently does. The historical aspect of interpretation is much more intensively felt and concretely expressed than in the discussions of *Geschichtlichkeit des Verstehens*, historicity of understanding by Heidegger, Bultmann, and others. For Royce, the hermeneutical phenomenon definitely has a social dimension and is completely integrated into the historical process, not over and above it, as in the hermeneutics of Heidegger and Bultmann. These two thinkers devalued the historical process to something objective and abstract out there, while the *geschichtliche Erfahrung*, the historical experience, was equally isolated and abstract on the subjective side. Despite their claims to the contrary, existential philosophy and theology have never overcome the ghastly trench between object and subject but have, instead, reaffirmed it. In his concept of the community of interpretation, Royce has again achieved the reconciliation of subject and object, thus repeating a feat Paul (and perhaps John) had already brought about. Thus, Royce reaches a quality of translation and interpretation that does credit to their true sense, namely, as a true carrying over and as integration, which neither Bultmann nor any professional exegetical scholar today have yet come to.

---

7. Time and space did not permit going any further into the substance of the second volume of *The Problem of Christianity*, where Royce's contribution to a communal hermeneutics is further developed.

As any modern interpreter, and especially every liberal one, Royce faces the difference between the New Testament thought world and ours. His claim is true that his answer to that problem is neither hostile nor apologetic. He anticipates Bultmann's program of demythologizing when he stresses interpretation instead of a trimming of texts down to what people still can believe today. Like Bultmann later, he integrates this critical reinterpretation into a general hermeneutical approach and theory. Like the existential interpretation, Royce sees the chances for a continued relevance of the Christian message in the fact that it is true to human nature. Royce and Bultmann both claim that the essential meaning of Christianity is not well maintained by preserving traditional Christianity but that the tradition needs to be critically reviewed, which is the same position Paul holds vis-à-vis Holy Scriptures and the Jewish tradition.

At the base of Royce's reinterpretation of the Christian message lies a critical rediscovery of the early church. There are constant references in Royce to changes in perception, especially as to eschatology. The issues of novelty and openness are rightly associated with that, but equally correctly they are seen not just as imagery but as indicators of the basic intent of the eschatological orientation of the Pauline/early Christian message. Royce's understanding of openness (of the community process and most of all of its interpretative heartbeat) continues Paul's direction of reinterpretation of tradition as it shows in his eschatology. The major difference between Royce and Paul is that the former stresses the infinity of the process while the latter plays with the terminal date. However, it should be noted that Paul's "eschaton" is conceived of not as something intermediate. Royce takes the right to his reinterpretation from the infiniteness of Paul's notion of the heavenly communion with Christ and God. The concept of infiniteness is more guarded in Bultmann's eschatology, but it is there, too. Just as in Bultmann, the "eschaton" has been translated by Royce from a quantifying (spatial/temporal) concept to a qualifying (crisis/decision) one; Royce also knows of the decisiveness of the now (lecture 14). His emphasis on the will also stresses the importance of the present moment. As Royce interrelates the community and the time process and deals with the relationship between memory and hope, he professes to a degree of *Geschichtlichkeit*, historicity, that is much stronger than what Bultmann's hermeneutics would call for (lecture 5).

Royce integrates the hermeneutical problem and its resolution completely into history and the social process—comparable to Paul's approach in the Epistle to the Romans. This is different from Bultmann, who refers only to history of thought and that only as explanatory background for his hermeneutics, not as its true context, thus being even more of a reductionist than Martin Heidegger in *Sein und Zeit*. Gerhard Ebeling and especially Hans Georg Gadamer remedied this in part (following the later Heidegger's example to a degree, especially Ebeling), but they never exceed history of thought. They never touch the social process. Ernst Fuchs tries to relate to that process in an impressionistic fashion through his various examples and metaphors. His interpretation of Rom 7 is another attempt in that direction, but he achieves less for a historical understanding and integration of hermeneutics there than Royce's and Hans Jonas's interpretation of this chapter. Although Bultmann in his form criticism stresses a social approach and in his reconstruction of the history of the early church emphasizes the importance of the collective consciousness, in *Theology of the New Testament* two great individuals, Paul and John, nevertheless prevail, and in his hermeneutical theory something like Strauß's myth-producing collective consciousness is only marginally hinted at; it never moves to the center. The hermeneutical relevance of the social dimensions of form criticism has not yet been fully recognized.

Royce proves that historical continuity is a hermeneutical issue too (not only in a negative sense as Bultmann and Fuchs argue; lecture 15). Historical continuity for Royce is much more than a series of analogies (as it is for most other modern hermeneuticists; 2:364). Although Royce acknowledges the importance of the individual and emphasizes the now, his interpretation cannot be called an existential interpretation. Instead, it is a spiritual interpretation but not in any mystical sense. It is an interpretation that acknowledges the spirit of the community it studies. Since in the case of the Christian community "the Lord is the spirit," it is also a christological interpretation. It is quite consistent with this approach that the social contexts and conditions of the origins of Christian doctrines are reviewed too—a matter of little interest for hermeneutics since Bultmann and Heidegger—but very much corresponding to Paul's consciousness about the context of early Christianity (1:200).[8]

Royce's theory of cognition can easily be read as a metaphysical translation of the Pauline triad "knowledge, faith, love" (lecture 11). Just as in Paul (there in opposition to the Gnostics), the social character of knowledge is stressed. It shows first of all in the inclusion of the element of interpretation into knowledge, certainly also in the denotation of the true community as a community of interpretation (lecture 12).[9] For any interpreter of Paul, Royce's argument that love constitutes knowledge is

---

8. Compare the example of the revivified early Christian in the later lectures.

9. Royce acknowledges that he owes this concept to that of the "community of inquirers," better said, the "interpretive community," of his older friend Charles Sanders Peirce (1839–1914), himself quite hostile to the reigning individualism. Volume 2 of *The Problem of Christianity* shows even more prominently both the dependence of Royce's hermeneutics on Peirce and its gained independence from the friend's hermeneutics.

most intriguing (lecture 14). The connection of interpretation and counseling reminds one strongly of the character and function of exhortation as encouragement and empowerment in Paul's own correspondence.

Paul's understanding of sacrament and even more John's use of it can be compared with Royce's theory of signs (lecture 14).[10] The sacraments of baptism and Eucharist and the sacramental character of proclamation in Paul and even more clearly the concept of σημεῖον in John presuppose just like Royce's sign an objective expression, which transcends subjective experience but necessarily calls for interpretation, too. The basic objective expression relates to an active social consciousness, which provides the leads for the interpretation. Royce can illustrate the antecedent nature of the social consciousness and its expression by describing how the world's and our neighbor's interpretation of us precede and condition our perception and understanding.

Like Bultmann, Royce knows of the *Geschichtlichkeit*, historicity, of interpretation, but he knows also like Paul and more than Bultmann of the *Geschichtlichkeit* of the interpreting community (lecture 9). Likewise, Royce makes the interpreting community interrelate memory and hope. This interpreting community is not just a compounding of individual consciousnesses. The community as such transcends the individual.

4. THE CONCEPT OF COMMUNITY

Just as in Paul, Royce has the social body precede and constitute the individual body (lecture 14). The individual gains personal experience in and through the corporate experience. In his description of the community as a prior experiential unit, Royce translates the nineteenth-century notion of personality to the community. Here Royce especially follows Wundt. He is aware of the fact that his discussion of the individual and the collective is a reconsideration of the ancient, especially Platonic, philosophical problem of the relationship between the one and the many, the part and the whole (lecture 13). It is clear that the popular-philosophical discussion of that issue has influenced a text such as 1 Cor 12, too.

Royce understands Paul's body of Christ correctly as collective corporate consciousness in action. The essential function of proclamation in the early Christian, especially the Pauline, community is repeated in Royce's understanding of the community as essentially communicating

---

10. Its dependence on his friend C. S. Peirce's theory of signs should not be overstressed. Royce has also given the concept of signs his own touch.

(in the continuous interpretative process; lecture 10). Royce's understanding of the community as spiritual does not imply any ethereal or spooky nature but a concretely living corporate existence (1:66–74). This community is spiritual because it is formed and led by the Lord, who is the creative, living, and directing spirit. The risen Lord/Spirit interprets the historical Jesus (1:196–99). In the constant interpretative process (the activity of the Lord/Spirit) the community finds its self-perpetuation (lecture 8).[11]

This authentic corporate experience is contrasted with the phenomenon of society as governed by law. Royce gives a fascinating portrayal of the modern industrial society in an equally authentic discussion of Rom 7, again anticipating exegetical insights of Rudolf Bultmann and Werner Georg Kümmel about Rom 7, namely, that this famous text does not speak of the individual Paul at the date of writing the Epistle to the Romans but of the corporate experience of humanity before the epiphany of grace, as seen through the eyes of faith (1:110–59). Royce in line with Paul depicts the law not only as the divine will but as the social will to which people consent. However, this social role actually creates and encourages self-consciousness, selfhood, division of labor ("works of the law," in Paul's formulation), place hunting, and so conflict and divisiveness (1:132–35). In a moment of genius, Royce speaks of the much-debated original sin in Christian doctrine as that of contentiousness (1:144). This is well in line with Paul's (and Bultmann's) assertion that sin is essentially καύχημα, although Royce draws a more colorful picture of it than Bultmann does. Royce is aware that Paul's allusion to the temptation story ("You shall all be gods"), also betrays awareness of the competitive and combative pride against fellow humans (1:156–57).

As Royce, like Paul, relates the origin of sin to social development and training, not just to individual growth and education, he gives a spellbinding description of Paul's vision of the conflict between two laws; it is the conflict between social will and self-will, one born by the other but necessarily falling into hatred against its very originator. Royce follows Paul's suggestion in Rom 7 of drawing even conscience into the vicious circle—making it neither an aloof arbiter nor a savior, as liberal theology wanted to have it (1:137). Conscience grows out of the chaos of intersecting social contrasts. It is no wonder that Royce sees in Rom 7 individualism and collectivism calling for each other and creating an impenetrable maze. Thus, the social role creates a community of hatred (1:144). The cooperation born out of the social will does not radiate love but competitiveness among essentially divided people (lecture 10).

---

11. See also the discussion about Jesus and Paul in 1:74–106.

Thus, Royce is able to get Paul's point that flesh is not just a part of the individual nor moral evil but is sinful activity, this competitive and divisive strife under the social will, and thus destructive power and slavery (1:177–78). The social process breeds conscious as well as conscientious sinners. The "natural community" is a "community of sin."[12]

Royce did not need all the religious-historical discussion New Testament scholarship had to undergo to discover that Paul can use "grace" and its equivalent terms and motifs in a temporal, a spatial, and a qualitative sense (1:165–79). It is the new age,[13] but it is also a realm, an "aeon," as New Testament scholars would say (1:192), and it is a quality, the quality of new life. The individual is won over by saving love in and of the community. The redeeming spirit in the community saves one. Divine (and communal) love makes the person love others. This love is given, not a product of education (1:173–75). It is loyalty.[14]

The saved community is also reconciled (lecture 7). The new is strong and creative enough to integrate the old in an innovative fashion. One notices here a resemblance to Hegel's play with the ambiguity of the German word *aufheben*[15] (1:182). One is reminded, too, of Philo's notion of the encyclical education, that is, encyclopedia in its literal Greek sense, as paradoxical preparation for the spiritual vision. According to Royce, the experience under the law is made to work positively in the new existence of hope. Reconciliation is in effect interpretation, and an even more active and constructive description of the activity of the spirit is presented than Hegel would give. But Royce lacks neither Paul's nor Hegel's universalism. Since reconciliation is salvation through interpretation it does not concern itself with the individual alone, as Royce's pietistic background would have it;[16] it is concerned with the world at large as well (lecture 14). Thus Paul's new creation is correctly interpreted as a cosmic affair (lecture 13), and the gist of Rom 5:10 and 2 Cor 5:18–20 and their respective contexts is well presented by Royce.

One of Royce's real departures from the theology of Paul can be

---

12. This is an attack on the impacts of Augustineanism, particularly also those of its major offsprings, Lutheranism and Calvinism, fountainheads of Western capitalist society. Also related is Royce's attack on the subjectivism of pragmatism in 2:304; important also is the observation that there is something like the self-righteousness of christocratic asceticism, an anticipation of the problems of neo-orthodoxy.

13. The new Jerusalem in 1:58; Paul's new community in 1:91–106.

14. A definition of loyalty is given in 1:158. It is the consciousness of one who loves the community, the latter seen and understood as a person.

15. To terminate as well as to lift unto a higher plane or even to integrate and preserve.

16. Where reconciliation is that of the individual.

found in his double discussion of sin, one centering on Rom 7, the other an elaboration of the sin against the Holy Spirit of Mark 3 (and Synoptic parallels)—with no real attempt to reconcile the two (lecture 5). The two issues can be kept apart, and they can be seen together. This is the only time that Royce uses the Synoptic Gospels to modify Paul. It is not entirely a correction. Royce seems to be aware of the difficulty Paul has in coping with the sinning of church members, especially with the existence of heresy. Royce, therefore, ingeniously takes the sin against the Holy Spirit to be treason, apostasy from the community. It is the unthinkable sin, the unforgivable violation and destruction of the essential fabric of the community and of the moral self, of loyalty. It is the suicidal severing of all bonds with the community, therefore sin unto death, the hell of the irrevocable: tragedy and chaos in the community. All this is an interesting analogy to Paul's description of the character and result of heresy in Gal 5; Phil 3; and 2 Cor 10–13.[17]

Royce's other departure from Paul's theology is consistent with the previous one (lecture 6). It is Royce's separation of the discussion of grace from that of atonement, although he can unite them under the heading of reconciliation. For Paul, atonement, reconciliation, and grace are one. They precede any individual experience too. Royce's radical reinterpretation of Pauline eschatology makes him see the problem of enmity, rebellion, and chaos not only as the past of but also as the constant threat to and the experience of community—an imaginative and re-Paulinized version of the Augustine-Luther concept of the *simul justus et peccator*. Although treason is irrevocable damage, the beloved community is able to overcome this deadly blow by the creative combination of vicarious suffering (under and from the tragic apostasy). It is also the imaginative integration of the trauma of apostasy into a more mature and expansive corporal experience. Hegel's notion of the dialectic necessity of sin shines through in this statement of Royce: "The deed of atonement shall be so wise and so rich in its efficacy, that the spiritual world, after the atoning deed, shall be better, richer, more triumphant against all its irrevocable tragedies than it was before that traitor's deed was done." Paul's transformation of the death and resurrection of Christ into functional structures of his own career and communal life,[18] his hope that his christologically oriented surrender as fool might engender corporate repentance and restoration, and the conciliatory handling of the case of apostasy in 2 Cor 2 and 7 are excellent anticipations of Royce's translation of the Christ

---

17. It is surprising that, contrary to Royce, Bultmann never gives a theological assessment of the phenomenon of heresy in Paul or early Christianity.

18. Esp. in 1 Cor 3 and 4 and 10–13; 2 Cor 4–6; and, in its own curious way, 2 Cor 10–13.

event into a continuous structure of community life.

In his Christology Royce sides with the position of Lessing regarding revelation and against Kierkegaard, whose position is adopted by Bultmann. Like Lessing, Royce doubts the continued viability of the idea of complete and universal revelation in one particular moment of history (1:423). He cannot work with the notion of the historical uniqueness of the god-man Jesus. The saving event of the cross has completely turned into a principle—not entirely foreign to Paul, who, in 1 Cor 1:17–25, for instance, discusses the cross of Jesus in very close association with the principle-oriented structure of wisdom speculation. Royce retains the importance of the particular (individual and historical) in his translation of the two-nature Christology into a two-level Christology. The level of the individual and that of the community are in a dialectic relationship. Royce's entire book *The Problem of Christianity* is the interpretation of a particular but continuous movement as universally relevant, which continues Royce's previous interest in the dialectic understanding of particularity, especially in his *California*[19] and his discussion of provincialism. Therefore, although Bultmann with his insistence on the "that" of the revelation in Jesus is literally closer to Paul, Royce's imaginative and far-ranging historical dialectic matches that of Paul more than Bultmann's refusal to elaborate on the "what" of revelation.

Royce's description of the community of interpretation as universally expanding through its interpretation (lecture 12) is an almost exact translation of the Pauline church as being a consciously missionary church. Interpretation as Royce sees it, namely, worldwide generalization and integration, actually a world of interpretation, is the analogy to Paul's missionary activity as described primarily in Rom 1:9–17 and Rom 15. Paul takes his preaching to the nations as a worldwide hermeneutical mission. One can even find the same enthusiasm about the universally gratifying character of this hermeneutical mission (especially in Rom 15) in Royce's portrayal of the worldwide community (lecture 13).

The contrast of the two different worldviews in Rom 1–3 and 5 is found in Royce's description of the universal community and its context, too. Both Paul and Royce try hard to eliminate any chauvinism from their universal mission, Royce with an even clearer perception of the danger of imperialism,[20] but both find it necessary to speculate globally. This constructive thought is not done in the abstract but is closely related to the

---

19. Being a study in the American character.
20. See his attitude toward Germany, particularly also its tragic turn in his last book, *The Hope of the Great Community* (New York: Macmillan, 1916).

communal life of people, actually understood as part of the collective enterprise itself.[21] The many anticipatory visions of Paul—his concrete expressions of justification and hope—in structure, function, and context find a very interesting parallel in Royce's concept of hypothesis (lecture 16).[22] It is the community reaching out in both cases. The critical reader even notices closer parallels to the idea of the *homo absconditus,* the hidden human, in Ernst Bloch. There is no cheap optimism in Royce, but we find a conscious, constructive defiance of the isolation and blindness of individual and society (1:145–58).

It is in line with Paul's own intentions, especially in his last letters, particularly in Romans, when Royce replaces the all too familiar but destructive concept of theodicy-oriented theology with a community-oriented theology. The Pauline correspondence had already radicalized the early Christian understanding of the church as not only representing the new creation but as participating in God's creation. Paul's idea of the church is even more that of an *ecclesia concreatrix,* a cocreating church (lecture 14). Exactly this is Royce's community too. "The true church is the one believing in and furthering the unity of mankind, advancing the universal community." The fact that Royce first developed his "magnum opus" not only for but also in exchange with a *lay audience,* mostly of women,[23] should help us be lenient toward the traces of male chauvinism still present in his language. In practice, he was moving beyond that already, more than most of his academic peers. Royce demonstrates to us defeatist theologians that our tradition is more critical and progressive than that of Max Weber, for instance, and that a forgotten Harvard philosopher is a more challenging partner for the necessary dialogue of tomorrow than Habermas of Frankfurt, so often quoted among modernists, camouflaged conservatives as they are.

---

21. Royce's utopian dream did not end with *The Problem of Christianity* but stayed alive and moved beyond it; see his last book as mentioned in the previous note.

22. Again, partly based on Peirce.

23. Both speaker and audience were excellent demonstrations of the fact that lay theology, the greatest heritage of the Reformation, still has promise in the modern world.

17

REASON, RELIGION, RESPONSIBILITY: REFLECTIONS ON THE FRANKFURT TILLICH

1. PREFATORY REMARKS

Transgression of borders is a major expression of academic vigor and a major ingredient of the sanity of the university. Such courageous and imaginative transgressions are major contributions of the universities to their urban environment. The following chapter deals with another academic transgressor who worked on both sides of the Atlantic. This person who liked to transgress established border and frontiers and did so most prominently at the only citizens' university in Germany, the university of Frankfurt, was Paul Tillich, a theologian by training, a philosopher and sociologist out of passion. His engagement at this university in its social and political context made him a *persona non grata* for the Nazis, who drove him out of his job and out of Germany. His warnings about their demonic mythology that turned blood and soil against enlightened urban consciousness proved to be all too true. Tillich remains a model for academicians of tomorrow, certainly for all those who want to live and think in urban contexts.

2. ACADEMIC THEOLOGY IN FRANKFURT NOW

I thought apt the title of this chapter when I was approached about a contribution to the Tillich Luncheon. The triadic alliteration seemed best

---

* This paper was originally delivered at the Harvard Tillich Luncheon, 21 April 1997.

to characterize the profile of the Frankfurt Tillich, not only as a historical person but also as a paradigmatic figure for us today. You might ask why I left out "culture." Not because it does not start with an *r* but because culture would have been for the Frankfurt Tillich pretty much the mix of all three: reason, religion, and responsibility. Therefore, I cannot proceed to treat them one after the other. Rather, with the Frankfurt Tillich they were interdependent and interactive. I put "religion" between the two other terms because religion is for Tillich the vital link between the two other concepts or, better, perspectives, reason and responsibility. Tillich does not consider any of the three themes, reason, religion, or responsibility, to be all-embracing. Each is to be seen and practiced in a dialectical fashion. This dialectical approach has to take into account that any generalization of any of these terms would bring out their demonic, even, corrupting and destructive, dimensions. This would even be true for responsibility. The Frankfurt Tillich, although himself a very active person, often and strongly stresses the theme of justification by faith, reading it in its Lutheran understanding of justification by faith alone, not by works.

I must ask for indulgence for what I am going to present. One must take me as a curious amateur in matters of Tillich, as a *Liebhaber*, not as a *Kenner*, to use Tillich's native tongue. And I speak here as a citizen of Frankfurt, as a professor of the university that appointed Tillich in 1929.

Tillich's fame and memory were of major importance in our arguments for creating a school of Protestant theology in Frankfurt in the 1980s, a Fachbereich Evangelische Theologie, as it is called in modern German academic lingo. Since the 1970s the Johann Wolfgang Goethe University in Frankfurt had a department of Religionswissenschaft.[1] This department, however had no legal title to train persons for the ministry or the priesthood due to the peculiar German law governing state-church relations. In Germany, such training presupposes a definite orientation of the school in question toward either Protestantism or Catholicism. In the case of the training for the ministry, it needs a school of Protestant theology; in that of training for the priesthood, a school of Catholic theology. In 1987 the two schools of theology at the Johann Wolfgang Goethe University were founded.[2] I was the founding dean of the Protestant school

---

1. This was different from the U.S. departments of religion because it had a Protestant and a Catholic section. This division within the department, however, did not satisfy the legal requirements for the training for the ministry and the priesthood.

2. Unfortunately, even after the separation, the Roman Catholic Church objected to concur with the state in granting the newly founded school of Catholic theology the right to train for the priesthood. A drawn-out court battle was in the end lost by the state and the university. The Catholic Church won.

and the first administrative dean for common affairs of both schools of theology. This was the first time since the Reformation that a Protestant and a Catholic school of theology had a common administrative bond. This included even elements of a common curriculum and a shared Ph.D. program, with programs in history of religion, comparative religion, and philosophy of religion. We were unable also to establish a school of Jewish theology. Thus we did not fully succeed in finally bringing about what many had hoped and worked for at the founding of Frankfurt University in 1914: the establishment of three schools, and faculties, of theology. However, we were able to secure the full sponsorship of the Protestant provincial church for a continuous visiting professorship in Jewish philosophy of religion at the school of Protestant theology. This visiting professorship carries the name of Martin Buber. Attempts to found a Tillich chair for systematic theology and philosophy of religion at the Frankfurt University have remained unsuccessful to this day.[3]

Still, what we achieved would have been to Paul Tillich's liking, even more since the connection with the school of philosophy did not break off. On the contrary, after many years' efforts, an Institute for Philosophy of Religion was established, jointly administered by both schools of theology and the school of philosophy.

Tillich would be excited, too, if he could see our introductory program for the Master of Divinity. Here incoming students learn to see their studies themselves as societal praxis, not as theory. This appropriates and integrates the approach of Tillich and of the Frankfurt School to praxis and its relationship to theory. With these models before them, students learn early to turn their studies into a socially and politically engaged acquisition of theology. They learn to grasp theology within the larger context of the university's and the church's attempts to analyze and interpret the past and the present for the future.

3. TILLICH'S LIFE IN FRANKFURT

This shows that there is an afterlife of Tillich in Frankfurt. We can now move on to the topic proper. Paul[4] Tillich was born in 1886. As noted

---

3. In approaching potential donors in Germany and the United States, I found much interest, and Hannah Tillich expressed her support by way of telephone and writing, but there were no financial results. Still, our Protestant school, through the efforts of Professor Yorick Spiegel, has continued to conduct seminars on Tillich, within and outside of the curriculum. Tillich research is continued through these seminars.

4. The baptismal name was "Paulus."

already, he came to Frankfurt in 1929. That means he was already in his forties. He had been teaching as a professor for five years, first in Marburg and then in Dresden. His appointment was in philosophy, more exactly in philosophy and sociology, including social pedagogy. He was also made the director of two institutes, those of philosophy and of pedagogy. This meant that the youngest and most progressive German university, still in its building phase, saw this systematic theologian as an all-purpose person. He was taken as someone who could replace none less than Max Scholar in philosophy, who could also bring life into pedagogy and particular into social pedagogy, not necessarily the most common subjects of theological training. It implied, too, that administrative duties were expected from this theologian, who to many of his contemporaries must have appeared to be more of a dreamer. The Prussian curator Riezler, practically the head of the university, must have seen through the dreaming eyes of this theologian and discovered a realist. This was a discovery that some other Prussians using their Nazi glasses four years later forcefully denied.

This Prussian curator had appointed Tillich against the will of the Frankfurt faculty. Tillich, however, quickly gained the trust of the whole department of philosophy, and in 1932 he was voted dean of the school of philosophy, in those days comprising not alone the philosophers but closer to a school of arts and sciences in the United States, at least as far as the arts were concerned. Tillich proved to be what Adorno later praised him for, a *pacidius,* a peace lover.

Tillich was persuaded to leave Dresden for Frankfurt for various reasons. The fact that Frankfurt was a real university, not only a technical university (as Dresden was), certainly proved attractive. This was given weight by the challenging task of dealing with the combination of philosophy and sociology as a theologian, and this at a university that possessed a strong anticlerical tendency. Attempts to found three theological schools, Protestant, Catholic, and Jewish, had not succeeded at the new university. Two other features of this young university at Frankfurt, founded in the year in which World War I began, set it apart from all other German universities. The university in Frankfurt was the only German university founded on money given by citizens of the town. The foundation was initiated and chaired by the mayor of the city of Frankfurt. Jewish citizens of Frankfurt gave much of the money. Frankfurt had the second largest Jewish community in Germany after Berlin, the largest in proportion to the population. Frankfurt was not only the native town of Goethe but also hometown to the Rothschilds and many other major Jewish figures of commerce, industry, and culture. The newly founded University of Frankfurt became the first German university that admitted Jewish students and appointed Jewish professors in greater numbers.

Famous names were among them, such as Paul Ehrlich, Karl Mannheim, and Martin Buber. Since 1923 Martin Buber had taught as an adjunct professor at the university, first for the Jewish study of religion. In 1930 he was appointed for the study of religion in general. After Tillich's appointment to Frankfurt, Buber and Tillich soon became quite close.

This strong Jewish contribution to the population and life in and of Frankfurt had not only strengthened the banking and trading and industrial dimensions of this old imperial but now strongly republican city but had also enriched its cultural life. This town had a strong and cultivated bourgeoisie but also a strong proletariat, and there were Jewish citizens belonging to either of the two or to both.

It is often overlooked that the training and research center of German trade unions, the academy of labor, was a part of Frankfurt University. It also opened the university as a whole to members of the working class. At this academy, one of the inspiring figures was Ernst Michel, a lay theologian from the left wing of the Catholic Church. He attracted other people of the same persuasion. This meant that progressive, critical Catholics were not rare in Frankfurt either.

In the same peculiar Frankfurt blend of philosophy and sociology, Tillich, through his chair, was to represent a group of young academicians of Jewish background assembled around the Institute of Social Research. Director of this institute became Max Horkheimer. Another person of this group was Theodor Wiesengrund, later known as Adorno. I am speaking of an institute and a group that became famous as the "Frankfurter Schule." Theodor Wiesengrund Adorno practically became the assistant of Tillich and under his guidance wrote his second, his *habilitation*, dissertation on Kierkegaard.[5] A good number of these members of the Frankfurt School later became friends of Tillich, especially Max Horkheimer.

Another important element of Frankfurt University was the work of the anthropologist Leo Frobenius, well known for his cultural history of Africa, in which he analyzed and interpreted corporate mythical consciousness as culture creating reality. Heavily influenced by Frobenius was the classical philologist at Frankfurt, Walter F. Otto, who interpreted the Roman and in particular the Greek mythical world as an overwhelming and motivating force, as an epiphany, powerful and creative.

All this was hard to match anywhere else and strongly attracted Tillich and his wife. They quickly felt at home among university colleagues, some of them already mentioned, and many others could be added, rather famous ones among them. The Tillichs had regular access to a

---

5. For academic teaching credentials, German universities require not only a doctoral degree but in addition a *habilitation* with another dissertation and a trial lecture.

group of artists, journalists, and writers but also to a circle that Paul and Gabrielle Oppenheimer used to entertain in their house. The Tillichs enjoyed their life in the newly built part of the city between the opera and the university, where the upper-class bourgeoisie of Frankfurt lived, among them many Jews.

I already mentioned that Tillich's active concern for the proletariat was not at all astonishing for these acquaintances and friends of the upper-class bourgeoisie. Many of them shared at least a passive interest in understanding and improving the conditions of the working class in Frankfurt. The latter was numerous and strong in Frankfurt. The members of the proletariat lived not far away from the university, actually to the southwest of it. Frankfurt industrialists, especially of the various chemical factories, and here again especially Jewish entrepreneurs, had built social housing in settlement style, extraordinary and exemplary for the remainder of Germany. This was topped by the famous architect and city planner May. He built large, inexpensive quarters for workers and other low-paid people in an open style, under modern hygienic as well as aesthetic principles. This was thoroughly modern social city planning that was hard to find anywhere in Germany or elsewhere.

On the other hand, it was and is peculiar for Frankfurt University to this day that it is a foreign element to the section of the city of which it is officially a part, namely, to Bockenheim. Here the population was and is mainly lower middle class. Tillich later self-critically confessed that he and his friends and colleagues had failed to relate to these people around them.[6] They left them to the Nazis, who received their strongest support, numerically and in terms of energy, from this class. These people were never reconciled to the university built in their midst. It remained an unwanted foreign body. This provided the sociopsychological background for the turbulent Nazi takeover of the university in 1933, after Hitler had come to power.

4. THE CHALLENGE TO THE BOURGEOISIE

In looking back to Tillich's arrival in Frankfurt in 1929, we must note that Tillich's concern for the proletariat was essential for him. He was not satisfied with the kind of exotic or benevolent interest in the poor that many intellectuals showed to cover their bad social conscience. Tillich saw the need for challenging the bourgeoisie in his own surrounding and in the church. Long before he came to Frankfurt, he had begun to attack

---

6. The "petite bourgeoisie," as they were contemptuously called in Marxist terminology.

the ideological pope of Protestant bourgeoisie, Albert Ritschl, as did the representatives of dialectical theology at the same time (e.g., Karl Barth, although under different perspectives).

In liberal theology as represented by Ritschl, Tillich sees a lack of "depth and paradox."[7] In the same essay Tillich accuses this liberal theology of being "a typical escape theology."[8] "The moral principle came in instead of the truth question."[9] Tillich argues that the kind of liberal Protestantism that Ritschl represented considered it a main function of Christianity to enable morality. Tillich charges that Ritschl and others suspended theoretical for practical reason.

Wenz also quotes another statement of Tillich in which he brought his criticism of Ritschl to a climax: "We did not want to accept the defeat of metaphysics and did not wish to take as inevitable the flight into the defense lines of the theory of values. We wanted the 'Sein.' And the experience of being as 'being power' became the existential experience from which the most part of my later thinking grew." This criticism of Ritschl turned into a criticism of Neo-Kantian philosophy, still very prominent in Germany at the time. Tillich criticized the Neo-Kantian approach to thinking for its panlogism, formalism, interest in quantifiability, and practical usability. He wanted to recover the true Kant against the pseudo-Kant of the Neo-Kantians.

Much of what Tillich stood for as philosopher and as university professor during the time of his arrival and teaching in Frankfurt showed up in his contributions to the second edition of the theological encyclopedia, *Die Religion in Geschichte und Gegenwart*.[10] In his article there on philosophy, Tillich argues for the complete independence of philosophy, its subjects, objects, methods, and its way of questioning.[11] Still, philosophy

---

7. Paul Tillich, "Der Werdergange Eines Deutschen Theologen: Ein Brief an Thomas Mann," in idem, *Gesammelte Werke* (ed. Renate Albrecht; Stuttgart: Evangelisches Verlagswerk, 1959–75), 13:24.

8. Ibid., 13:25.

9. Paul Tillich, "Vorlesung über die Geschichte des christlichen Denkens II: Aspekte des Protestantismus im 19. und 20. Jahrhundert," in *Ergänzungs- und Nachlassbände zu den Gesammelten Werken von Paul Tillich* (ed. Ingeborg C. Henel; Stuttgart: Evangelishes Verlagswerk, 1972), 2:179.

10. Tillich wrote for this encyclopedia the articles "Mythos und Mythologie," "Philosophie," "Offenbarung" (revelation), "Religiöser Sozialismus," and "Wissenschaft," the latter used here in its German sense, which comprises all of scholarship, not only "science" in the sense of natural senses. Given the space limitations of this essay, I cannot deal with these articles at all.

11. Quite remarkable for a theologian, that is, a representative of a discipline that has all too often either claimed philosophy to be dependent on theology or theology to be dependent on philosophy.

for him is anything but an abstract, general, ahistorical, or otherwise sterile exercise; it is embedded in history, is an essential part of it; it changes with history; the changes of history are its fate. Tillich had already worked out this particular idea of the timeliness of authentic philosophy in his inaugural lecture in Frankfurt for the 1929 summer term, entitled "Philosophy and Fate."

Tillich's demand to restore metaphysics appeared at first sight out of touch with the philosophy of the time. Tillich's teachers, the systematic theologians Lütgert and Kähler and then the idealist philosopher Schelling (subject of both of Tillich's dissertations) had all contributed to Tillich's conviction to demand to regain the metaphysical dimension of philosophy. He also considered Kierkegaard to be in support of this demand. In Tillich's eyes, dialectical theology and existentialist philosophy had misunderstood Kierkegaard when they used him as support for their disregard of metaphysics. In the article on philosophy, already quoted, Tillich says, "Either metaphysics is philosophy itself, or it is nothing." Yet the metaphysical dimension for Tillich is essentially bound up with the existential one; they are inseparable. The upshot of this is that Tillich in his advocacy of philosophical reasoning takes leave from rationalization. Rationalization, contrary to its claim, is for Tillich the opposite of what he understands as continuous radical questioning, reasonable reasoning. Reason and transcendence are interdependent for him.[12]

5. THE SOCIALIST DECISION

I shall concentrate now on the one major book that Tillich wrote and published in Frankfurt: *Die sozialistische Entscheidung* (*The Socialist Decision*).[13] Originally it had been a paper that Tillich had given under the same title at the "Hochschule für Politik" (the Academy for Politics), in Frankfurt on Main in October 1931.

In this book the suspenseful concurrence of καιρός and λόγος happens,[14] that of philosophy and fate, of theology and mission. Reason, religion, and responsibility coincide in a prophetic analysis and challenge of society, of a culture at the brink of catastrophe. Tillich calls his own class as much as traditional socialism to a radical change, away from

---

12. In his Frankfurt period Tillich wrote and published mostly papers, essays, and articles. A good number of them were collected and published under the title *Religiöse Verwirklichung* (Berlin: Furche, 1930).

13. Die Sozialistische Aktion 2; Potsdam: Protte, 1933.

14. The two terms mean the appropriate moment and the reason and speech that accompany it.

comfortable accommodation and proud orthodoxy, both fateful if continued. The book has a deceptively academic tone and complexity. Under this cover there is high drama. Tillich's long occupation with symbols and myth as being formative but also critical realities finds its preliminary fulfillment here. It is more than merely a direct response to the preoccupation of Nazis with myth, demonstrated especially by Alfred Rosenberg's *The Myth of the Twentieth Century.*

Tillich's *Die sozialistische Entscheidung,* very timely at its date of writing, is still one of his most relevant contributions to our age, a period of resurgence of the so-called New Right all over the Western world as well as in the region of the former Soviet Union. *Die sozialistische Entscheidung* is a passionate plea both for appreciating socialism and for reforming socialism, a response to the danger of the alliance of bourgeoisie, capitalism, and fascism, prophetically foreseen by Tillich.

Tillich by that time had gained considerable experience and versatility in dealing with the issue of myth. His critical discussion of Schelling's philosophy had been a major but not the only source for that. Tillich had published on myth and symbol in Frankfurt, too. Still, the work on *Die sozialistische Entscheidung* opened further dimensions.

They evolved out of religious-historical as much as out of psychological insights into the primeval basis and the primal functions and relations of myth. Tillich now uses the term *Ursprungsmythos,* that is, primeval as much as primal myth. Any myth has that character. It states and explains the whence as much as the where of human existence, collective and individual. It communicates that existence is bonded to the power of myth. This kind of myth promises security. Thus, conservatives tend to go for it in romantic preoccupation.

This conservative romanticism Tillich sees as a major obstacle and opposition to the realization of true justice, which can be achieved only in freedom. This freedom is lost if the primeval myth dominates. Freedom and justice, contrary to the primal myth, look ahead to the "whither" of human existence and experience. In order to get to this "whither" of freedom and justice, prophetic power is needed. Tillich sees it evolve as a critical force in the biblical as well as Jewish tradition. There prophets preached against the fetters of primal myth. Christianity adopted that, too, although Christianity later showed a recurring tendency to fall back into the bonds of the *Ursprungsmythos* proper, thus losing the "whither," freedom and justice, from sight. In prophecy, Tillich sees the *Ursprungsmythos* retained to a degree, but in a broken form, interpreted with the eyes pointing ahead.

Tillich takes up ideas of Lessing's *Education of Humanity,* so important for the evolution of the idea of progress and of education in the United States. Tillich sees Reformation and Enlightenment in sequence and in a hereditary connection with the biblical Jewish prophecy mentioned. Tillich incorporates the bourgeoisie and its development into this prophetic tradition. In the evolution of the bourgeoisie, Tillich sees a principle at work, the bourgeois principle, which he defines, as the result of the prophetic humanist attack on the primeval myth that had governed the Middle Ages. The bourgeois principle opened new dimensions for human activity.

Yet it fell back into tendencies of primal myth due to its belief in harmony and balance, achieved not the least in and through the market. Productivity and trade were pushed ahead and demonstrated a new sense of realism. This was a real gain but at the same time a new bondage, namely to *Verdinglichung,* to "re-alism,"[15] or, as we usually but imprecisely say, materialism.

Socialism, in Tillich's eyes, builds on the bourgeoisie, its humanist prophetic momentum, idea of harmony, and materialism. But socialism goes beyond that in a critical manner. This happens most of all through socialism's increased interest in the "whither," through its prophetic element. In its prophetic inclination socialism stridently proclaims that bourgeois harmony promises did and will not fulfill themselves, that disharmony evolved instead—in the form of the alienation of the working class, the proletariat. Thus the latter justifiably wants to go beyond bourgeoisie to a form of freedom and justice that transcends bourgeois materialism. The three categories I started out with, reason, religion, and responsibility, are combined here by Tillich, though using different terms. For Tillich, socialism as a process combines rationality with prophetic religion and with responsibility for a just and human society for all.

As all creative movements before, socialism is a movement of inherent contradictions. It lives with the absolute contrast of radical pessimism toward the past and of radical optimism toward the future. Both elements need to be reconciled. This can happen through the use of religious tradition, for this can provide the forces of faith and engagement.

The next contradiction inherent in socialism resides in the socialist hope that the changes of social circumstances will change humanity. This presupposes a mechanistic anthropology, actually an antisocialist concept. Instead, so Tillich argues, a holistic image of the human is necessary, a consciousness that is free to live out of the depth of being. Personhood and people at large are to be seen in a dialectical relationship.

Another contrast in socialism is that of achieving the powerless society through the extreme use of force. This misconception needs to be overcome by basing power on democratic structures that control power

---

15. Play of words on the Latin background of realism: *res* = thing (*Ding* in German).

and guarantee justice for all groups. Contrary to the present forms of democracy, such democratic structures must be included in the economy and the market. Both are at present not really democratically controlled. The economy and market must be made reasonable and humane through a democratizing process, quite different from state control.

In *Die sozialistische Entscheidung* and in the contemporary *Ten Theses*, Tillich develops an important and still relevant theory of fascism. He sees fascism in general, and so-called National Socialism in particular, steered by forces of the bourgeoisie that have lost trust in the bourgeois principle. This kind of anxiety is particularly strong in the lower middle class, the major source for fascist recruitment. There are hints in *Die sozialistische Entscheidung* and elsewhere in Tillich that he had a realistic fear of the proletariat being increasingly affected by petit-bourgeois dreams, which make people interested in finding satisfaction in a pseudoharmony within the smallest possible circle—while at the same time hoping for the strong military and police state that can secure such harmony. For Tillich, nationalistic, chauvinistic, indeed reactionary romanticism is at the heart of fascism, is the major element of its fascination. Tillich correctly observes a tendency among leading circles of the bourgeoisie and of leading capitalists toward an alliance with fascism and with a strong state because these circles expect that a better protection of their interests could come from such an alliance.

I can now forgo a further detailed presentation of the new insights that Tillich developed in Frankfurt with respect to symbol, myth, the principle of Protestantism, religious socialism, culture, and so forth because they all culminate in *Die sozialistische Entscheidung*. This presentation of Tillich's important as well as complex book, *Die sozialistische Entscheidung*, needed to be brief, all too brief. I hope that I was nevertheless able to communicate the gist of it.

6. TILLICH IN NEW YORK

Union Theological Seminary has invited me to research and to teach for this year in the name of Bonhoeffer. Doing this where both Tillich and Bonhoeffer were at relatively the same time makes me raise the question as to what it was that made the very same environment radicalize Bonhoeffer and soften Tillich.

Bonhoeffer came to New York with a kind of neo-orthodox theology and with a political mindset that, in German terminology, was called national liberal, in fact, conservative, with a nationalist and an antidemocratic tendency. People like him and Karl Barth were open to a kind of fascism that Mussolini represented. Protestant theology provided enough stimuli for an anti-Jewish dimension, for an antilegalism, which was prone to irrational emotionalism.[16] Yet New York changed this all. Bonhoeffer encountered the drastic racist and class dimensions of a capitalist society, the bloody consequences of which worsened because of the ongoing depression. He experienced the potential for change inherent in democratic institutions and practices.

Contrary to Bonhoeffer's Union years, those of Tillich did not radicalize but, on the contrary, softened him. The whole socialism theme moved into the background. This is quite strange and disconcerting. The Frankfurt Tillich coming to New York was more than a radical thinker. He saw himself as active in a radical practice, represented by his German, in particular his Frankfurt, contacts, his teaching, and his writing. *Die sozialistische Entscheidung* had brought it all to a head. This book, together with other writings of Tillich, had been committed to the fire after the takeover of the Nazis by a mob of students led by the Frankfurt student chaplain, right in the center of town, on the Römerberg. Tillich's writings were confiscated, too, in the bookstores and the publishing houses. *Die sozialistische Entscheidung* had been shredded and turned into pulp.

Thus Tillich came to New York as a proven radical, fully prepared to look through and behind the social programs of the U.S. Democrats as highly deceptive measures. Much of the New Deal was comparable to Bismarck's social policies, antisocialist both in theory and in fact. Despite all that preparedness and foreknowledge, Tillich did not pick up where he had left off in Frankfurt. *Die sozialistische Entscheidung* was put on hold, became a matter of the past and of the archives.

How can this contrast between Bonhoeffer and Tillich be explained? A very insufficient but common explanation is the claim that there is a major breach in Tillich's thinking, as if there had been a younger and an older Tillich. I agree with Günter Wenz that there are too many continuous strands in Tillich's works to allow for such a division. However, it is significant that Wenz speaks of the Frankfurt Tillich in mere passing. He selects from that period mostly Tillich's discussion of myth. The deep connection of Tillich's understanding of myth with *Die sozialistische Entscheidung* is not taken seriously enough by Wenz, let alone the new contributions that this book made to Tillich's understanding of myth, most of all with respect to the primal, the *Ursprungs* myth.

There was definitely a retreat from *Die sozialistische Entscheidung* when Tillich came to New York, although this book would have been as timely in New York in 1934 as it had been in Frankfurt in 1933 and

---

16. Certainly an extreme misunderstanding of the concepts of gospel and freedom.

beyond. The blend of tact and fear of an immigrant in a host society, accompanied by the simple challenges and chores of settling with a family in a new country and culture, working hard on the new language—all these are offered as another set of explanations, certainly understandable.

It is certain, too, that the personality of Reinhold Niebuhr, the friend who had made the emigration and immigration possible, played an important role in this change of a revolutionary into a moderate democrat. A supportive argument for this could be that in 1945 Tillich had thought that the destruction of fascist imperialism in Europe and in Asia would bring about a radical change, a new beginning of a revolutionary nature. His bitter disappointment that this did not come about made him desert active politics and concentrate more on philosophy of religion, religion, and culture, and on systematic theology. The existence of this disappointment in 1945 may prove that upon arrival in the United States twelve years earlier Tillich had not surrendered his political hopes, only delayed them due to the circumstances.

A further explanation may have been the experience he had at the seminary with two colleagues. I am referring to the increasing difference, dissent, and finally hostility between Reinhold Niebuhr and his colleague Harry F. Ward, like Niebuhr an ethicist. Bonhoeffer had attended seminars that Ward and Niebuhr still taught jointly. When Tillich came to Union, the relationship between Niebuhr and Ward had started to change, initially to everyone's surprise. Niebuhr was also a member of the Socialist party. He had been the founder of the Fellowship of Socialist Christians and, in 1935, the editor of its journal, *Radical Religion*. In 1935 Niebuhr broke with the pacifists of the social-gospel movement and with the pacifist Fellowship of Reconciliation. Niebuhr increasingly criticized socialism, in particular its communist form. His colleague Ward, on the other hand, was a radical socialist who had developed enthusiasm for Soviet socialism. He was an avowed and nationally known anticapitalist. He even defended the pact between Stalin and Hitler.[17]

One additional cause for the retreat of much of the Frankfurt Tillich into the background may already be evident in *Die sozialistische Entscheidung* itself. Tillich here does not show any interest in the development of socialist practice and ideas in the United States. He shared this lack of

---

17. This conflict found expression in a novel by Edward Fuller, *Brothers Divided* (New York: Bobbs-Merrill, 1951). Elizabeth Dilling, *The Red Network: A "Who's Who" and Handbook of Radicalism for Patriots* (Kenilworth, Ill.: self-published, 1934), finds Union Theological Seminary suspicious. She reports that among some it carries the nickname "The Red Seminary" (Robert T. Handy, *A History of Union Theological Seminary in New York* [New York: Columbia University Press, 1987], 193; on 191–93 he reports on the conflict described).

appreciation with most of his social-democratic comrades in Germany, especially those of the intelligentsia. If they mentioned it at all, they unfairly belittled U.S. socialism as being no real socialism because it lacked theory and truly socialist praxis. This was more ignorance than arrogance that knowledgeable people of Massachusetts and of New York, for instance, could have easily corrected. However, Tillich seems not to have made great efforts to correct his little knowledge of U.S. socialism when he arrived in the United States.

Looking at the present social and political situation in the West, in the German Federal Republic as much as in the United States, especially the rise of the New Right, *Die sozialistische Entscheidung* turns out to be the most modern of Tillich writings. After doing away with a few dated historical references, phrases, and arguments, the remainder of *Die sozialistische Entscheidung* is more than an Evergreen. It is a precise description of our present social and political situation, its dangers and its promises. Certainly, the problems and dangers have increased, not the least because the lower middle class has been successful in sucking up the proletariat, as Tillich had foreseen and feared. Solidarity of workers and their unions with the increasing number of unemployed has not really come about, on the contrary.

I have to come to a close. At the present time there is constant talk about change of paradigms. I am an elderly, retired professor. Therefore, I feel entitled to resist such a current fad. I have been an academic administrator and university politician, too. Inculcating the hereby-gained experience and conviction and reflecting on the Frankfurt Tillich, I am inclined to call for a return to authentic paradigms, indeed, to the model presented by the Frankfurt professor that I have talked about today. He took on the beast as it was about to swallow everything. He presented a paradigm of corporate consciousness and responsibility for professors and students. Even under duress and danger, he exhorted all on both sides of the Atlantic to follow this. Contrary to that, many professors today have taken the entrepreneur as the role model to follow. They increasingly turn into hobbyists, at least partly publicly financed. They are possessors, not professors. I am old-fashioned and call for the return to Tillich's paradigm. I am for professors who profess.[18] Professing can be dangerous, but it has the promise to gain life—for all of us.

---

18. That would be in correspondence, too, with the concept of "corporation," so dear to Harvard University, yet it would improve on it, namely, in the direction of its authentic biblical, that is Pauline, meaning, the corporation meaning the entire community and including and empowering all its members, not only its leaders.

18

PRAXIS AND THEORY IN THEOLOGICAL EDUCATION: IS SCHOLARSHIP "HOT" OR "COLD"?

This chapter now goes from model professors to academic education as such. The paper was consciously conceived as stimulation for curriculum reform in a training center of theologians in one of the major urban centers of the United States. What vision should form the curriculum of such a divinity school, not only its master programs but also its doctoral program and the teaching related to these programs? The ideas expressed

---

* This essay appeared in this form in print in the *Harvard Divinity Bulletin*. Then dean of Harvard Divinity School, George Rupp had invited me to give this paper as the key address to a faculty curriculum retreat of Harvard Divinity School in North Andover, Massachusetts. I conceived the paper as a meditation on Marx's "Thesen über Feuerbach" (Theses on Feuerbach) and its interpretation by Ernst Bloch in *Das Prinzip Hoffnung* (*The Principle Hope*), this book having been written by Bloch in Cambridge, Massachusetts, during his immigration days in the Hitler period. The printed form of this essay is an abbreviation of the actual paper. All references to Karl Marx and Ernst Bloch made in the oral presentation were left out in the printed version, at the request of the editor. In the meantime, the original typescript is lost. The above text is scanned from the printed version. Those initiated into the thoughts of Marx and Bloch will recognize the traces of their line of argument, although I have turned it in the direction of a theological reflection. The paper is dedicated to the memory of Bill Sampson (M.T.S. 1973) who was murdered on 3 November 1979 in Greensboro, North Carolina, by members of the Ku Klux Klan when he tried to reconcile the praxis in North Carolina's paternalistic industry with the theology he had learned at the Divinity School, not the least in the M.Div. seminar cotaught by Arthur McGill and myself. Theology can be a very dangerous enterprise. As I reread and adjust these lines of old I do this also in Arthur's memory. My collaboration with him who died so prematurely is reflected in this essay and in this book.

in the following essay have consequences for the setting and shaping of theological research at large too.

Praxis itself both contains theory and demands theoretical deliberation and scholarship. Consciousness, as reflection, will, intention, projection, communication, and dialogue, is present in all of religious praxis and experience. Praxis is question, both spoken and unspoken, and it is response. It is a continual challenge to claims, offers, and plans made in theory. It is a stunning collage of former theories that have been expressed and realized in the life and experience of many observers. All of us carry in our minds the reflections of past generations. We are moved still by condensed forms of older battles. These presuppositions or prejudices, if you will, are the lifelong baggage of any person or scholar. They inform our thought and become our praxis, religious and otherwise. They can be motivating, inspiring, stifling, liberating, or repressive. In no way is praxis innocent or mute. In no way is it "over there," outside."

We have learned about imperialism, racism, sexism, and many more oppressive and repressive phenomena. We have become aware, too, of the contributions of religion and the participation of theology and scholarship in these phenomena. Praxis, too, is full of repressive ideologies, dogmas, and structures, conceived by scholars and now eternalized and petrified, either oppressive at birth or over time by their having become petrified, hurting as they confine people, demonized because they have become objects of worship. Religion is one of the predominant sources of alienation, but we also know that religion has often been the means of survival of the victimized, supporting them, giving them dignity, providing them inner food when other food was denied. Religion can be the heartbeat of resistance to oppression and the heartbeat of revolution.

The preserving and protecting aspects of religious life and religious experience can turn into reaction. The moving, questioning, and challenging aspects of religion can turn into revolution. All this is and has been embodied in religious jobs being necessary praxis. But what about the future? Will these dynamics continue to operate in the same way? Praxis offers many options as well as a dialogue among those options, and we are inextricably involved in that dialogue.

Scholarship would be misconceived if it presumed to take a distant position pretending noninvolvement and claiming adjudication. We take sides whether we want to or not. Our very scholarly deliberations and our scholarly debates express in various dialogues our involvement in that lively practical exchange and battle where the options for the future are clarified and decided upon. For example, our uneasiness about the situation of minorities and about women and our embarrassment about imperialism could already be a decisive turn in this taking of sides, in this choosing among options for the future. Yet uneasiness and embarrassment are too little. Imperialism, racism, and sexism could be seen as merely minor distortions and defects with only a repair job being necessary. In that case we conceded that the situations we are in, especially the religious and academic ones, were basically sound, with only a few adjustments required.

However, we could also go forward with the solid eschatological heritage of our religious and theological tradition and decide that liberation and revolutionary change are our task as religious people and as theologians within that religious praxis. We could take the mysteries of faith we celebrate in worship, particularly in the sacraments, as platforms or starting points that reflect riddles to be resolved, problems to be worked on, experiences with trends and tendencies not yet understood but with directions to be clarified and followed, mysteries not as celebrations of puzzles and darkness for puzzle's and darkness' sake but mysteries with the challenge and promise of change and with the encouragement toward our participation in that change,

There is, allegedly, a humble and respectful approach to such complex and confusing praxis. Religion and religious life in that view are considered organic, understood as a world of organic "units." These units are allegedly appreciated only by way of respectful, acritical, and positive emotional descriptions with a perception more sensual than intellectual. Associated with that view is another one that appears, upon the surface, to be a most contradictory approach, namely, a detached one, interested only in isolating, measuring, listing, and quantifying data. Both approaches are merely receptive, at most descriptive. They stay on the surface of the phenomena and the appearances they encounter. They do not penetrate to the heart of the matter. Whether they look at religious praxis as an assemblage of organic units or split it up into isolated facts and data, they have in common that they work with boxes into which they put the realities that they observe. The difference between the two kinds of approaches is that one keeps the object alive while the other kills it and dissects it, sterilizing and petrifying it for the future. But whether the unity of the object described is one of an organic nature or of a mathematical, statistical, and mechanical character, in neither case is it the unity of real life. In both cases praxis is put in a museum, and whether the museum is a live one, a zoo, or a dead one, an archive of fossils, is of minor difference. Praxis merely described is praxis murdered. It is praxis in the abstract, praxis misunderstood, praxis not participated in. Romantic and empiricist or positivist scholarship in fact led to an increase in alienation that is already abundant in practice.

Praxis calls for a kind of critical inquiry that penetrates to the heart of the matter. This kind of scholarship does not celebrate distance and abstraction, but empathy and participation. It is critical scholarship, associated with the *logos* in its double sense, that of "reason" and of "word."

As Protestants we have a tradition to defend here, too, with respect not just to scholarship and theory but with respect to praxis itself. For us religious experience and religious praxis are not without *logos*. Interpreting religious life as being without *logos* in the sense of reason and word confirms and increases the human alienation and repression of which religion has been the servant and guardian so often. Theory and scholarship are not cool, but hot, not aloof, but engaged. Scholarship is always partial, whether we concede it or not. Let us be rather open about that instead of being devious.

Scholarship reflects upon reality. In so doing it is involved in the movement and momentum of reality itself, of praxis proper. The truth of theological scholarship does not show as such, but it appears in the oscillating seams of the living contact between theology and religious praxis, the encounter of scholarship with reality in general. Here in that oscillating encounter we are dealing with the essence of reality. That essence demonstrates itself in the direction and clarity of praxis and in the power and concreteness of thought. Religious praxis and theological scholarship both experience truth, but truth is not a thing. Truth is a process. Truth creates its own momentum and its own tools. It resists manipulation and control. Truth is not beyond praxis, but praxis contains truth. Truth cannot be isolated in theory but only participated in.

Scholarship will destroy itself whenever it tries to isolate and intern truth, either by way of contemplation or by way of scientific recording. Truth is active, not passive. It invites the person willing to be active, to labor, and to wrestle, but also willing to let go. Truth is not for keeps, but it is leading on, always ahead, not so much reality as it was, as reality as it will be. Scholarship, and scholarly life are always incomplete, eschatological. In the end Hegel was less monstrous than Kierkegaard because Hegel, struck by cholera, left a fragment while Kierkegaard left a work complete, up to the last full stop.

Theological scholarship conceived in this spirit constantly interferes with its own temptation to collect and control. Contact with religious praxis and with the reality of life keeps it on its toes. Religious praxis is different from the obedient application of theological theory. It is a constant challenge and enticement to that theory. Religious praxis does not want to be application of the abstract but rather to be a witness to the concreteness of scholarship and of theological education as much as to the concreteness of life. The invitation of praxis to theory will be all the more heeded if theological thought is active in constantly uncovering the petrefacts, obstacles, errors, fetters, deceptions, and manipulations that kill its very life and drive. Right theological thought and right religious action are not foreign but akin to each other, and they are often one and the same. A theological seminar can be religious praxis just as much as a sermon or a prayer can be a theological exercise. As scholars we have a mandate to be truthful, but this means that we have to let truth work. We are merely to assist in a process that is not ours. We do not receive this mandate from a single group or from a single institution, not even from a society or a church. Neither does it come from the worldwide communities of scholars or believers, although they have a stake in it. This mandate comes from humankind at large—dead, alive, and yet unborn. That is where our responsibility and accountability rest.

The mandate of truth calls us to put probing and daring questions to reality, questions that challenge established views and structures and leave them in force only if they prove to be nondeceptive and nondestructive. These probing and daring questions are in concord with the open nature of reality. Reality, religious and otherwise, is eager to be prodded and to be communicated with. Scholarly questions raised that way are not disinterested. And the answers are at the edge of knowledge. Such oscillation between praxis and theory calls for an ever-lively chase between question and answer, analysis and synthesis, at the very brink of reality and existence. Theological inquiry can be and should be at the head of critical inquiry, not hiding behind the backs of other colleagues in other disciplines of the community of scholars but leading them in continuous critical investigation.

Inquiry is a process of questions and answers in a moving, live system. It complies with the momentum of the object observed. Reality does not allow dominance or exploitation, but it invites assistance, collaboration, and participation. Reality yields to the patient and trusting observer whose imagination has become attuned to its momentum. Critical scholarship is not a destruction of reality but an assisting, collaborative understanding of it. Scholarship is constant adventure, dangerous as well as rewarding, participating intensively in the adventure of life. This collaboration is neither blind nor static. It is alive, highly personal, and therefore not without voice or opinion, full of consent and dissent. It is a critical force vis-à-vis any distortion, manipulation, or exploitation discovered. It is an angry attack upon anyone, person or group, who claims ownership and hold over the reality described. Theological scholarship thus conceived enables the growth of religious experience and praxis and, as a result, the growth of a better world. Scholarship since ages old has had a midwifing task. This is hard labor, calling for engagement, in fact, an enthusiastic engagement. And it is moral engagement, too.

It is obvious after all I have said that teaching cannot be primarily and mainly a transfer of information. Teaching is an invitation to participate actively in the adventure described, the adventure of scholarship, the adventure of real experience. In this kind of setting the teacher is not a repressive authority representing the establishment and communicating established thoughts. The teacher is the first student in class, and it is to be hoped that he or she is also the best student in class. Any attitude of the teacher as veteran would be deadly; so would be any encouragement of academic consumerism. Academic discipline cannot enforce and reward regurgitation.

Teaching is an exposure to the momentum of praxis and theory in their continuous dialogue, the spreading of a critical awareness and experience of the goal of that process. It is an exposure to the ethos and flavor of that lively exchange. The true teacher is no external authority in this experience but a living example. Any controlling external or bureaucratic approach to this internal order and discipline would undermine the power of the momentum described. The process carries its discipline and its justification within itself.

19

EN ROUTE TO AN URBAN THEOLOGY: CAN THEOLOGY HELP US UNDERSTAND URBAN SOCIETY?

1. INTRODUCTORY REFLECTIONS

Given the prominence of "praxis" in what has been said before, the reader is definitely entitled to have his or her question answered that would ask the author how he is implementing such critical understanding of the social existence of urban theologians and all these challenging reflections in a concrete academic setting. The answer to such questions is given in a position paper that reflects the situation of the Protestant School of Theology at Frankfurt University, the place where not only Paul Tillich taught but also Martin Buber and the founders and members of the "Frankfurt School," the representatives of the "critical theory." That

---

* The following is the reworked version of a paper whose original version I wrote as a proposal for a position paper to be discussed, amended, and approved by the faculty of the new School of Protestant Theology at the Johann Wolfgang Goethe University in Frankfurt on Main. I wrote the proposal as the founding dean of that school. Additions were made to the proposal in the final chapter, where the individual fields of the school were represented. These supplements were provided by my colleagues Yorick Spiegel, Dieter Stoodt, and Edmund Weber. The faculty accepted the proposal in this supplemented form as its own position paper. In the meantime, retirements and new appointments have changed the situation in the various disciplines of the School of Theology. Modifications and innovative improvements have taken place in all the disciplines. Justice could be done to these changes only through extensive detail. This would also surpass my capability and entitlement since I have meanwhile been retired. Thus, I have returned to my initial draft and improved it. Therefore, the position paper's last chapter, which dealt with the individual disciplines, is not to be found here.

position paper grew out of the experience of a praxis-oriented introduction into the study of theology as it had been worked out in the Protestant section of the School of Comparative Religion, the predecessor to the two present schools of theology at the university, the Protestant and the Catholic one.

Frankfurt on Main played an important role in the Reformation, as did other free imperial towns. In this context, plans for new theological developments were drafted. German Protestant theology, however, did not settle down in these cities but, instead, preferred small towns. University theology has, in fact, remained there to the present day. The Humboldt University's school of theology in Berlin remained an exception, yet it was never city-oriented in an institutional sense but was rather capital-oriented, national. The schools of theology in Leipzig and then also in Halle and Breslau overslept the change of their environments into cities. After the Second World War, several theological schools were established in different major cities of the Federal Republic (Hamburg, Munich, and Bochum). If one compares these institutions' conception of themselves with those of others in rural or small-town settings, however, the difference in location seems to be one of pure chance. The institutional consciousness of these new schools evolved with little or no regard for their social location.

The fourth Protestant theological school in a major city of the Federal Republic after World War II was founded in Frankfurt on Main.[1] Will this school, too, pursue an individualized small-town bourgeois theology, as all Protestant schools have so far been tempted to do?[2] Will it respond to the chance provided by the new foundation, and will it develop an urban theology in an institutionalized effort within a metropolitan context? This is as much a matter of consciousness and will as of organization.

2. THE SITUATION

2.1. In General

In a city such as Frankfurt, it can be expected of all institutionally organized academic disciplines to see themselves and their university

---

1. There is also another Frankfurt in Germany, that on the Oder River.
2. This does not deny that individual university theologians have attempted to use an urban perspective. However, these counterexamples have remained individual exceptions. They have not become institutional reality.

context structurally as well as functionally in a regional social context to which they correspondingly offer their particular contributions. In a large city, theology needs to face the special social, political, and cultural situation created by this high accumulation of people with all their activities and needs. Theology must deal with the mobility of people and the flexible infrastructure and social web created for and by them. The long history and important role of Christian traditions in a town as ancient as Frankfurt are not sufficient reasons for founding a theological school there; even less do they provide sufficient guidelines for the future. Today Frankfurt's old ecclesial tradition is merely one of many factors making up the city, in the eyes of many, a factor even reduced to marginal importance. The large number and mobility of the inhabitants of Frankfurt are more important for this metropolis than the age of its Christian heritage.

In the past, cities were cultic centers and/or seats of rulers, frequently protected against and isolated from the surrounding countryside by fortifications, and theology almost always served this thinking in terms of fortress and rulership. Cities such as Frankfurt, however, gained importance relatively early as seats of trade and centers of communication. Today they are, especially the large ones, multicultural conglomerates. Their function as trade and market centers has come much more to the fore—alongside their importance as industrial centers.

The urban situation at the end of the second millennium, which still measures time according to the birth of Jesus—although hardly oriented toward this—has developed in a rather explosive manner and is characterized by radical transformation. As a result, unreasonably hectic activities leave an uncountable number of often seemingly insoluble problems unresolved. This development is further aggravated by the dissolution of old patterns of order, such as the nation-state. The old ideological patterns, including the denominationally oriented ones, do not function any longer.

The high density of habitation has led to an increased lack of oversight, and its consequences are often felt to be no longer manageable. This situation is accompanied by an indigestible flood of stimuli and worsened by on-the-job stress and frustration. Defense mechanisms are thereby caused on the personal as well the group level, such as isolation, crawling into anonymity, and increasing loneliness—accompanied by alienation, despair, and apathy. On the other hand, we also find reactionary, chauvinistic aggressiveness—this also a sociopathological consequence of the situation described. In many cases, the multiformity of urban self-presentation and experience aggravates this problematic situation.

2.2. Consciousness and Identity

Theology works with consciousness, is critical scholarly study of consciousness. It reflects with scientific methods collective consciousness as well as the consciousness of persons, that of small as well as of large groups, and of institutions, too. Objects of inquiry and study are not specific religious phenomena alone. Their wider contexts, conditions, motivations and goals are analyzed and interpreted as well. Religious phenomena do not exist in a vacuum. They possess origins and relations in time and space. They exist in contexts of past, present, and future and have material dimensions as well. They are part of the manifold human web of personal, transpersonal, and institutional relationships. Consciousness is to be found within all of that. Thus, consciousness as an object of theological scholarly reflection is passive as well as active, related to praxis. It comes from these broad areas of human praxis, and it again aims at praxis.[3]

Theology works with consciousness as an active phenomenon and thus constantly deals with processes, in which identities originate, are modified, and are lost. All this is the concern of theology, too. Objects of theological inquiry are shaped by life itself, so also by life in the big cities of today. A theology that deals with these themes is not merely a theology for the city but is also itself an expression of urban consciousness. Theological analysis and reflection thereby become active parts of the life of urban society, elements of the political process in the city. They relate to much more than the religion(s) of individuals.

In the cities, especially in the large ones, the closeness and togetherness of social groups has often caused contradictions, irritations, and tensions. These have been frequently glossed over by a kind of local patriotism that was supposed to work as a facade. There is no question that religious factors have repeatedly served as instigators of these troubles, yet they have also functioned more than once in a reconciling manner. In

---

3. "Praxis" is here understood in the sense that the famous "Frankfurt School" perceived it. Ernst Bloch has contributed to this as well, not the least in the book he wrote in Widener Library during his days as a refugee in Cambridge, Massachusetts. Praxis is understood as activity that is undertaken in personal responsibility. It originates in social conditions, which define the nature of contemporary existence. It is the given historical reality. This form of nature is to be taken as challenge and task, not as fate. Praxis, thus conditioned and moving, is reflected and condensed in theory, which is clearly an afterthought, but a necessary one. Theory does not precede praxis but originates in it, preceding and stimulating the reality of tomorrow, as its sketch, as it were. It anticipates the future. In this understanding of praxis and theory, the future is considered to be the platform of liberation. In this liberation, the world is changed through the concrete union of thought and action.

the latter case, religion has often been used with the goal of an inauthentic social peace. Yet there are authentic acts of straightening out of difficulties and differences caused by multicultural differences, and this balancing often evolved into new possibilities for the city and its groups.

Today these urban tensions have been increased and extended by a degree of mobility that exceeds what cities were accustomed to, and this has occurred in an explosive intensification. In the upper sectors of society, those of the well-to-do, mobility has increased relatively peacefully because it is seen as furthering the establishment, the resources, as well as the revenues of those who have the means to pay for such mobility and to exploit its benefits. On lower social levels, these tensions are often full of irritation, even hostility and hatred.

Already in the Middle Ages the geographic and social mobility of persons and groups had interregional and interreligious, sometimes even transcultural, character. However, all kinds of mobility have grown tremendously in modern times, with an incredible increase during and since World War II.

In the light of these drastic changes, cities everywhere find themselves in a process of renewed search for their identity. The radical rearrangement of economic structures is exerting further pressure in this direction. Old and new groupings are involved in this process, some of their own free will, and this often not merely actively but rather aggressively. Others are forced and only passively involved. All these groups, both the active and passive ones, experience this redefinition of their group identities.

It is all too obvious that people often do not consider it easy to find or keep their own identity in the city. This has been increasingly so since the time of industrialization, and it has intensified in the period that is called the second industrial revolution. The uncertainty often starts with the question of what one's first seat of residence is. Actual citizenship is less and less clear. The identity of traditional groups and groupings is no longer a matter of course either. New ones originate, often without a clear understanding of themselves, even less with a resilient one. Whether the interrelationship within the groups is more confusion or concert quite often remains unclear.

Thus, the search for identity is a task on all levels, of the city as a whole, of its larger and smaller groups, and of each family and each citizen. It is a matter of fact that even the smaller associations can no longer be sure of their members, the larger ones, such as the churches, even less. It is disputed whether a possible antidote would be an increase in the groups' internal liberality. This could include the encouragement of greater differentiation within the group, with greater autonomy of the individual sections and greater personal self-determination of the members. Churches in particular are discussing this. An urban theology would have an important task in such reflection and creative imagining.

2.3. Identity and Integration

Churches in cities are traditionally organized into parishes. Recently church administrations have started to fuse smaller parishes into larger ones. This has increased the abstract regionalization of congregations. These enlarged parishes are even more removed from people's real lives than before. The abstract parish structure, small or large, is traditional, yet its biblical-theological foundation is highly questionable. There are, however, some socially relevant strengths of such partitioning:

The U.S. experience with congregations based on personalized membership teaches, for instance, that such completely person-oriented organizations have great difficulties absorbing and resolving deficits of social migrations that are caused by social mobility in the cities today. The real parishes in the United States, those that are geographically, not personally, defined are better able to fill the void caused by their richer members fleeing to the suburbs and their poorer members staying and increasing in number in the inner city, by way of reproduction and through immigration. These local parishes can often substantially help to strengthen their impoverished parishioners. In addition, they can give their threatened communities something like a social spine. In this way, the parish system can, in areas of social tensions in major cities, provide social defense, stabilization, and even improvement. It can provide assistance and support to socially and economically disadvantaged people. In this, there is social help, rehabilitation, and empowerment, including economic hope for impoverished people who were marginalized by mainstream society.

The history of the word *parish* hints at a decisive alteration, a social as well as theological and psychological change that happened when the church became state religion. This change of the nature of the parish for the most part was destructive for nature and life of the church. It implied a complete contradiction to the understanding of congregation and church in the New Testament and the early church. The Latin word *parochia* is a direct loanword from New Testament Greek, where the term παροικία[4] does not mean the local congregation, even less in the sense of a

---

4. "Sojourning existence, stay as a stranger in a foreign country" in 1 Pet 1:17 speaks about the circumstances of the existence of the church; compare the naming of the members of the church with the synonym πάροικος, "stranger, foreigner, migrant," in 1 Pet 2:11. In

geographically restricted sector. Instead, it refers to noncitizens staying in a foreign place, even in a foreign country, and indeed refers to migration into foreign lands. Παροικία is the exact opposite of settledness, of being at home.

As the church in the first century adopted this Greek term παροικία, it characterized mobility as its major structural principle. More was in view than the desert and nomad model that could be easily romanticized and allegorized.⁵ The New Testament associates concepts of sojourning with those of the city.⁶ Urban life and wandering here do not exclude each other, on the contrary. The assembly of citizens is the early church's societal frame of reference, not the garden of paradise. The language, style, and thematics of the New Testament writings testify to embeddedness and to interest in urban, indeed metropolitan, culture as a phenomenon that depends on mobility and enhances it. The congregations provide shelter, rest, motivation, and orientation for the sojourners' further pursuits.

The New Testament writings and those of the so-called apostolic fathers were directed to an urban public, not to a rural one. The emphasis of these writings on sojourning presupposed that one could not be too sure of being securely settled in one's present location. One had to take into account the possibility of moving on. Many different reasons could be the cause, not the least economic ones. The majority of the population of the cities, in particular of the larger ones, knew this mobility from their own experience—especially the members of the lower classes. The early church interpreted this being on the move with its constant readiness for a new turn as something essential and even beneficial. This mobility was

---

Heb 11:9, the verb παροικεῖν, "migrate, sojourn" is used for the nomadic existence of Abraham and his family, prefiguring the way of life of the adherents of the early church.

5. It could be easily romanticized and allegorized and is so until today. In this fashion it is still used as cliche for an internalizing antiurban interpretation of the message of the New Testament and its concept of community.

6. Just a few references must suffice. In Gal 4 Paul associates the biblical Sarah, like her husband Abraham a wandering person, with the heavenly Jerusalem. In his very urban first letter to the Corinthians, Paul uses in a central chapter (10) the exodus motif in order to describe the existence of the congregation addressed. In the Epistle to the Hebrews, the motif of the wandering of the believers—the dominant theme of the document—is especially elaborated in chapter 11. The heavenly city as the goal of this sojourning is already hinted at in 11:10, then mentioned again in 12:22 and 23, here together with some major elements of the Hellenistic city: the city council, the people's assembly, the registry (of properties, taxable persons, and taxable income). The book of Revelation refers to cities and urban matters many times, and it concludes with two visions of the new Jerusalem. On the other hand, John describes in his central chapter 12 the existence of the church on earth (the children of the heavenly woman) as straying in the desert.

not always a physical phenomenon, yet it was at least a mental one. The experience of being foreigners, alienated in many different ways, was elevated by the early church into a more general anthropological category with a deeper meaning behind it. Being on the move, experiencing alienation was no longer seen as merely negative and deficient but was understood as a fundamental human experience, interpreted as an essential condition for freedom and for authentic future, necessary elements of a liberating process full of dynamism.

The documents that speak of such παροικία presuppose life in the big city. The big city in such texts is not demonized; even less is rural or small town life glorified. The emphasis of the early church on far-reaching communication, indeed a cosmopolitan reach, belonged to the Hellenistic city, especially the big one.

The parochial system as we know it has been common in the church since Constantine's reform. It was intended for rural and small-town situations. It met the needs of rural and small-town people in that period and worked within the structures of their local lives and relations. The village and the small town, however, remained the mental and social models and structural perspectives of Christian congregations to this day, in the cities as well. These models and perspectives were and are unable to reach or meet the structural and substructural system of the big cities with their diversity and mobility. However, whatever the organizational structure of the urban and metropolitan congregations of tomorrow, it needs to retain the sense of belonging and engagement that the parish model could provide. Its inherently abstract nature can be overcome by democratic qualities of personal responsibility, communal concern and solidarity, inspiration, and empowerment.

Therefore, it is still an essential as well as an unfulfilled task for a school of theology in a big city, even more in a metropolis, to discover the city for theology, recognizing its peculiar character, demand, and promise. Its difference from village and small town has to be recognized as regards the togetherness and interweaving, the antitheses and conflicts, the remedies and chances, the religious praxis, its attitudes, customs, insights, fears, and hopes. The organizational situations, the necessities, and the potentials of the city need to be studied. Such an undertaking will be a rediscovery of responses, insights, and evolutions of the church of the first and second century C.E.

Theology can no longer belittle or even overlook the relevance of the correlation of church members and religious praxis to the life of the big city, its problems and chances, its failings and its strivings. The reality of the big cities has to be consciously faced and researched. Critical historical and systematic comparisons of comparable situations of earlier religious praxis within the church and outside of it belong to that. In such comparison, the potential for structures of shared and corporate consciousness can be discovered and encouraged. Communal motivation and condensation in the face of multiple differentiation must be studied. Mutual relations of personal, group, and societal identity are to be considered, too, as well as the nature and potential of integral tendencies. The latter exist despite and within all differentiation. Theology can do this only if theological subject matters are interpreted in their own right too. Their relation to sociological and sociopsychological conditions and interpretations needs to be scrutinized. Theologically informed critical analysis of sociological and sociopsychological phenomena and their atheological interpretations is also obligatory. The result of such analysis will be that the nonideological and nonreligious pretensions of such phenomena and of their secular interpretations are most often questionable. These interpretations reveal their hidden ideological, religious, and indeed theological presuppositions and perspectives all too frequently to the eye sharpened by theological criticism. It must also be asked what consequences this hiding of religious and theological elements and aspects entails for the relevance of the disciplines involved and for the life of the city. The hidden ideological or even theological presuppositions, camouflaged by objectivity and alleged neutrality, influence in an uncontrolled way the description of the city's inhabitants and institutions by scholars trying to ignore the discipline of theology.

A critical debate of the existing Christian image of the city, particularly its parochial structure, will help one to understand anew the phenomenon of neighborhood in an authentic, nonideological, and unsentimental fashion. Neighborhood constitutes an important factor of integration and stabilization in the larger community of the city. The neighborhood is also—quite unromantically—a potential bridge to larger entities of identification: the area around the city, home, and homeland, regional and transregional culture and history, province, nation. The neighborhood can be seen as plurality and can be further developed in this differentiated fashion. This diversity needs to be embraced and experienced. At the same time, neighborhood could be a momentous element in the reconciliation between the big city and nature that has not yet been achieved anywhere. Neighborhoods can function also as interlocking forces, not limited to the city itself but stretching beyond its borders into other communities.

Thus, the concept of neighborhood is not necessarily a reactionary one. The same is true with so-called local patriotism. It is not by necessity isolationist and chauvinist. In an urban context, the concentration on the locally particular can function as potential for the acknowledgement of societal mobility and transparency. This could fertilize as well as brace urban life, not only in its small contexts, but it could also be effective on a broader level. The city and the larger society need such support in order to gain a more livable future for themselves and for society at large. In these more particularistic aspects and phenomena of urban life, dynamic power exists that cities require in order to function as a force of transcendence beyond the pathetic halo, the idiosyncrasies and the inordinate controls of the national state. The latter is more hindered than furthered by its controlling tendencies and powers and by its stifling centralism. Cities, which activate their particularities, can evolve into true links between nations, in a more democratic European and in a worldwide society. They can be strengthened in this approach by the oldest international institutions, the universities, the churches, the synagogues, and the mosques.

The universities can be even more effective in this process than the others mentioned. The universities have a tradition that has already proven its ability to transcend the crusts of many hundred years of Christian chauvinism. The individual universities have been members of a universal academic republic since the Middle Ages, and they are still supposed to be that. Some of this can still be observed today in the forms of international academic cooperation and even more in border-transcending student protests. A theology that understands itself as an essential, even a founding member of such global academic community can and must contribute to the universities' critical dialogue with the sins of centralism, of which nationalism and imperialism are as much part as is the increasing global economic monopolization.

Mercantile globalism, contrary to its propaganda, is a new centralizing threat caused by a steadily decreasing number of increasingly powerful companies. They are dividing the world among themselves and making states and state organizations their faithful satellites and vassals. In order to counteract this threat, theology must do its part in stimulating the assessment of the dangers and potentials of the economic situation and its development. Theology can encourage practitioners and theoreticians to meet and exchange their views on these matters and to work out suggestions that promise improvements. This cannot be done responsibly without the participation of other academic partners and practitioners. The fact that the city is part of the global village is an essential perspective of such exchange. Critical assessment cannot be the only response to the development of world economy. Constructive consultation must grow out of such criticism.

The city must be turned into a conscious laboratory of experimentation in the meeting of cultures, forms of cultures, languages, religions, industries, trades, and banks. In this collaborative experimentation, a school of theology can contribute to creating a common language between the different parts. Such a language is much more than an accumulation of linguistic elements. It must be an expression of a multifold consciousness of identity among all citizens, not only as persons but also as members of their various groupings. This will stand at the end of the road of experimentation. It will mean a praxis of understanding beyond the borders, which had been set by previous divisions of culture, religion, economics, and politics.

Therefore, an urban theology needs to be an ecumenical theology. It must be open toward other institutions and forms of religion beyond the borders of the larger established Christian churches and toward non-Christian partners in the interreligious dialogue. Such ecumenical exchange will not succeed if it maintains the disrespect for the traditions of others so common today. The denial of authentic identity to these so-called "sects" and "foreign" religious bodies would be detrimental to the community of the cities of tomorrow. The continuation of such neglect of other religious bodies is to this day a form of continued Christian colonialism. It still insists on the other side's surrender of its own face and heart. There is another danger, however: an all too quick generalization and untested claim of commonality among these bodies. All of them, the churches included, have to muster the will to listen and understand the others in all their foreignness. This will take much time and patience. The necessary understanding and interpretation will have to overcome the individual particularism. It will have to deal with the often-hostile facades of isolation and pride and will have to cultivate the virtues of curiosity and respect—even in relation to one's own tradition, the value of which outsiders very often recognize more easily than insiders.

2.4. Community/Labor/Production/Civilization

The main concern of urban theological scholarship and teaching is consciousness that is relevant for the community. There is a dialectical relationship typical for urban life: people have more contacts, and at the same time they are living farther apart and are more alienated. These features of urban life cause its attraction and its offensiveness. As theology reflects on them, it has to consider the basic dialectic between the personal and the communal as well. There is a tension between rightful personal privacy and an all-exclusive isolation, between healthy community life and social pressures. The city stands for accumulation as well as for differentiation. It could become an agglomeration into collectivity, which would destroy persons. The other danger for a city is that of atomization. The city offers a continuous unevenness between history and future, passing over too fast or holding on too firmly, between neglect for the personal strengths of the many and overattention to the excessively praised gifts and achievements of some few. Arrogance and failure, pretentious might and weakness, idealist upswing and corruptibility—these common features of urban life are all proper topics of theological discourse.

The critical-analytical and the synthetic constructive forces of urban theology will have to prove themselves in the discovery of the theological equivalency of these themes and their various modifications. An internal discourse and interdisciplinary and societal exchange will be the place where such discoveries occur. The diagnostic and therapeutic abilities of theology and its visionary potential will have to manifest themselves in this. In its ability to formulate challenges and to balance apparent imbalances, theology will have to demonstrate its capability for peace making.

An urban theology will have to dig even deeper into the concrete problems of the city if it wants to do justice to the fact that theological problems are not situated in heaven but are out there on the street. It has to reflect critically and constructively on the history and transformation of the means of production. The intensive differentiation represented by the division of labor will be a subject of such inquiry, so also the arrangements and rearrangements of production-related groups. The city is primarily the socially organized space and environment in which production, in particular industrial production, is at home. It is also the location where most of the exchange of the goods of production takes place and where an essential part of their consumption is enabled and indeed occurs. Theology cannot deal with all of this sufficiently without extensive and intensive interdisciplinary cooperation.

Theology must ask whether and how in such processes the Christian conception of personal gifts and their free and creative unfolding and sharing can be realized or is interfered with if not altogether prevented in its necessary egalitarian accomplishment. This includes the old and ever-new question of how being an authentic person relates to performance and whether and how far personal achievement is constitutive or destructive for personal identity and society's health.

Production, division of labor, and exchange of goods of production were already in antiquity essential elements of "civilization," civilization in the true sense of the term, namely, the *civitas* and the *cives*, presuppositions of a society of *citoyens*. Certainly the evolution of *bourgeoisie*, related to the *borough*, more in the sense of *bourg/burg* in the Germanic sense of an isolated and fortified place, had its origin in such understanding. Even today, this association of *civilization, civitas/city,* and *civis/citizen* is not completely forgotten. This is true despite the fact that in the Middle Ages the ancient notion of the town or city was rather transformed, indeed falsified.

Other essays in this collection deal with the fact that organized Christian religion and Christian theology as institutionalized scholarship have had an essential part in the misunderstanding, transformation, and corruption of the associations described. Their positive prospects were not sufficiently appreciated, and their negative potentials, such as rugged individualism, not recognized; instead, the latter were brushed over and hidden by other, more imagined dangers. Therefore, the truly negative potentials were corrosive under cover and all the more dangerous. Christian religion and theology have caused many of the catastrophic developments we face in the cities of today, although theology and religion hardly feel responsible. Responsibility was, rather, covered up or altogether avoided by noble retreat, an allegedly spiritual way out.

Although it neglected the urban situation institutionally, academic theology is not separable from these processes, neither as a whole nor in any of its disciplines. It cannot be disassociated from the reality in the cities. It must see itself as an element in the city's increasingly self-differentiating production that brings about an ever-growing expenditure of administration, police, taxes, and the like. In addition, the public and private services expand. Urbanity is the origin of politics; thus urban theology is necessarily political theology whether it encounters all of these circumstances, causes, and developments consciously or not. Theology needs to become more aware of its essentially political nature.

An urban theology that in this light reflects critically religious phenomena and ecclesial institutions and issues must find it interesting that since World War II all essential economic, social, and political movements and developments have evolved within big cities. Many of these movements and developments have been processes of a religious or pseudoreligious nature. An exception was the evolution of liberation theology in basic rural communities in South and Middle America.

2.5. Living Together

Churches and congregations have in the past always been related to the family as a basic social unit. The idea of an inner relationship of the οἰκία to the biological family and the understanding of the church as *familia dei* has been active in the church since the second century. This has provided the essential model for the social self-understanding of the church. To this day churches tend also to offer this model to their surrounding as the one and only social pattern. The interest in securing one's own biological future has also served as a major purpose of the church, although not always consciously conceded. The church thereby became interconnected with economic production and biological and social reproduction—without being sufficiently critically aware of this. The result was a tendency to multiply obedient subjects of the politically, socially, and economically powerful. Thus, the church contributed to the conservation of what alleged to be the established order, the seemingly stable and beneficial condition. The church repeatedly defended what had long outlived itself. In doing so, the church had robbed itself of its visionary ability and task, thereby betraying the future-oriented nature of the gospel and its accompanying trust and mission.

The dwelling motif has been a significant symbol in biblical thinking from the start, a motif related to the divine as well as to the human. Biblical texts use the motif not in a merely figurative sense, even less in an introverted fashion. They rather describe the dwelling as something concrete, often utterly physical. This makes it appropriate for theology to reflect on questions of settlement, existing as well as future ones. Aspects of social ethics also belong to this. Concepts, plans, and norms of housing developed by various entities of society, both public and private, need to be included in theological considerations too. Concentrating housing in relatively small spaces, as is characteristically done in cities, creates a mental and religious climate that should be the concern of theological attention and inquiry. Academic disciplines, among them theology, need a lively and creative intellectual fervor. Such atmosphere requires healthy housing conditions. All too often intellectual life and pursuit have been slowed down, damaged, or killed by inhumane urban living conditions.

This demands that theology accompany city planning and urban architecture in a foresighted manner. The building needs of local churches should be subordinated to this wider concern in which interdisciplinary contacts are again of cardinal value. By means of such discussions, adequate building models for appropriate future dwelling can be found. In the field of architecture, church and theology have to this day limited their common concern too much to church-owned buildings, especially the architecture of churches, often with incredible neglect for the surrounding environment. Cheapness and humaneness, private wealth and common weal all too often come into conflict in the context of building and housing. Moderating these tensions and conflicts is more than a question of mere technical and economic calculations; it is also one of consciousness, motivation, communication, and structure. All these areas should be home territory for theology.

The bureaucratic planning of the city and of city districts is part of organized dwelling. Traffic planning and regulation belong to this. All of these are phenomena of communication. There is hardly any other human book that is more interested in communication than the Bible. All aspects of human mobility and of exchange of opinion and information are to be critically and constructively reviewed there, also including physical movement and its means. In a world taken over by the media and their images, church and theology can bring to the fore their age-old acquaintance with symbols. Urban symbols, for instance, among many others fill the Bible from its first chapters to its last. The tower of Babel and the "heavenly" Jerusalem are the most prominent yet not the only ones. In the last book of the Christian Bible, John the seer turns the megalopolis into an entity that saves the world.

Since olden times theology has had to deal with symbols and myths. It has had and still has experience with demythologizing efforts and with the critique of ideologies. Academic theology, therefore, is able to deal with the symbolisms and ideologies of our modern cities and metropolises, not only with the expressed but also with the hidden ones.

The social, mental, and cultural climate of a city—and the religious life within it—are areas of concern. Cities consist not only of public, commercial, and industrial buildings but also, and to a higher degree, of living quarters. Today the latter are increasingly segregated. We have personalized buildings on the one hand and uniform apartments and houses of cheap mass production for the less well-off on the other. The elite have individualized houses, apartment buildings, and settlements that are more and more fortified. Perhaps mixed solutions could be possible, such that reduce the social polarization. Increasing contrasts mark the current situation: on the one hand apartments accumulate in high-rises, and on the other hand the city expands horizontally. It extends into suburban and satellite settlements. Can this expansion really improve the sense of community? Does it not achieve the opposite? The suburban sprawl threatens to erode the sense of communal identity, and so do many high-rises. And what about the environmental costs? On the other hand, is a concentration of city dwelling in a smaller space an answer to the suburban sprawl? Do centralization and decentralization necessarily stand in conflict with each other, or is a reconciling compromise possible? It is quite obvious that city centers are all too often drained of any living quality and downgraded to office holdings. Excessive cost saving, often combined with corrupt profiteering, has turned cheap housing into slums and ghettos in most countries. The hope for easier access to social and economic success in the cities—misused by the advertising industry all over the world—has encouraged land flight and overcrowding in the cities, which contributed to a disastrous development.

2.6. Living Together in the Flow of Time

A theology that is conscious of its situation in society can contribute a good deal to the definition and analysis of health and normality. It possesses a wide and differentiated tradition of debate and experience. It has a rich contemporary practice of charitable services, too. All of this needs to be better integrated into concerted endeavors of a new urban and metropolitan theology. Questions of public health are not only issues for medicine and politics and for the social activity of the church. No, they are natural questions of theology in its complete range, not of practical theology alone.

It is a matter of course that the rich biblical and ecclesial discussion about disease, about the normal and the anormal and abnormal, about the valuable and the worthless, and about the strong and the weak belongs into this context. A great deal of social-critical explosiveness is present in these discussions. Paul has debated such problems under the metaphors of refuse and garbage—and this in the context of his understanding of justification by Christ.[7]

There is some connection with the modern insight that municipal refuse is not merely a negative phenomenon entailing more or less complete removal. Growing ecological consciousness has helped to increase the awareness of the need for differentiation. The situation has moved in a positive direction. The objective has become less that of re-fuse than that of re-use. The problem of trash does not start with garbage removal; even less does it end there. Isolating persons in sanitariums, reformatories, and prisons can pertain to it as well. This relates to the difficult issue of the distinction between the dispensable and the indispensable, which has many different faces. The medical profession knows this. The problem of "triage," the selection of those considered worth saving, is not limited to epidemics and other catastrophes. It is more common, and other professions are involved in such decisions, too. How are they made? Who defines the values operative in them?

The ever-expanding cemeteries in cities are also phenomena of urban clearance. They become more and more expensive, not only in terms of monetary expenses but also in terms of demands on space and other resources. In the cemeteries themselves we meet curious mixtures of extreme personalization and utter anonymity. We find glaring class distinctions as well. How much memory does a city owe to its former citizens? Is a place in the cemetery, even more a costly epitaph, the final climax of human justification? This has become as much an economic as a financial problem, another element of the discussion of wise use of resources. This is a question that is appropriate in a city's management of its monuments, too.

---

7. Most prominently in the first part of Phil 3.

The two preceding paragraphs may have been too drastic for the taste of many readers not accustomed to have all of these very concrete themes juxtaposed so closely. *Normally* these issues are kept widely apart. However, a theology informed by the concepts of incarnation and the justification of the godless needs to emphasize that these details of urban life are quite concrete and relevant for everyone and are closely interrelated.

The observation of these relationships, too often covered up, makes something else obvious: communities again and again experience transitions, entry and exit, birth, marriage, divorce, remarriage, other forms of bonding, death, hiring and firing, moves and removals, and so forth. Today the big question is whether communities are still able to publicly recognize these transitions. Can a city afford all that any longer? Issues of sexual, racial, social, and cultural identity and relations play into this as well and have been distorted by discrimination all too often and too much, frequently caused or at least supported by religious and theological opinions and actions.

It is traditional that religions, the churches included, played and play an essential function within society with respect to the "rites of passage." In former times, religious rites functioned in such instances in place of public law. Today the need for proper recognition of the actual realities of transience has become infinitely complex. The reality is multifarious and multileveled, conditioned by ever-diversifying traditions, expectations, and norms. The radical variety of existing cultures and traditions and of social changes and new desires calls for extensive reconsiderations in which theology as an academic discipline has a legitimate place. It is knowledgeable about rites.

Such reconsiderations cannot be done abstractly. They need to include urban reality, consciousness, and identity, and they are changing as well. A radically reformed understanding of the many "rites of passage" in general and in particular could become an important therapy against the pathetic tendency toward anonymity in our big cities. The multifaceted complex of transition always includes memory and remembrance. Recognizing their particular character and function contributes to the understanding and preserving of identity. This can provide antidotes against societal disintegration. The Bible and the Jewish and the Christian traditions are full of cases and practices of remembering. The same is true with Islam and other religious groups.

2.7. The City in Context

Cities have lived at the expense of the surrounding countryside since ages past, the more the bigger the city was and is. Cities tend to use the countryside as a reservoir for personnel, goods, and services. The countryside buys and consumes the goods produced by the city as well. Degradation of the surrounding villages and small towns has all too often been a result of the growth of the city. The communities around the growing cities frequently experienced the urban expansion as an attrition of their own substance and identity. Their own integral potentials and abilities were emptied too.

Today, under ecological perspectives, the problems of the city environment are being taken more seriously in the urban debate. The customary urban disregard for the countryside surrounding the cities and of the environment at large threatens to avenge itself on the cities themselves. Their rather fragile infrastructure is in many cases close to collapse, especially that of the megalopolises. Theology has recently rediscovered ecology. Outside influences were responsible for that discovery, not own insight, despite some very interesting and imaginary strands in the Jewish and Christian tradition.[8] Urban theology needs to comb through the church's history, assessing the manifestations, experiences, and necessities of religious connections and dissociations, conflicts, and solutions in the ecology of urban life. This research will be done in a historical-critical and a systematic-critical way of which theology has proven to be capable, although so far all too little in an urban perspective. Such constructive rethinking will include concern for ecologically healthy conditions and relations in the future. An ecologically conscious city will contribute to modifications not only of urban but also of regional infrastructures.

Theology has had and still has a hard time understanding the problems of industrialization. Even less has it proven its ability to reflect on industrialization constructively. This reflection demands cooperation with other relevant academic disciplines and with city planners and politicians. Mental, spiritual, and cultural values stand behind the possibilities of work and of gain-seeking for all citizens. To this day, this has been considered merely under economic and political perspectives, not under religious and theological ones. The theological discipline of social ethics has reviewed this mostly in reaction to relevant nontheological scholarly fields, all too often merely depending on them. The questions of

---

8. The book of Genesis and the Psalms could have given different directions already. The most challenging example that theology and church have completely covered and forgotten is Rom 8, where Paul discusses the human corruption of nature in the context of justification, of slavery and liberation, of inspiration and resistance, and of communal promise and hope. The individualizing interpretation of the Bible was the main means by which such perspectives were buried.

the essence and of the possibilities of technology have been almost consistently ignored in the fields of theology at large. At best, they were looked at from an arrogant distance. When the ecological debate started and high tech knocked on the door, theologians reacted more with sentiment and emotion than with reason. The now so fashionable service industry has as yet never been exposed to an intensive value discussion. If anyone has given it some deeper thought, then only some specialists among social ethicists. Generally, one took it for granted that the traditional general values could be applied to this new outgrowth of the second industrial revolution. The cause of such insufficient reactions was the lack of appropriate preparation.

The new tasks of sciences and technology, including the issues of gene manipulation, in the context of global urbanization need the critical accompaniment of the entire university, including the humanities. This will result in a constructive impact on the society of tomorrow. Urban theology can and must play a role, too. It can fulfill this task most efficiently if it is sufficiently aware that it is situated in and a part of its urban surrounding. Mutual dialogue between the academic disciplines will improve such awareness.

Theology had even greater difficulties with respect to issues of money, economy, finances, and the university discipline of economics. These difficulties are surprising, since the most important writer of the New Testament, Paul, a thoroughly urban figure, invested much energy and thought in a major financial enterprise, the collection for Jerusalem, and wrote extensively about it. In addition, he again and again reflected about remuneration, performance, and achievement and about their proper and improper relations. He did so under an aspect that Protestants had from the very start considered of greatest importance, the issue of justification. To this day, however, there is no sufficient theology of money. It is left by default to Christian economists and bankers, who have to come up with theological answers from scratch, with little possibilities of exchange with academic theology, if at all.

2.8. Quality of Life

The modern city is not only a production center but also a center of consumption, education, communication, and entertainment. Arts in all forms are also at home there, active arts as well as their reception. Religion and churches have a place in the city since ancient times, yet to this day theology, especially Protestant theology, has great difficulties appreciating, let alone integrating, aesthetics as an intellectual enterprise. Aesthetics represents a blend of values and of hermeneutical issues that is not too far removed from theological discourse. Still, it has almost never become a relevant subject in theological reflection, only occasionally in practical theology. Even there it is most often reduced to the aspect of its immediate applicability in the area of church and religion. It is especially hard for theology to deal with merely indirect religious and theological expressions. Arts, especially modern arts, are full of the dogmatically imprecise, the heterodox, or, even more, the interreligious. This is one of the reasons theology, which is too much concerned with the theologically correct, has a hard time dealing with the arts intellectually.

Since its beginnings, Protestant theology has occupied itself quite actively with the problem of education. One could call the Reformation an adult education movement. It encouraged lay theology, and the most prominent dogmatic to this day was produced by a layman, John Calvin. Unfortunately, the Protestant movement turned its attention more and more to the education of children. Lay theology practically died out. Pietism tried to revive adult education and lay theology but with no long-range success. In the last century, adult education and lay theology were energetically revived first in Denmark, then in Great Britain, the United States, and Germany. However, this discussion and the ensuing practice have succumbed in the meantime.[9] An urban theology worth its name must reverse this trend. It can give adult education and lay theology a new chance. Divinity schools in Germany and the United States have sufficient proof that lay people are interested in theological courses over a lifetime. These people need to be taken more seriously. Their mature life and judgment and their professional experience need to be integrated. Theology can benefit if such persons are encouraged to participate in the theological discourse. Cooperation with other disciplines and agencies will improve the dialogue and increase the input that theology can get from these lay persons. If theological faculties will pontificate less, listen more to a mature laity, and ask for their contribution to theological inquiry, the educational situation in the city of tomorrow will be reshaped. The potentials of the urban setting will be much enhanced.

It is curious that so little has been thought and discussed in the church and in theology about the proper location of institutional education. What appeared as given was taken as a matter of course, and this location was that of small towns and villages. The larger cities of Germany, Switzerland, France, Great Britain, the Netherlands, and Scandinavia, although

---

9. It almost never addressed the city as such. An exception could be found in the days of the young University of Chicago after the big fire, with George Mead as the most prominent example. Parker, the president of the university, was of public influence in Chicago and the nation as well, especially in the areas of theology and church.

often very active in the origins of the Reformation, never adopted a leading stance in the educational enterprise of Protestantism. The urban dimension of Geneva in the long run did not color its contribution to the Protestant world either, not even in larger Presbyterian communities. The transfer of the Presbyterian experience to the American colonies happened through Puritans who had their origin in urban settings but who had lost the urban perspective that they had originally acquired.[10]

This neglect of the social-geographical location of education in general has remained almost completely true in Germany after 1945 as well, with drastic consequences for the pedagogy of religion and for religious instruction in public schools. The social milieu of the schools and their wider context in an urban society remained theologically almost completely undisputed. The inner and organizational connections between religious instruction and other fields were not reflected under the aspects of urban contexts. Within the study of pedagogy, the active communication between the various fields is left to the students, all the more the reflection of the function of these fields and their connections within the social context of the life in the city.

This is even more the case in the area of continuing and adult education. How can the corruption of the general and religious education of children be stopped? How can it be changed from a blessing for what is established and conformist to a creative instrument in unfolding free personalities able to think freely? How can this be enhanced on all levels of education in all classes of society?

The public nature of theology and church, especially with respect to social and legal privileges, can no longer be taken as a matter of course, the least with respect to contents and forms.[11] Church and theology

---

10. This was in contrast to some of their forebears, who under the Bloody Mary had been refugees to Frankfurt on Main and other cities on the Continent and had undergone major experiments in liturgy and polity that were in fact revolutionary. I have written on the English refugees in Frankfurt, whose pastor John Knox was for a while; see Dieter Georgi, "Demokratische Experimente englischer Flüchtlinge 1554–1559," in *Gott in Frankfurt? Theologische Spuren in einer Metropole* (ed. Matthias Benad; Frankfurt am Main: Athenäum, 1987), 59–64. One could call this experimentation attempts in urban theology, quite different from and opposed to the inclinations and developments in Anglican and Lutheran theology and polity, that therefore led to the local difficulties of the refugees' congregation.

11. Everything in this paragraph is of particular relevance in Germany, Scandinavia, and Great Britain, where various remnants of established state churches still exist. However, the argument that this does not apply to the United States at all is a great self-deception. Civil religion is in the United States not only more pervasive than anywhere in Europe but also has many legal sides and political presuppositions and consequences, usually camouflaged but all the more effective.

should be the first to open the debate on all this; they should not wait for the public or the state or other religions to push for that. Intensive experimentation and theoretical efforts with new forms of the public nature of religion are required.

All of what has been mentioned last belongs in the context of theology and culture, a frame of reference that for many decades was taboo in Protestant Germany due to the criticism of *Kulturprotestantismus* by dialectical theology, especially that of Karl Barth. Today a theology of culture is possible again, indeed highly desirable. A school of theology like that in Frankfurt committed to an urban theology in the fashion described is predestined to produce such a theology of culture. Paul Tillich's heritage should be a local as well as an international challenge to fulfill such task.

Entertainment and leisure belong to an urban culture, too. Protestant theology has not paid much attention to these phenomena. They were considered below esteem. The Sabbath command belongs here, yet it has been heavily neglected by antilegally inclined Protestant theology. When the aspects of relaxation have been considered at all, then under narrowly religious aspects, rarely under the perspectives of entertainment and leisure. Other biblical suggestions on entertainment as they are to be found in the rich narrative material of the First and Second Testaments are not taken seriously either. An encouragement of the lighter muses or a theological justification of them so far is even less likely. Protestant theology felt and feels committed to seriousness. The many biblical examples of humor and irony and of play and drama that scriptures share with their cultural environments need to be rediscovered and evaluated.

Citizens need to be assured that the city lives, and it cannot live without the active participation of the citizens. An urban theology, especially a metropolitan one, needs to understand itself as part of this life. An active interest in democratic structures and procedures, indeed institutional and personal participation in the democratic process, are essential for urban theology. The theological dimensions and problems of urban and metropolitan life must be recognized, pointed out, and debated. Such observations, findings, criticisms, and suggestions must be communicated to the municipality, personally as well as through institutional channels. A closer interconnection and networking between university and city and between school of theology and municipality is necessary to provide a platform for intensive exchange with the urban/metropolitan society. The churches and other religious entities in the municipality and its surroundings need to be included in this.

3. CONCRETE ANTICIPATION OF AN URBAN THEOLOGY IN FRANKFURT ON MAIN

Since the 1960s, the Johann Wolfgang Goethe University had a Department of Religion with a Protestant and a Catholic section. Attempts were made to appoint scholars who showed an understanding of the urban situation of the department. A differentiated understanding of past and present social realities, developments, and interconnectedness was expected of the teachers. A certain acquaintance with the academic conditions of the Frankfurt area was considered desirable, that is, with the interdisciplinary transparency traditional at Frankfurt University, especially the heritage of the critical theory of the "Frankfurt School."

The ecumenicity within the department in 1987 was carried over into the setup of two new schools of theology, which took the place of the old Department of Religion. German laws on church-state relations required a transformation of the Protestant section of the Department of Religion into a School of Protestant Theology, since otherwise the training of candidates for the Protestant ministry would be impossible. Such training needed to be confessionally distinct and institutionally separate from the newly formed School of Catholic Theology (the Catholic section of the former department). The Roman Catholic Church unfortunately denied the new Catholic school the right to train candidates for the priesthood. Nevertheless, both schools established and maintained a certain degree of institutional ecumenical cooperation unheard of between schools of theology in Germany since the Reformation.[12]

The School of Protestant Theology in Frankfurt has adopted a program of praxis-oriented introduction into the study of theology. Students are stimulated from their first term on to understand and utilize their own academic study of theology as their societal praxis and thus to prepare themselves for their profession in scholarly as well as social responsibility. The church's role is seen as a major interface in this relationship between university, society, person, church, and profession. The critical imagination of the students as well as their confidence in the communicative process are instigated as essential elements of urban theology and its mediation. Students get acquainted with the phenomenon

---

12. There are common affairs in teaching, research, library, and other elements of administration between both schools that call for close cooperation on the level of deanship, faculties, and committees. The administrative deanship on common affairs alternates between the deans of the Catholic and the Protestant schools. Possibilities for further developments and changes in existing state-church relations could not be realized but can be envisaged on the basis of the Frankfurt experiment.

of alienation, learn to analyze relevant social and psychological situations, and discover how to respond to them. They are encouraged to design their own studies as their own creative praxis, as something that has its own integrity and importance beside the praxis of their teachers and the academic and clerical staff. This takes shape as a rehearsal of democratic processes.[13]

Theology must appreciate anew that biblical proclamation and religion did not originate in niches but at the thoroughfares and junctions of a large world. The authors of the writings of the First and Second Testaments were conscious of this, as were their readers and listeners. They knew the problems of living in foreign lands and of interstate relations. Already during Israelite times, a strong Diaspora developed that grew explosively in Jewish times. Israelites and Jews, including the Jewish writers and readers of the Second Testament, cultivated and tested models of communal life. They had an impact on their environment. This remained a fact with the church as well, for the better and for the worse. A school of theology in a metropolis will have to learn these lessons about failures and successes. Based on this, it will have to engage itself in the praxis of the city today and tomorrow, not only passively as a beacon and buoy, but also actively as an icebreaker and pathfinder.

---

13. The ideas described above have caught on. Union Theological Seminary at Dasmariñas in the Philippines is establishing an Interdisciplinary Learning Center for A Livable World. In its program, the seminary students who are training for the ministry will cultivate the arable grounds of the school, which exists in an environment of explosive urbanization and industrialization. This will help to finance their own studies, their families, and the seminary. Ecological gardening, fish breeding, and similar means of production will be practiced in the context of shared learning and action. In shared reflection on this and of the radically changing social context of their lives and that of the seminary, the students participate in a learning process together with seminary faculty and experts, practitioners, and researchers of rural and urban background and concern, who will join the center for a certain time. Cooperation with the communities around is an essential part of the enterprise. Such exchanges of past and present experience and contemporary problems will constitute a praxis in which all participants can contribute and partake responsively and responsibly. Since this center will also be a spiritual community conducting retreats and training camps, church people at large will be enabled to take and give. This will enlarge the experiential dimensions of the center. A doctoral program will be an active part in this praxis-founded enterprise. It will encourage the students actively to view their own past and present experience and activity as essential elements in the shaping of theological research and teaching of tomorrow. The graduates of the various programs will thus be enabled to function as multipliers of such experiences in the professional situations that they will enter, most often in the milieu of social minorities, yet with great expectations not only from their fellow believers but also from those of other persuasions.

20

ON SOJOURNING

The final chapter presents a commencement address that speaks to an audience of graduating students about the existence of an academician inside and outside the university as sojourning toward the city as an encouraging as well as challenging utopia with knowledge as the most open and most unfinished accompaniment in the experience of life.

On a day like this it is proper to look back. Therefore, I want to start this address by remembering the teacher who influenced me most, Ernst Käsemann. Thinking of his teaching, I chose the scripture text from Heb 13.

Ernst Käsemann's study on the Epistle to the Hebrews, *Das wandernde Gottesvolk* (*The Sojourning People of God*), was a book that brought theory and practice together for his students. Käsemann participated in the resistance of the church in Germany during the Nazi period and was put in prison; part of his work on the sojourning people of God was written there. This book and Käsemann's teaching instilled in us the awareness that scholarship and life belong together, that theology is not an isolated exercise of individuals but that theology is theology of the people of God on the way. This noon I learned through a letter from my father-in-law that the daughter of Ernst Käsemann, Elisabeth, was shot dead in an Argentine prison after having been tortured. Theology is *theologia viatorum*, and the road is full of unanswerable questions.

Actually, I did not become a scholar in the classrooms of Käsemann, Bornkamm, or Bultmann. It happened before that, on the road as a boy. It happened between March 1944 and May 1945, when I was fourteen and

---

* This is an abbreviated form of the Baccalaureate address given at Harvard Divinity School on 15 June 1977, as printed in the *Harvard Divinity Bulletin* (October/November 1977).

fifteen years of age, during the months between my confirmation in the church and my discharge from the German army. I became a scholar in air-raid shelters, on railroads, in army camps, and on battle roads.

In these fourteen months I saw my own hometown, Frankfurt, go up in flames, a city dating back to Charlemagne, with the largest integral medieval city center in all of Germany. A few months later I stood in the midst of another city when it experienced its hell of fire—Dresden, the largest and best preserved German Baroque city. I saw the collapse of my country and nation. I learned of the annihilation of the Jews, of the destruction of lives by the hecatombs; I experienced the disappearance overnight of values that had taken centuries to build, bare survival by the skin of my teeth, the experience of human nature at its core, where the beast shows, but also the angel.

However, what I remember most of all from that period is my reading. With school being more off than on and with no books being printed, I recall poring over the classical authors in my mother's library. During innumerable nights and days in the air shelter, I encountered tragedy and comedy as it had received focus by these writers. Most of all, I was fascinated by the works of the romantic German poet, Eichendorff. I still remember the fascination of his most delightful novel, *From the Life of a Good-for-Nothing*. Some of you may still see the impact of that reading on me. Out of the world of this poet, Eichendorff, an image stuck with me: that of the sojourning scholar, the perennial student, always on the road, never through with studies, never satisfied with the particular manifestation of truth in the alma mater at hand, always looking ahead toward the city of truth, which happens to be an amalgamate of the heavenly Jerusalem and the eternal Rome.

So, long before I started my university career, I learned on the hard benches of life that the scholar can be an image of what life is all about, a metaphor for the experience of people, nurtured by hundreds and thousands of years of human experience before them, but not resting on that experience; instead, restlessly moving ahead.

From Ernst Käsemann I learned that this metaphor of sojourning is particularly appropriate for the life of faith. I learned that the people of God is a community of sojourners, constantly on the road, never taking possession, always seeking the city that is to come.

The verse that I read from Hebrews is preceded by an interesting statement and admonition: "Jesus ... suffered outside the gate in order to sanctify the people through his own blood. Therefore let us go forth to him outside the camp, bearing abuse for him." Faith in Jesus does not call for a religious establishment, fortified by orthodoxy and protected by the extermination of heretics and unbelievers. The community of believers is an open community, a community on the move, by definition unorthodox, irreverent vis-à-vis every self-righteous and oppressive establishment, full of love for all creatures of God.

As I prepared for this address, I looked, as some of you will have anticipated, for counsel in the writings of the person I consider to be the greatest American theologian, William Faulkner. I looked through his *Hamlet*, but I found *The Reivers* of particular help for our meditation right now. Here Faulkner narrates the story of an eleven-year-old boy, Lucius Priest. One day in 1905, he borrows, together with the part Indian Boon Hogganbeck, the car of Lucius's grandfather, one of the first automobiles in the county. They want to reach their dream city, Memphis—not the one in Egypt but the more famous one in Tennessee. They don't really have permission for such a ride. Unwillingly, they take along the black stablehand, Ned William McCaslin. On their way, grandfather's car is traded for a racehorse of dubious quality, a horse that is satisfied with always coming in second. Lucius is made the jockey, and Ned makes the horse win with the most curious kind of dope: a can of sardines.

This hilarious outing can be read as a powerful allegory of life's sojourning ... and as an allegory of the university, too. Here in academia we have borrowed reality. We take it on a ride, not with full permission. As we ride on, we pretend to be masters of reality, at least for a short while. Then comes the desperate attempt to trade reality for a substitute, the substitute of our scholarship and learning.

However, it is not the experienced adults who bring things together again. It is the eleven-year-old boy; it is his innocence that makes things go and keeps the world of Faulkner's story together. The innocent has more insight than the learned. The innocent has more trust, and, because of that very trust, integrity is restored to the people, and human dignity returns to them.

All of you have lost your academic innocence by now. The parable of *The Reivers* may help you to look at your studies with a humorous eye, to understand your academic experience as a liberating image for your mission as sojourners ahead. *The Reivers* is about integrity. The integrity of the world cannot be preserved. It can only be regained, again and again. The integrity of the world can be regained only through the trust and hope of the innocent ones.

The real miracle of the kingdom of God is to become like children again. Never feel too good to be beginners again. Stay perennial students, true scholars, that is. Never take possession of anything, not even of the insight of your own answers. Never triumph over anyone. Trust that here is a goal that you have neither to invent nor to protect. Trust in people. Trust in the process people are involved in. Don't take it as a rat race but as the road to the city of God. There is weeping and chuckling on the road.

It is not knowledge that is to be found at the end of an academic career but wisdom. The wisdom that makes a scholar is made up of innocence, trust, and hope. And when all is said and done in academia, we have to confess with the greatest pun ever: Οἶδα οὐδὲν εἰδώς, "I know that I don't know anything." Goodbye.

Milton Keynes UK
Ingram Content Group UK Ltd.
UKHW041813170124
436213UK00001B/24